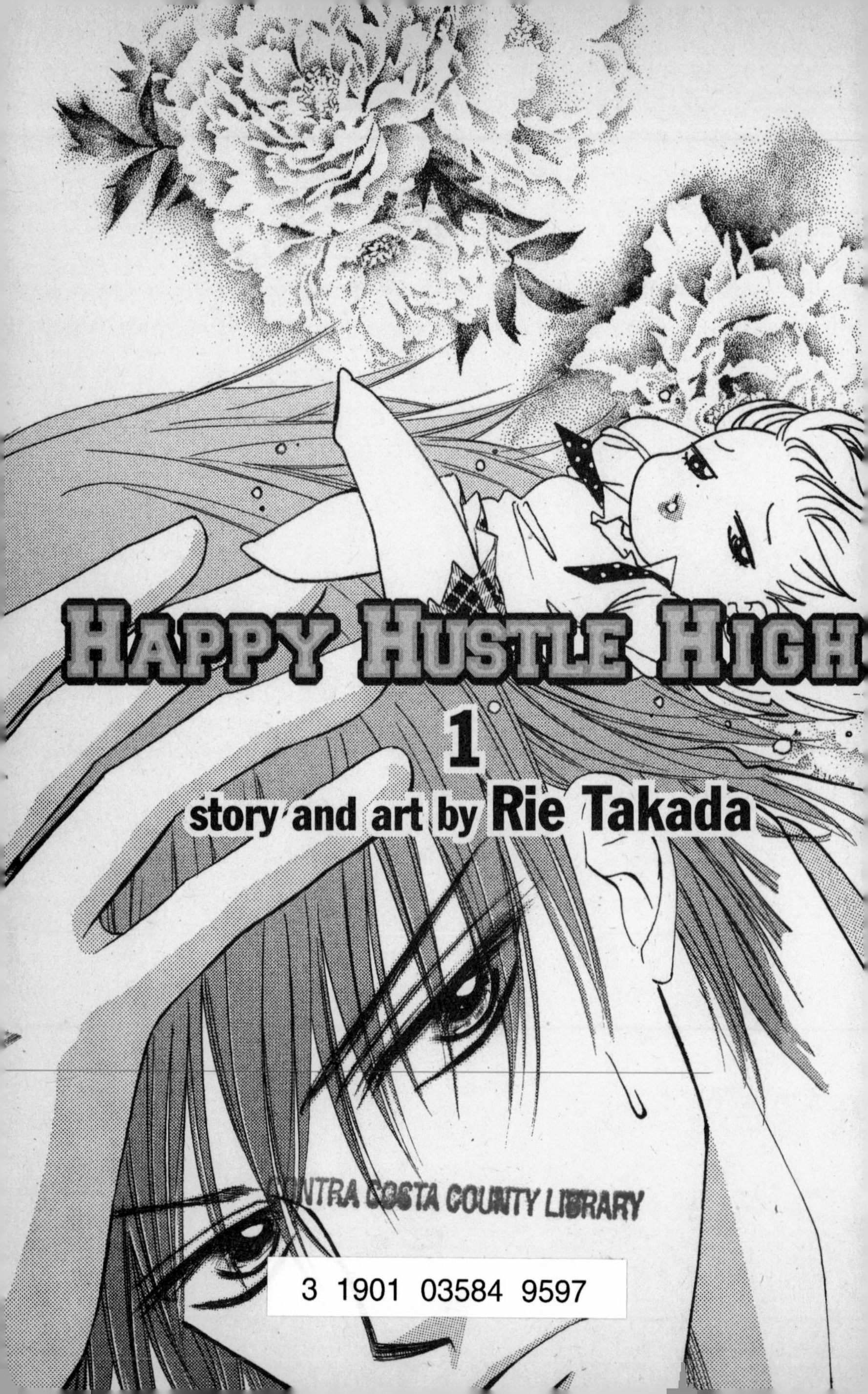

HAPPY HUSTLE HIGH

1

story and art by Rie Takada

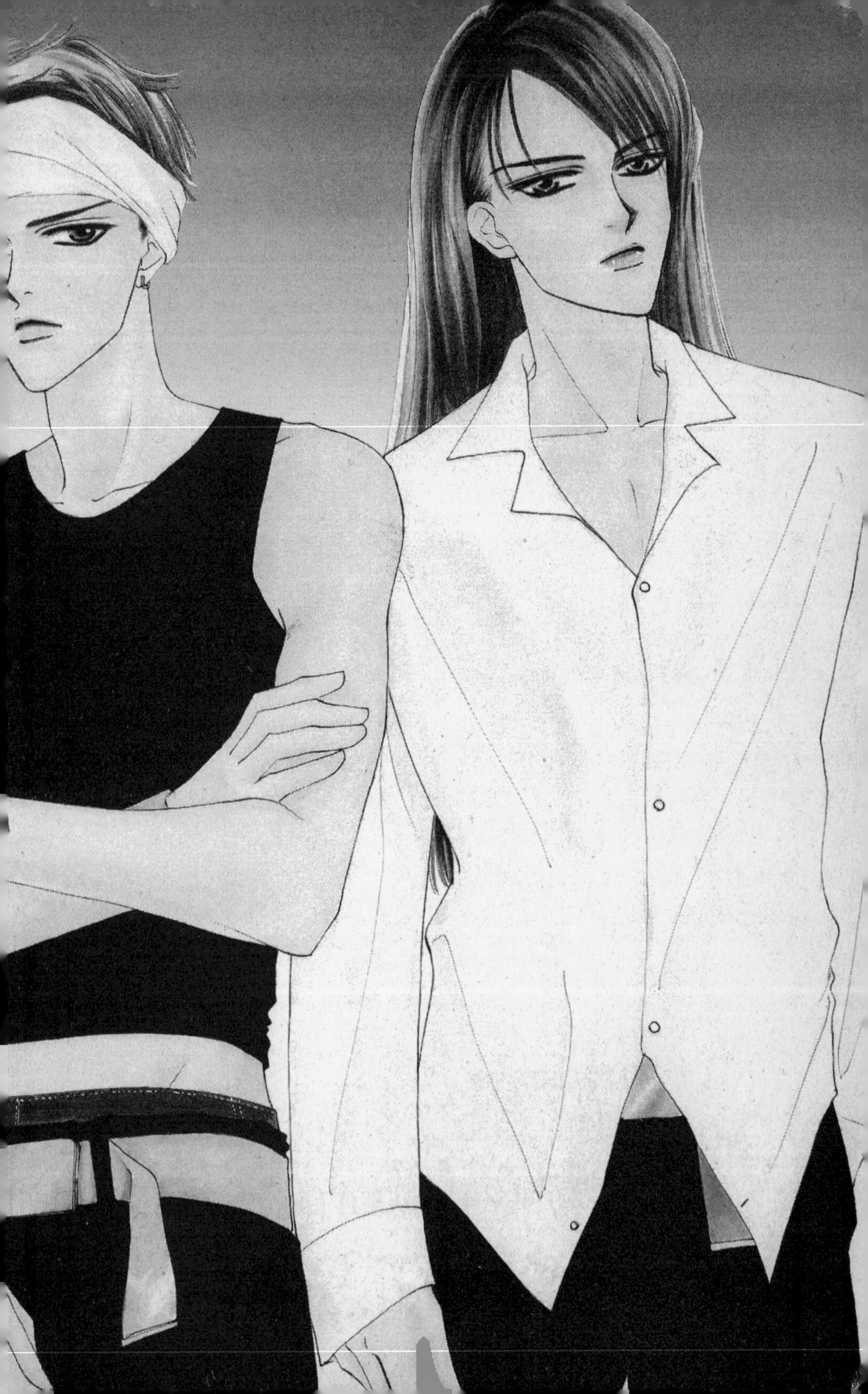

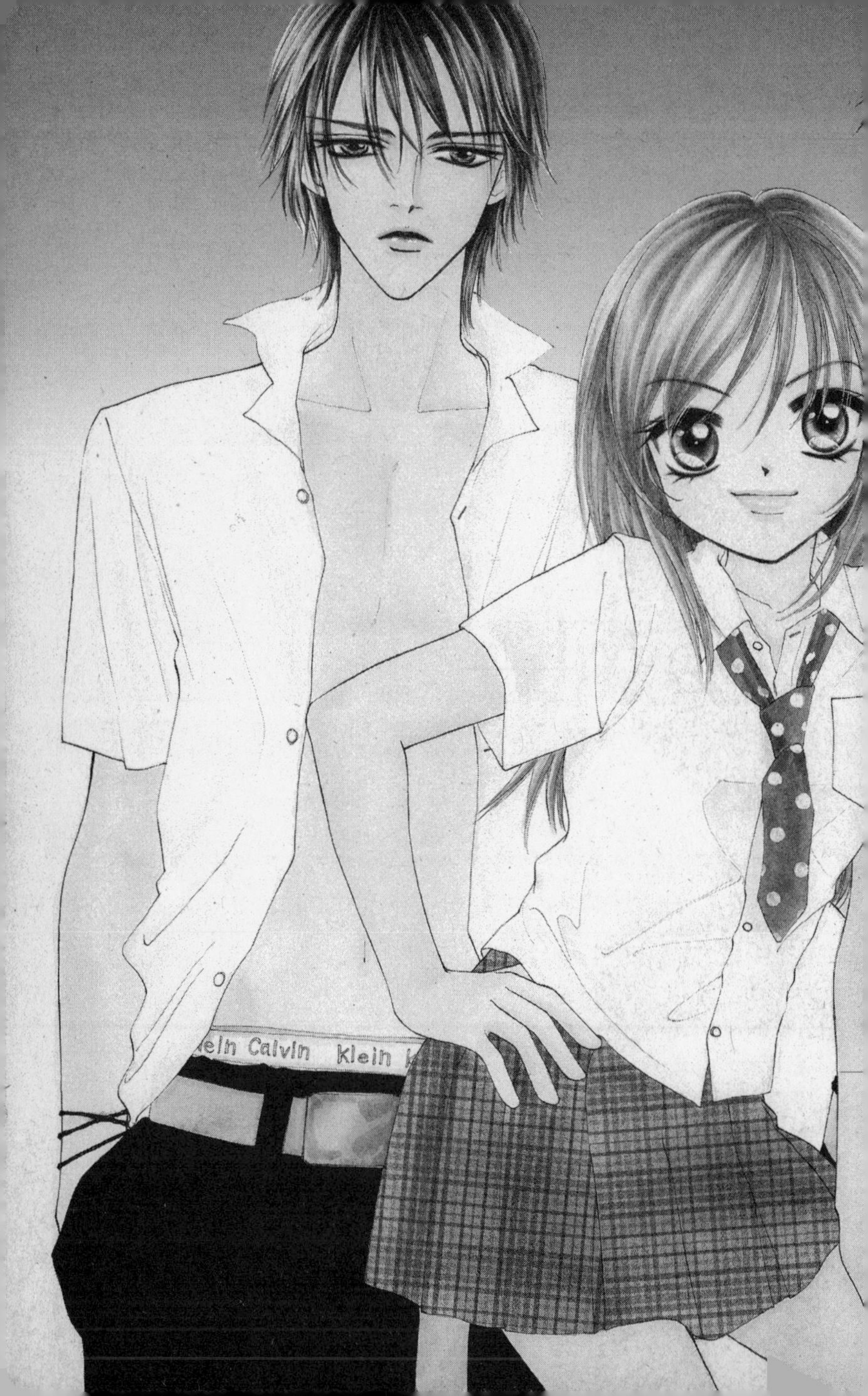

Klein Calvin Klein

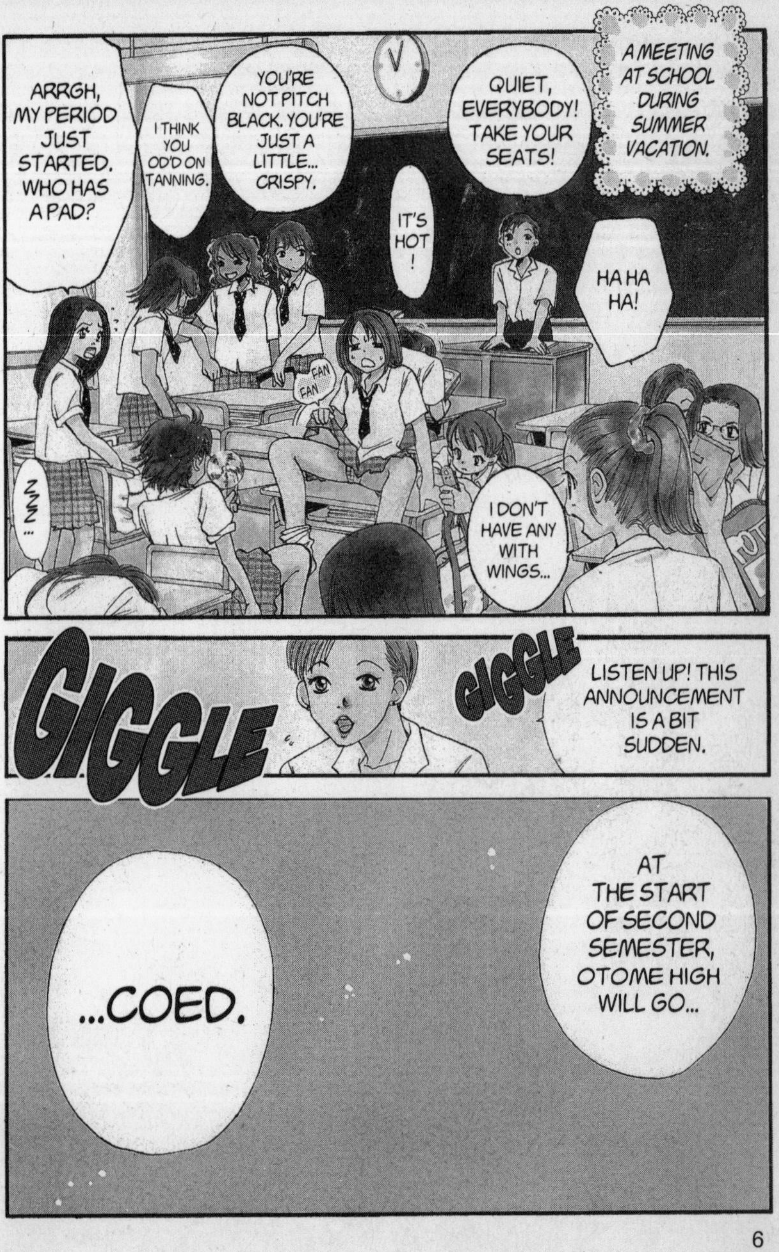
A MEETING AT SCHOOL DURING SUMMER VACATION.
QUIET, EVERYBODY! TAKE YOUR SEATS!
HA HA HA!
IT'S HOT!
YOU'RE NOT PITCH BLACK. YOU'RE JUST A LITTLE... CRISPY.
I THINK YOU OD'D ON TANNING.
ARRGH, MY PERIOD JUST STARTED. WHO HAS A PAD?
FAN FAN
I DON'T HAVE ANY WITH WINGS...
ZZZ...
LISTEN UP! THIS ANNOUNCEMENT IS A BIT SUDDEN.
GIGGLE
GIGGLE
AT THE START OF SECOND SEMESTER, OTOME HIGH WILL GO...
...COED.

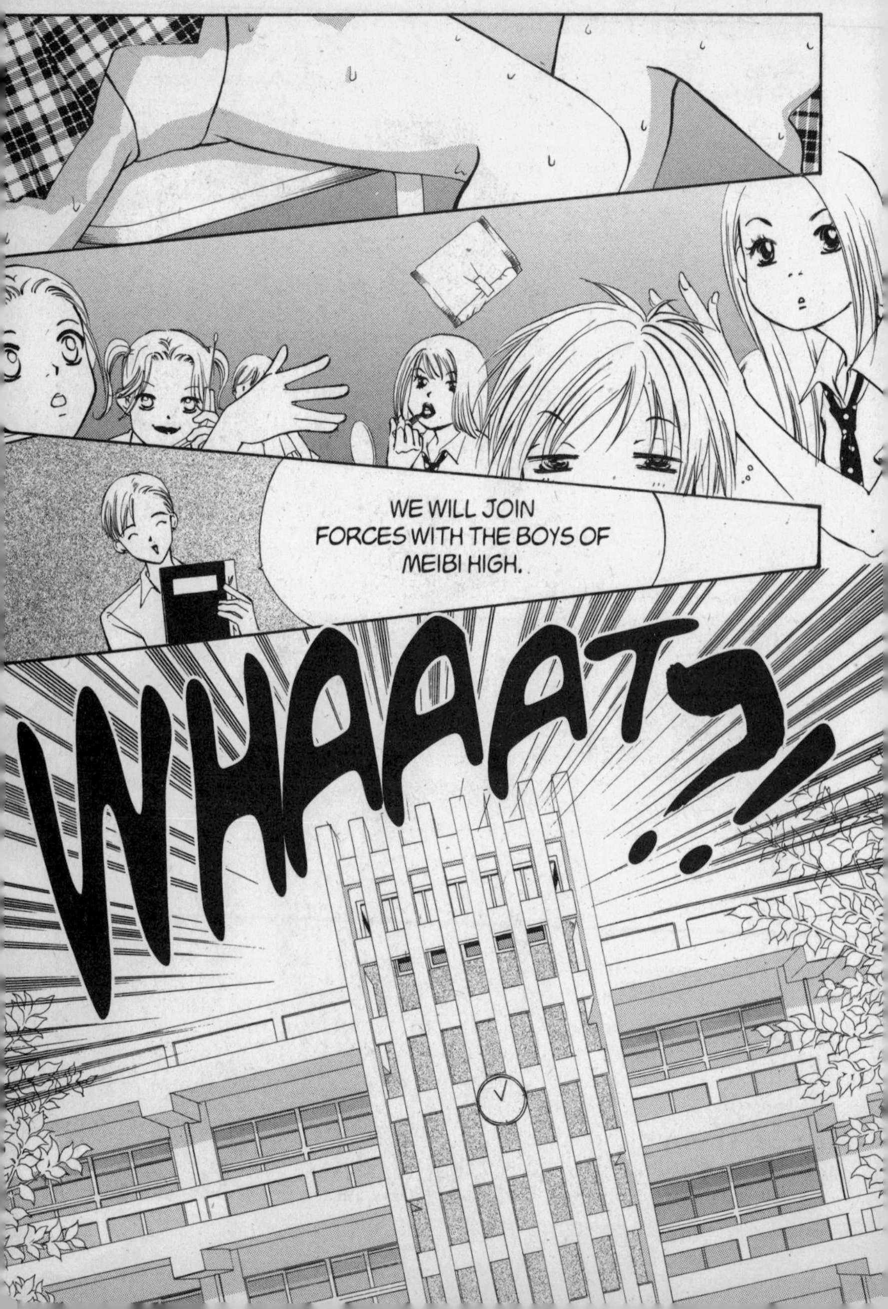
WE WILL JOIN FORCES WITH THE BOYS OF MEIBI HIGH.
WHAAAT?!

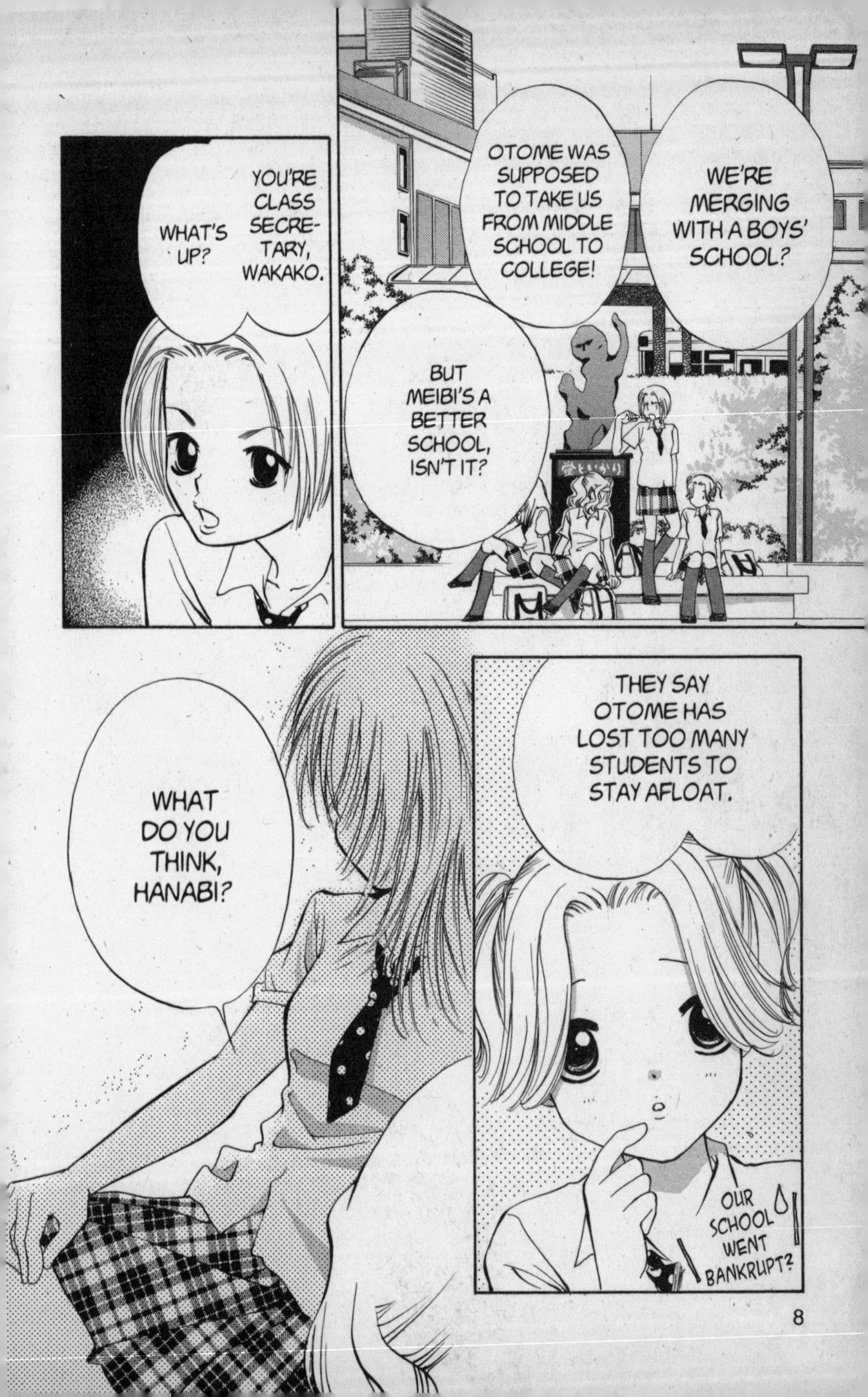
WE'RE MERGING WITH A BOYS' SCHOOL?
OTOME WAS SUPPOSED TO TAKE US FROM MIDDLE SCHOOL TO COLLEGE!
BUT MEIBI'S A BETTER SCHOOL, ISN'T IT?
YOU'RE CLASS SECRE-TARY, WAKAKO.
WHAT'S UP?
THEY SAY OTOME HAS LOST TOO MANY STUDENTS TO STAY AFLOAT.
OUR SCHOOL WENT BANKRUPT?
WHAT DO YOU THINK, HANABI?

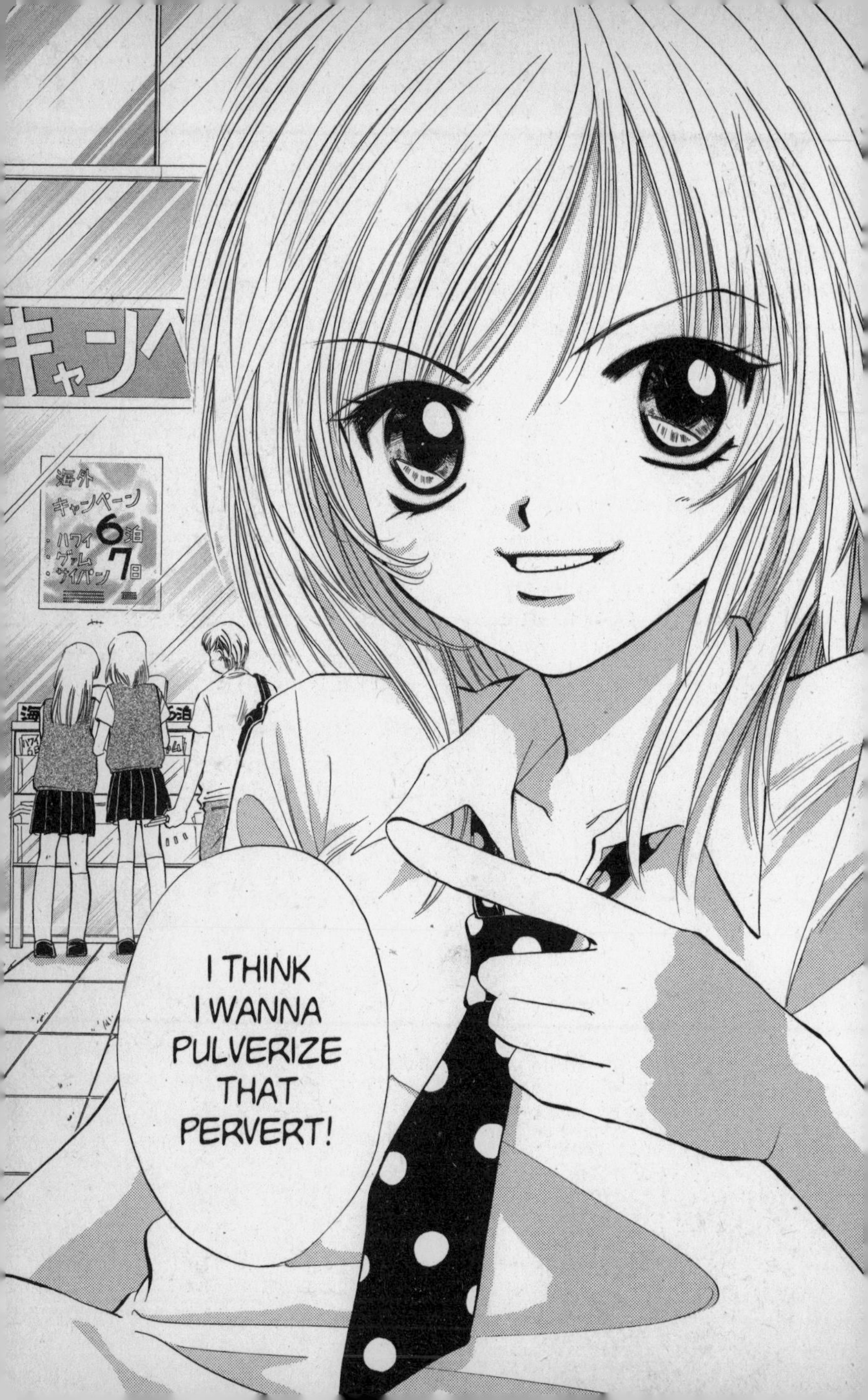
海外
キャンペーン
・ハワイ 6泊
・グァム 7日
・サイパン
I THINK I WANNA PULVERIZE THAT PERVERT!

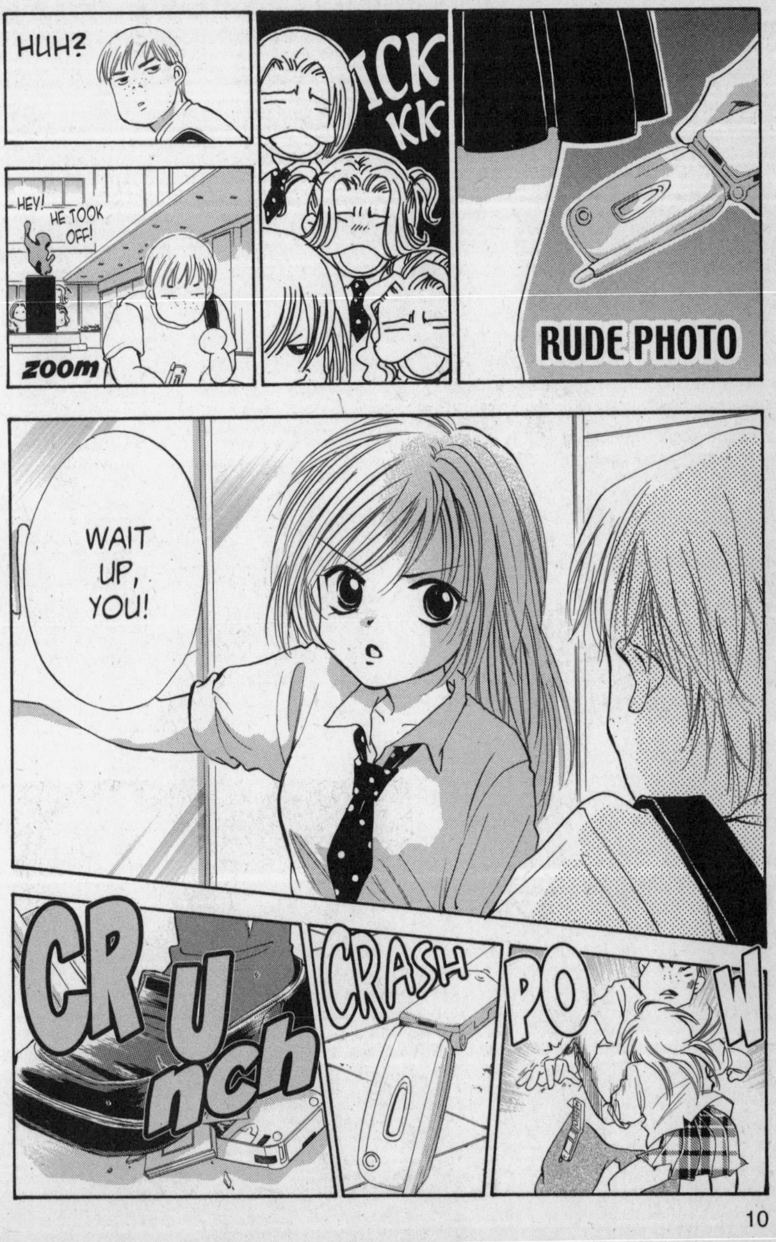
RUDE PHOTO
ICK KK
HUH?
HEY!
HE TOOK OFF!
ZOOM
WAIT UP, YOU!
POW
CRASH
CRUNCH

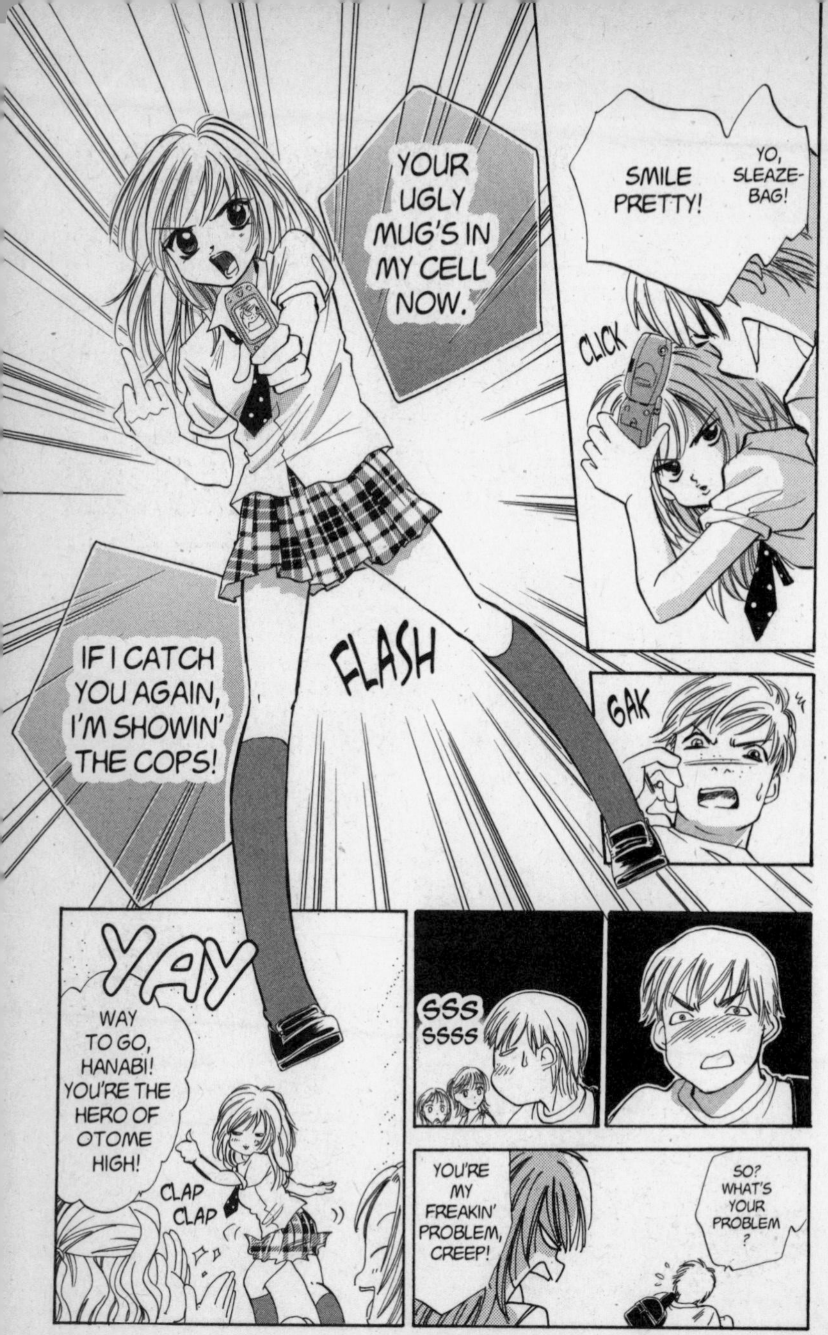
YO, SLEAZE-BAG!
SMILE PRETTY!
CLICK
GAK
YOUR UGLY MUG'S IN MY CELL NOW.
FLASH
IF I CATCH YOU AGAIN, I'M SHOWIN' THE COPS!
SSS SSSS
SO? WHAT'S YOUR PROBLEM?
YOU'RE MY FREAKIN' PROBLEM, CREEP!
YAY
WAY TO GO, HANABI! YOU'RE THE HERO OF OTOME HIGH!
CLAP CLAP

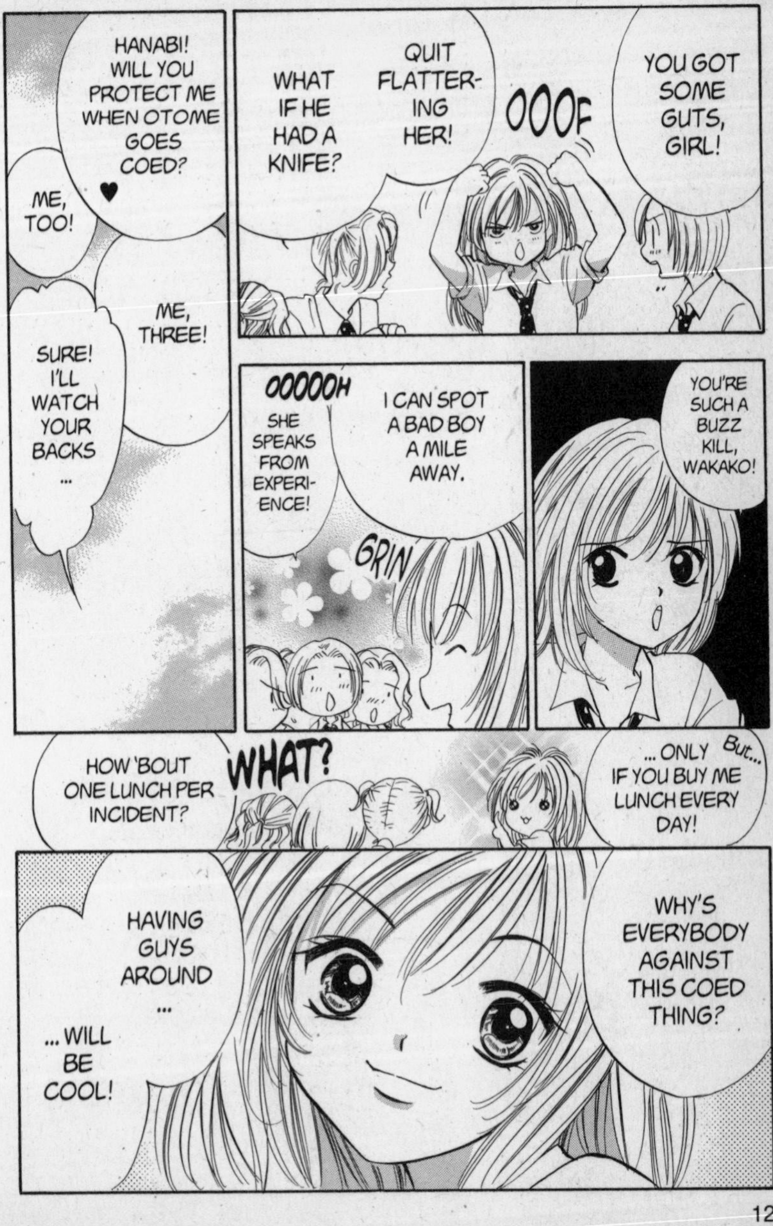
YOU GOT SOME GUTS, GIRL!
OOOF
QUIT FLATTER-ING HER!
WHAT IF HE HAD A KNIFE?
YOU'RE SUCH A BUZZ KILL, WAKAKO!
I CAN SPOT A BAD BOY A MILE AWAY.
OOOOOH
SHE SPEAKS FROM EXPERI-ENCE!
GRIN
HANABI! WILL YOU PROTECT ME WHEN OTOME GOES COED? ♥
ME, TOO!
ME, THREE!
SURE! I'LL WATCH YOUR BACKS ...
But...
... ONLY IF YOU BUY ME LUNCH EVERY DAY!
WHAT?
HOW 'BOUT ONE LUNCH PER INCIDENT?
WHY'S EVERYBODY AGAINST THIS COED THING?
HAVING GUYS AROUND ...
... WILL BE COOL!

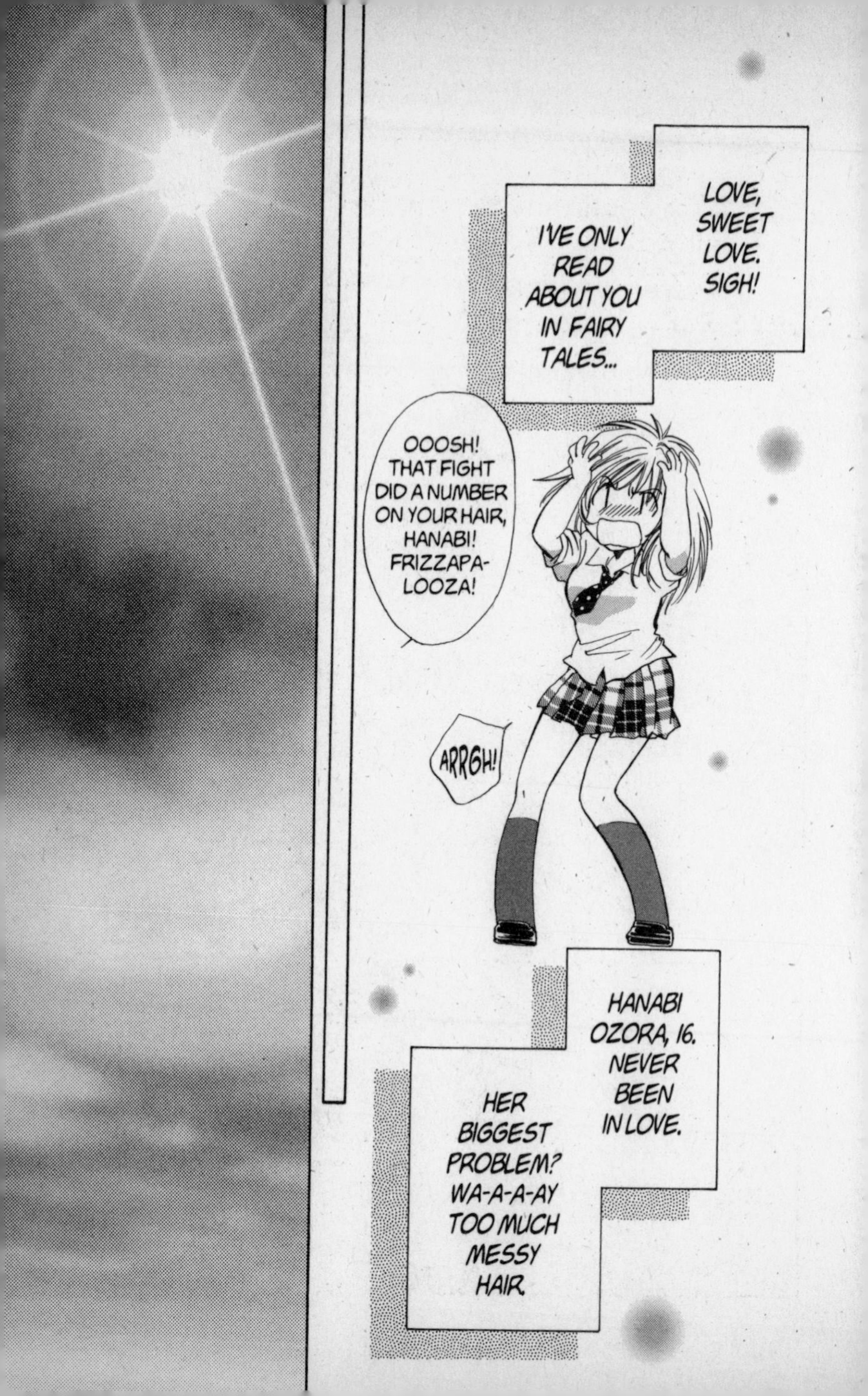
LOVE, SWEET LOVE. SIGH!
I'VE ONLY READ ABOUT YOU IN FAIRY TALES...
OOOSH! THAT FIGHT DID A NUMBER ON YOUR HAIR, HANABI! FRIZZAPA-LOOZA!
ARRGH!
HANABI OZORA, 16. NEVER BEEN IN LOVE.
HER BIGGEST PROBLEM? WA-A-A-AY TOO MUCH MESSY HAIR.

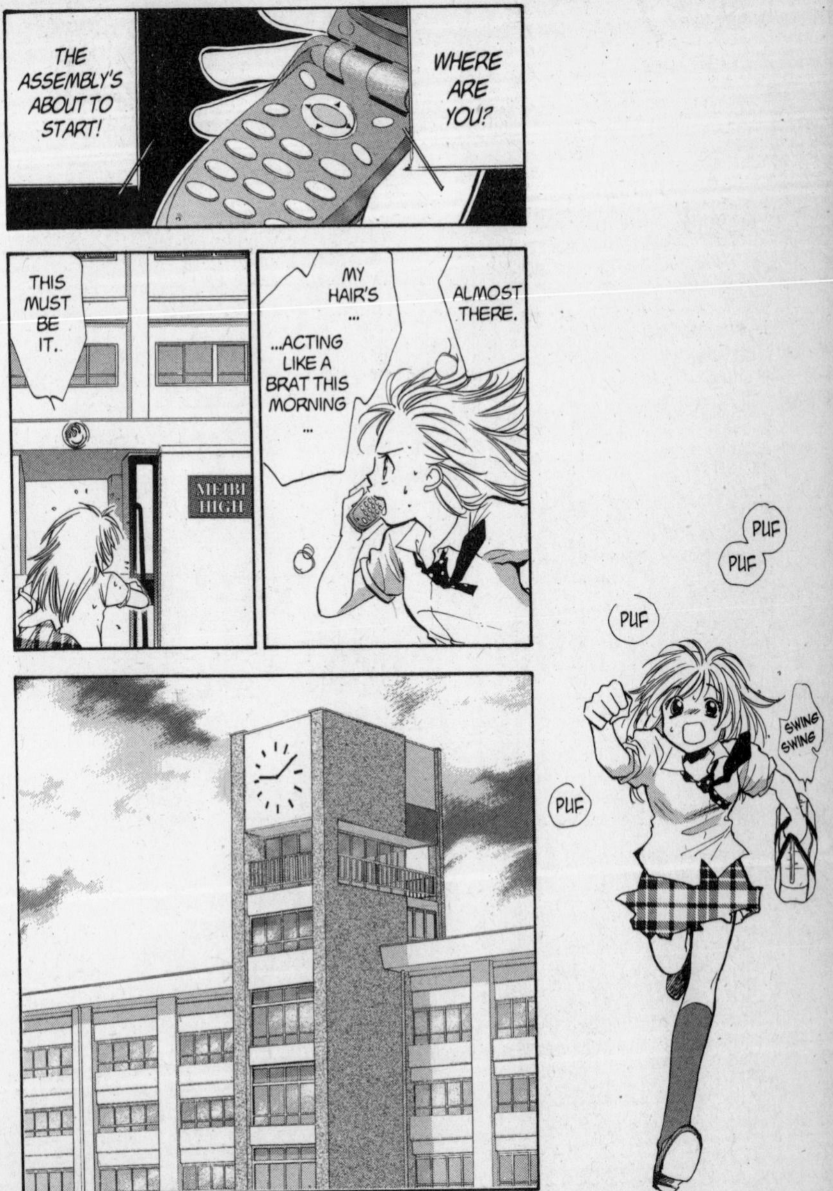
WHERE ARE YOU?
THE ASSEMBLY'S ABOUT TO START!
ALMOST THERE.
MY HAIR'S ...
...ACTING LIKE A BRAT THIS MORNING ...
THIS MUST BE IT.
MEIBI HIGH
PUF
PUF
PUF
SWING SWING
PUF

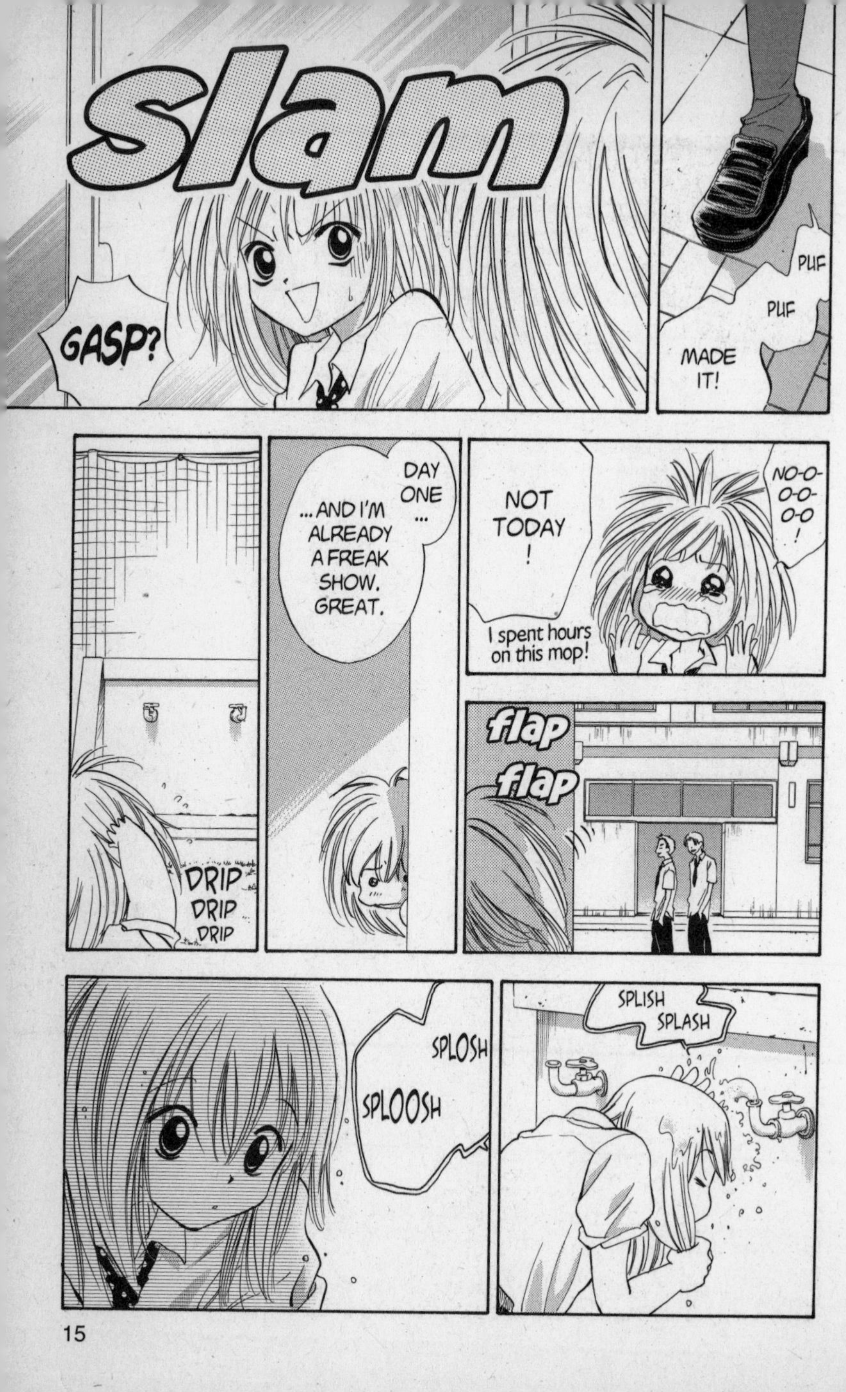
PUF
PUF
MADE IT!
slam
GASP?
NO-O-O-O-O-O-O!
NOT TODAY!
I spent hours on this mop!
flap
flap
DAY ONE...
...AND I'M ALREADY A FREAK SHOW. GREAT.
DRIP
DRIP
DRIP
SPLISH
SPLASH
SPLOSH
SPLOOSH

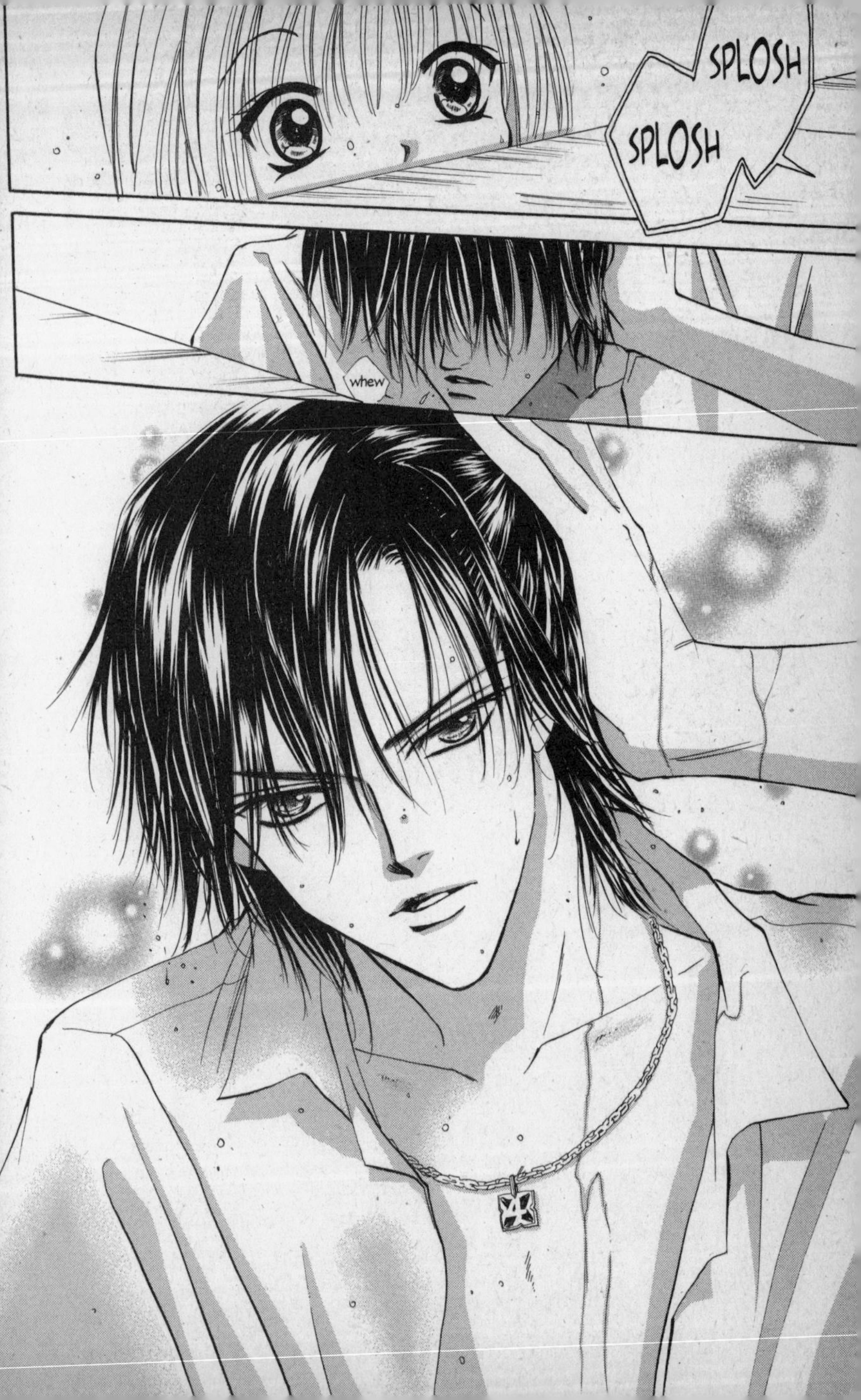
SPLOSH
SPLOSH
whew

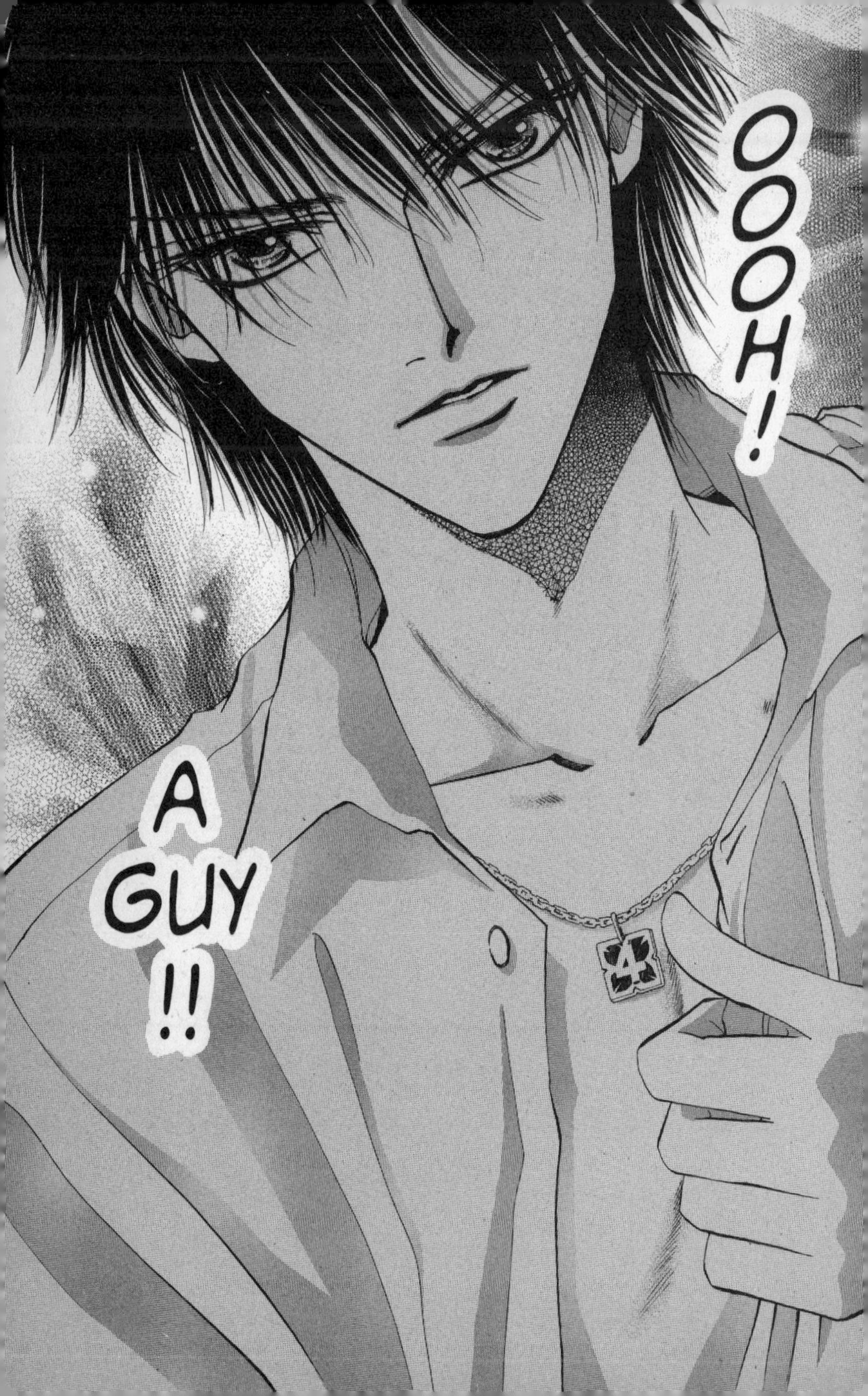
OOOOH!
A GUY!!

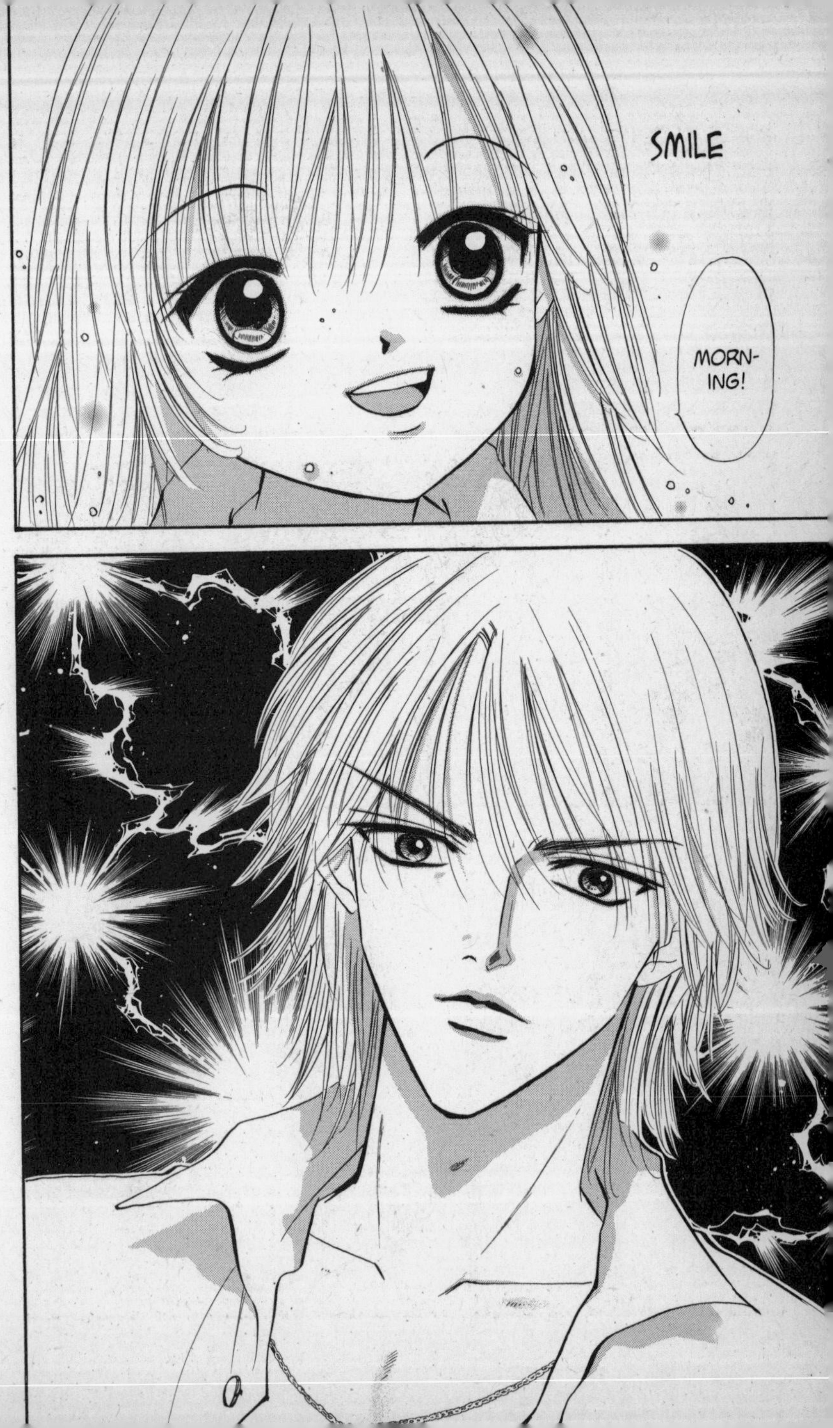
SMILE
MORN-ING!

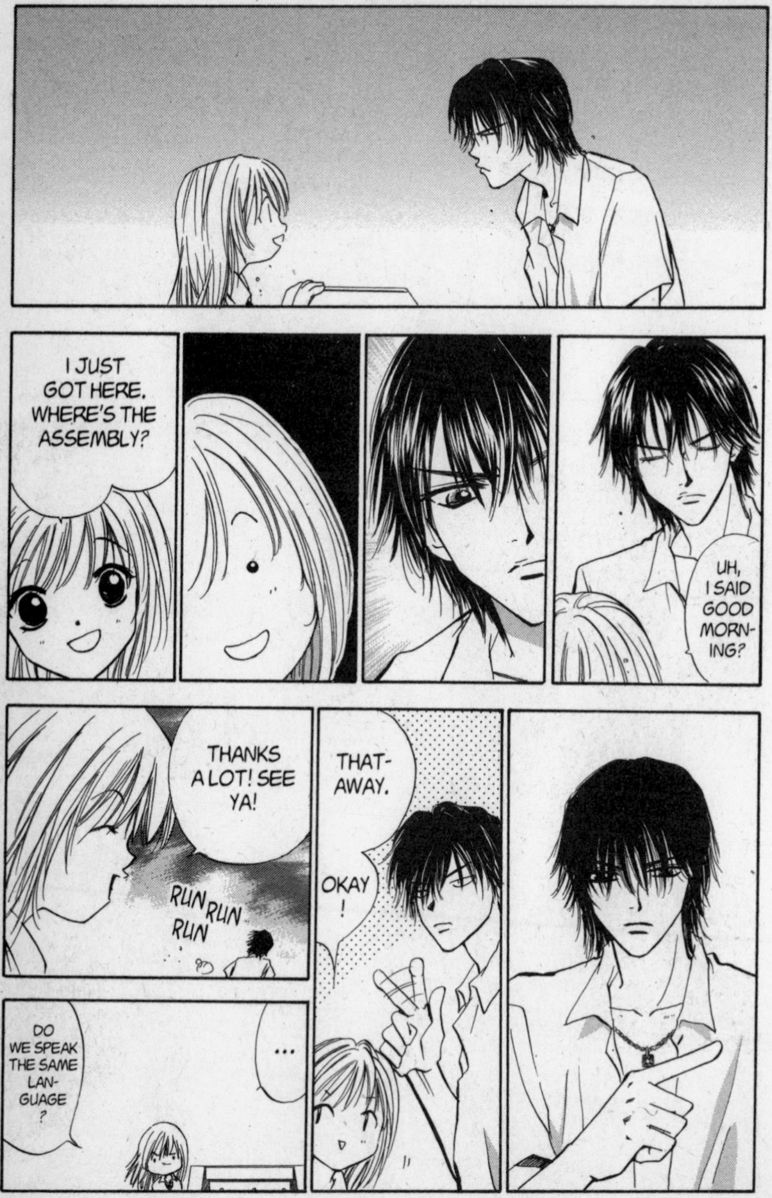
UH, I SAID GOOD MORNING?
I JUST GOT HERE. WHERE'S THE ASSEMBLY?
THAT-AWAY.
OKAY!
THANKS A LOT! SEE YA!
RUN RUN RUN
...
DO WE SPEAK THE SAME LANGUAGE?

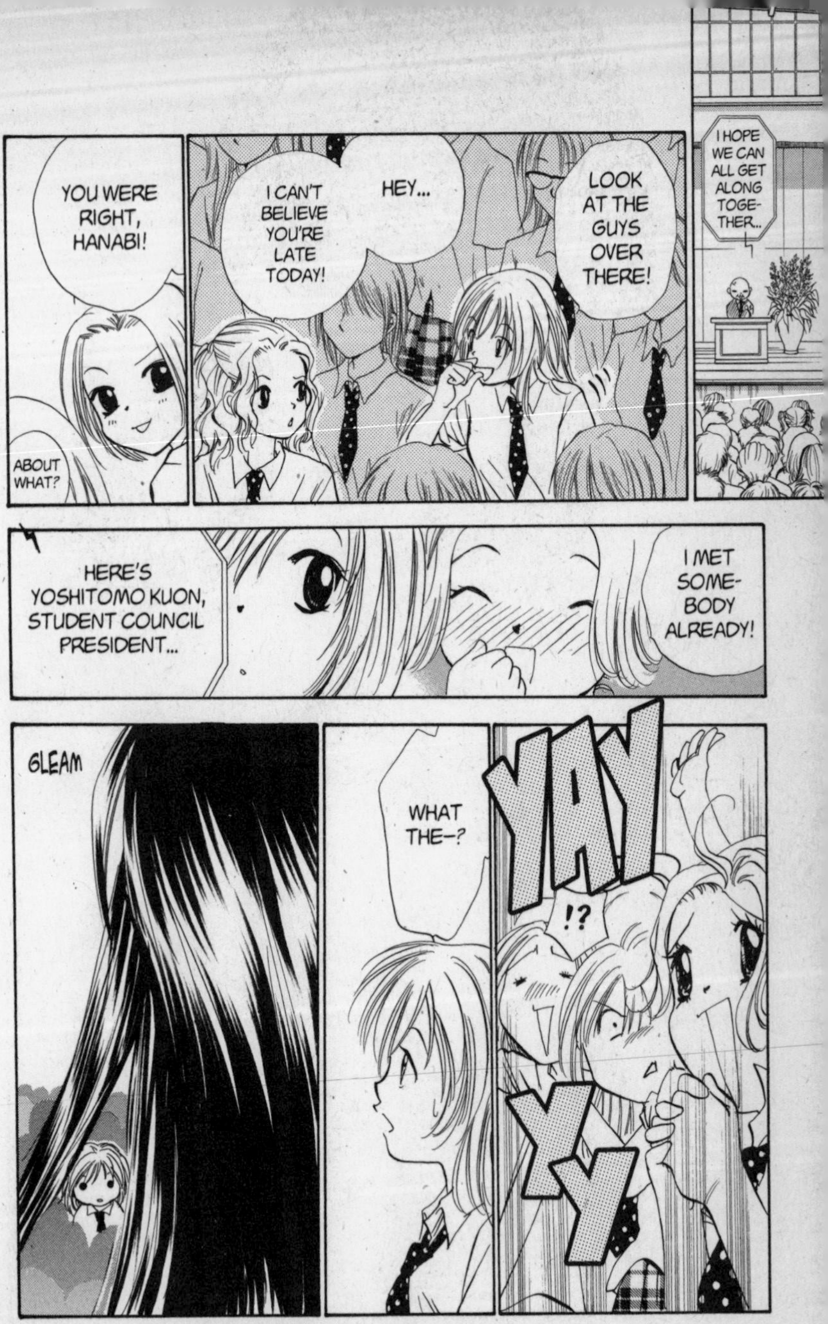
I HOPE WE CAN ALL GET ALONG TOGE-THER...
LOOK AT THE GUYS OVER THERE!
HEY...
I CAN'T BELIEVE YOU'RE LATE TODAY!
YOU WERE RIGHT, HANABI!
ABOUT WHAT?
I MET SOME-BODY ALREADY!
HERE'S YOSHITOMO KUON, STUDENT COUNCIL PRESIDENT...
YAY
!?
YAY
WHAT THE-?
GLEAM

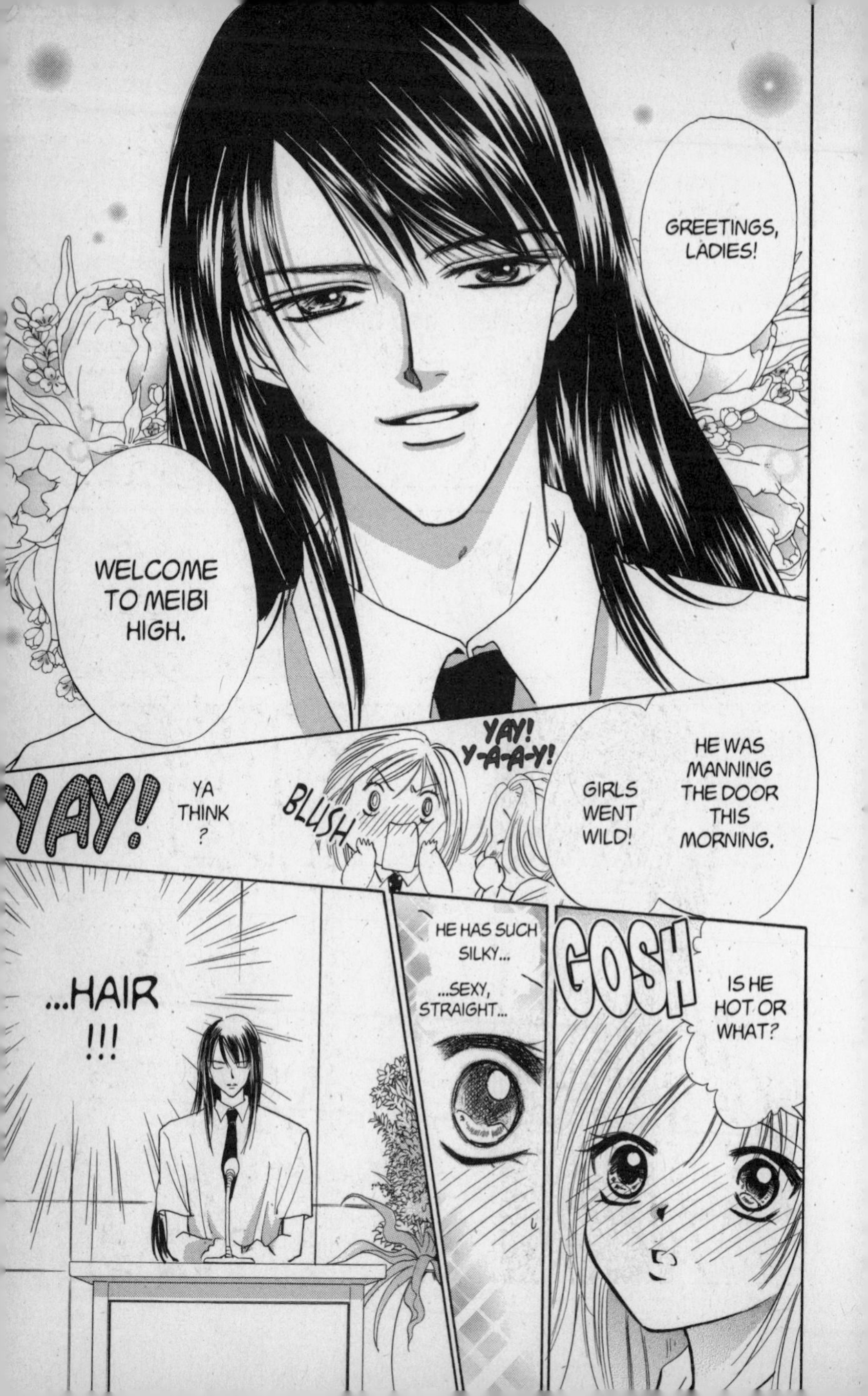
GREETINGS, LADIES!
WELCOME TO MEIBI HIGH.
HE WAS MANNING THE DOOR THIS MORNING.
GIRLS WENT WILD!
YAY! Y-A-A-Y!
BLUSH
YA THINK ?
YAY!
GOSH
IS HE HOT OR WHAT?
HE HAS SUCH SILKY...
...SEXY, STRAIGHT...
...HAIR !!!

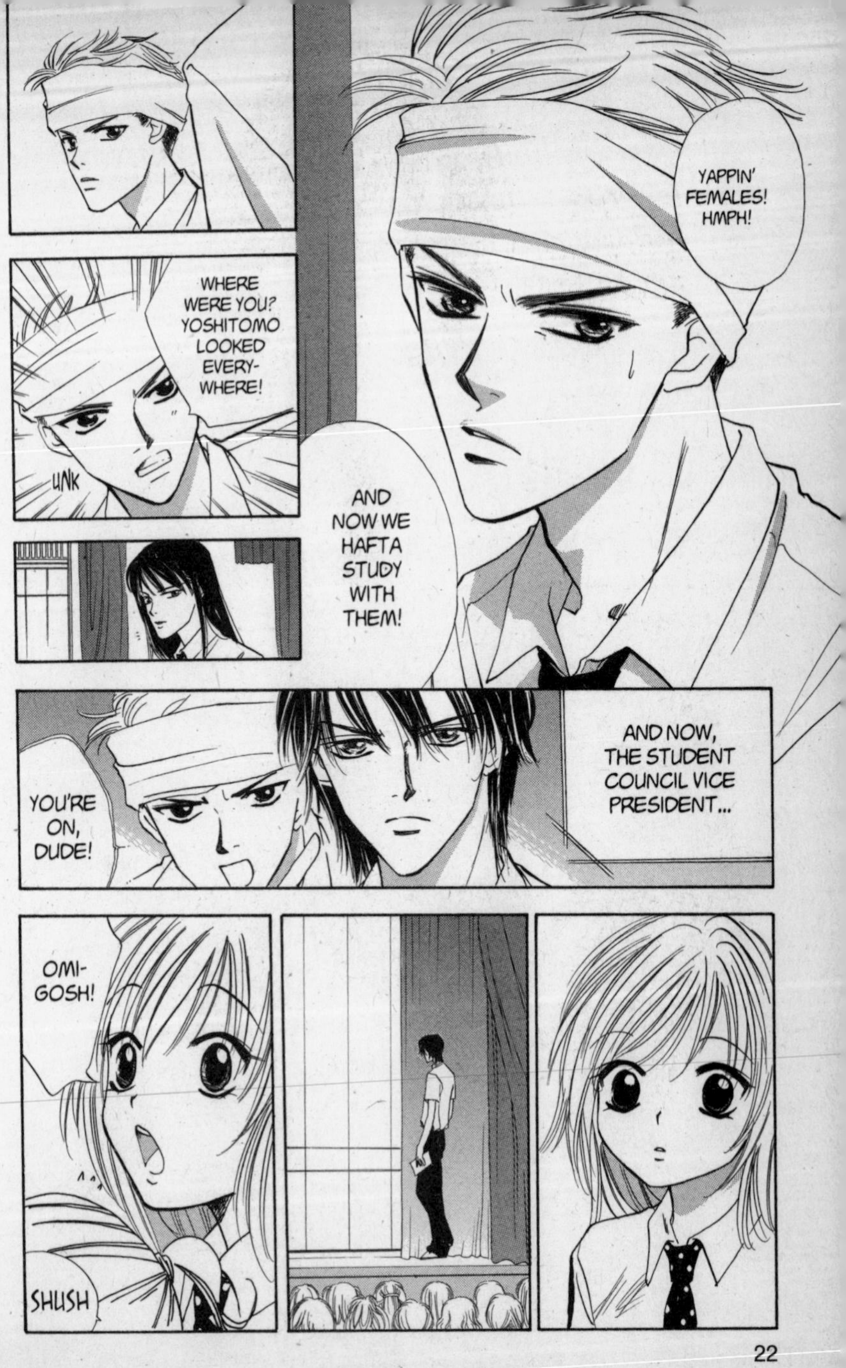
YAPPIN' FEMALES! HMPH!
AND NOW WE HAFTA STUDY WITH THEM!
WHERE WERE YOU? YOSHITOMO LOOKED EVERY-WHERE!
UNK
AND NOW, THE STUDENT COUNCIL VICE PRESIDENT...
YOU'RE ON, DUDE!
OMI-GOSH!
SHUSH

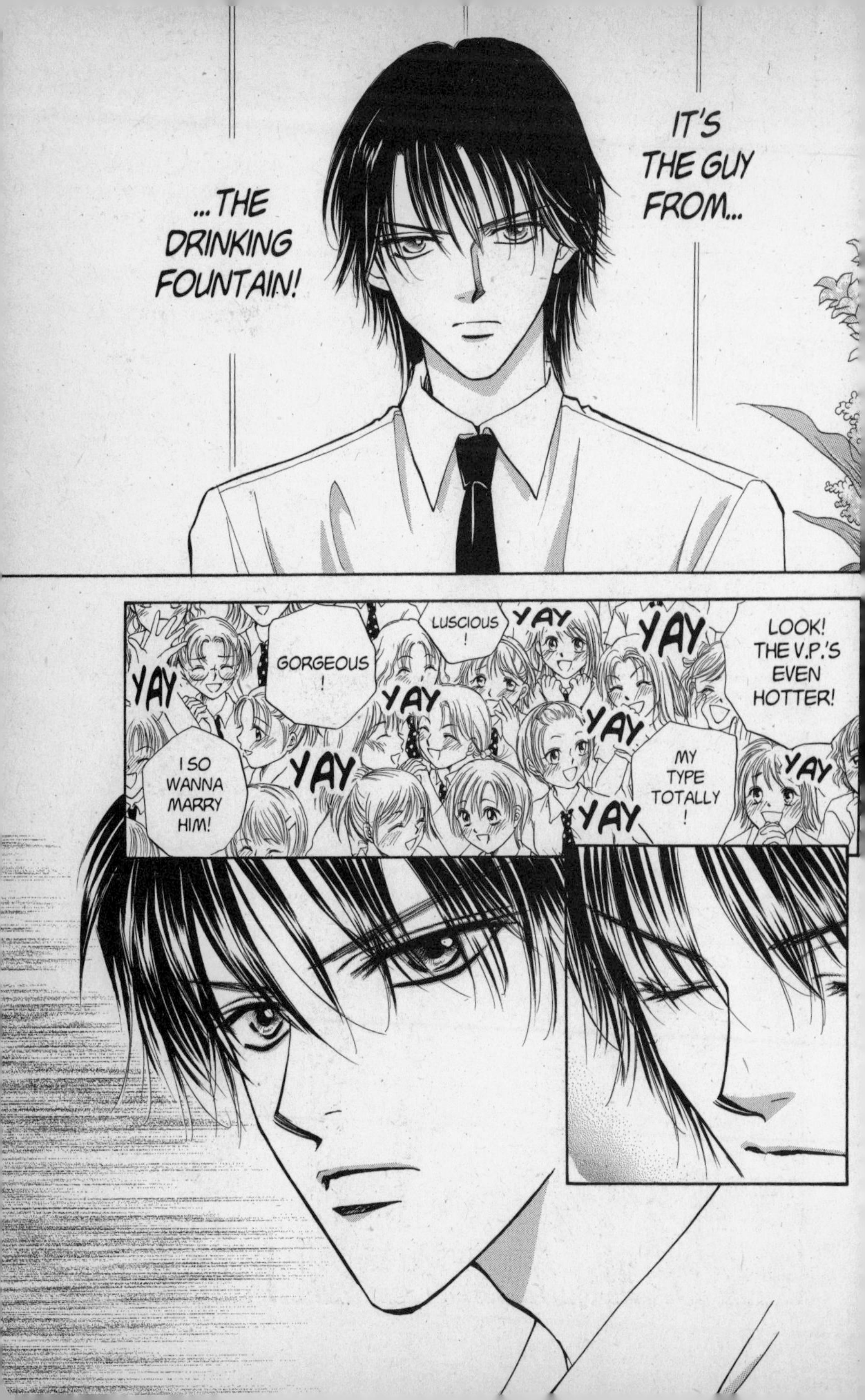
IT'S THE GUY FROM...
...THE DRINKING FOUNTAIN!
LOOK! THE V.P.'S EVEN HOTTER!
YAY
YAY
LUSCIOUS!
GORGEOUS!
YAY
YAY
MY TYPE TOTALLY!
YAY
YAY
YAY
YAY
I SO WANNA MARRY HIM!

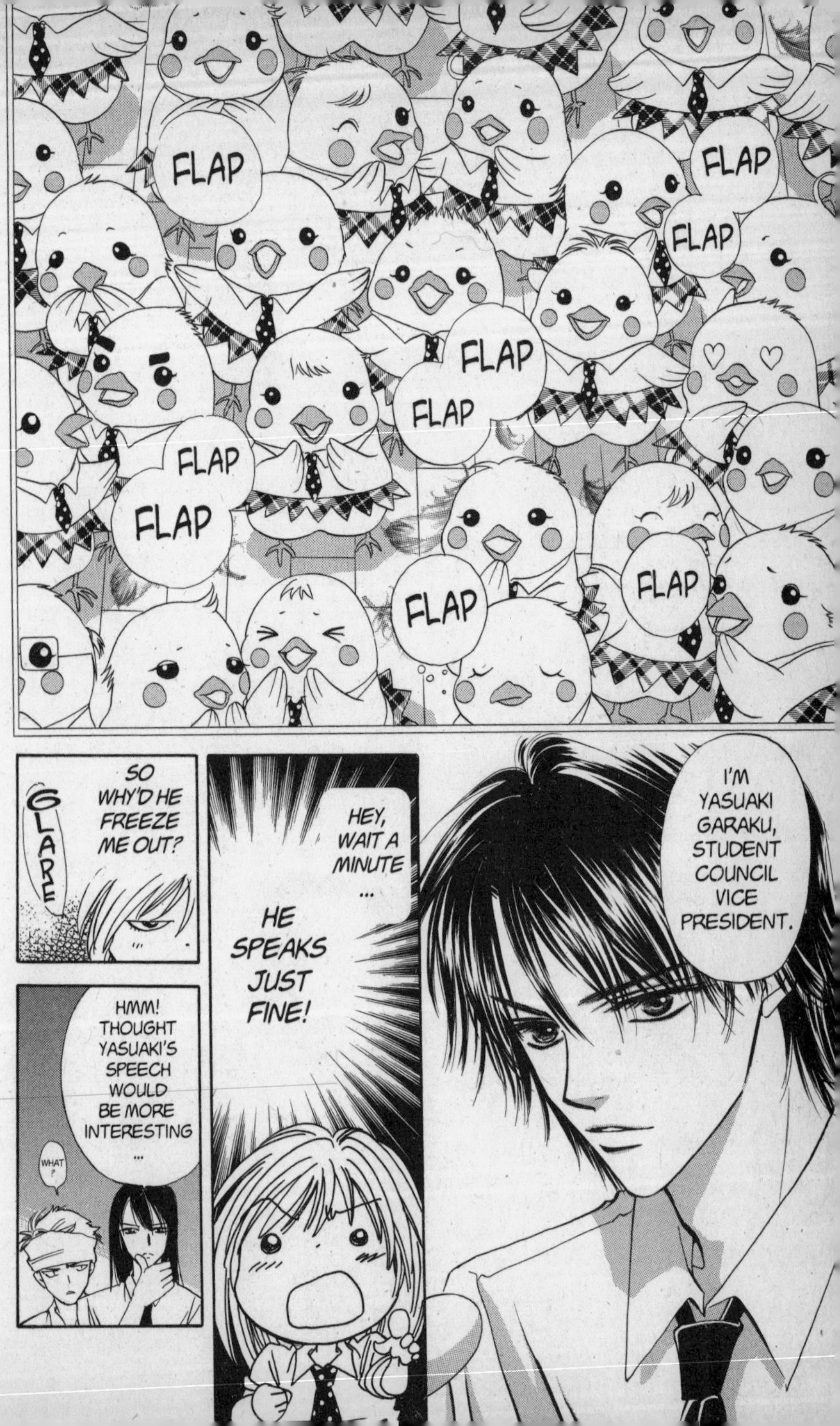
FLAP
FLAP
FLAP
FLAP
FLAP
FLAP
FLAP
FLAP
FLAP
I'M YASUAKI GARAKU, STUDENT COUNCIL VICE PRESIDENT.
HEY, WAIT A MINUTE ...
HE SPEAKS JUST FINE!
GLARE
SO WHY'D HE FREEZE ME OUT?
HMM! THOUGHT YASUAKI'S SPEECH WOULD BE MORE INTERESTING ...
WHAT?

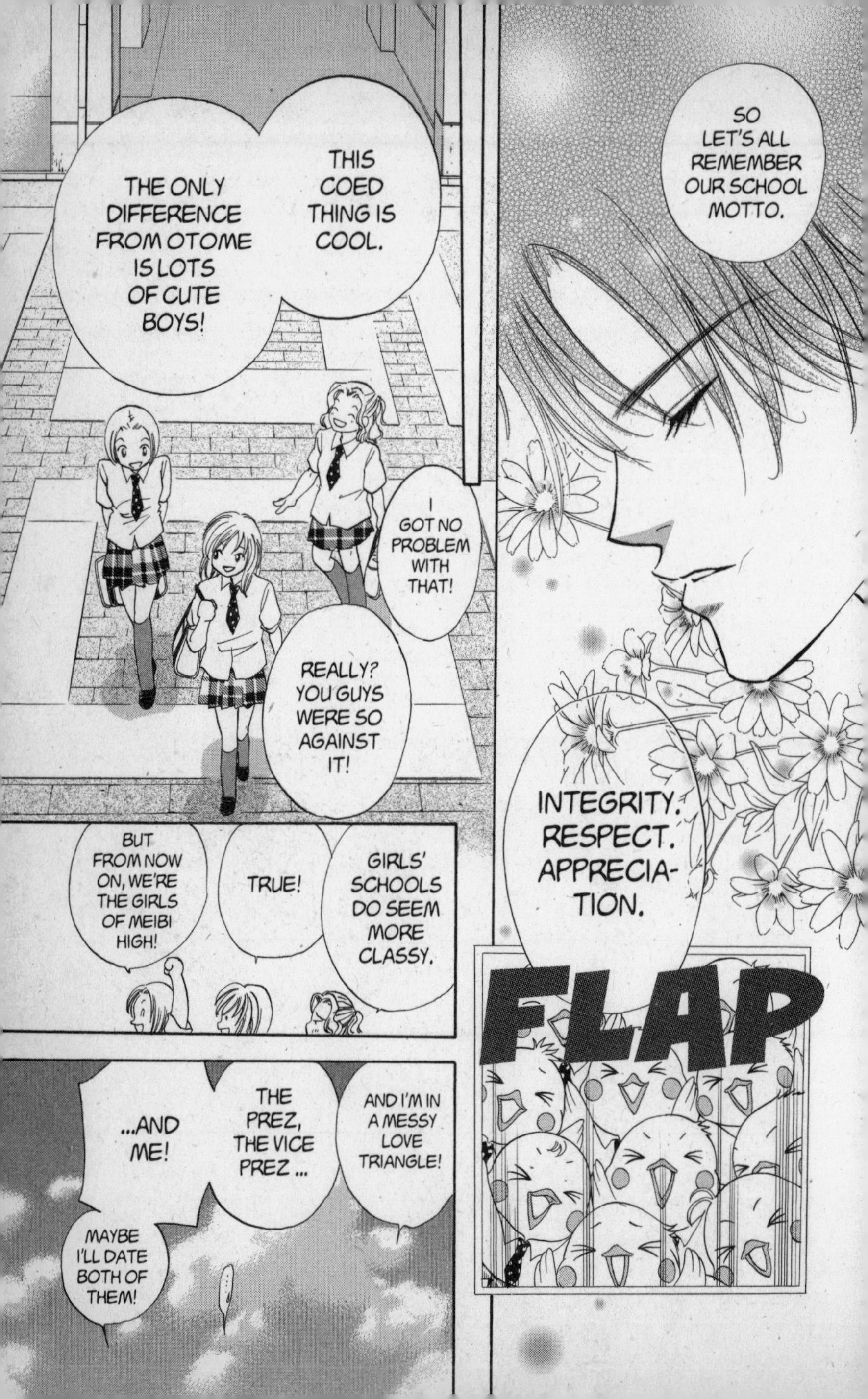
SO LET'S ALL REMEMBER OUR SCHOOL MOTTO.
INTEGRITY. RESPECT. APPRECIATION.
FLAP
THIS COED THING IS COOL.
THE ONLY DIFFERENCE FROM OTOME IS LOTS OF CUTE BOYS!
I GOT NO PROBLEM WITH THAT!
REALLY? YOU GUYS WERE SO AGAINST IT!
GIRLS' SCHOOLS DO SEEM MORE CLASSY.
TRUE!
BUT FROM NOW ON, WE'RE THE GIRLS OF MEIBI HIGH!
AND I'M IN A MESSY LOVE TRIANGLE!
THE PREZ, THE VICE PREZ ...
...AND ME!
MAYBE I'LL DATE BOTH OF THEM!
...

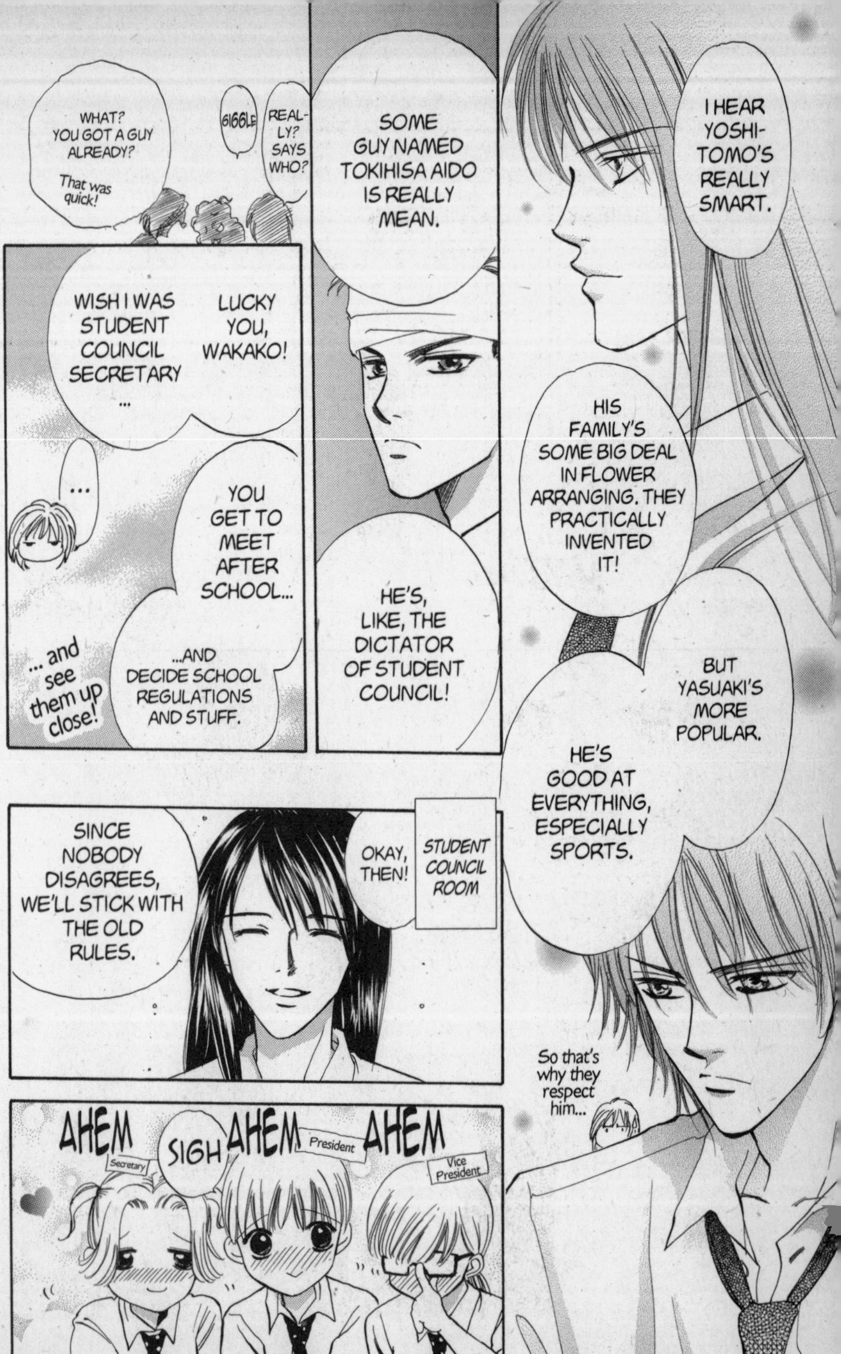
I HEAR YOSHI-TOMO'S REALLY SMART.
HIS FAMILY'S SOME BIG DEAL IN FLOWER ARRANGING. THEY PRACTICALLY INVENTED IT!
BUT YASUAKI'S MORE POPULAR.
HE'S GOOD AT EVERYTHING, ESPECIALLY SPORTS.
So that's why they respect him...
SOME GUY NAMED TOKIHISA AIDO IS REALLY MEAN.
HE'S, LIKE, THE DICTATOR OF STUDENT COUNCIL!
REAL-LY? SAYS WHO?
GIGGLE
WHAT? YOU GOT A GUY ALREADY?
That was quick!
LUCKY YOU, WAKAKO!
WISH I WAS STUDENT COUNCIL SECRETARY ...
YOU GET TO MEET AFTER SCHOOL...
...AND DECIDE SCHOOL REGULATIONS AND STUFF.
...
... and see them up close!
STUDENT COUNCIL ROOM
OKAY, THEN!
SINCE NOBODY DISAGREES, WE'LL STICK WITH THE OLD RULES.
AHEM
Vice President
President
AHEM
SIGH
Secretary
AHEM

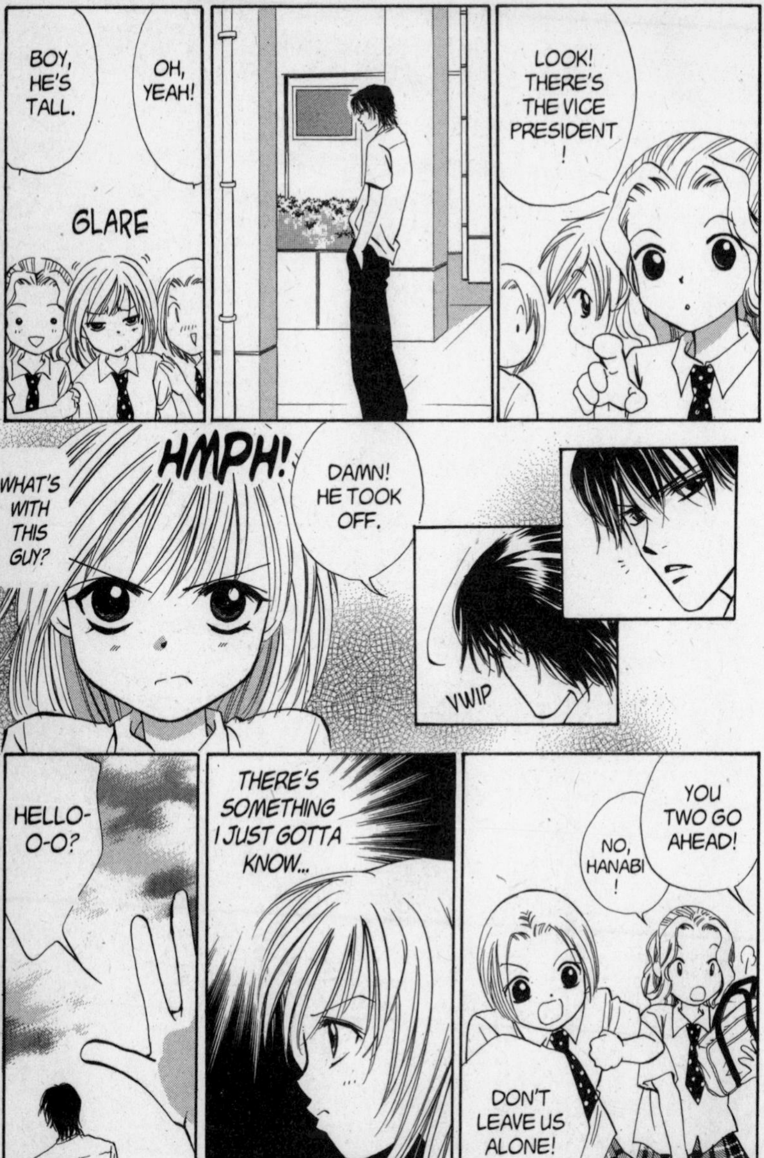
LOOK! THERE'S THE VICE PRESIDENT!
OH, YEAH!
BOY, HE'S TALL.
GLARE
VWIP
DAMN! HE TOOK OFF.
HMPH!
WHAT'S WITH THIS GUY?
YOU TWO GO AHEAD!
NO, HANABI!
DON'T LEAVE US ALONE!
THERE'S SOMETHING I JUST GOTTA KNOW...
HELLO-O-O?

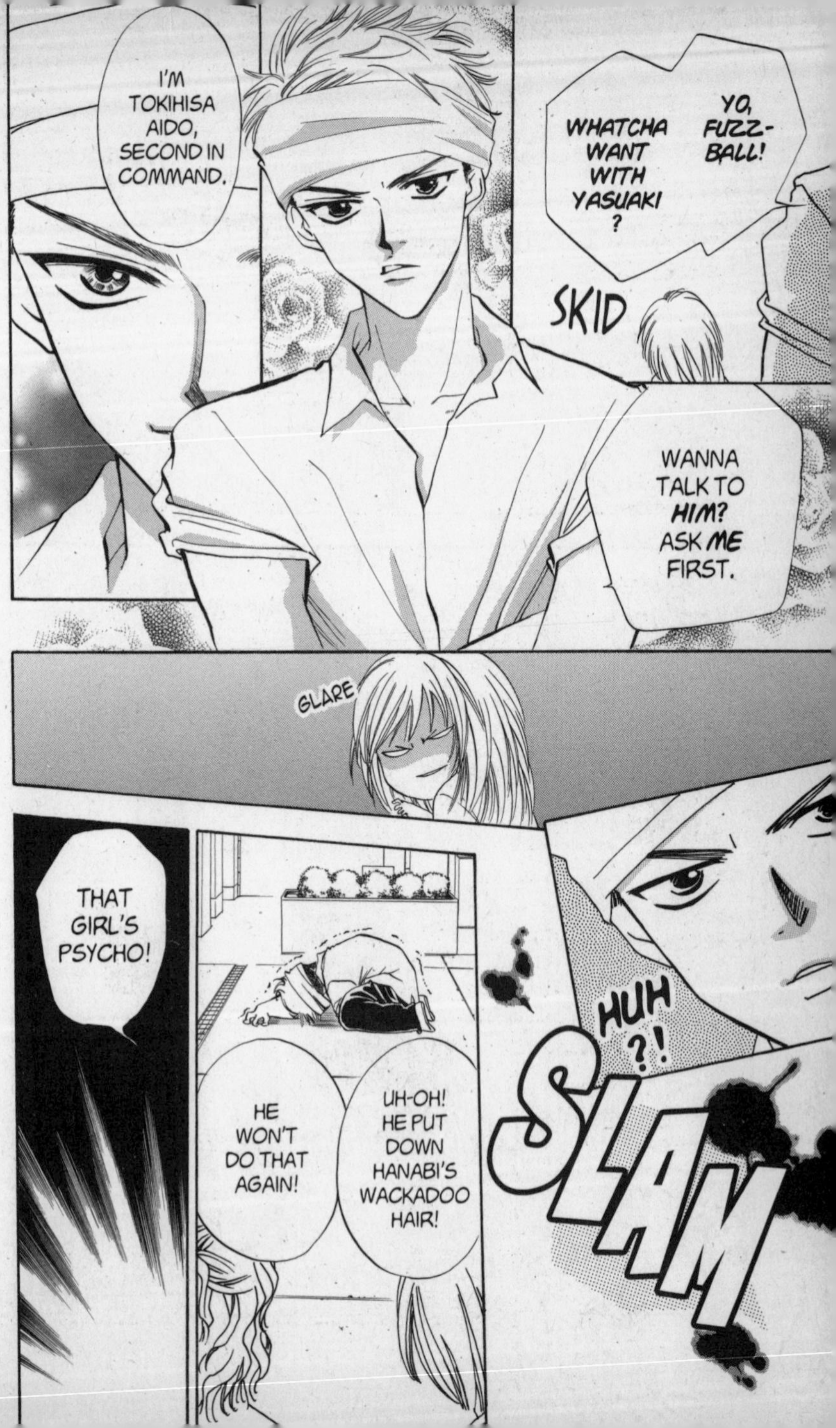
YO, FUZZ-BALL!
WHATCHA WANT WITH YASUAKI?
SKID
WANNA TALK TO HIM? ASK ME FIRST.
I'M TOKIHISA AIDO, SECOND IN COMMAND.
GLARE
HUH?!
SLAM
UH-OH! HE PUT DOWN HANABI'S WACKADOO HAIR!
HE WON'T DO THAT AGAIN!
THAT GIRL'S PSYCHO!

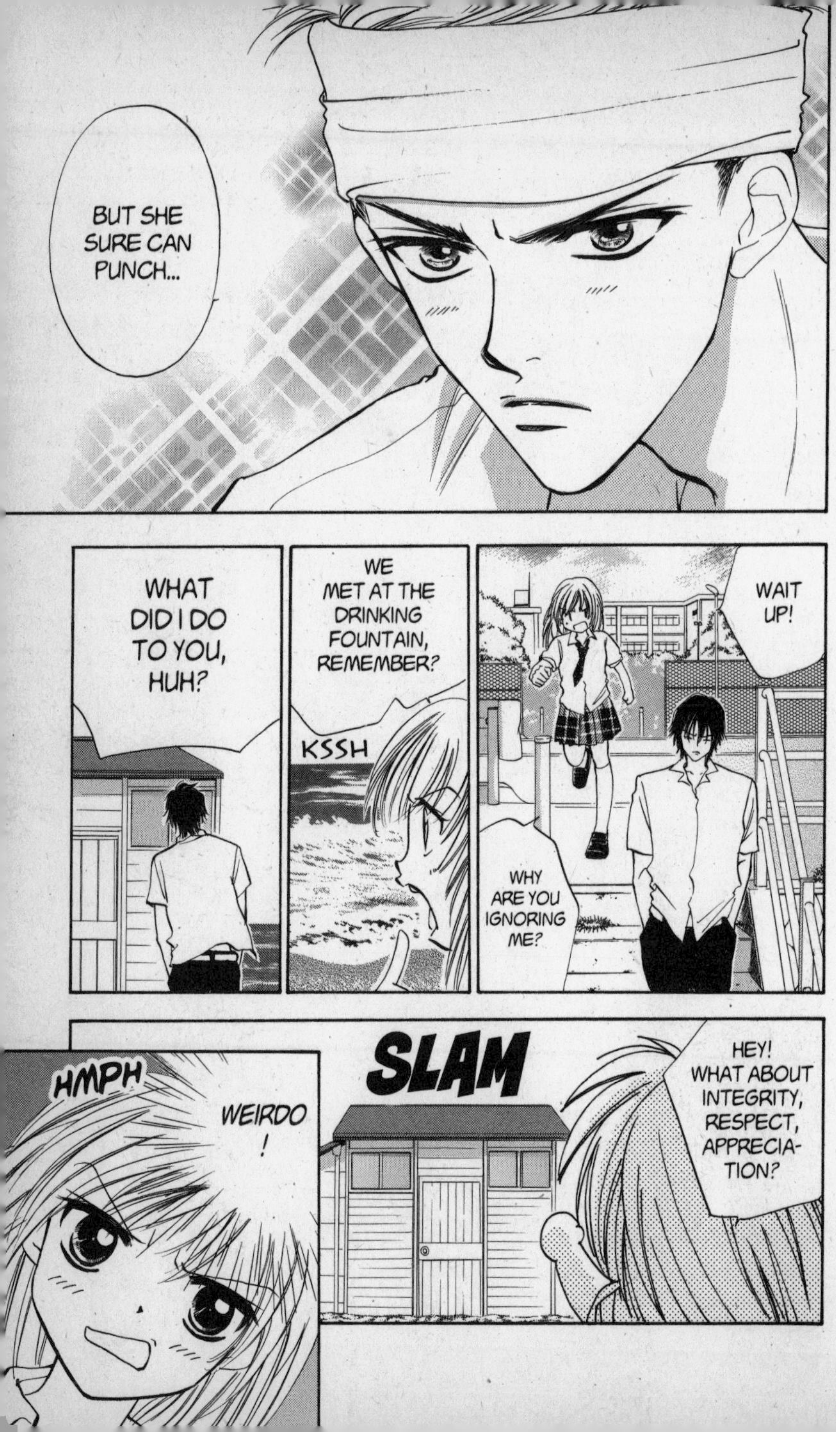
BUT SHE SURE CAN PUNCH...
WAIT UP!
WHY ARE YOU IGNORING ME?
WE MET AT THE DRINKING FOUNTAIN, REMEMBER?
KSSH
WHAT DID I DO TO YOU, HUH?
HEY! WHAT ABOUT INTEGRITY, RESPECT, APPRECIA-TION?
SLAM
HMPH
WEIRDO!

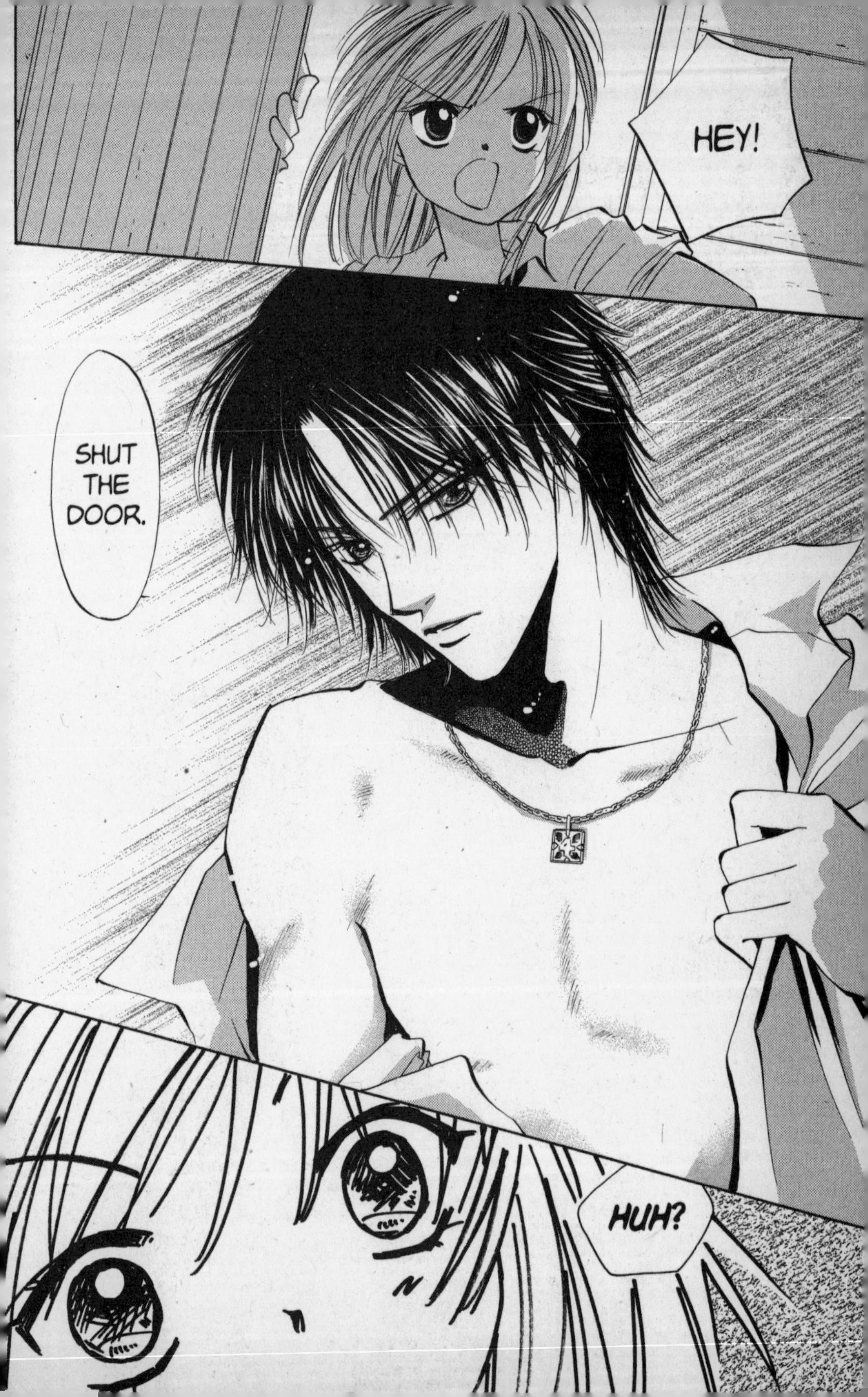
HEY!
SHUT THE DOOR.
HUH?

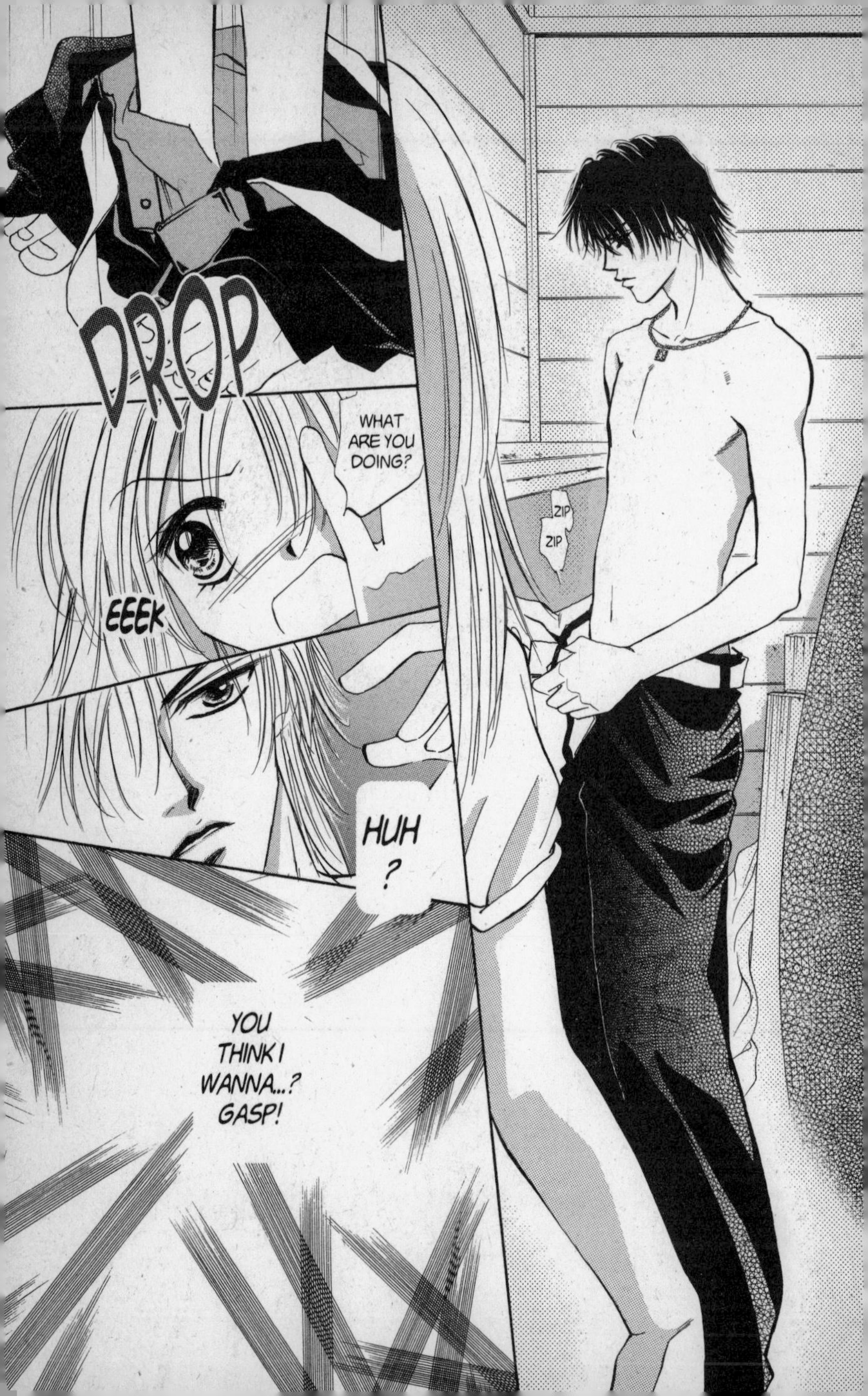

ZIP
ZIP
DROP
WHAT ARE YOU DOING?
EEEK
HUH?
YOU THINK I WANNA...? GASP!

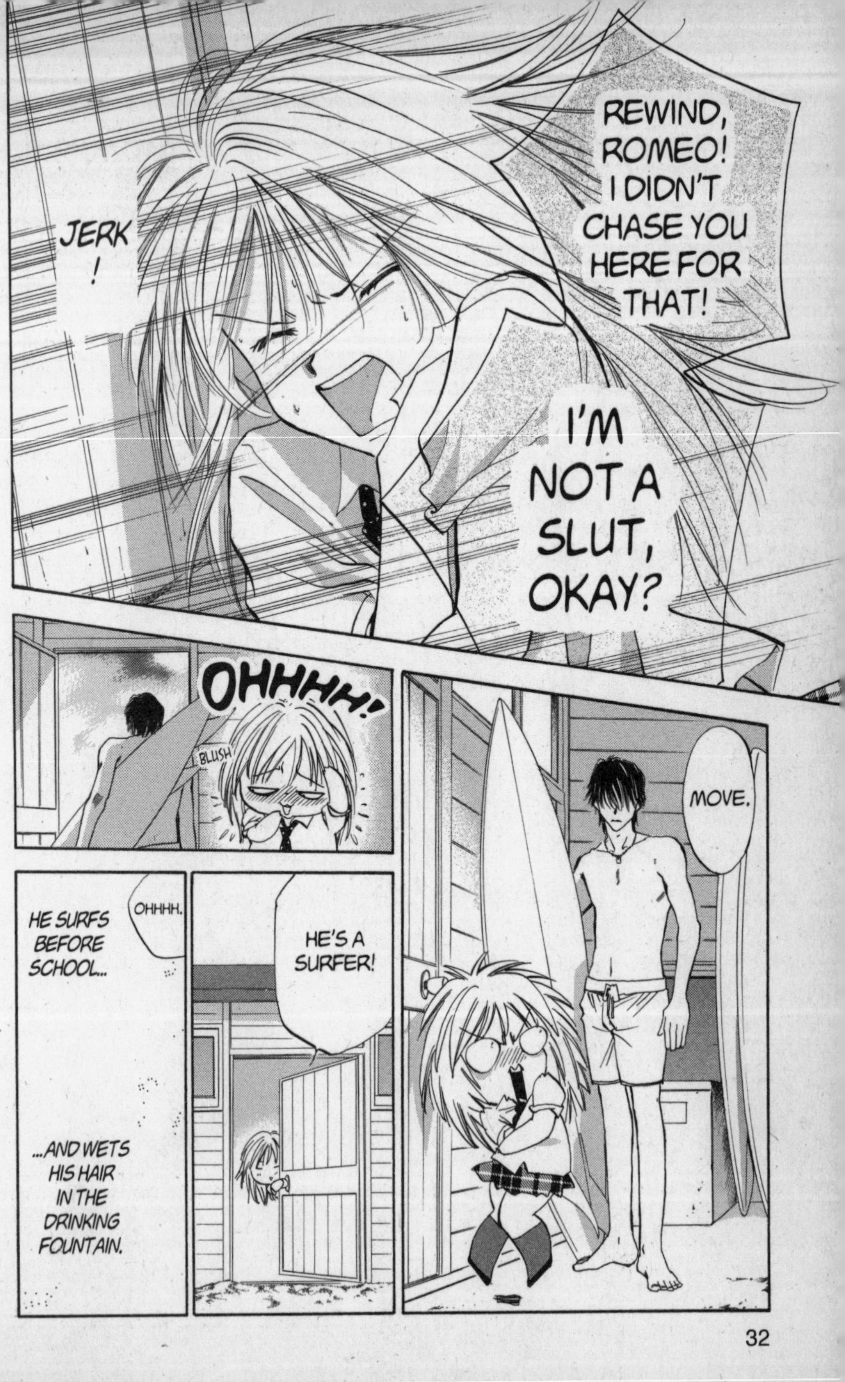
REWIND, ROMEO! I DIDN'T CHASE YOU HERE FOR THAT!
I'M NOT A SLUT, OKAY?
JERK!
MOVE.
OHHHH!
BLUSH
HE'S A SURFER!
OHHHH.
HE SURFS BEFORE SCHOOL...
...AND WETS HIS HAIR IN THE DRINKING FOUNTAIN.

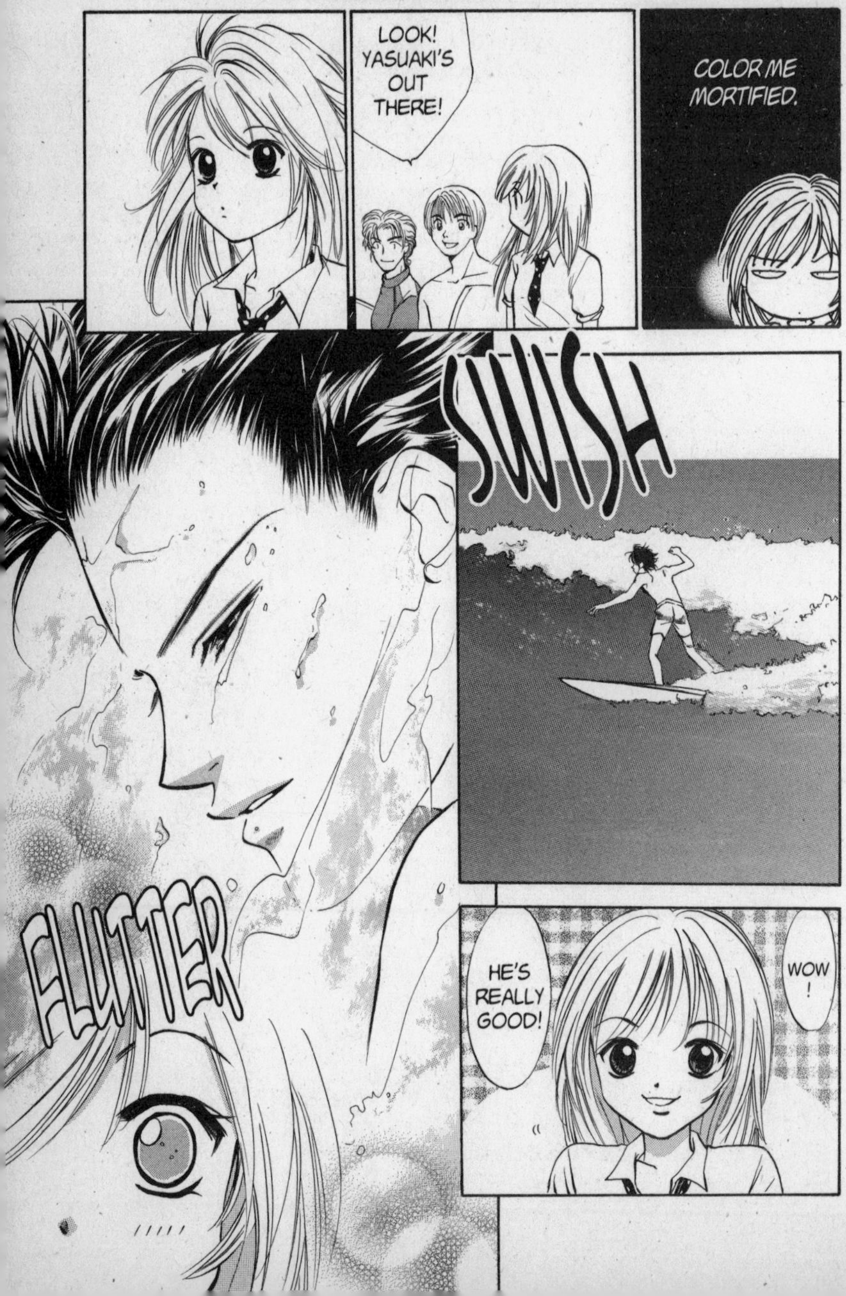
COLOR ME MORTIFIED.
LOOK! YASUAKI'S OUT THERE!
SWISH
WOW!
HE'S REALLY GOOD!
FLUTTER

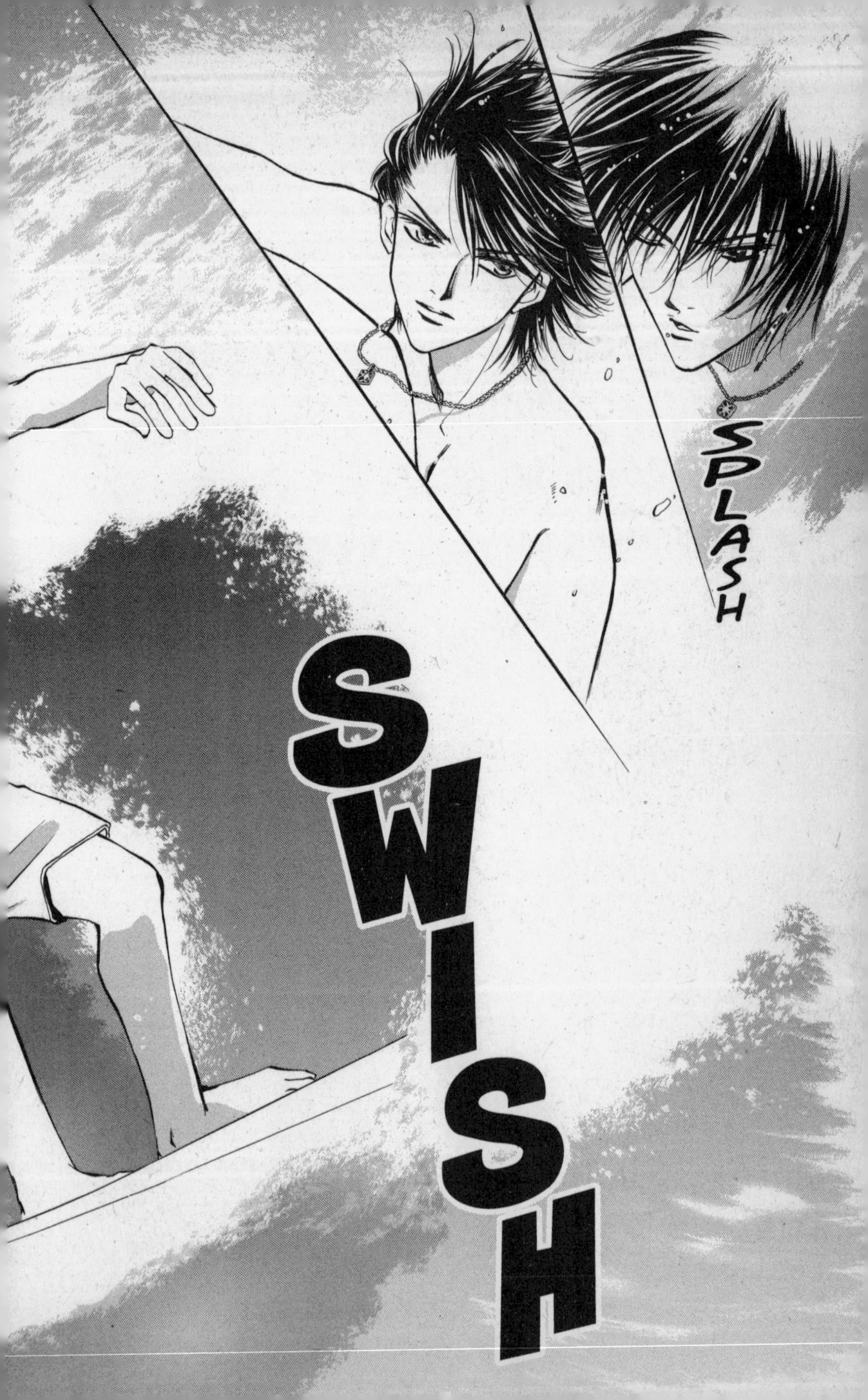
SPLASH
SWISH

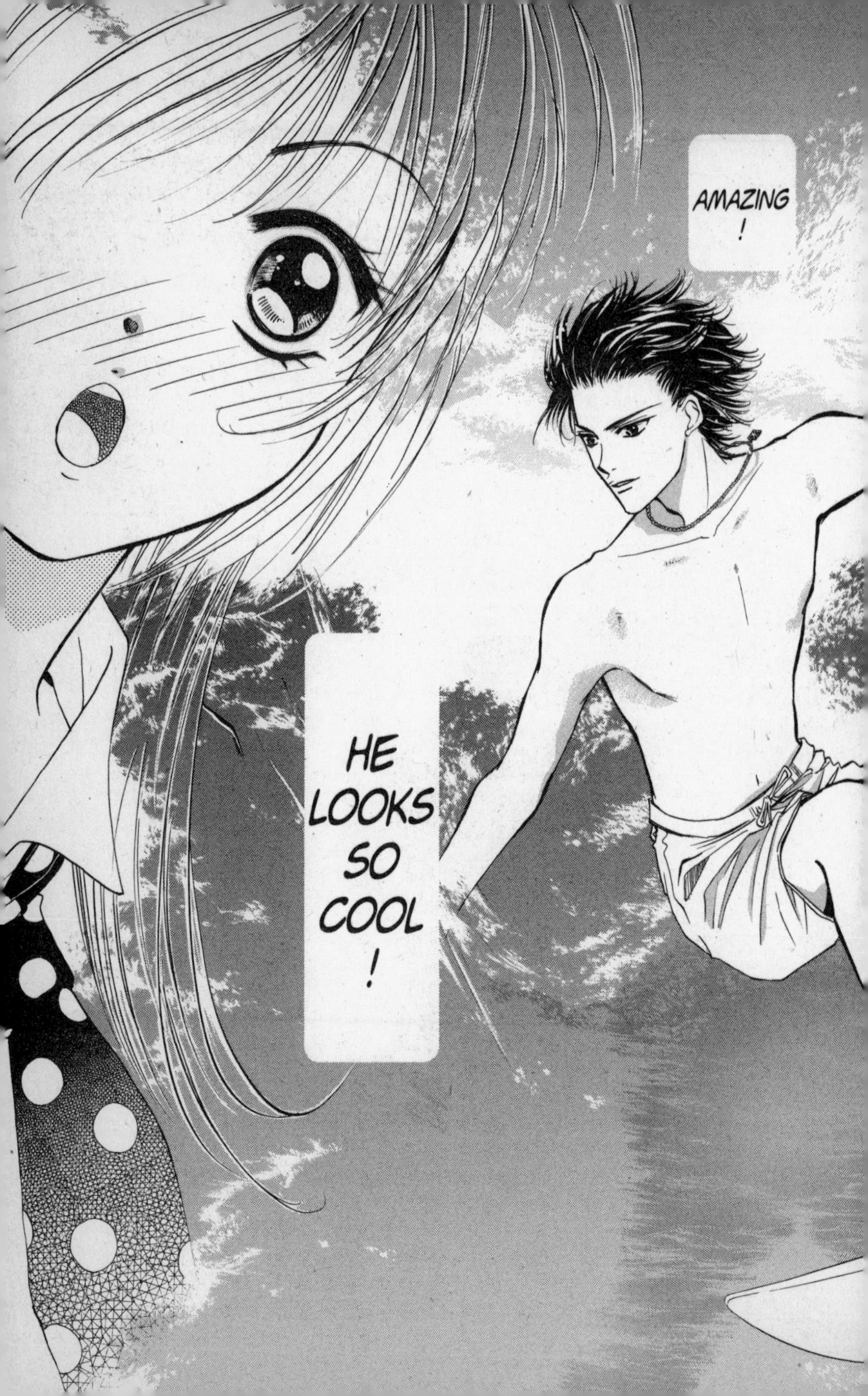
AMAZING!
HE LOOKS SO COOL!

BRILLIANT, YASUAKI!
NOT BAD, BUD!
How 'bout an encore?
......
TWEET
TWEET
YOU YASUAKI'S GIRL OR SOME-THIN'?
UH, NO, ACTUALLY.
WE GO TO THE SAME SCHOOL.

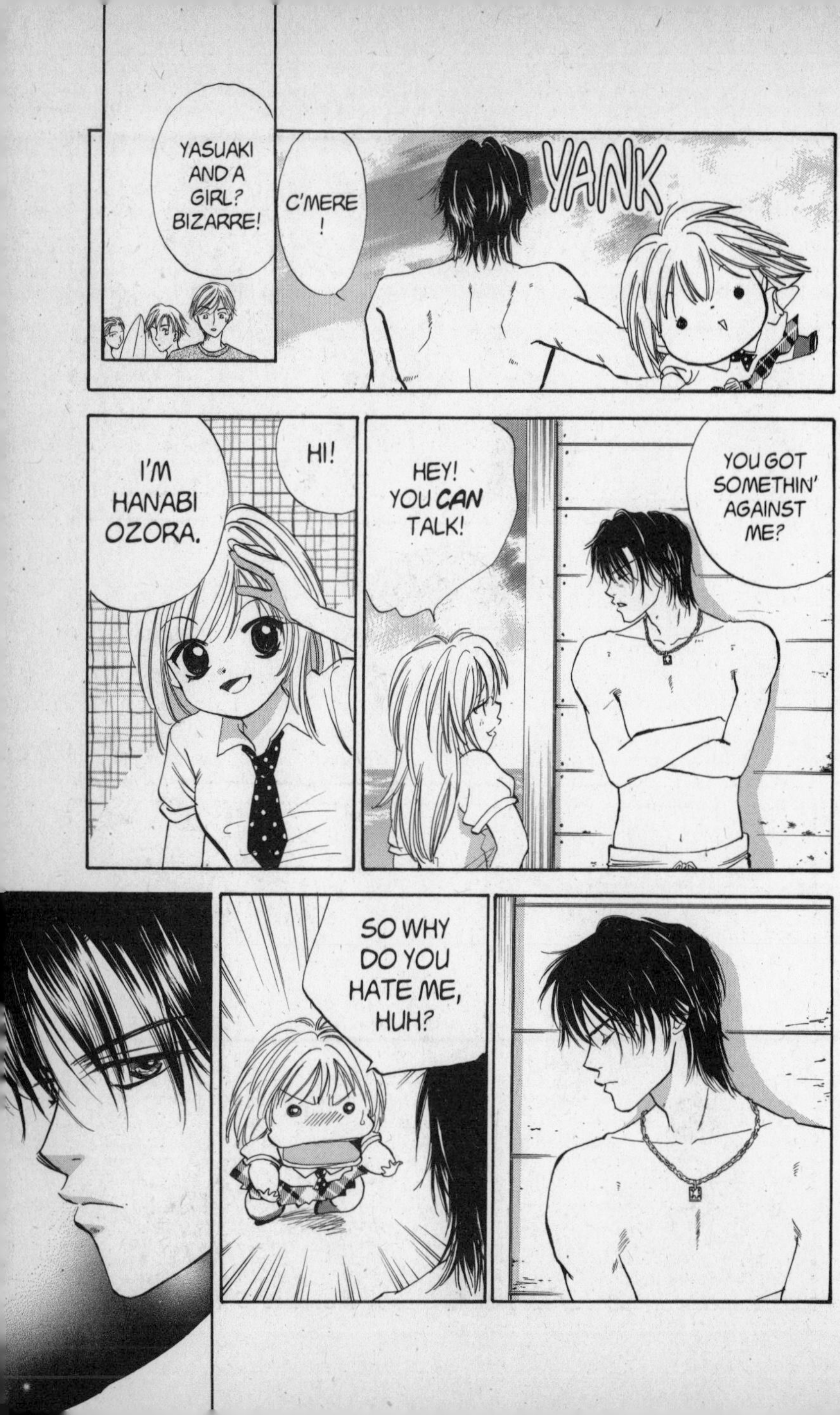
YANK
C'MERE!
YASUAKI AND A GIRL? BIZARRE!
YOU GOT SOMETHIN' AGAINST ME?
HEY! YOU CAN TALK!
HI!
I'M HANABI OZORA.
SO WHY DO YOU HATE ME, HUH?

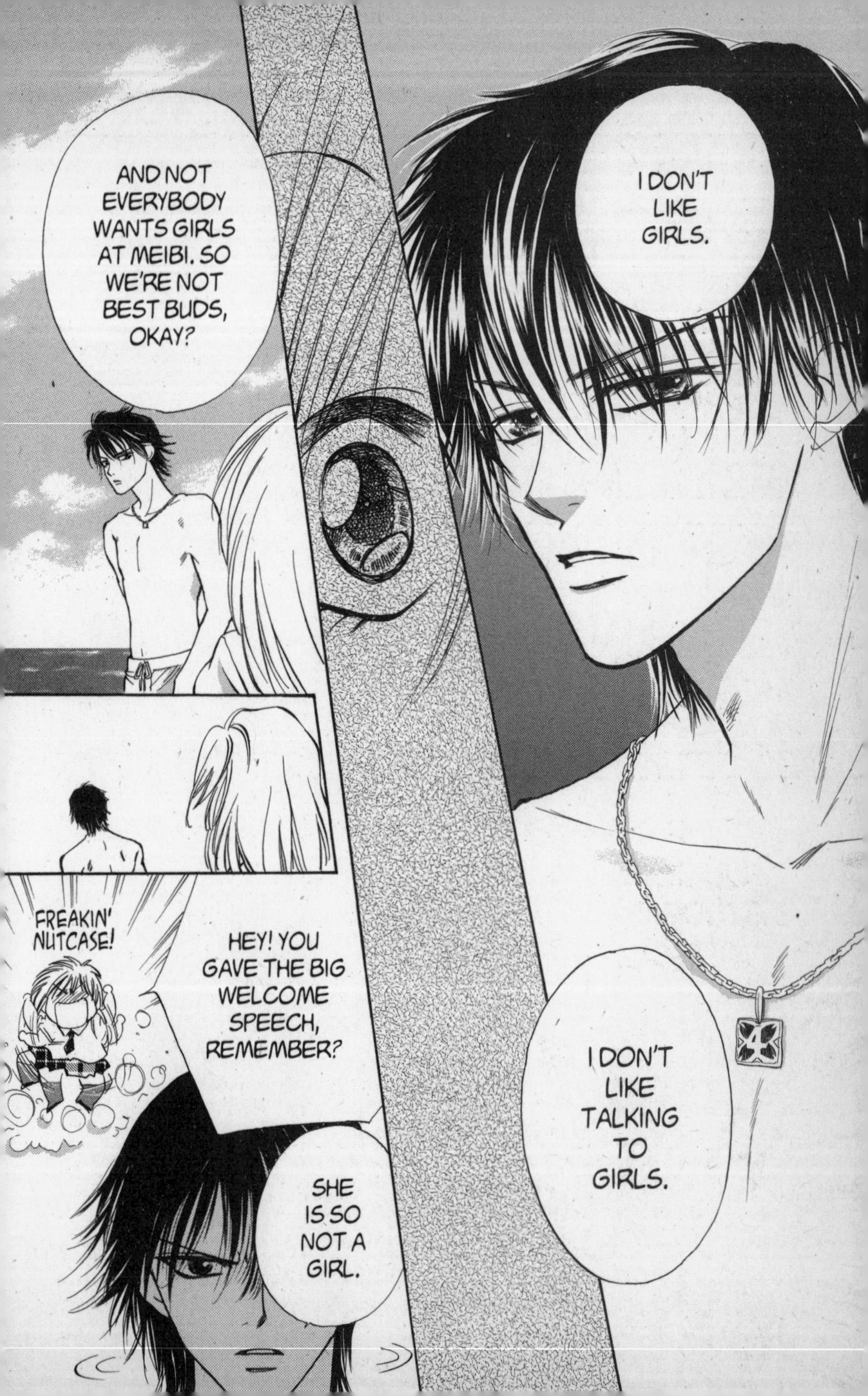
I DON'T LIKE GIRLS.
I DON'T LIKE TALKING TO GIRLS.
AND NOT EVERYBODY WANTS GIRLS AT MEIBI. SO WE'RE NOT BEST BUDS, OKAY?
HEY! YOU GAVE THE BIG WELCOME SPEECH, REMEMBER?
FREAKIN' NUTCASE!
SHE IS SO NOT A GIRL.

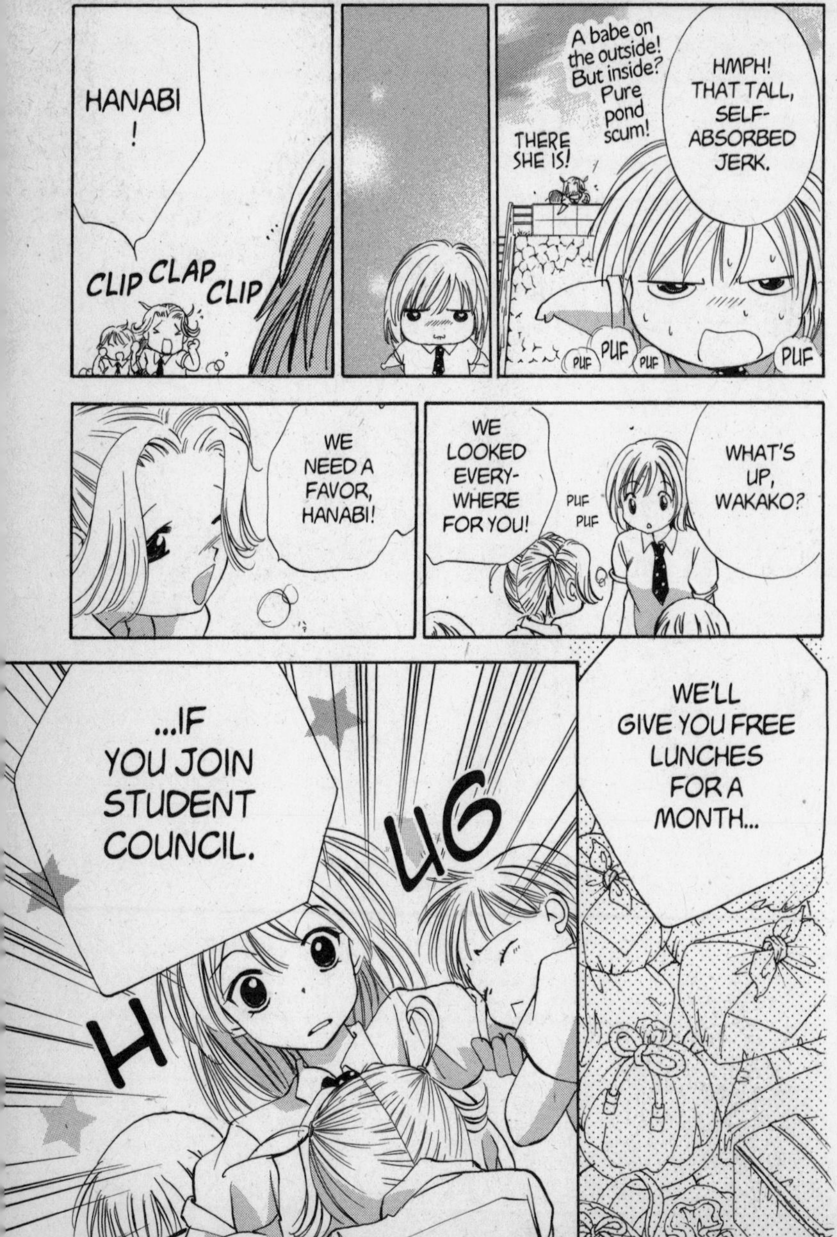
HMPH! THAT TALL, SELF-ABSORBED JERK.
A babe on the outside! But inside? Pure pond scum!
THERE SHE IS!
PUF PUF PUF PUF
HANABI!
CLIP CLAP CLIP
WHAT'S UP, WAKAKO?
PUF PUF
WE LOOKED EVERY-WHERE FOR YOU!
WE NEED A FAVOR, HANABI!
WE'LL GIVE YOU FREE LUNCHES FOR A MONTH...
...IF YOU JOIN STUDENT COUNCIL.
UG
H

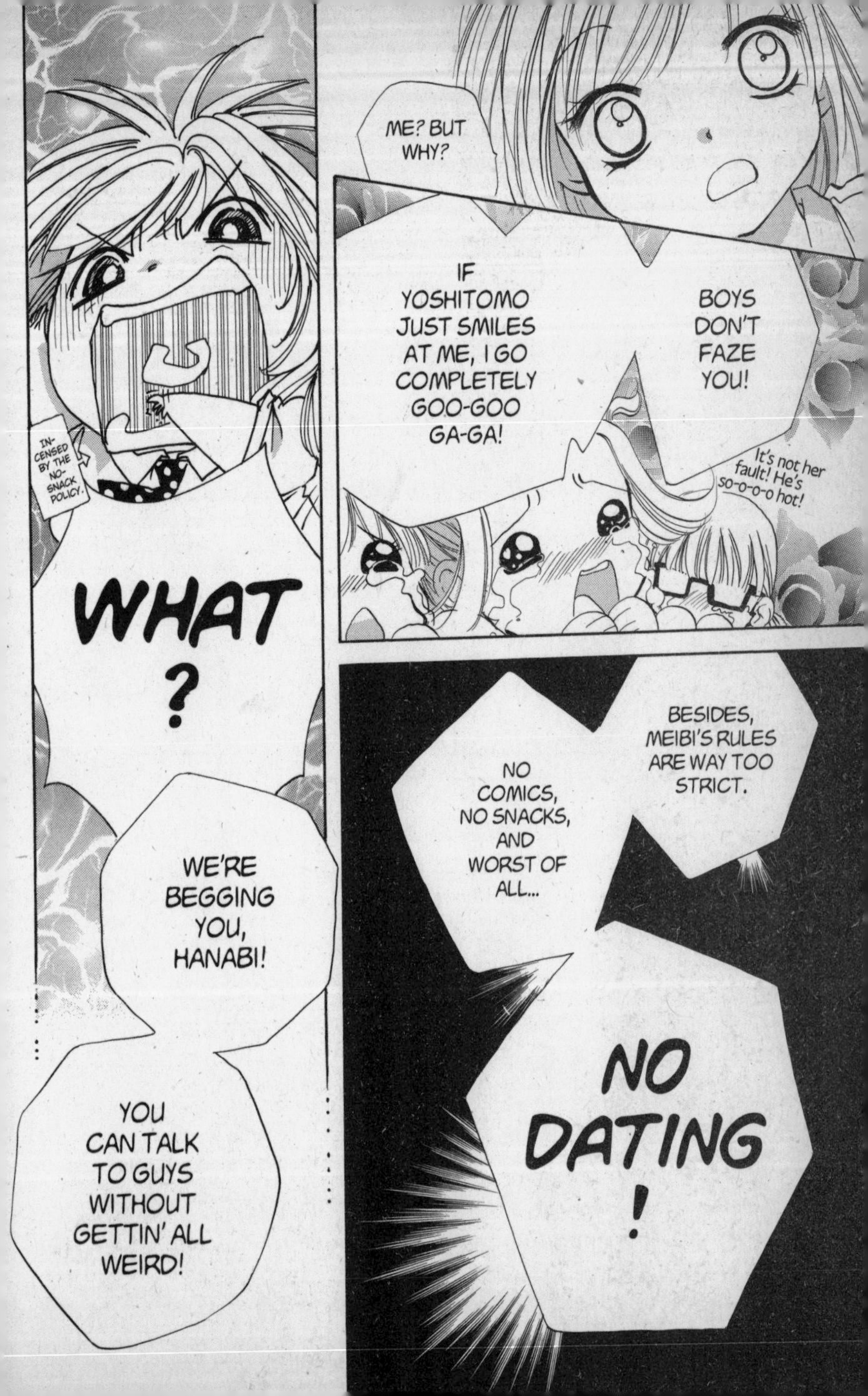

IN-CENSED BY THE NO-SNACK POLICY.
WHAT?
WE'RE BEGGING YOU, HANABI!
YOU CAN TALK TO GUYS WITHOUT GETTIN' ALL WEIRD!
ME? BUT WHY?
BOYS DON'T FAZE YOU!
IF YOSHITOMO JUST SMILES AT ME, I GO COMPLETELY GOO-GOO GA-GA!
It's not her fault! He's so-o-o-o hot!
BESIDES, MEIBI'S RULES ARE WAY TOO STRICT.
NO COMICS, NO SNACKS, AND WORST OF ALL...
NO DATING!

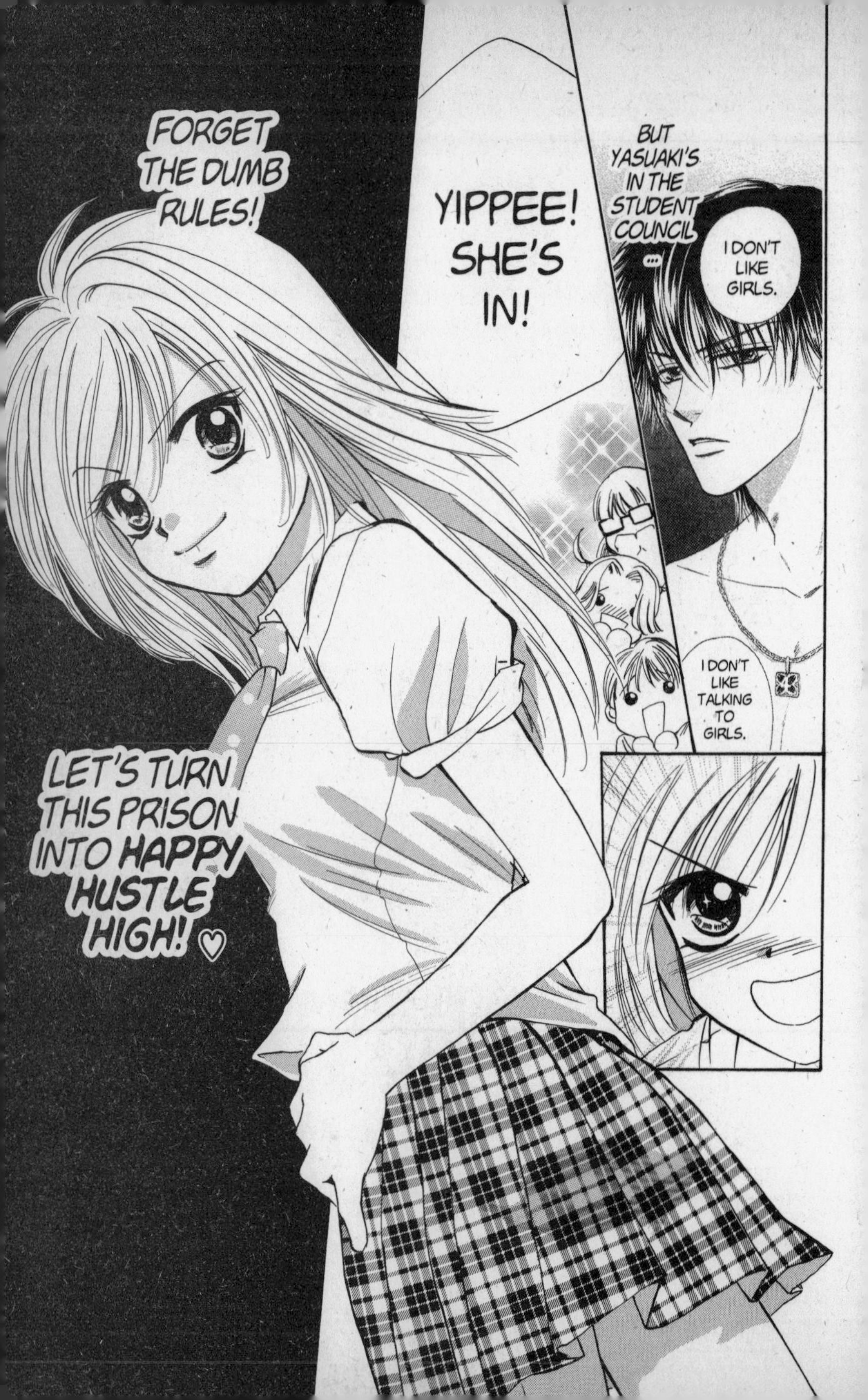
BUT YASUAKI'S IN THE STUDENT COUNCIL ...
I DON'T LIKE GIRLS.
I DON'T LIKE TALKING TO GIRLS.
YIPPEE! SHE'S IN!
FORGET THE DUMB RULES!
LET'S TURN THIS PRISON INTO HAPPY HUSTLE HIGH! ♡

HAPPY HUSTLE HIGH

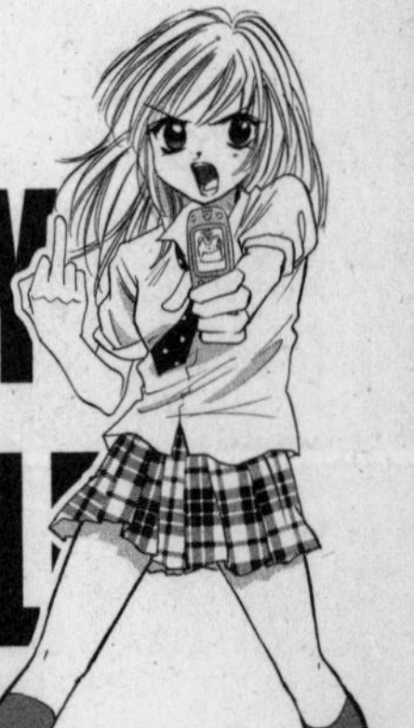

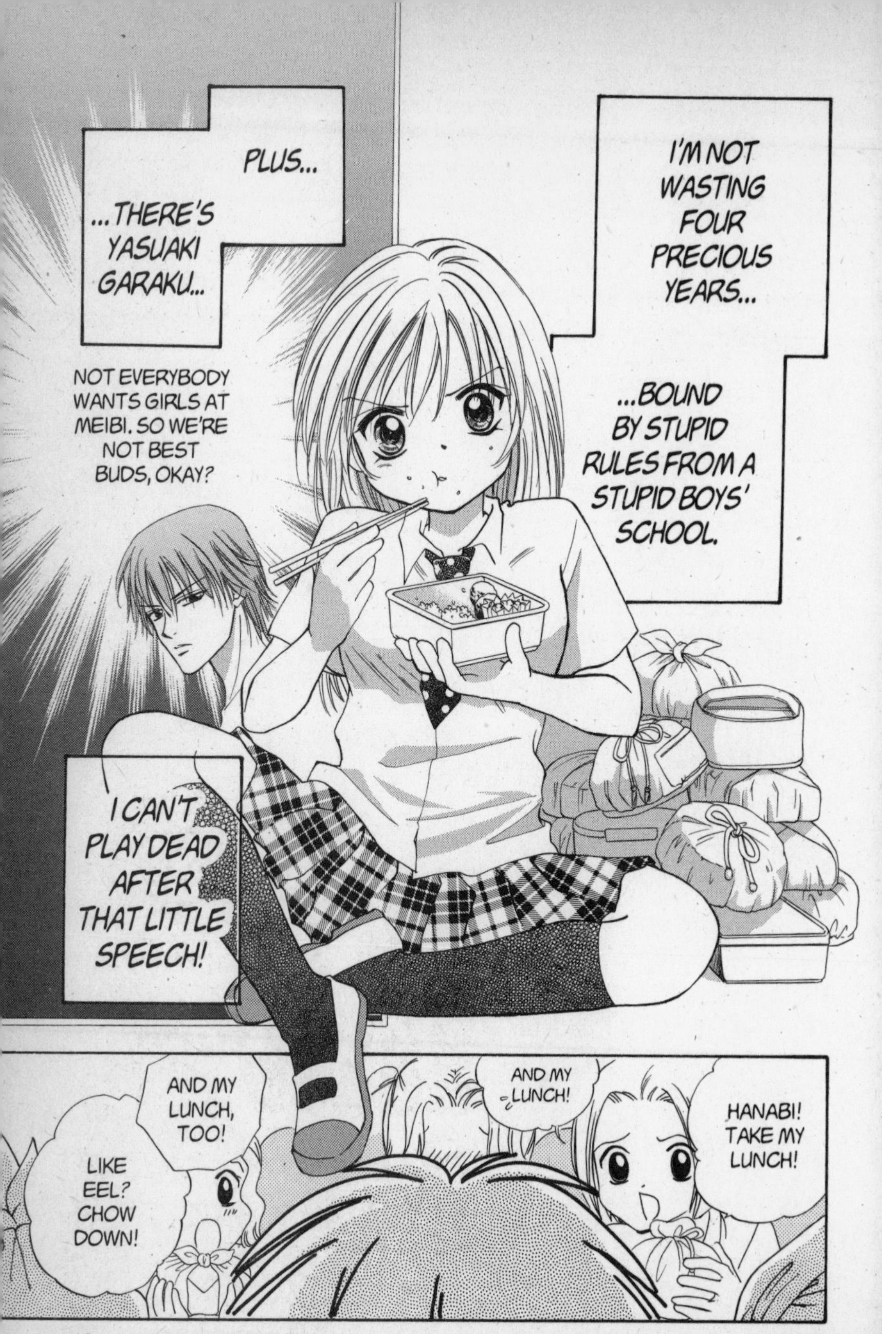
I'M NOT WASTING FOUR PRECIOUS YEARS...
...BOUND BY STUPID RULES FROM A STUPID BOYS' SCHOOL.
PLUS...
...THERE'S YASUAKI GARAKU...
NOT EVERYBODY WANTS GIRLS AT MEIBI. SO WE'RE NOT BEST BUDS, OKAY?
I CAN'T PLAY DEAD AFTER THAT LITTLE SPEECH!
HANABI! TAKE MY LUNCH!
AND MY LUNCH!
AND MY LUNCH, TOO!
LIKE EEL? CHOW DOWN!

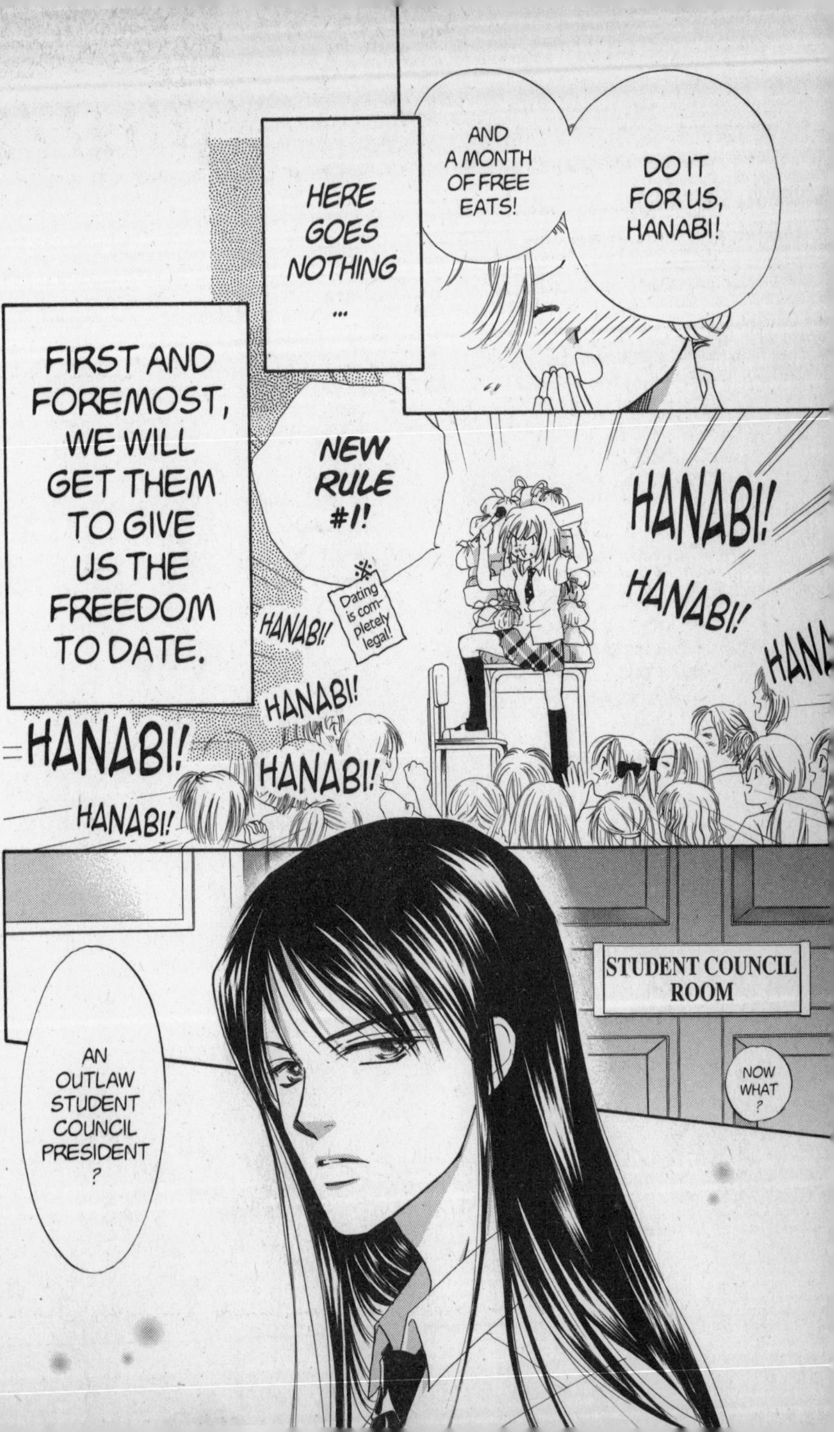

DO IT FOR US, HANABI!
AND A MONTH OF FREE EATS!
HERE GOES NOTHING ...
HANABI!
HANABI!
HANA
NEW RULE #1!
※ Dating is completely legal!
FIRST AND FOREMOST, WE WILL GET THEM TO GIVE US THE FREEDOM TO DATE.
HANABI!
HANABI!
HANABI!
HANABI!
HANABI!
STUDENT COUNCIL ROOM
NOW WHAT?
AN OUTLAW STUDENT COUNCIL PRESIDENT?

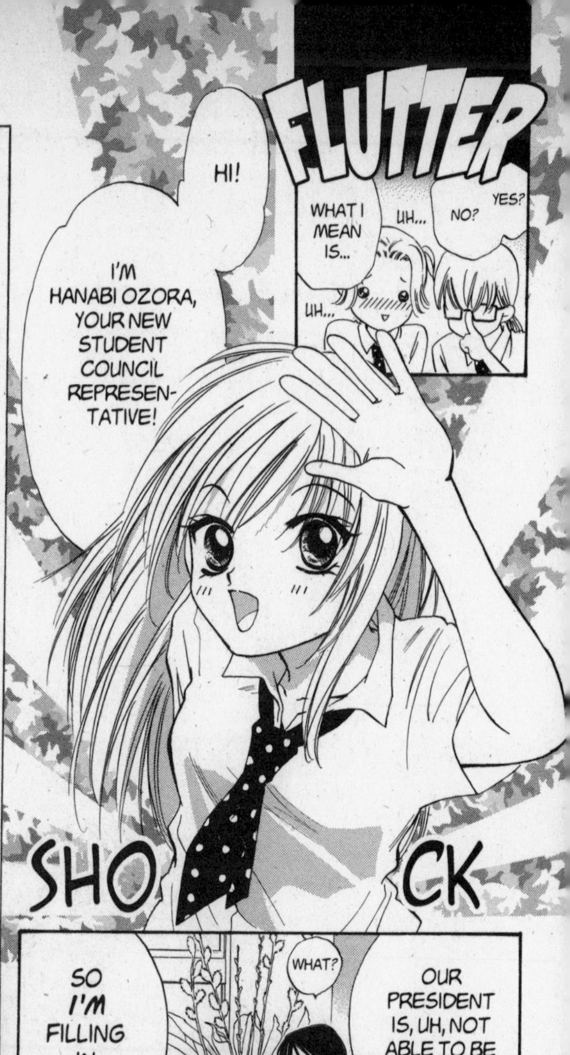
FLUTTER
YES?
NO?
UH...
WHAT I MEAN IS...
UH...
HI!
I'M HANABI OZORA, YOUR NEW STUDENT COUNCIL REPRESENTATIVE!
SHOCK
OUR PRESIDENT IS, UH, NOT ABLE TO BE HERE!
WHAT?
SO I'M FILLING IN TODAY!

I HOPE YOU ARE ENJOYING H3! I TOOK SOME TIME OFF BEFORE STARTING THIS SERIES. (I HAVEN'T KICKED BACK LIKE THAT SINCE ELEMENTARY SCHOOL!) NOW I'M FINALLY GETTING BACK INTO WORK MODE. JUST REALIZED SOMETHING RECENTLY—EVEN THOUGH I'VE DONE COMICS FOR TEN YEARS, IF I DON'T DRAW FOR A WHILE, I CAN QUICKLY FORGET HOW! AT ANY RATE, I HOPE YOU'LL READ HAPPY HUSTLE HIGH! THIS ROMANCE COMIC IS MY TRUE LOVE FANTASY!

-RIE TAKADA

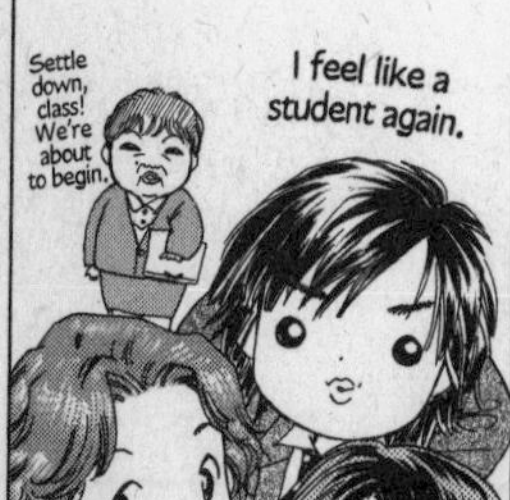
I feel like a student again.
Settle down, class! We're about to begin.

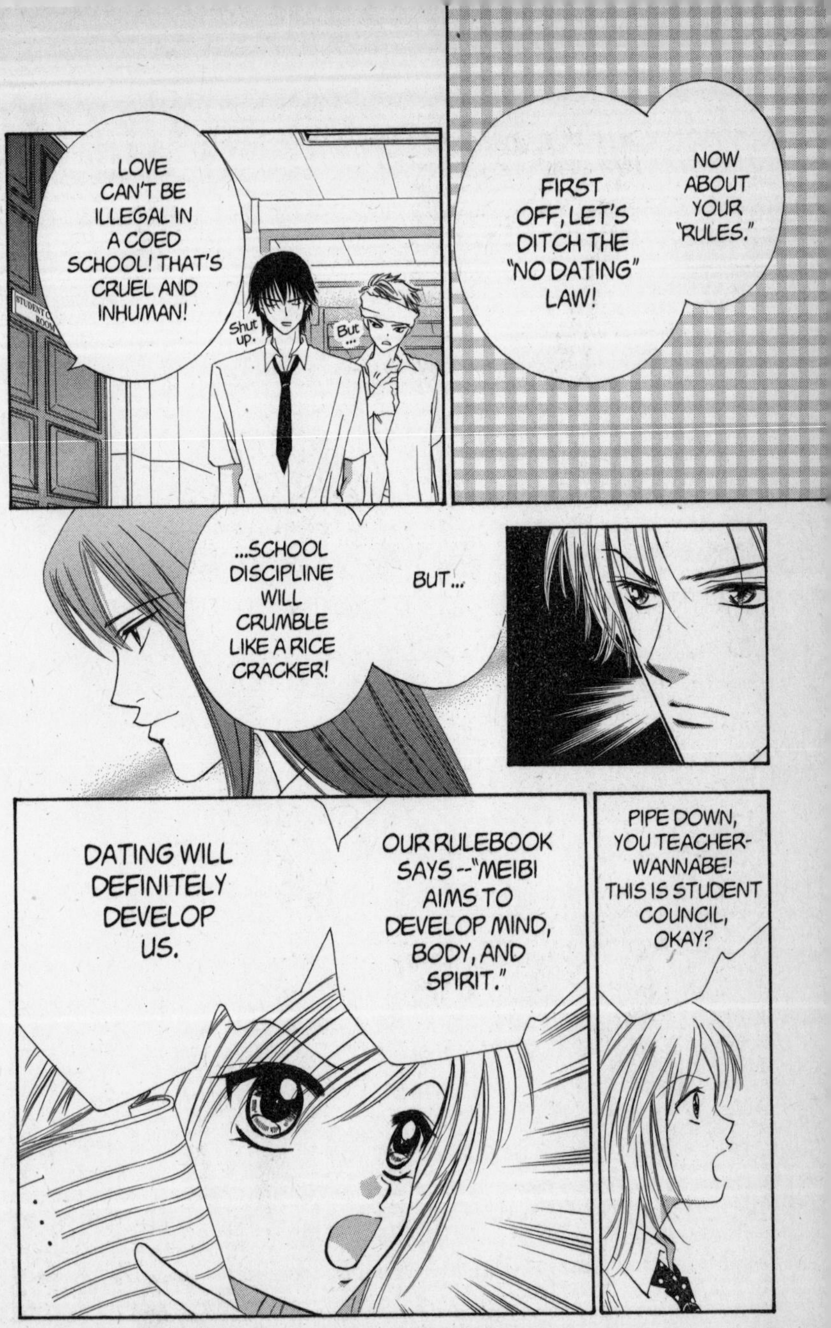
NOW ABOUT YOUR "RULES."
FIRST OFF, LET'S DITCH THE "NO DATING" LAW!
LOVE CAN'T BE ILLEGAL IN A COED SCHOOL! THAT'S CRUEL AND INHUMAN!
But ...
Shut up.
BUT...
...SCHOOL DISCIPLINE WILL CRUMBLE LIKE A RICE CRACKER!
PIPE DOWN, YOU TEACHER-WANNABE! THIS IS STUDENT COUNCIL, OKAY?
OUR RULEBOOK SAYS --"MEIBI AIMS TO DEVELOP MIND, BODY, AND SPIRIT."
DATING WILL DEFINITELY DEVELOP US.

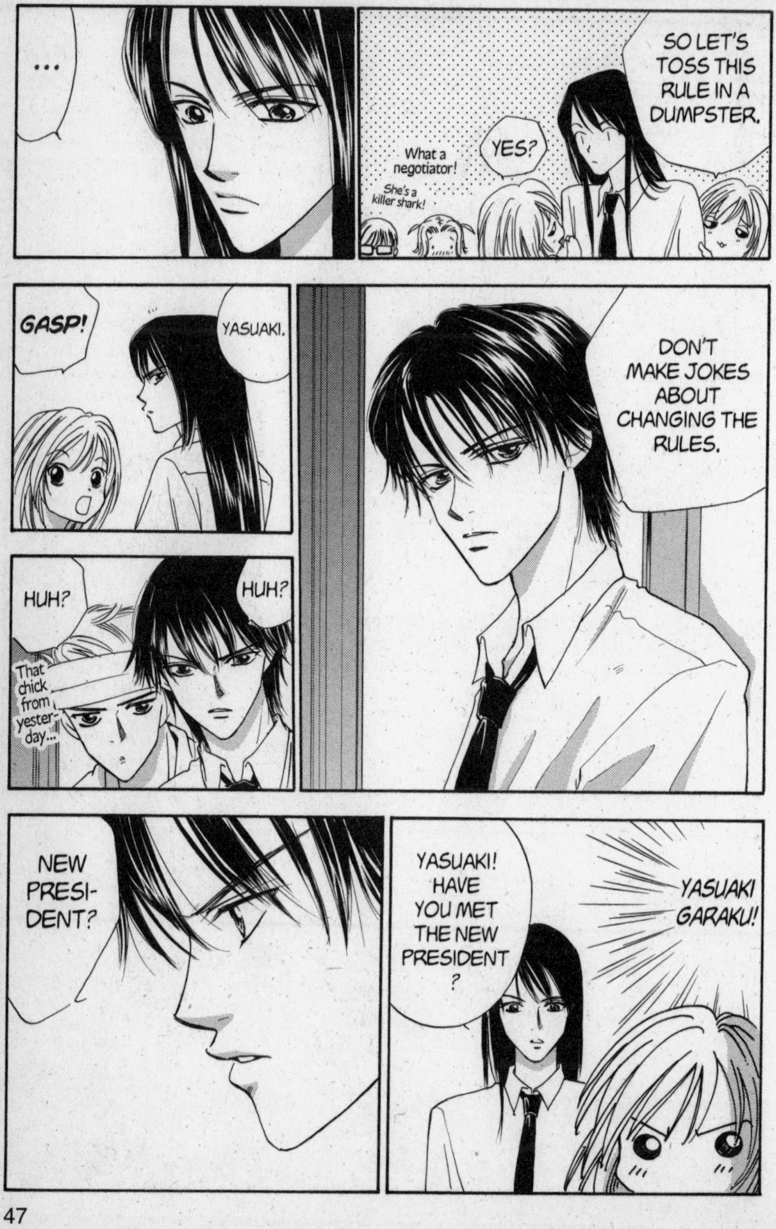
SO LET'S TOSS THIS RULE IN A DUMPSTER.
YES?
What a negotiator!
She's a killer shark!
...
DON'T MAKE JOKES ABOUT CHANGING THE RULES.
YASUAKI.
GASP!
HUH?
HUH?
That chick from yester-day...
YASUAKI GARAKU!
YASUAKI! HAVE YOU MET THE NEW PRESIDENT?
NEW PRESI-DENT?

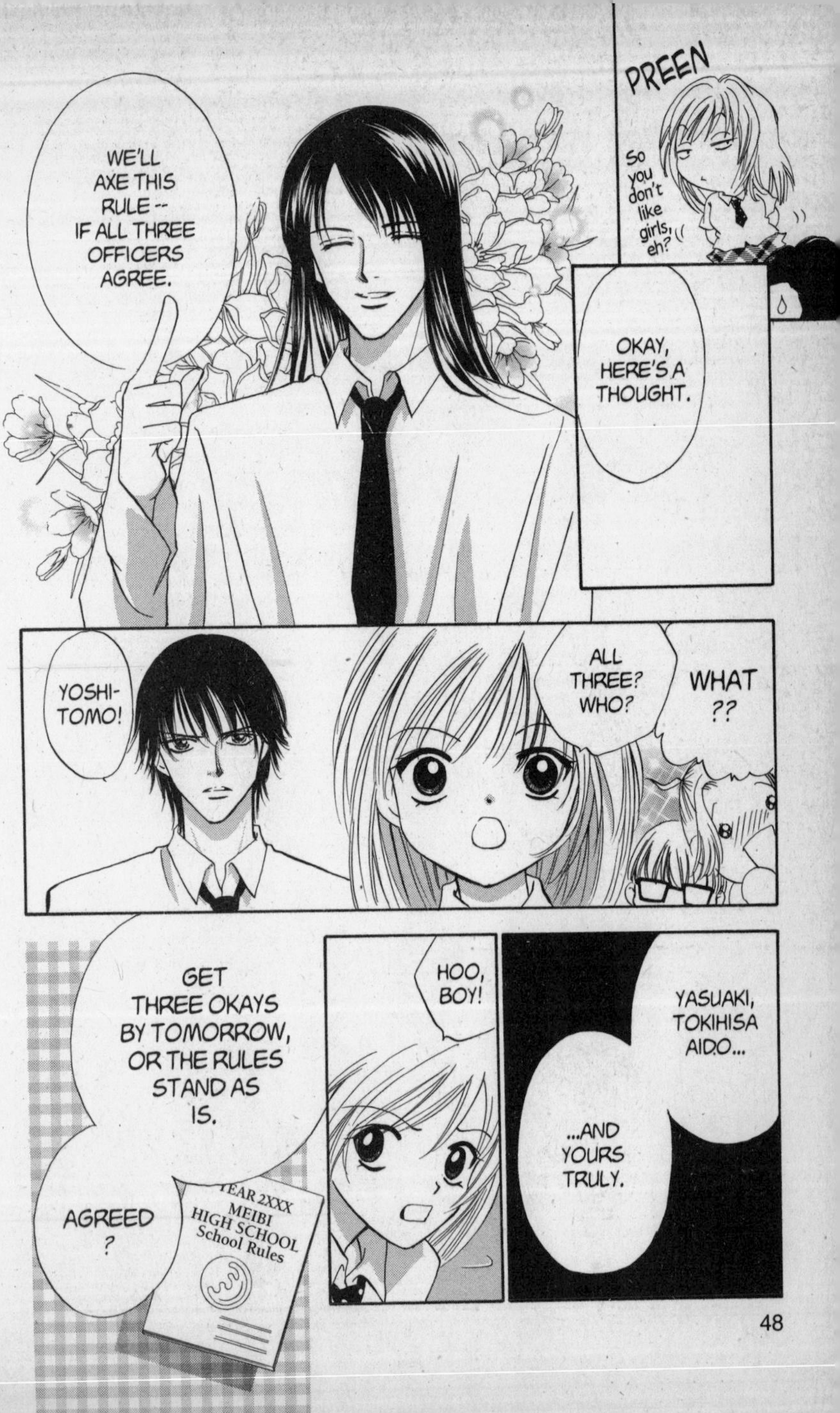
PREEN
So you don't like girls, eh?
OKAY, HERE'S A THOUGHT.
WE'LL AXE THIS RULE -- IF ALL THREE OFFICERS AGREE.
WHAT ??
ALL THREE? WHO?
YOSHI-TOMO!
YASUAKI, TOKIHISA AIDO...
...AND YOURS TRULY.
HOO, BOY!
GET THREE OKAYS BY TOMORROW, OR THE RULES STAND AS IS.
AGREED ?
YEAR 2XXX MEIBI HIGH SCHOOL School Rules

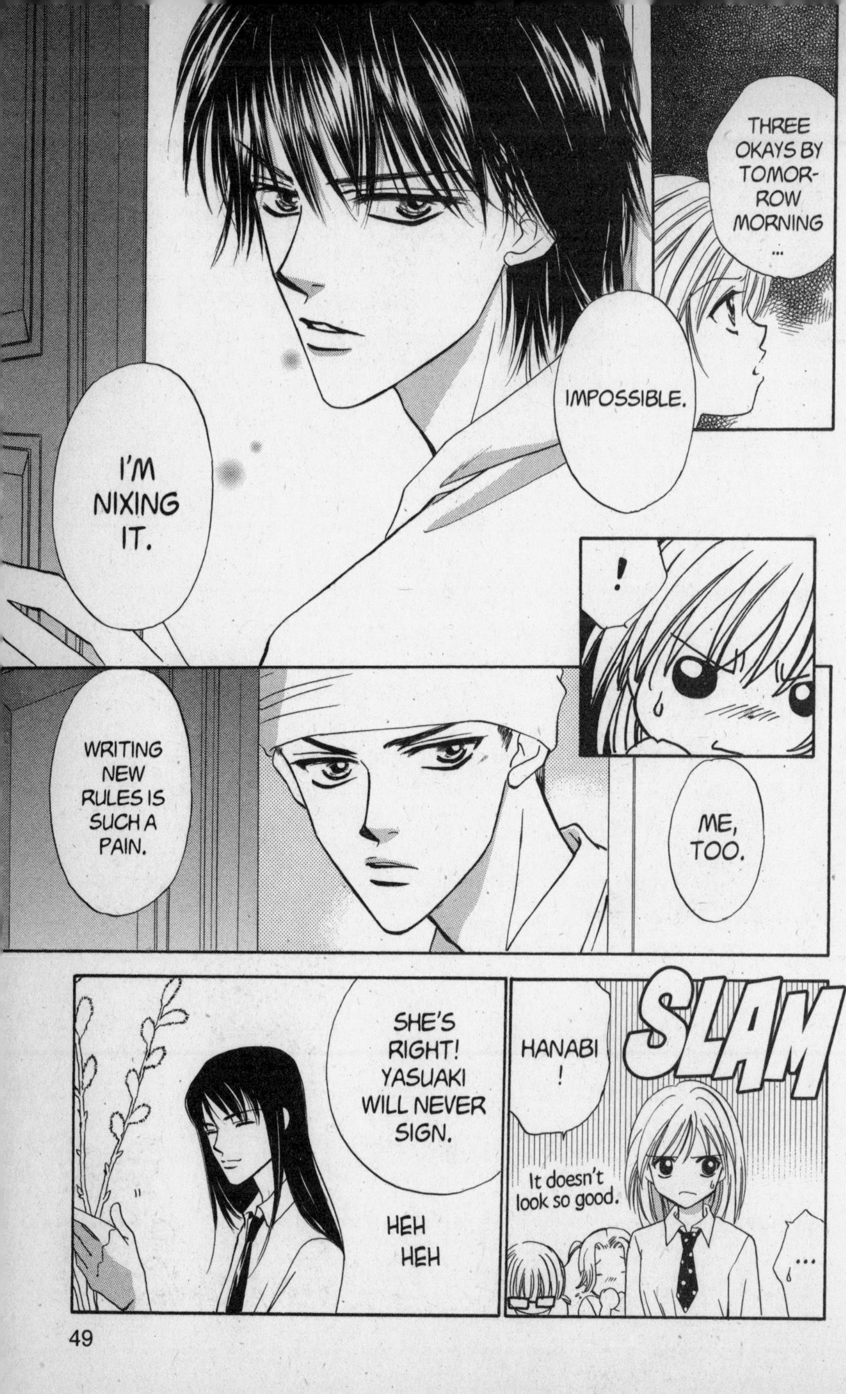
THREE OKAYS BY TOMORROW MORNING ...
IMPOSSIBLE.
I'M NIXING IT.
!
ME, TOO.
WRITING NEW RULES IS SUCH A PAIN.
SLAM
HANABI!
It doesn't look so good.
...
SHE'S RIGHT! YASUAKI WILL NEVER SIGN.
HEH HEH

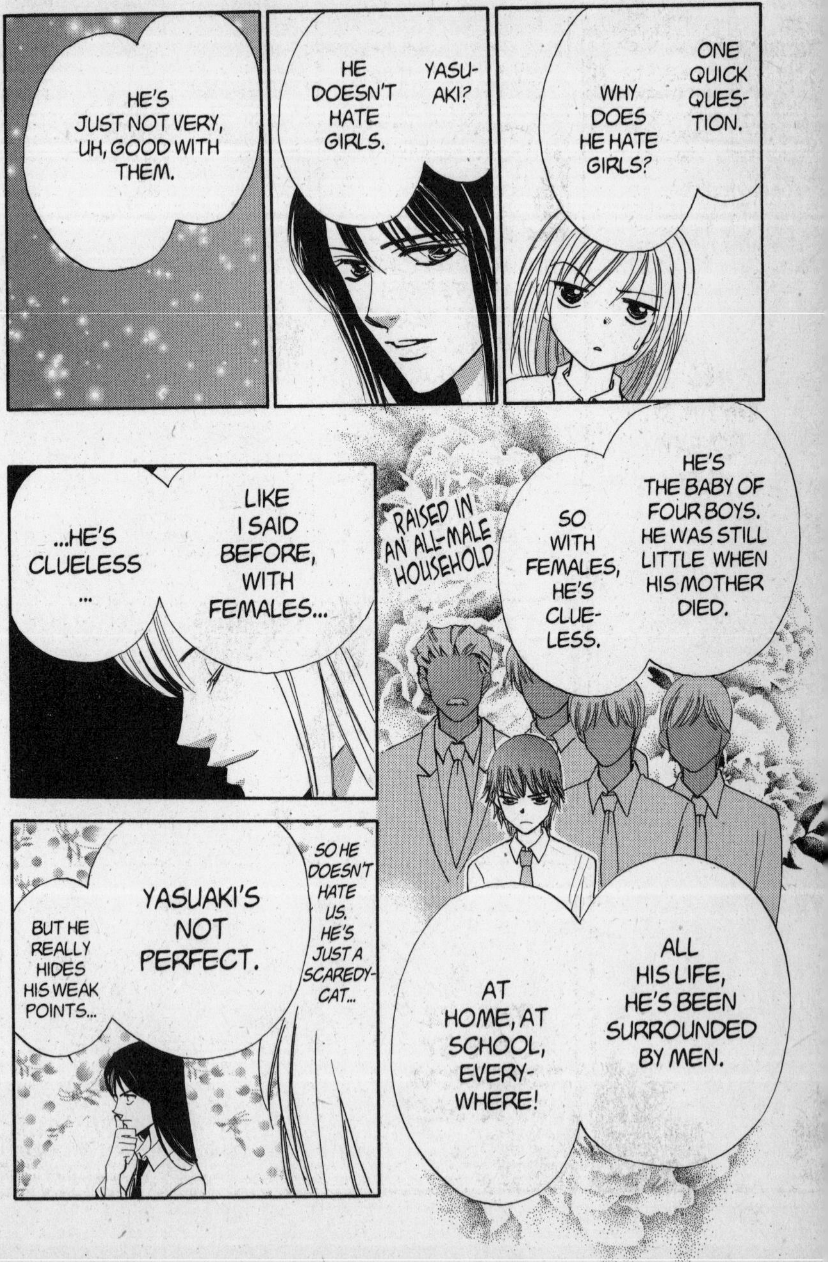
ONE QUICK QUES-TION.
WHY DOES HE HATE GIRLS?
YASU-AKI?
HE DOESN'T HATE GIRLS.
HE'S JUST NOT VERY, UH, GOOD WITH THEM.
HE'S THE BABY OF FOUR BOYS. HE WAS STILL LITTLE WHEN HIS MOTHER DIED.
SO WITH FEMALES, HE'S CLUE-LESS.
RAISED IN AN ALL-MALE HOUSEHOLD
ALL HIS LIFE, HE'S BEEN SURROUNDED BY MEN.
AT HOME, AT SCHOOL, EVERY-WHERE!
LIKE I SAID BEFORE, WITH FEMALES...
...HE'S CLUELESS ...
SO HE DOESN'T HATE US. HE'S JUST A SCAREDY-CAT...
YASUAKI'S NOT PERFECT.
BUT HE REALLY HIDES HIS WEAK POINTS...

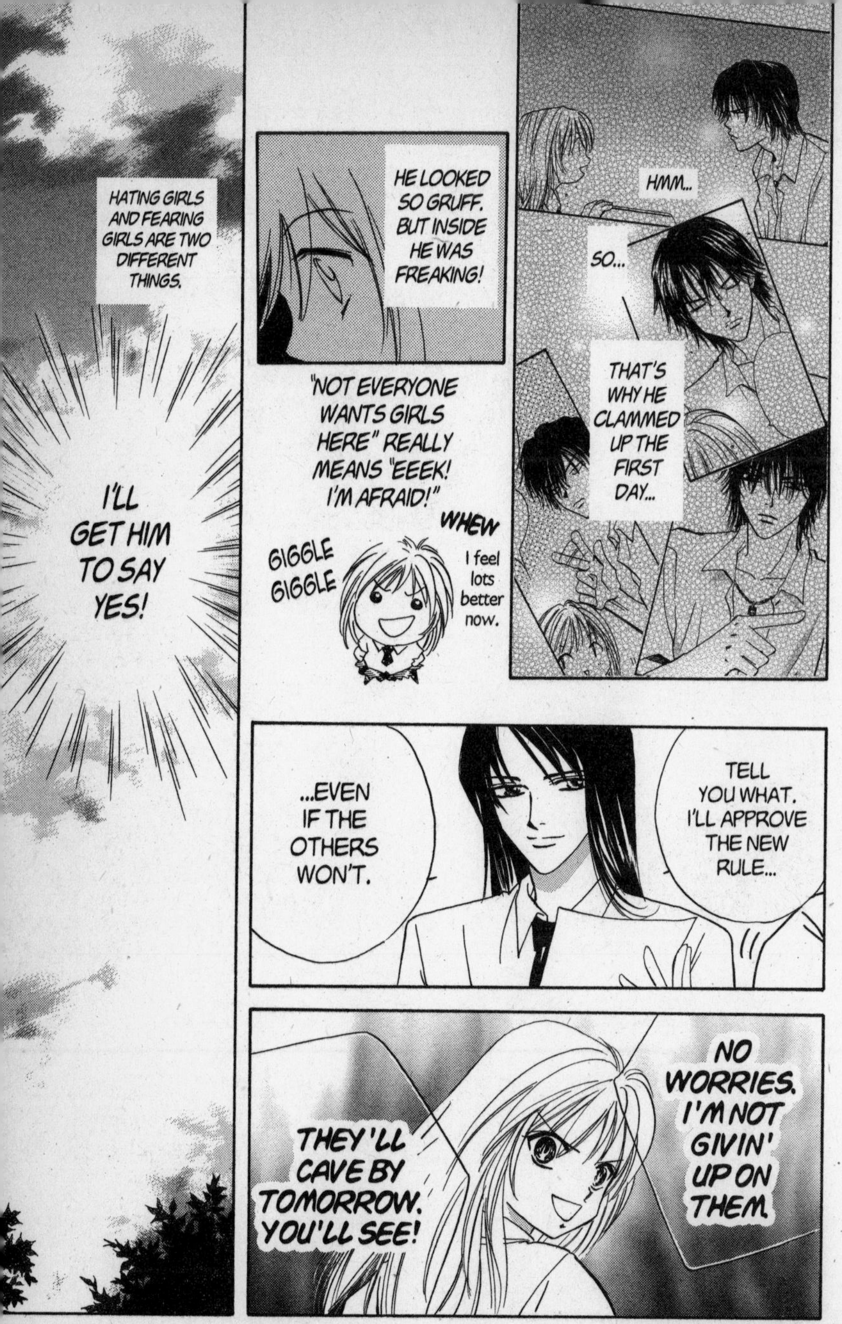
HMM...
SO...
THAT'S WHY HE CLAMMED UP THE FIRST DAY...
HE LOOKED SO GRUFF. BUT INSIDE HE WAS FREAKING!
"NOT EVERYONE WANTS GIRLS HERE" REALLY MEANS "EEEK! I'M AFRAID!"
WHEW
I feel lots better now.
GIGGLE GIGGLE
TELL YOU WHAT. I'LL APPROVE THE NEW RULE...
...EVEN IF THE OTHERS WON'T.
NO WORRIES. I'M NOT GIVIN' UP ON THEM.
THEY'LL CAVE BY TOMORROW. YOU'LL SEE!
HATING GIRLS AND FEARING GIRLS ARE TWO DIFFERENT THINGS.
I'LL GET HIM TO SAY YES!

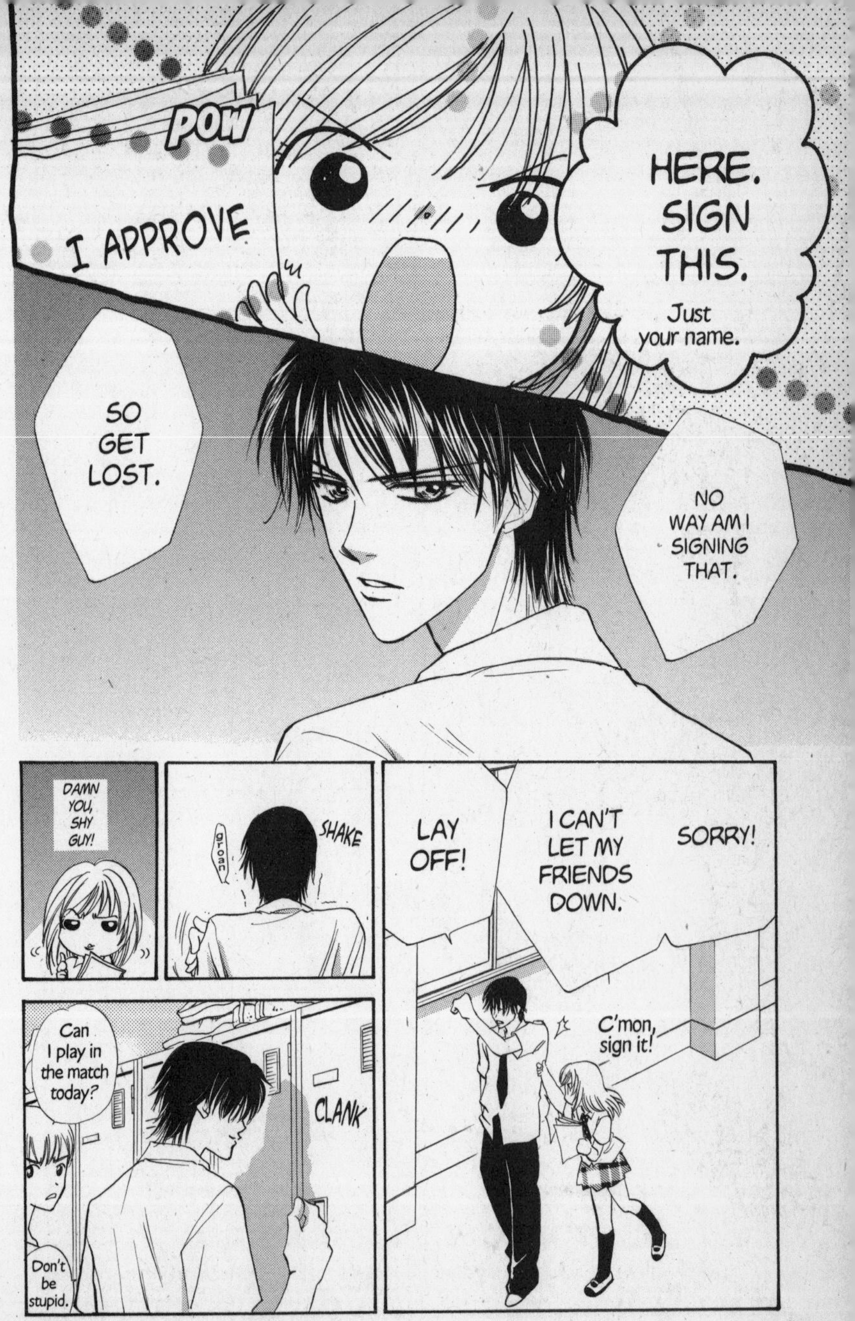
HERE. SIGN THIS.
Just your name.
POW
I APPROVE
NO WAY AM I SIGNING THAT.
SO GET LOST.
SORRY!
I CAN'T LET MY FRIENDS DOWN.
LAY OFF!
C'mon, sign it!
SHAKE
groan
DAMN YOU, SHY GUY!
Can I play in the match today?
CLANK
Don't be stupid.

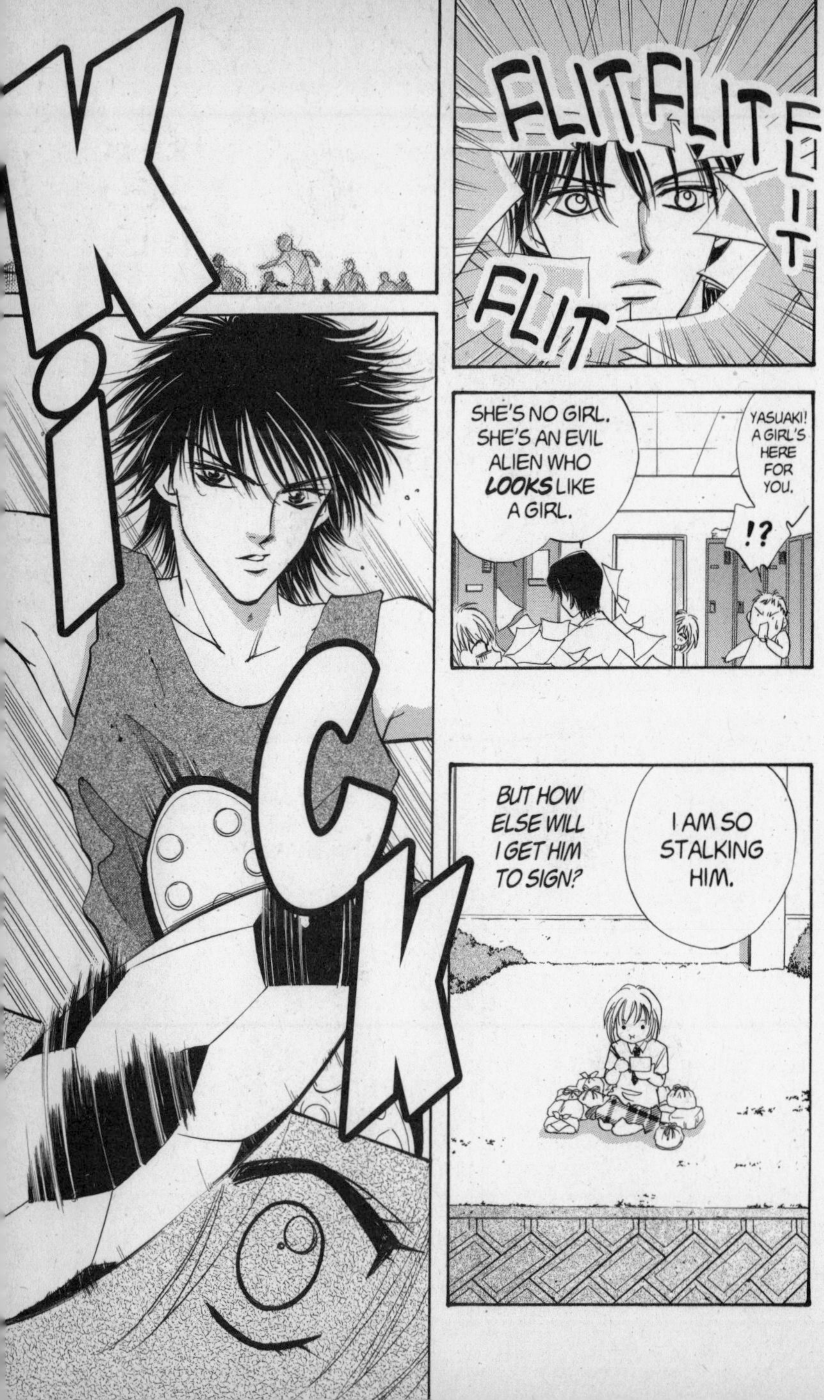
FLIT FLIT
FLIT
FLIT
YASUAKI! A GIRL'S HERE FOR YOU.
!?
SHE'S NO GIRL. SHE'S AN EVIL ALIEN WHO LOOKS LIKE A GIRL.
I AM SO STALKING HIM.
BUT HOW ELSE WILL I GET HIM TO SIGN?
KICK

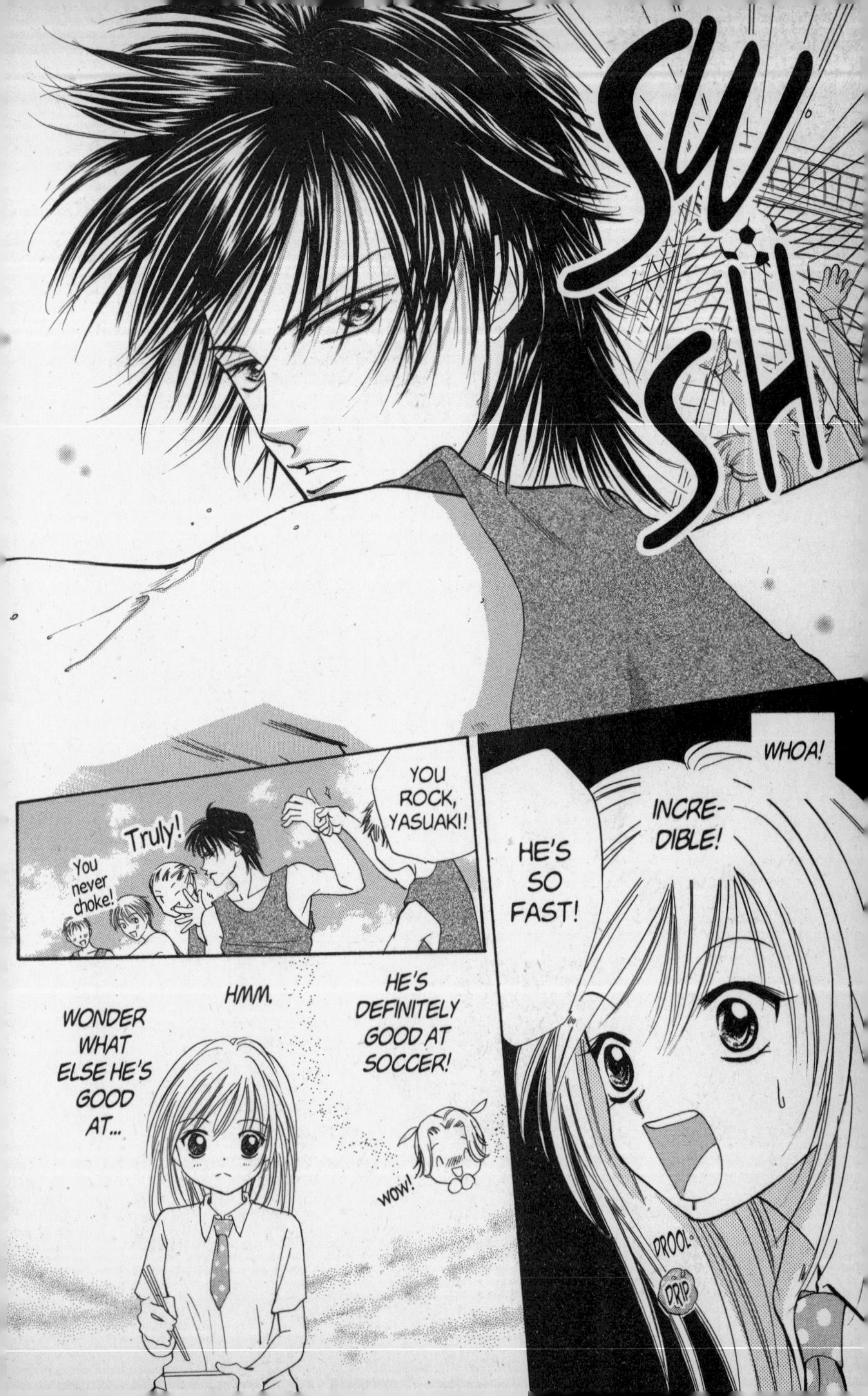
SWISH
WHOA!
INCRE-DIBLE!
HE'S SO FAST!
DROOL
DRIP
YOU ROCK, YASUAKI!
Truly!
You never choke!
HE'S DEFINITELY GOOD AT SOCCER!
HMM.
WONDER WHAT ELSE HE'S GOOD AT...
WOW!

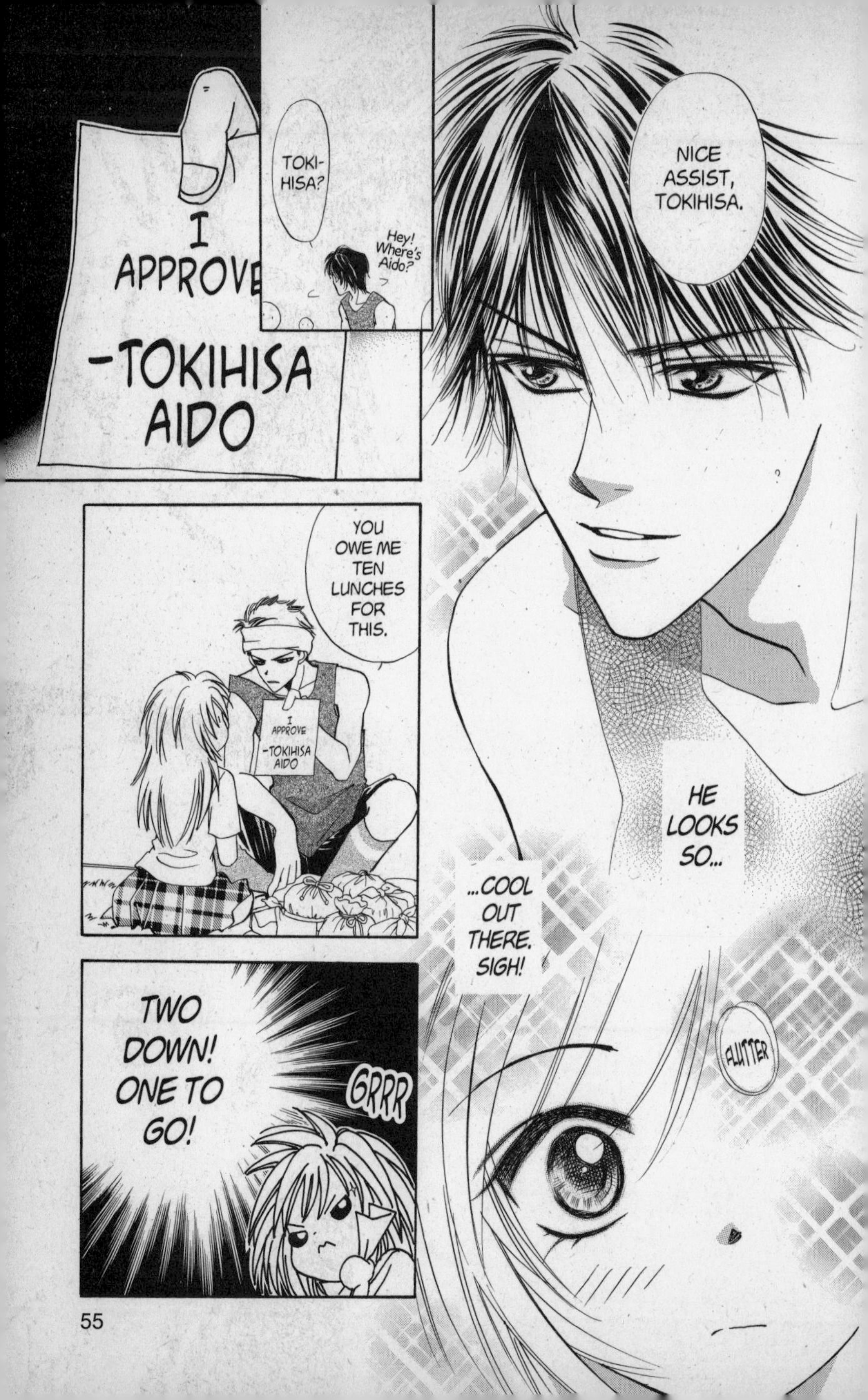
NICE ASSIST, TOKIHISA.
HE LOOKS SO...
...COOL OUT THERE. SIGH!
FLUTTER
TOKI-HISA?
Hey! Where's Aido?
I APPROVE -TOKIHISA AIDO
YOU OWE ME TEN LUNCHES FOR THIS.
I APPROVE -TOKIHISA AIDO
TWO DOWN! ONE TO GO!
GRRR

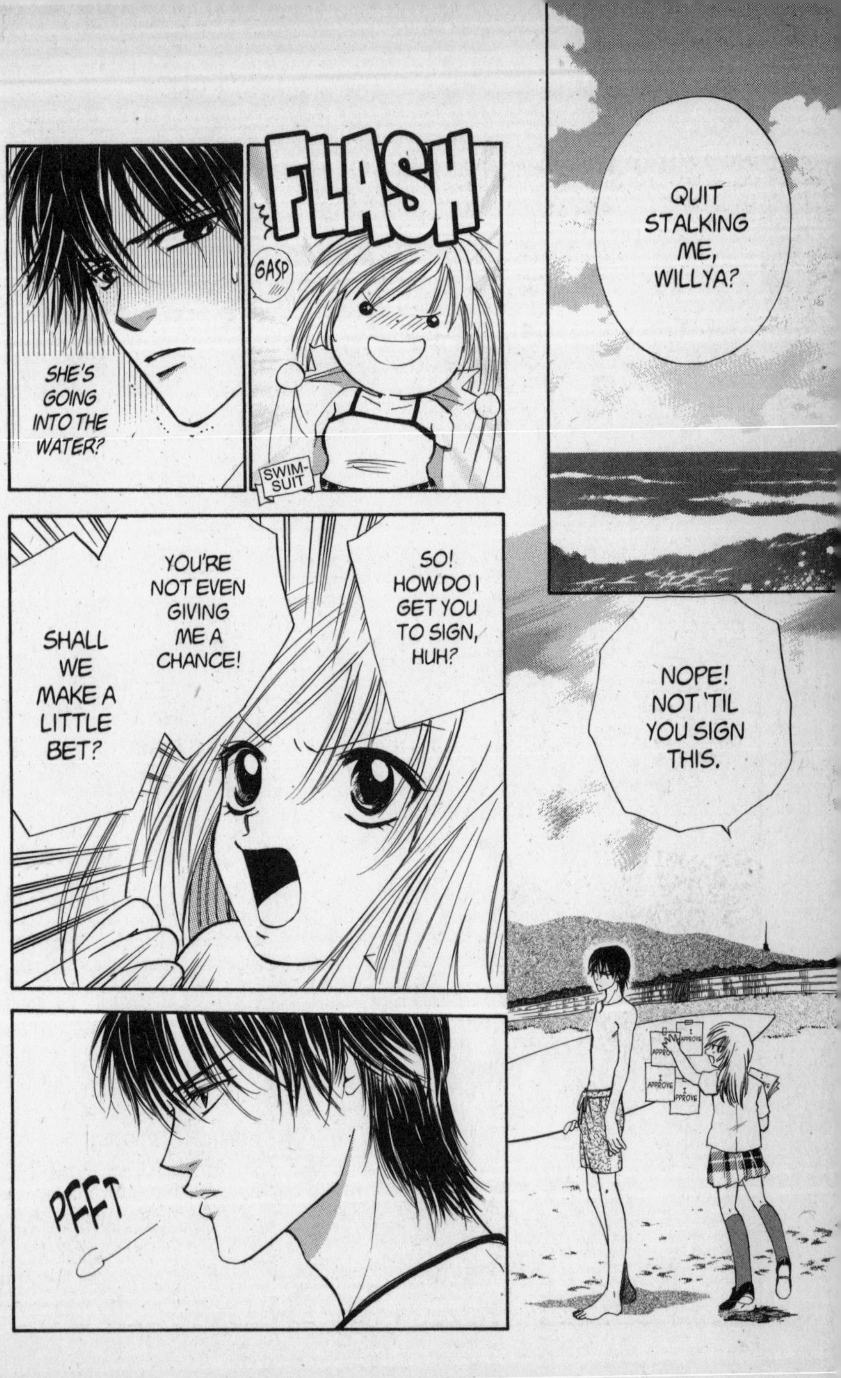
QUIT STALKING ME, WILLYA?
NOPE! NOT 'TIL YOU SIGN THIS.
FLASH
GASP
SWIM-SUIT
SHE'S GOING INTO THE WATER?
SO! HOW DO I GET YOU TO SIGN, HUH?
YOU'RE NOT EVEN GIVING ME A CHANCE!
SHALL WE MAKE A LITTLE BET?
PFFT

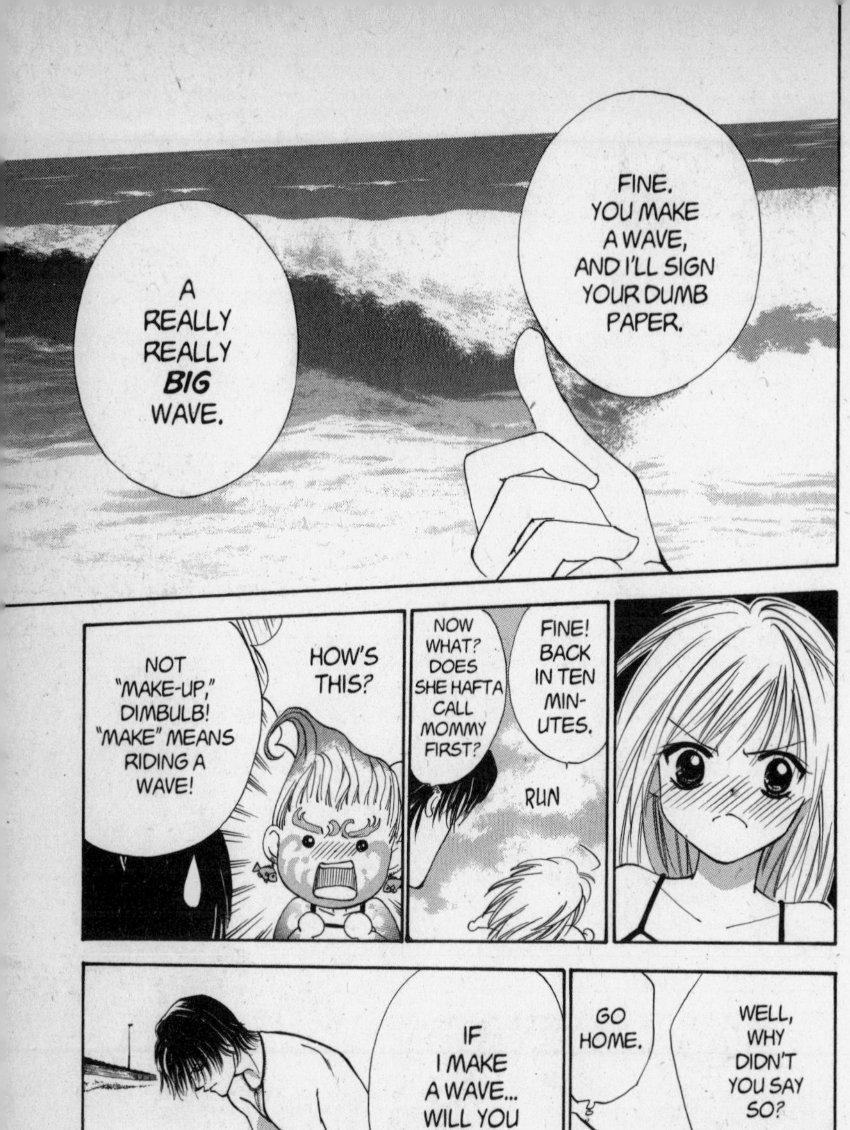
FINE. YOU MAKE A WAVE, AND I'LL SIGN YOUR DUMB PAPER.
A REALLY REALLY **BIG** WAVE.
FINE! BACK IN TEN MIN-UTES.
NOW WHAT? DOES SHE HAFTA CALL MOMMY FIRST?
RUN
HOW'S THIS?
NOT "MAKE-UP," DIMBULB! "MAKE" MEANS RIDING A WAVE!
WELL, WHY DIDN'T YOU SAY SO?
GO HOME.
SPLASH
SPLISH
HMPH
IF I MAKE A WAVE... WILL YOU SIGN?

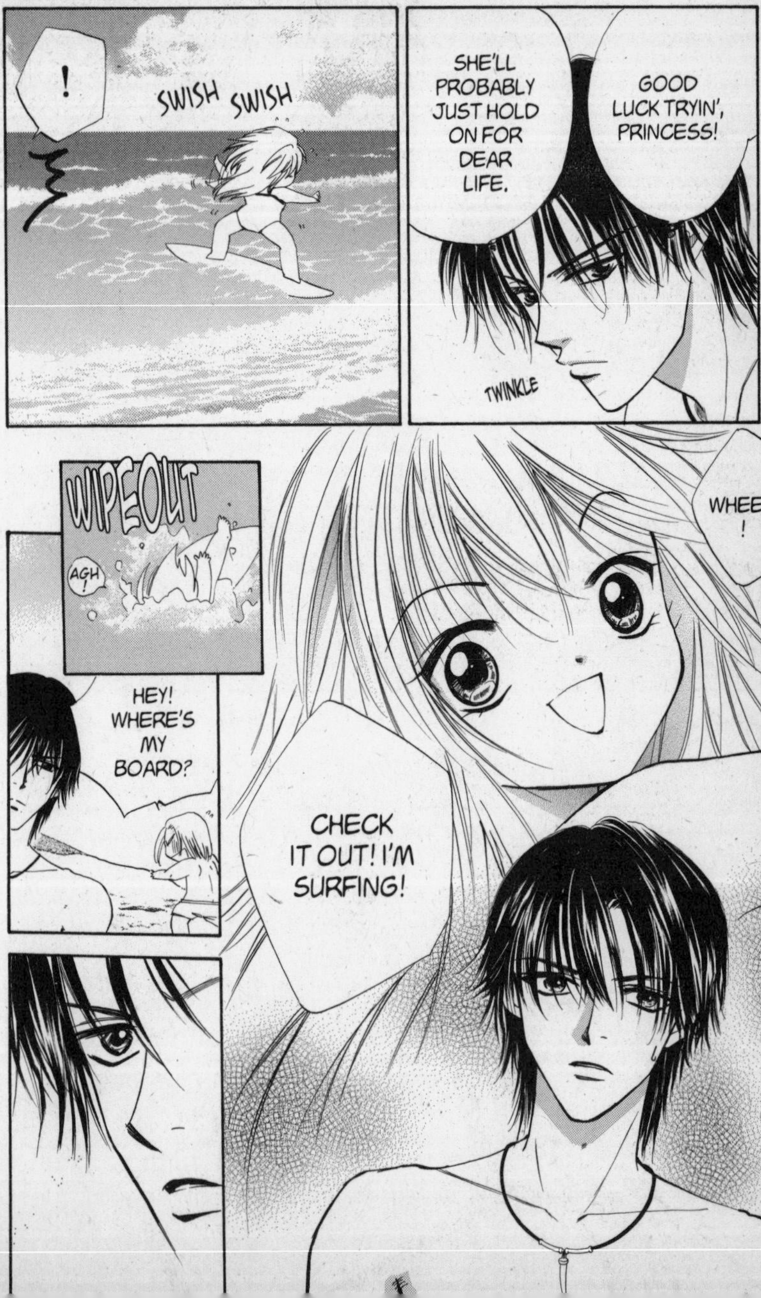
GOOD LUCK TRYIN', PRINCESS!
SHE'LL PROBABLY JUST HOLD ON FOR DEAR LIFE.
TWINKLE
!
SWISH SWISH
WHEEE!
CHECK IT OUT! I'M SURFING!
WIPEOUT
AGH!
HEY! WHERE'S MY BOARD?

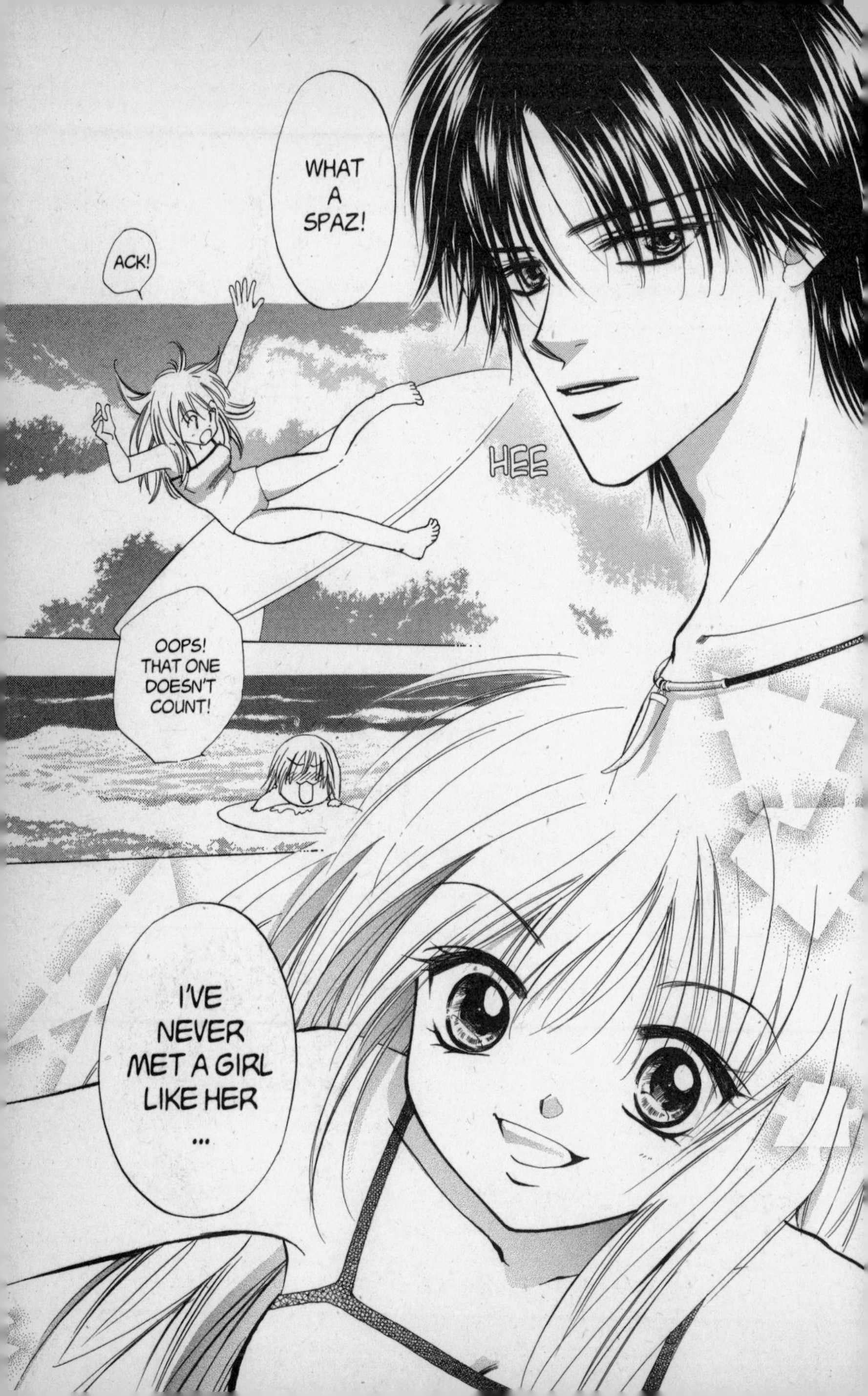
WHAT A SPAZ!
ACK!
HEE
OOPS! THAT ONE DOESN'T COUNT!
I'VE NEVER MET A GIRL LIKE HER ...

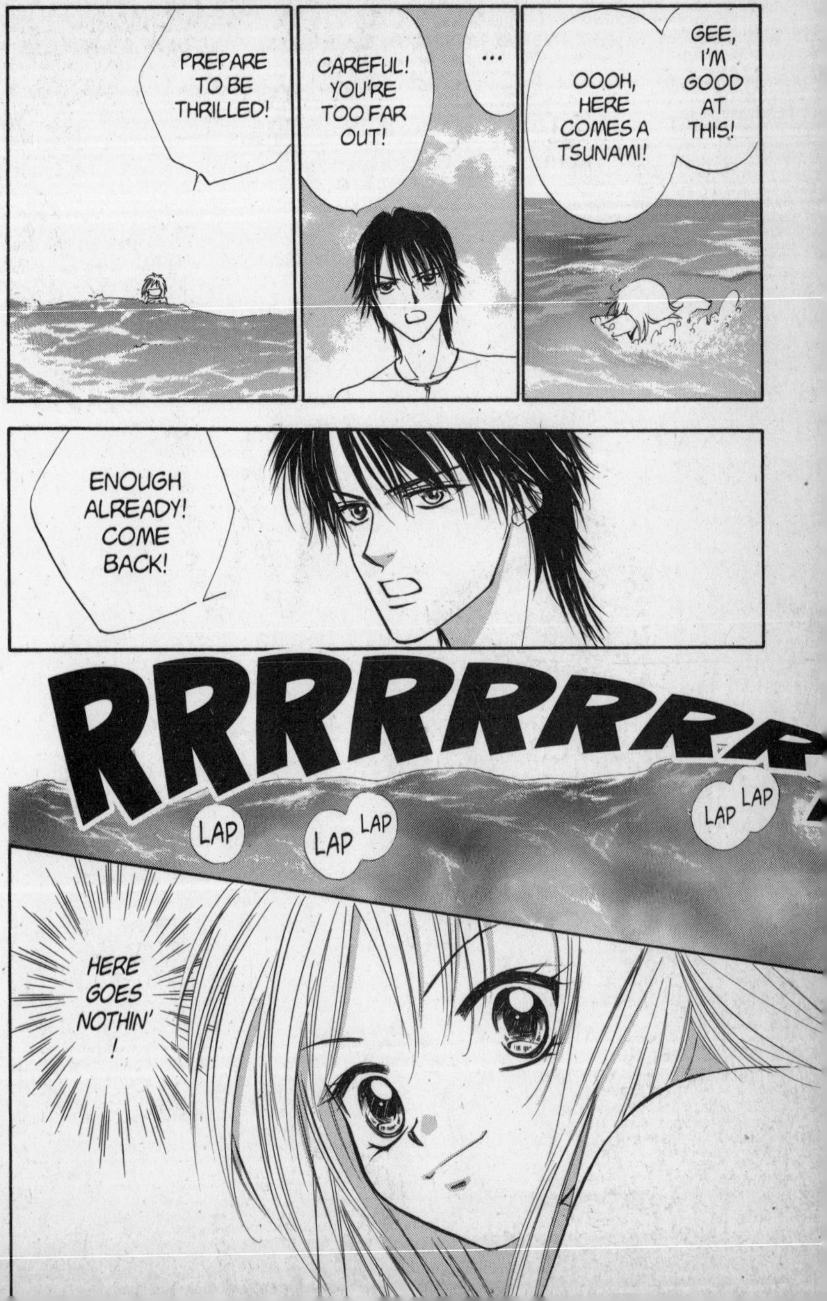
GEE, I'M GOOD AT THIS!
OOOH, HERE COMES A TSUNAMI!
...
CAREFUL! YOU'RE TOO FAR OUT!
PREPARE TO BE THRILLED!
ENOUGH ALREADY! COME BACK!
RRRRRRRR
LAP LAP
LAP LAP
LAP
HERE GOES NOTHIN'!

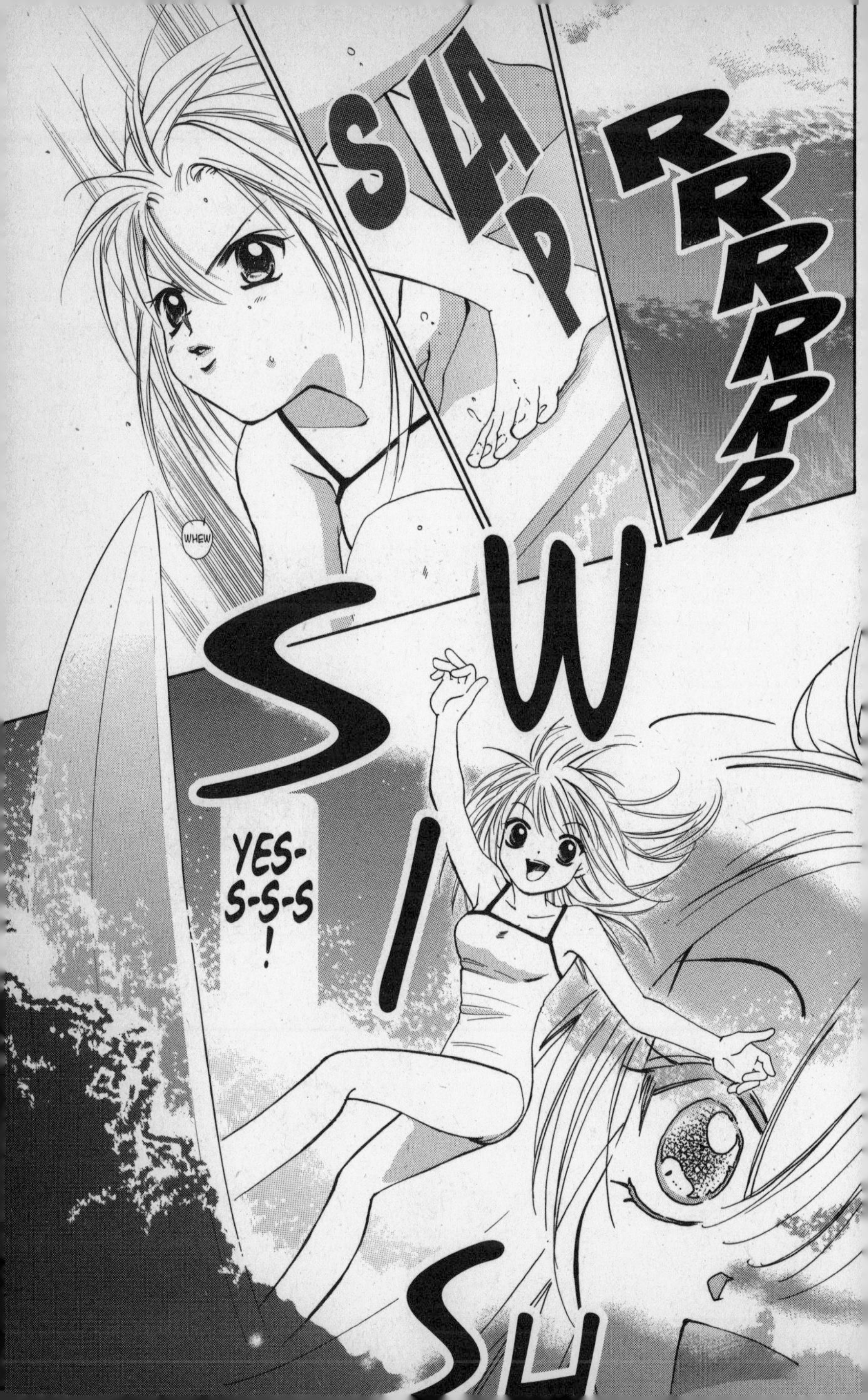
RRRRRR
SLAP
WHEW
SWISH
YES-S-S-S!

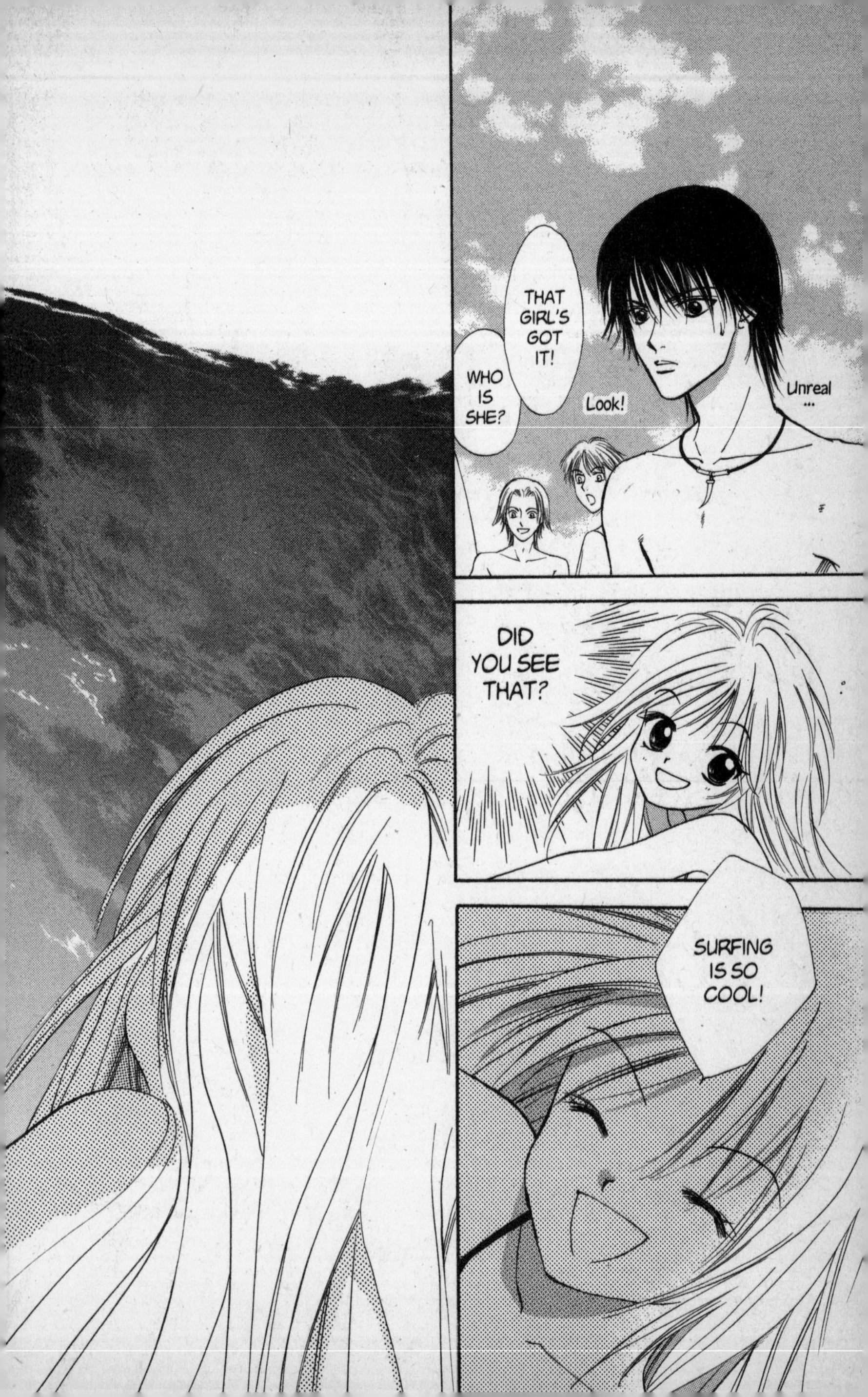
Unreal ...
THAT GIRL'S GOT IT!
Look!
WHO IS SHE?
DID YOU SEE THAT?
SURFING IS SO COOL!

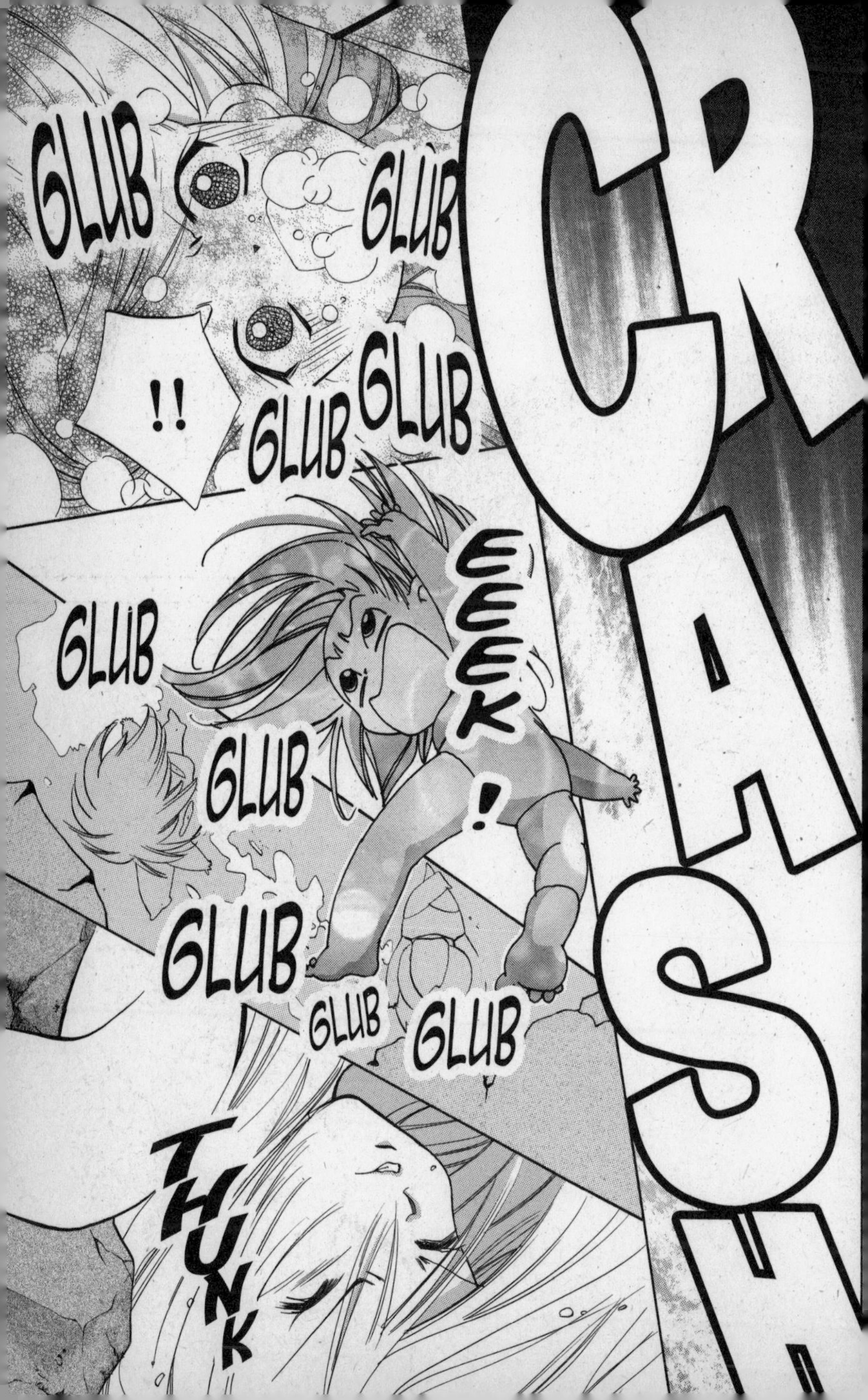
CRASH
GLUB
GLUB
!!
GLUB
GLUB
EEEK!
GLUB
GLUB
GLUB
GLUB
GLUB
THUNK

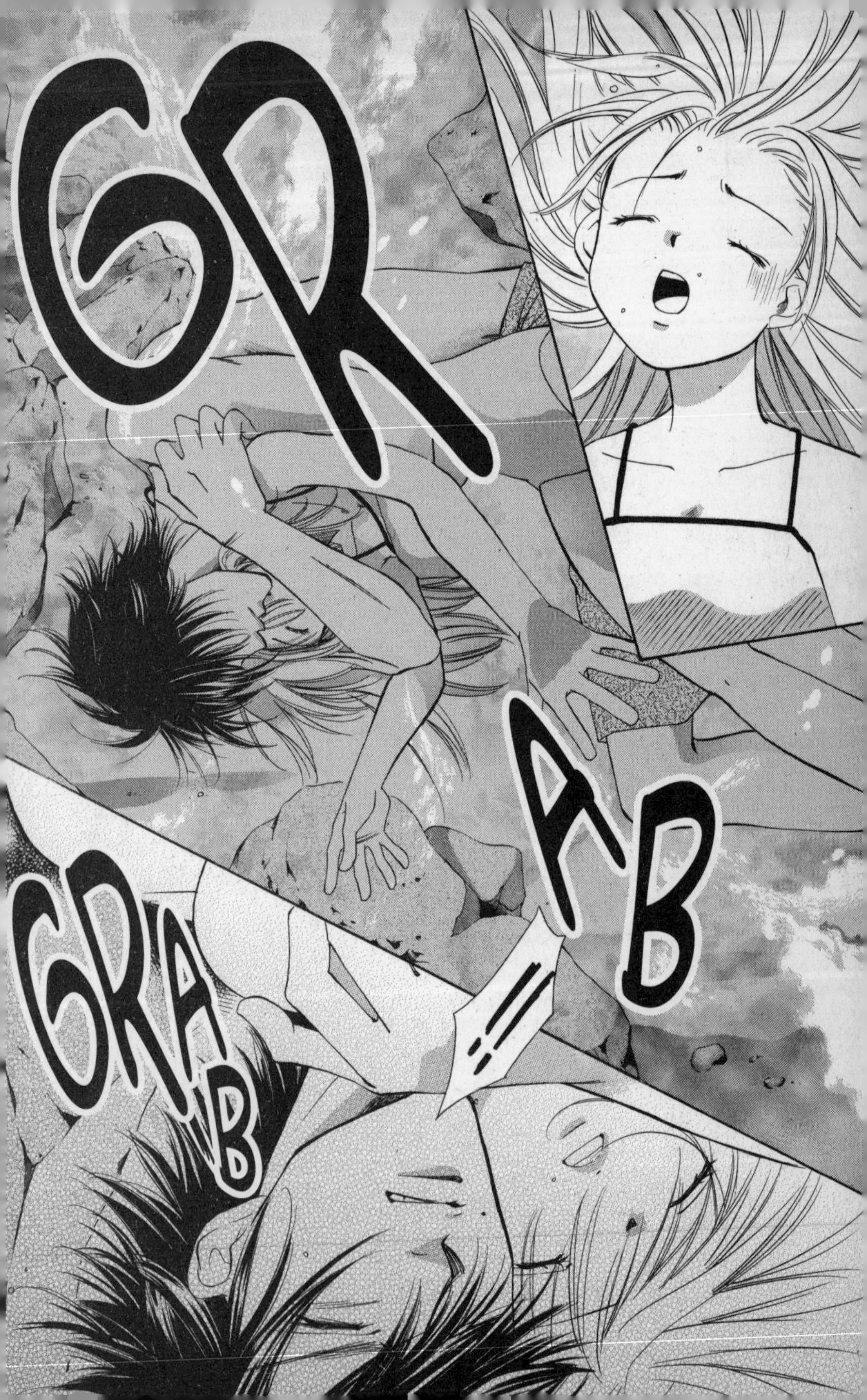
GR
AB
GRAB

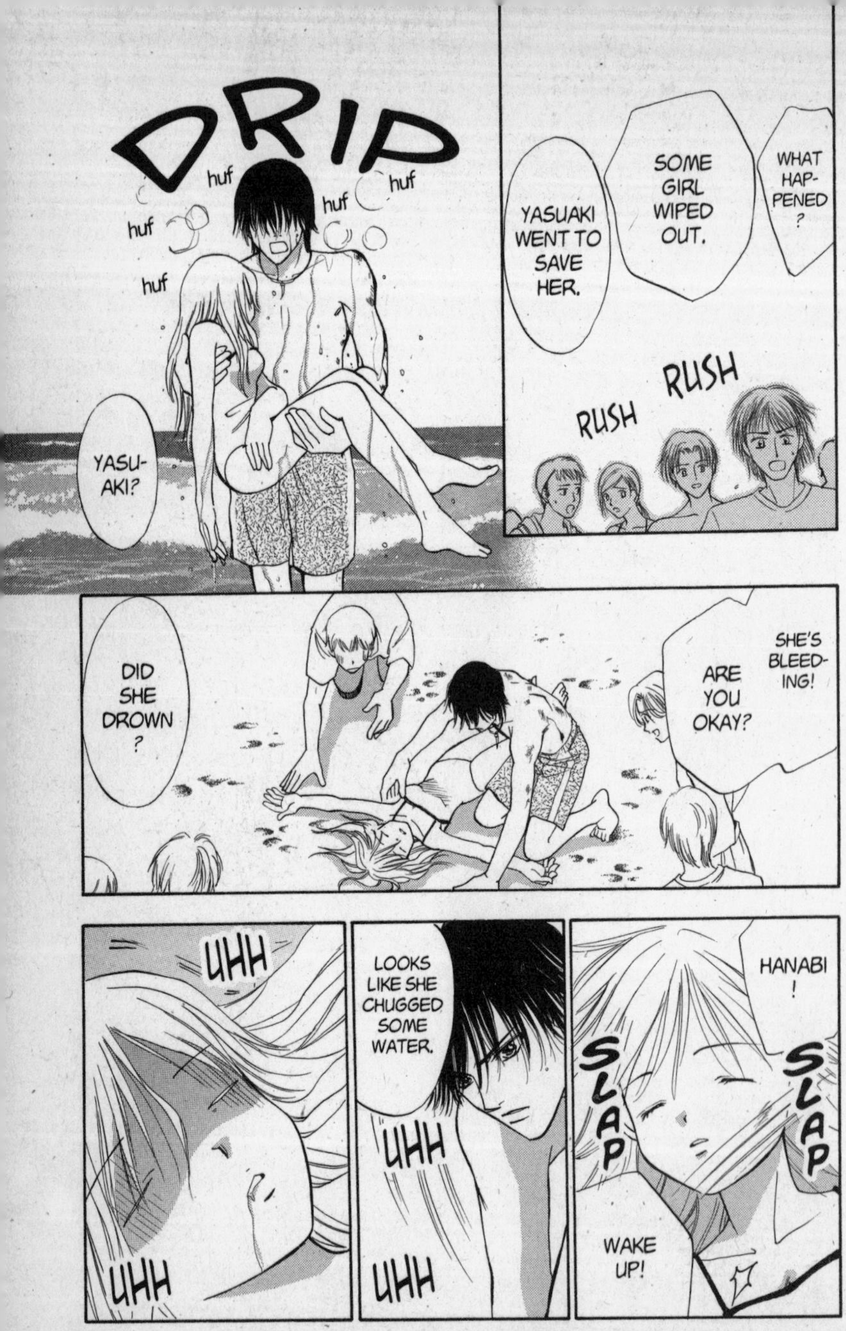
WHAT HAP-PENED?
SOME GIRL WIPED OUT.
YASUAKI WENT TO SAVE HER.
RUSH
RUSH
DRIP
huf
huf
huf
huf
huf
YASU-AKI?
SHE'S BLEED-ING!
ARE YOU OKAY?
DID SHE DROWN?
HANABI!
SLAP
SLAP
WAKE UP!
LOOKS LIKE SHE CHUGGED SOME WATER.
UHH
UHH
UHH
UHH

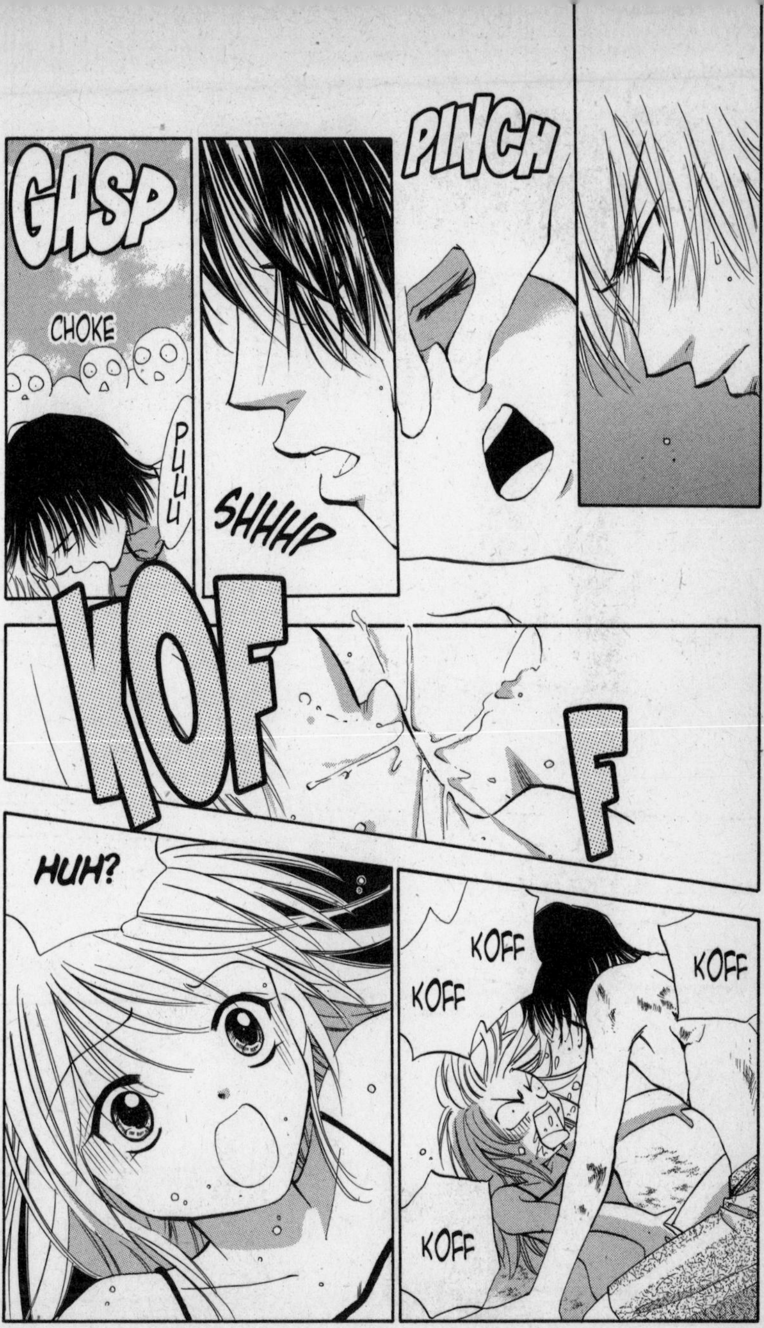
PINCH
SHHHP
GASP
CHOKE
PUUU
KOF
F
KOFF
KOFF
KOFF
KOFF
HUH?

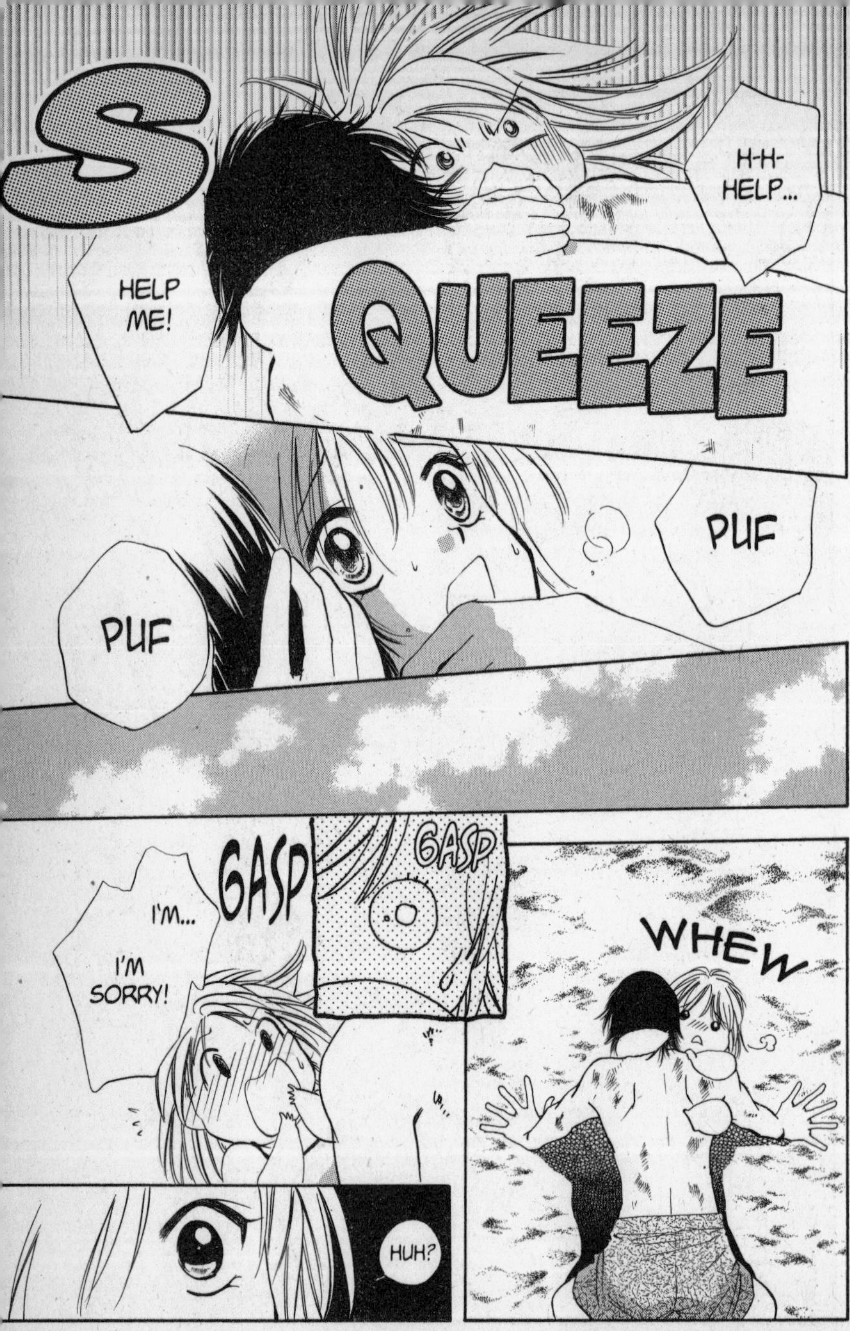
H-H-HELP...
S
QUEEZE
HELP ME!
PUF
PUF
WHEW
GASP
GASP
I'M...
I'M SORRY!
HUH?

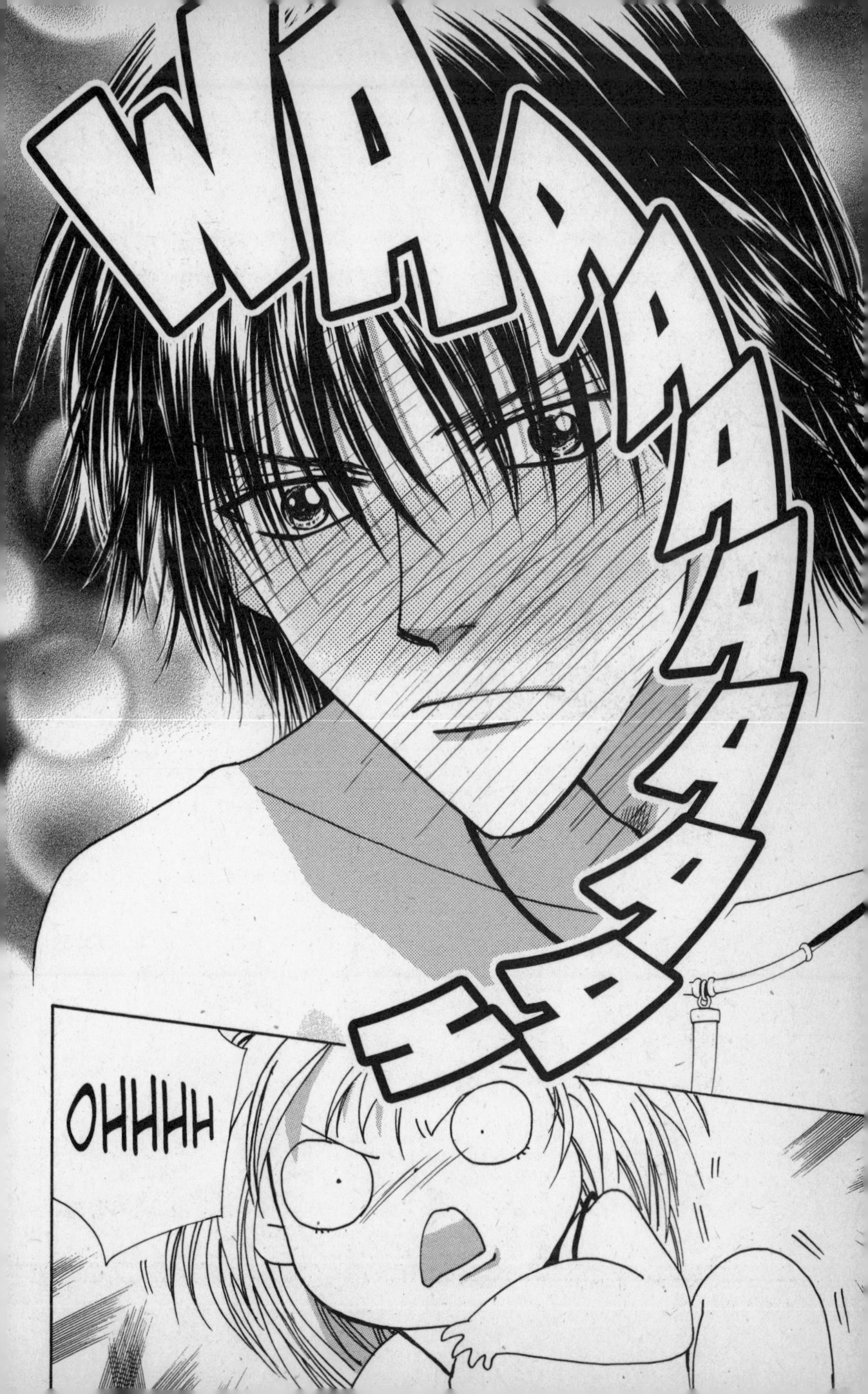

WAAAAAAAAA
OHHHH

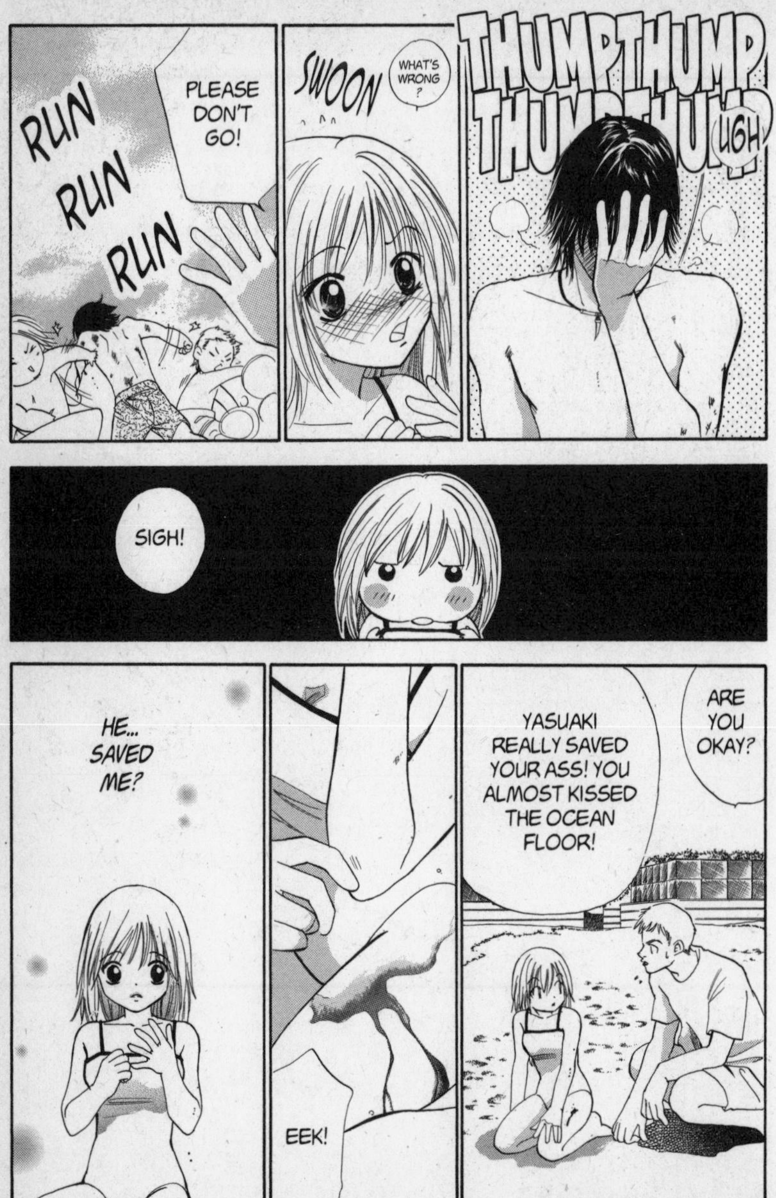
THUMPTHUMP
THUMPTHUMP
UGH
WHAT'S WRONG?
SWOON
PLEASE DON'T GO!
RUN
RUN
RUN
SIGH!
ARE YOU OKAY?
YASUAKI REALLY SAVED YOUR ASS! YOU ALMOST KISSED THE OCEAN FLOOR!
EEK!
HE... SAVED ME?

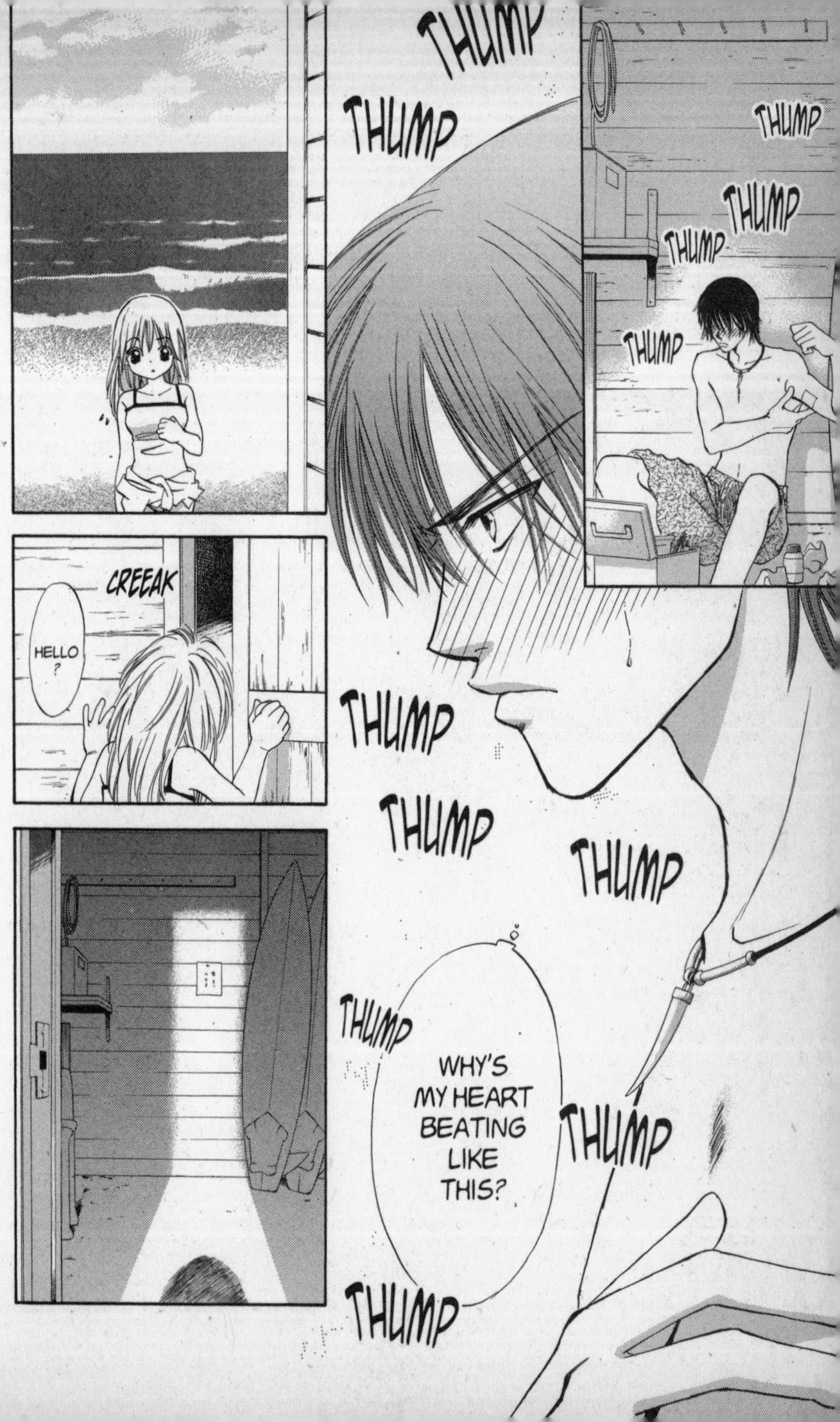
THUMP
THUMP
THUMP
THUMP
THUMP
THUMP
THUMP
THUMP
THUMP
THUMP
WHY'S MY HEART BEATING LIKE THIS?
THUMP
THUMP
CREEAK
HELLO?

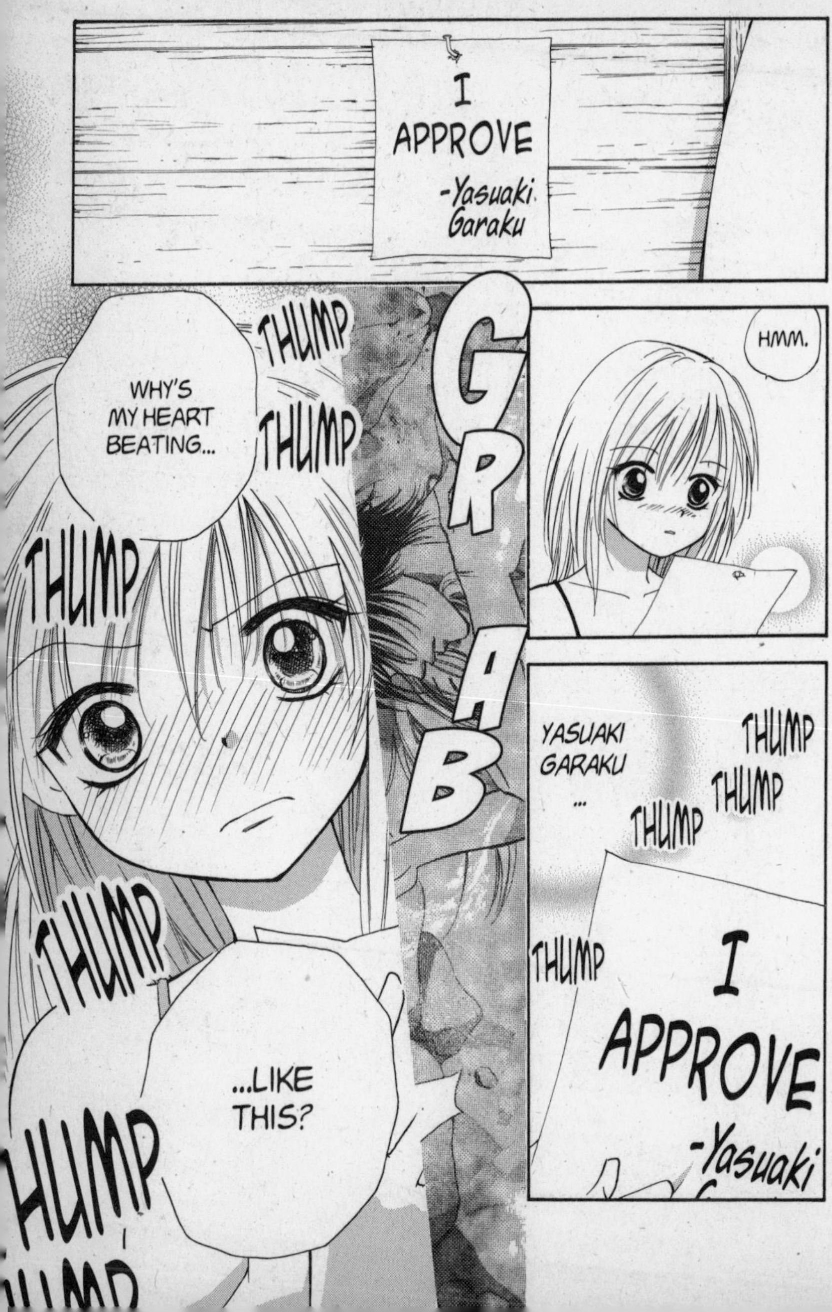
I APPROVE
-Yasuaki Garaku
HMM.
YASUAKI GARAKU ...
THUMP
THUMP
THUMP
THUMP
I APPROVE
-Yasuaki
GRAB
THUMP
THUMP
WHY'S MY HEART BEATING...
THUMP
THUMP
...LIKE THIS?
HUMP

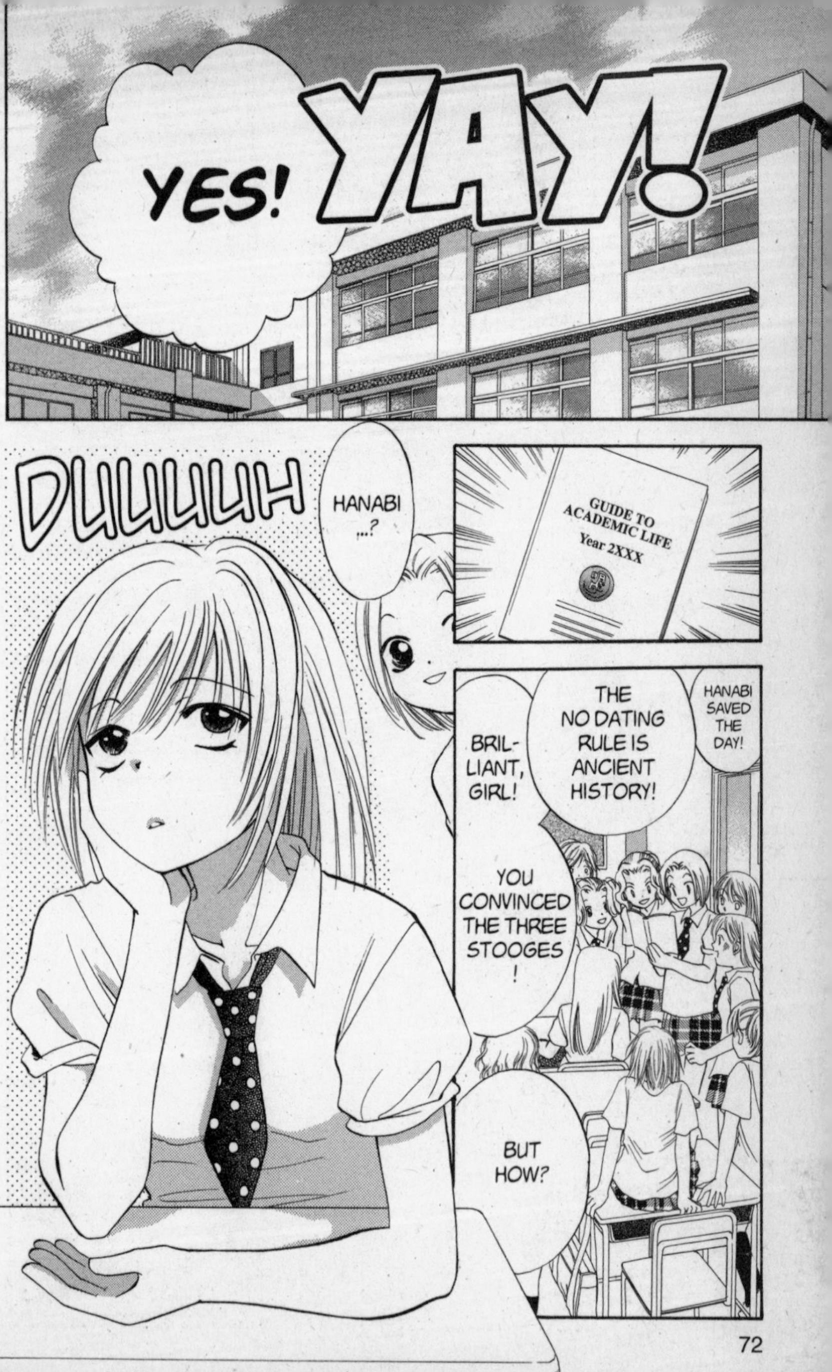
YAY!
YES!
GUIDE TO ACADEMIC LIFE Year 2XXX
HANABI SAVED THE DAY!
THE NO DATING RULE IS ANCIENT HISTORY!
BRIL-LIANT, GIRL!
YOU CONVINCED THE THREE STOOGES!
BUT HOW?
HANABI ...?
DUUUUH

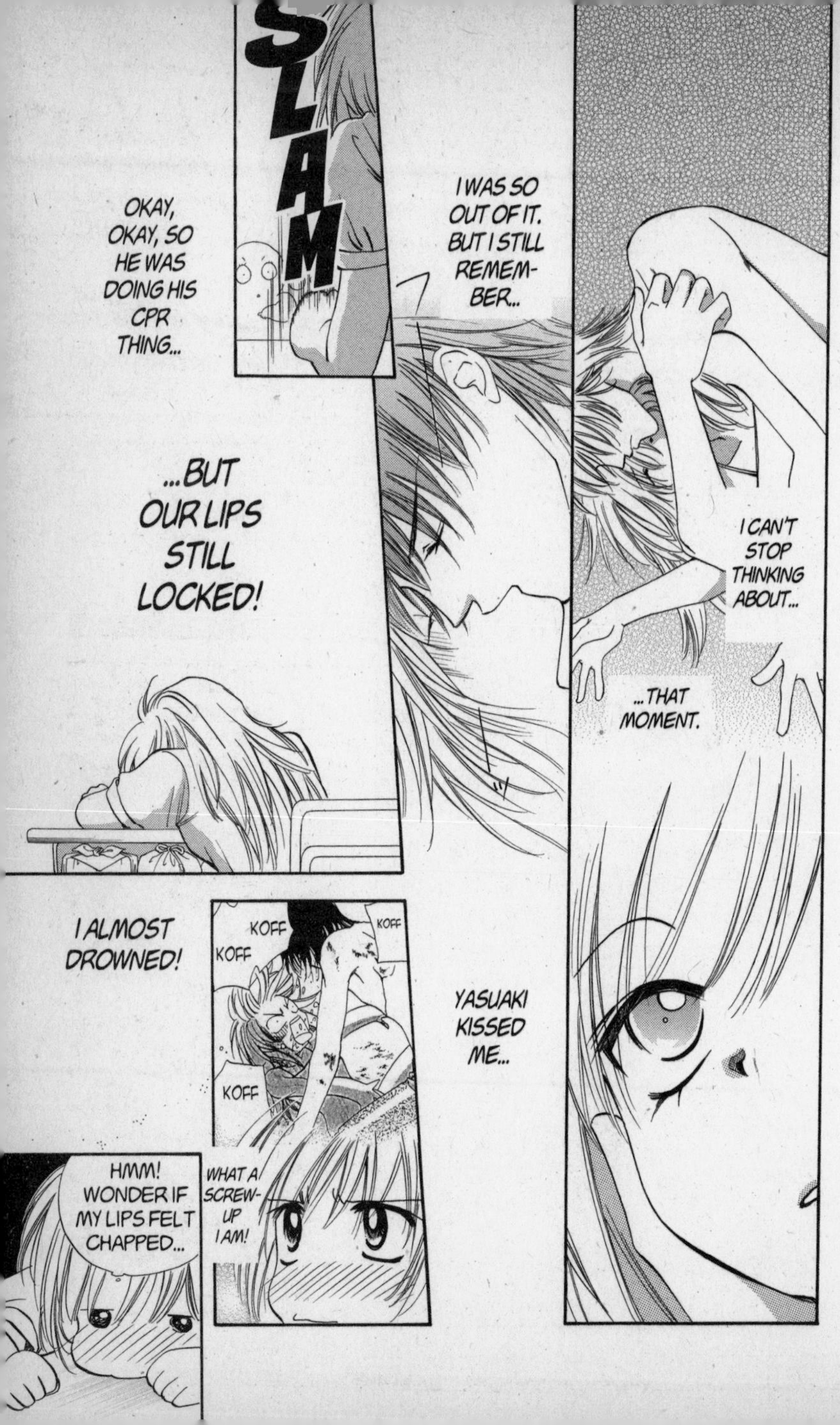
I WAS SO OUT OF IT. BUT I STILL REMEMBER...
I CAN'T STOP THINKING ABOUT...
...THAT MOMENT.
SLAM
OKAY, OKAY, SO HE WAS DOING HIS CPR THING...
...BUT OUR LIPS STILL LOCKED!
YASUAKI KISSED ME...
KOFF
KOFF
KOFF
KOFF
I ALMOST DROWNED!
WHAT A SCREW-UP I AM!
HMM! WONDER IF MY LIPS FELT CHAPPED...

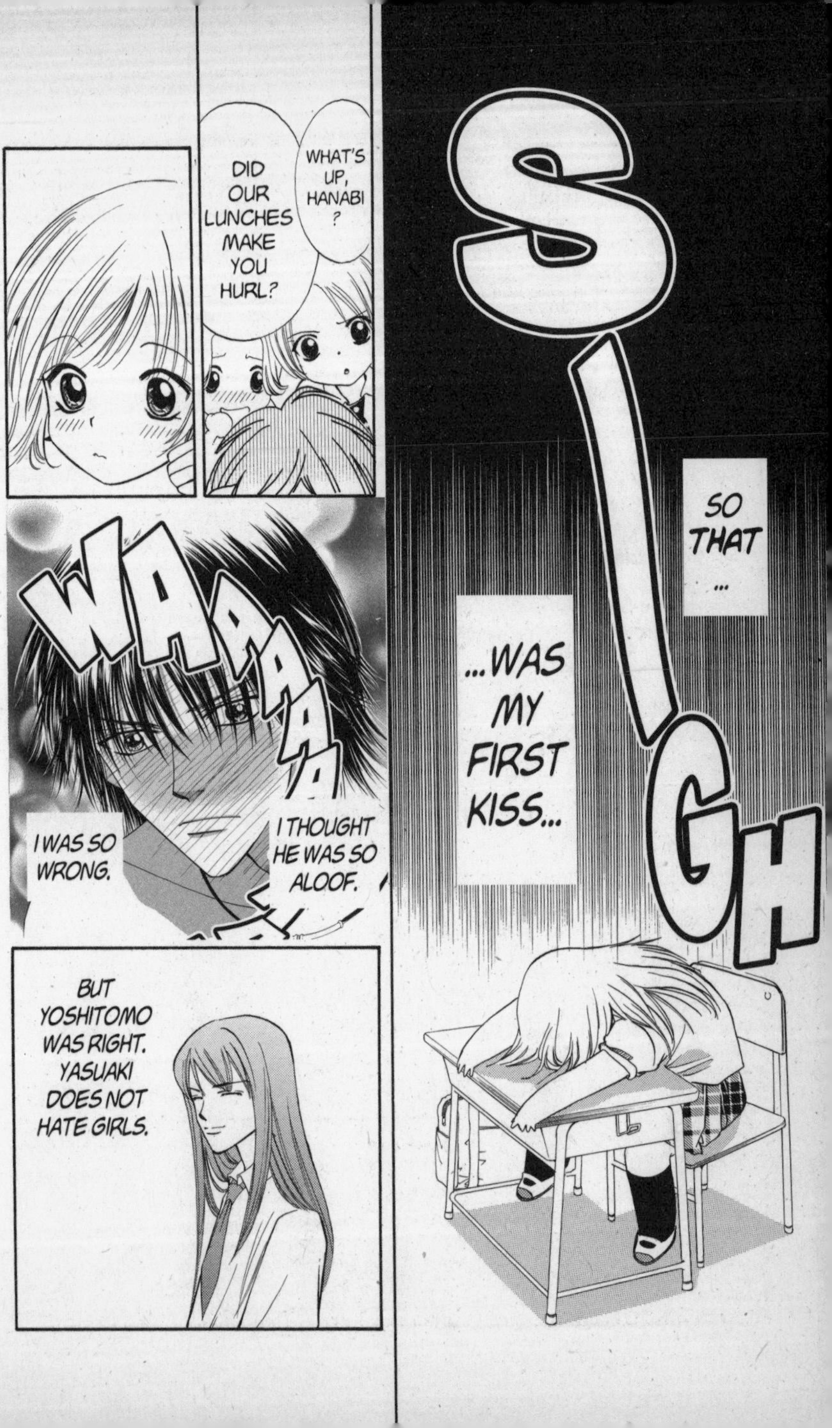
SIGH
SO THAT ...
...WAS MY FIRST KISS...
WHAT'S UP, HANABI ?
DID OUR LUNCHES MAKE YOU HURL?
WAAAA
I THOUGHT HE WAS SO ALOOF.
I WAS SO WRONG.
BUT YOSHITOMO WAS RIGHT. YASUAKI DOES NOT HATE GIRLS.

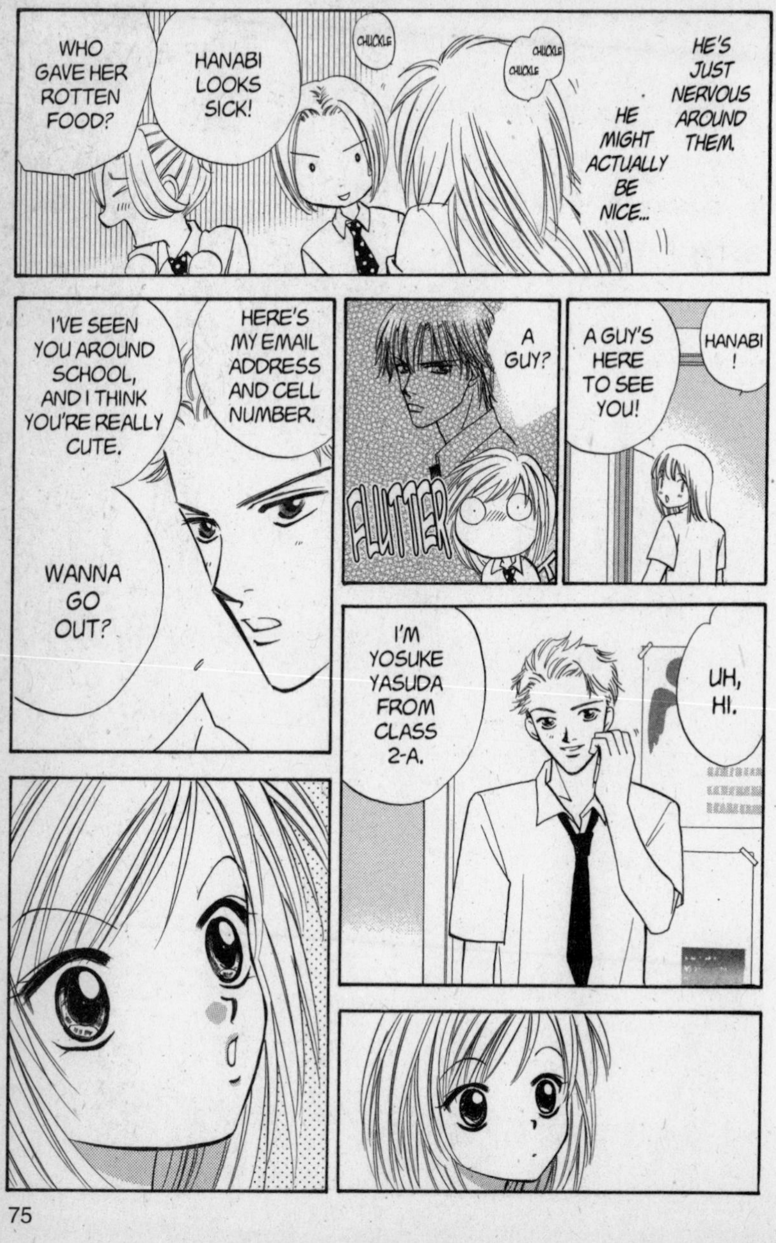
HE'S JUST NERVOUS AROUND THEM.
HE MIGHT ACTUALLY BE NICE...
CHUCKLE CHUCKLE
CHUCKLE
HANABI LOOKS SICK!
WHO GAVE HER ROTTEN FOOD?
HANABI!
A GUY'S HERE TO SEE YOU!
A GUY?
FLUTTER
UH, HI.
I'M YOSUKE YASUDA FROM CLASS 2-A.
HERE'S MY EMAIL ADDRESS AND CELL NUMBER.
I'VE SEEN YOU AROUND SCHOOL, AND I THINK YOU'RE REALLY CUTE.
WANNA GO OUT?

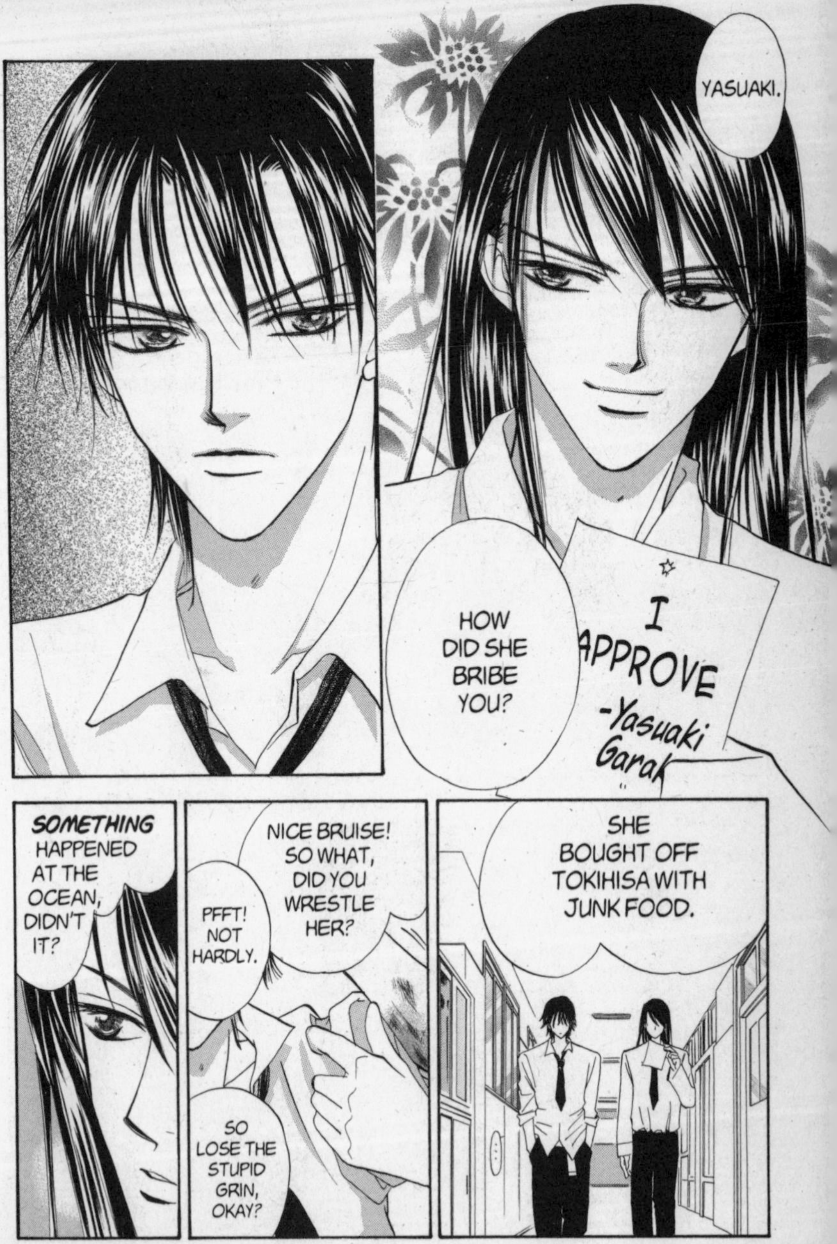
YASUAKI.
I APPROVE -Yasuaki Garak
HOW DID SHE BRIBE YOU?
SHE BOUGHT OFF TOKIHISA WITH JUNK FOOD.
NICE BRUISE! SO WHAT, DID YOU WRESTLE HER?
PFFT! NOT HARDLY.
SO LOSE THE STUPID GRIN, OKAY?
SOMETHING HAPPENED AT THE OCEAN, DIDN'T IT?

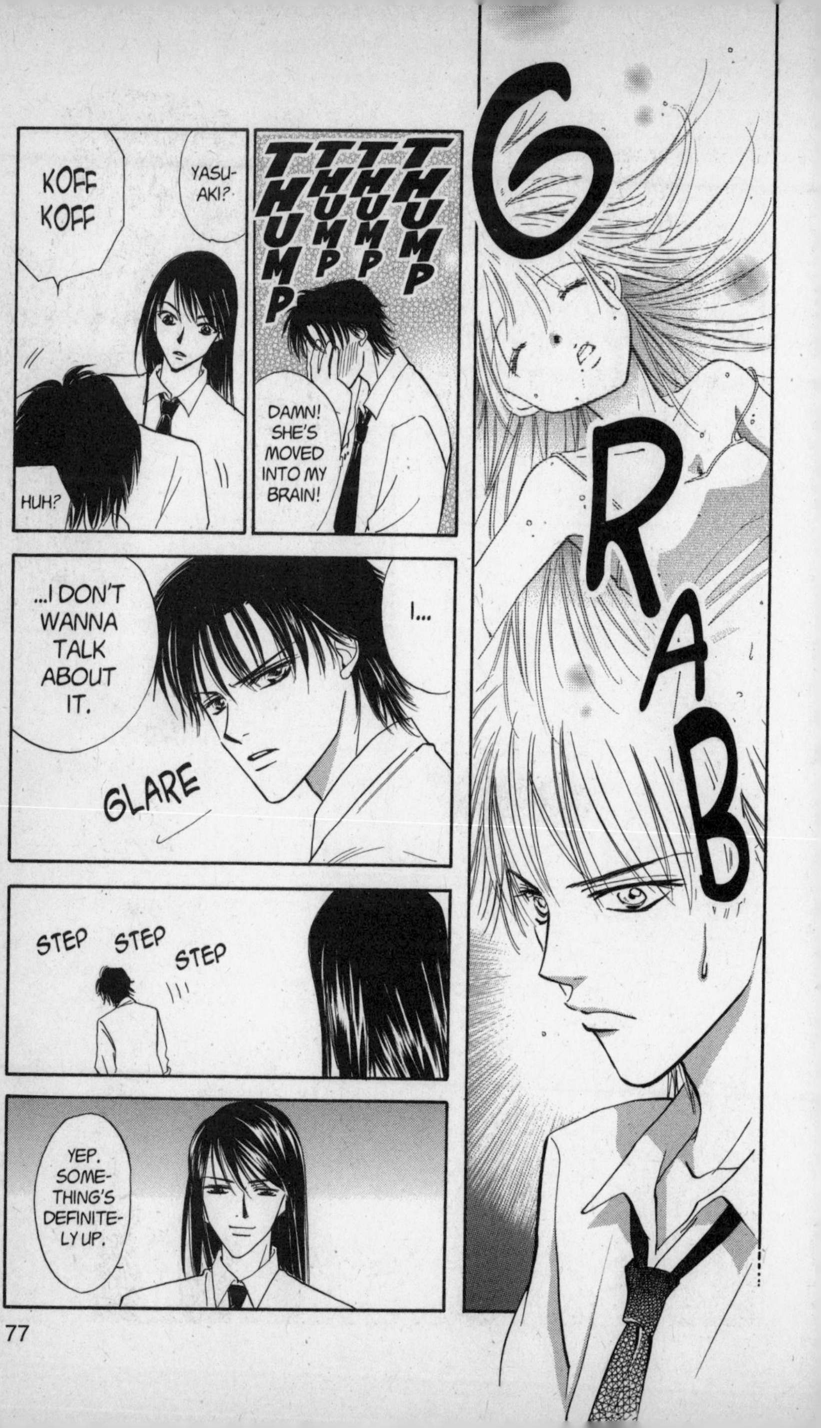
GRAB
THUMP THUMP THUMP THUMP
DAMN! SHE'S MOVED INTO MY BRAIN!
YASU-AKI?
KOFF KOFF
HUH?
I...
...I DON'T WANNA TALK ABOUT IT.
GLARE
STEP STEP STEP
YEP. SOME-THING'S DEFINITE-LY UP.

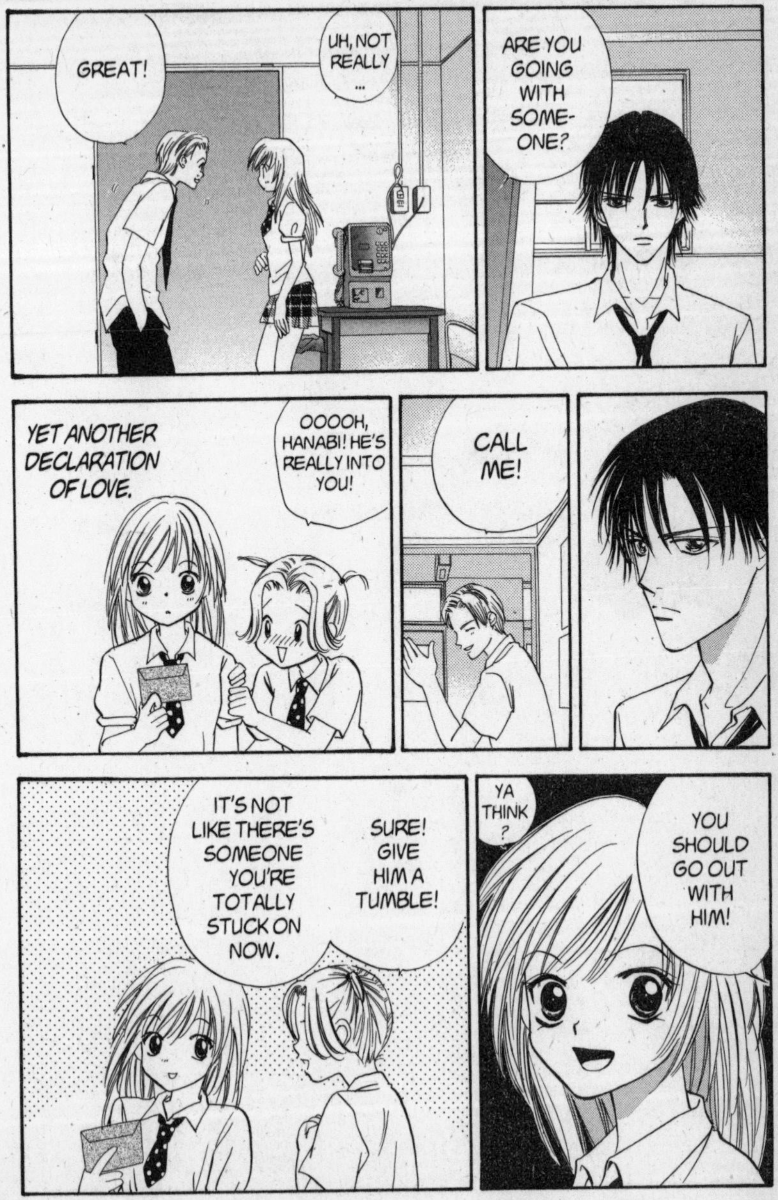
ARE YOU GOING WITH SOME-ONE?
UH, NOT REALLY ...
GREAT!
CALL ME!
OOOOH, HANABI! HE'S REALLY INTO YOU!
YET ANOTHER DECLARATION OF LOVE.
YOU SHOULD GO OUT WITH HIM!
YA THINK?
SURE! GIVE HIM A TUMBLE!
IT'S NOT LIKE THERE'S SOMEONE YOU'RE TOTALLY STUCK ON NOW.

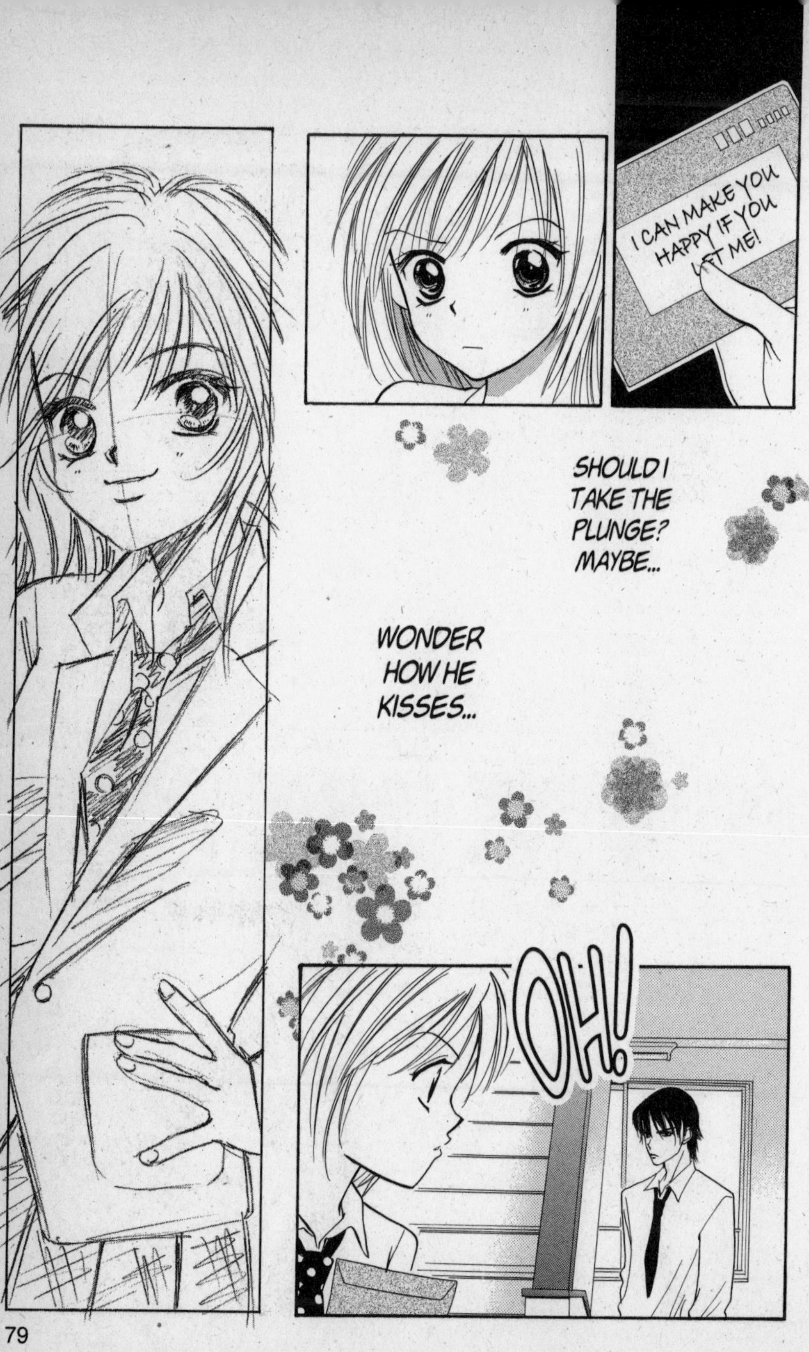
I CAN MAKE YOU HAPPY IF YOU LET ME!
SHOULD I TAKE THE PLUNGE? MAYBE...
WONDER HOW HE KISSES...
OH!

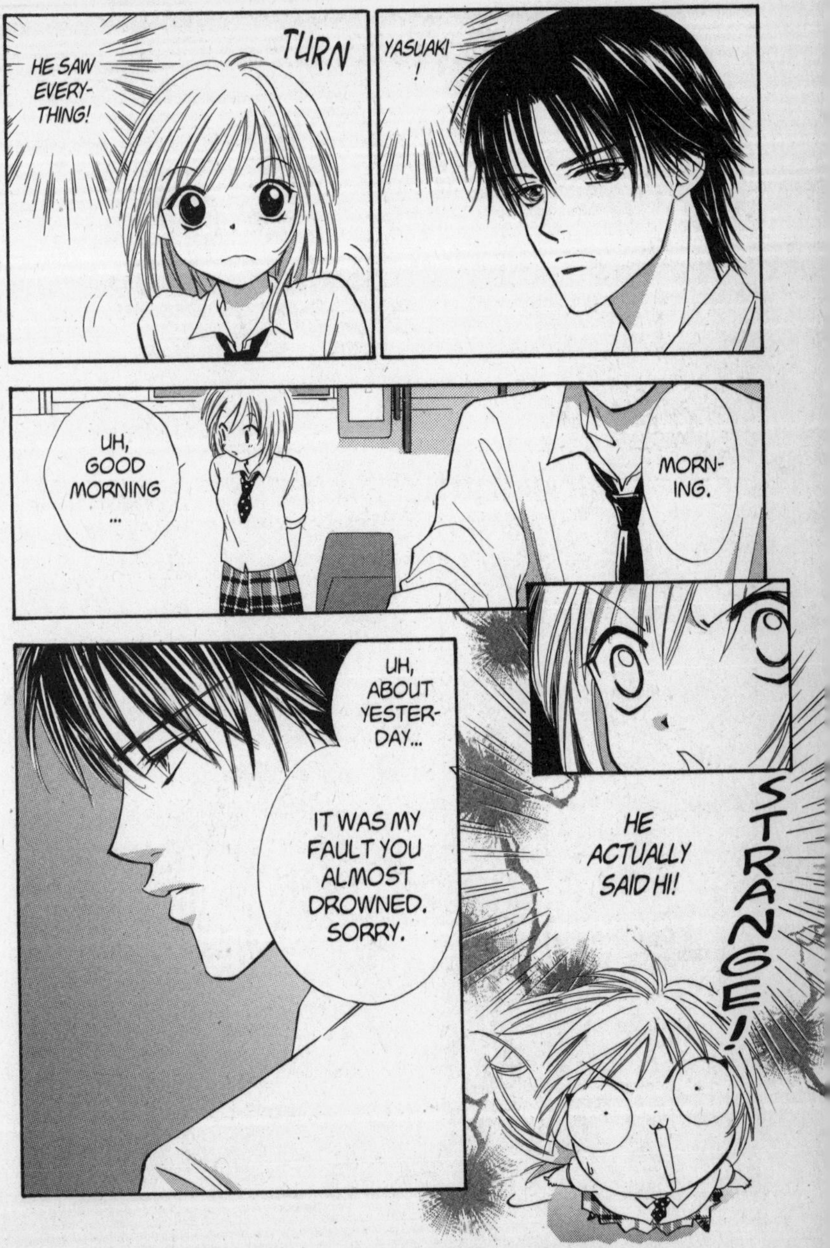
YASUAKI!
TURN
HE SAW EVERY-THING!
MORN-ING.
UH, GOOD MORNING...
HE ACTUALLY SAID HI!
STRANGE!
UH, ABOUT YESTER-DAY...
IT WAS MY FAULT YOU ALMOST DROWNED. SORRY.

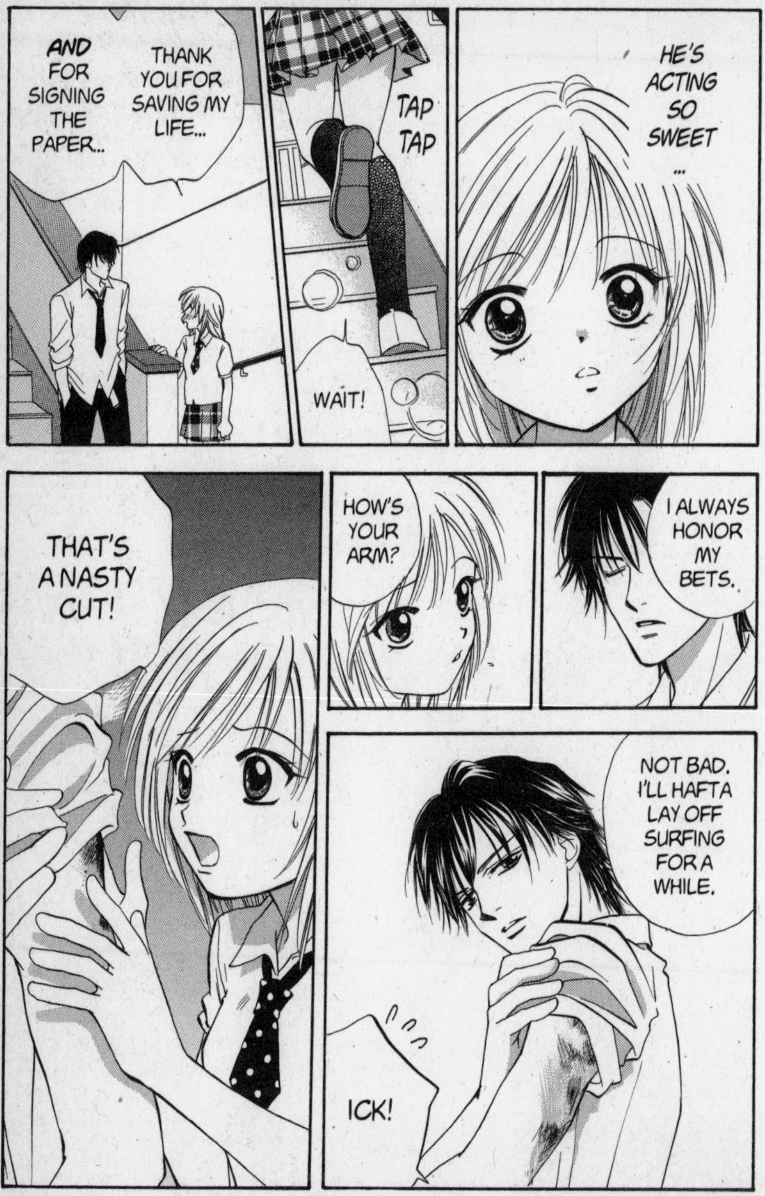
HE'S ACTING SO SWEET ...
TAP TAP
WAIT!
THANK YOU FOR SAVING MY LIFE...
AND FOR SIGNING THE PAPER...
I ALWAYS HONOR MY BETS.
HOW'S YOUR ARM?
NOT BAD. I'LL HAFTA LAY OFF SURFING FOR A WHILE.
ICK!
THAT'S A NASTY CUT!

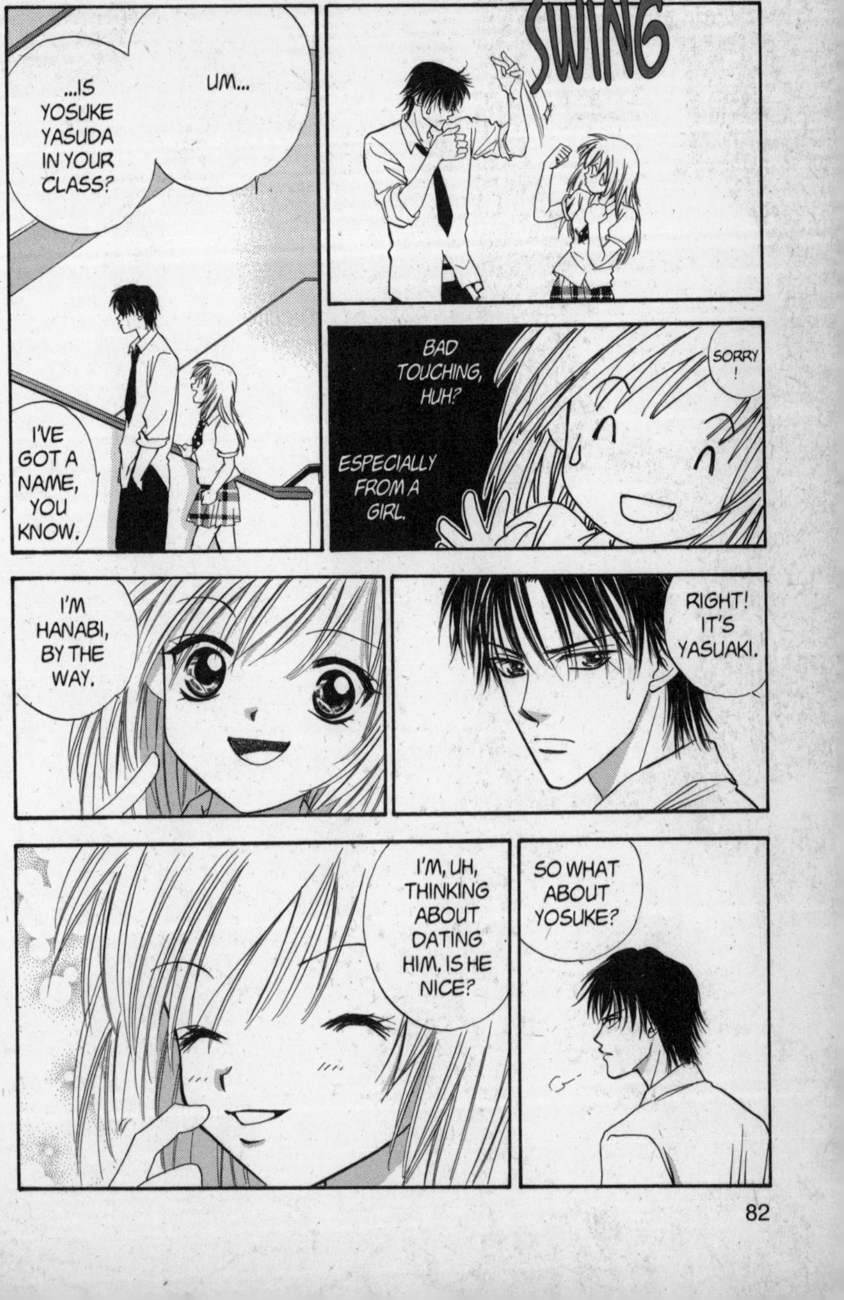
SWING
BAD TOUCHING, HUH?
ESPECIALLY FROM A GIRL.
SORRY!
UM...
...IS YOSUKE YASUDA IN YOUR CLASS?
I'VE GOT A NAME, YOU KNOW.
RIGHT! IT'S YASUAKI.
I'M HANABI, BY THE WAY.
SO WHAT ABOUT YOSUKE?
I'M, UH, THINKING ABOUT DATING HIM. IS HE NICE?

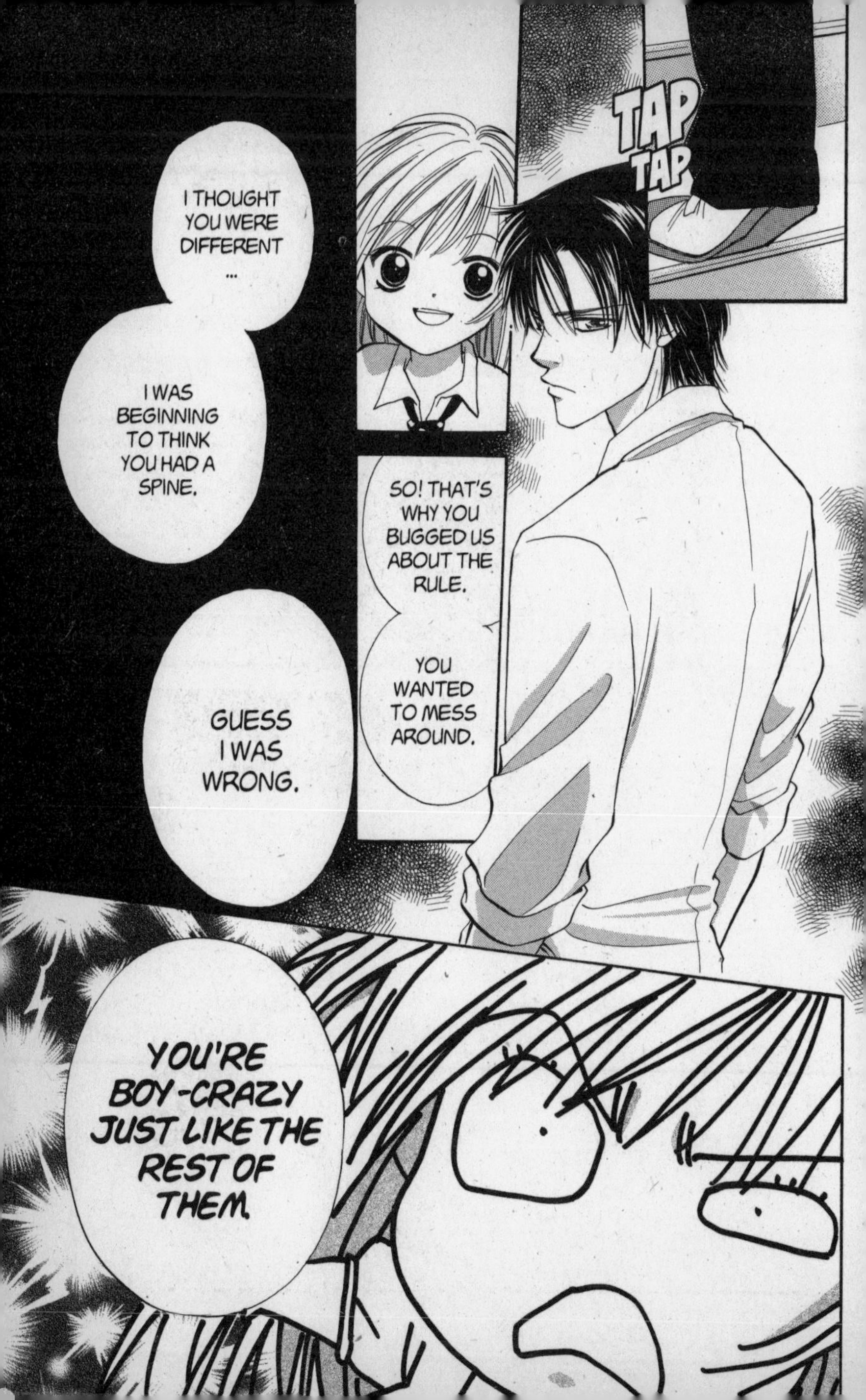

TAP TAP
SO! THAT'S WHY YOU BUGGED US ABOUT THE RULE.
YOU WANTED TO MESS AROUND.
I THOUGHT YOU WERE DIFFERENT ...
I WAS BEGINNING TO THINK YOU HAD A SPINE.
GUESS I WAS WRONG.
YOU'RE BOY-CRAZY JUST LIKE THE REST OF THEM.

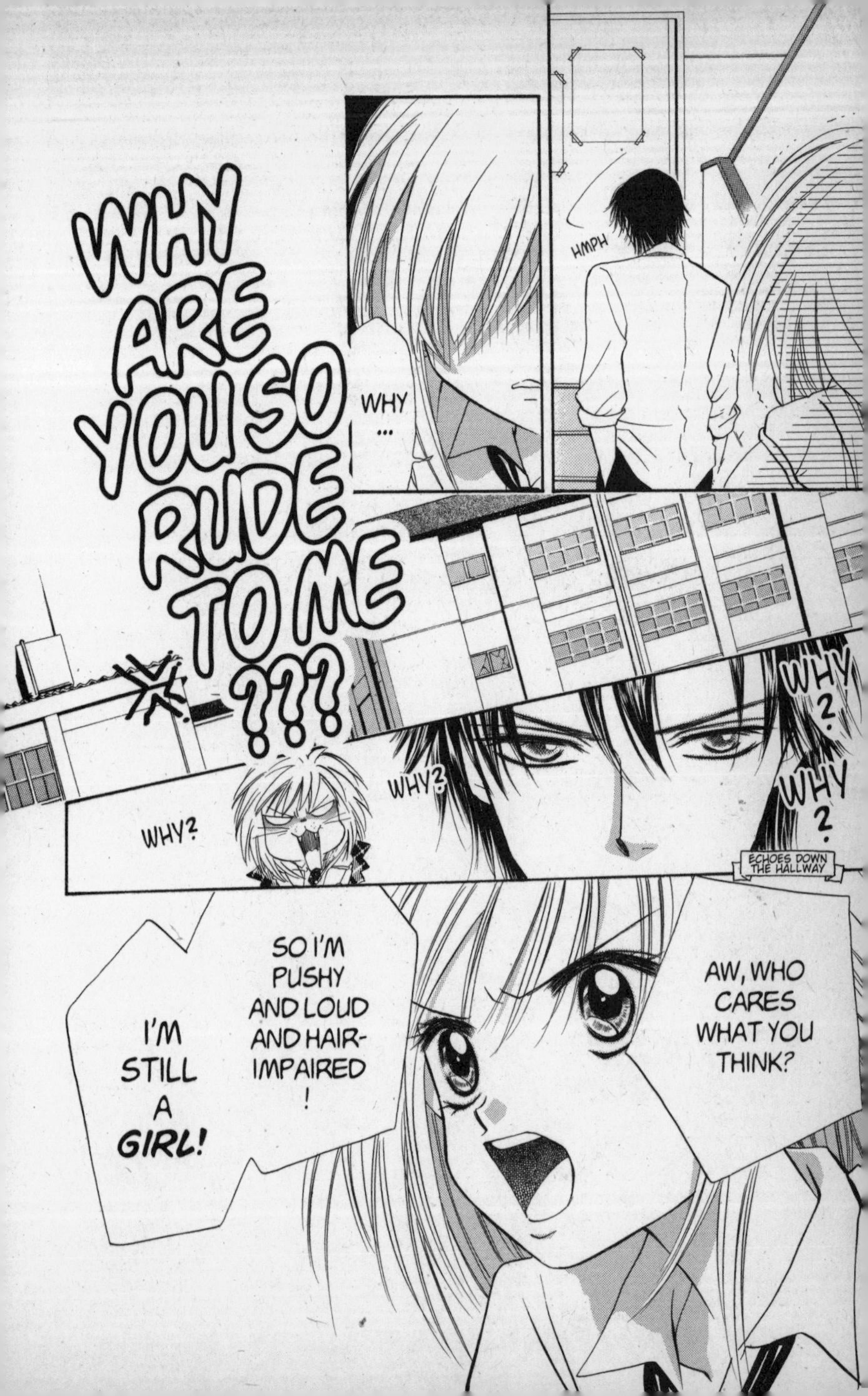
HMPH
WHY...
WHY ARE YOU SO RUDE TO ME???
WHY?
WHY?
ECHOES DOWN THE HALLWAY
WHY?
WHY?
AW, WHO CARES WHAT YOU THINK?
SO I'M PUSHY AND LOUD AND HAIR-IMPAIRED!
I'M STILL A GIRL!

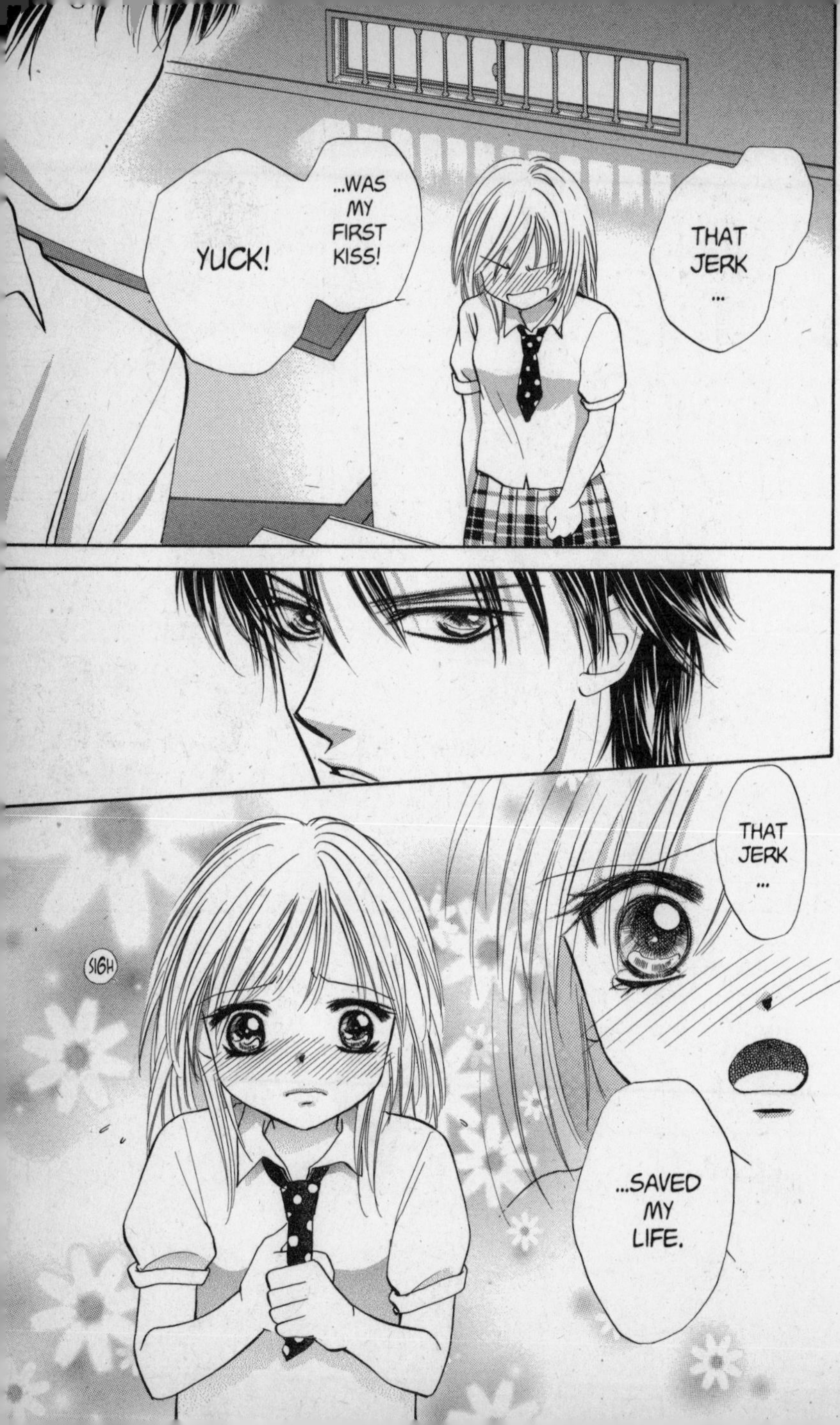
THAT JERK ...
...WAS MY FIRST KISS!
YUCK!
THAT JERK ...
...SAVED MY LIFE.
SIGH

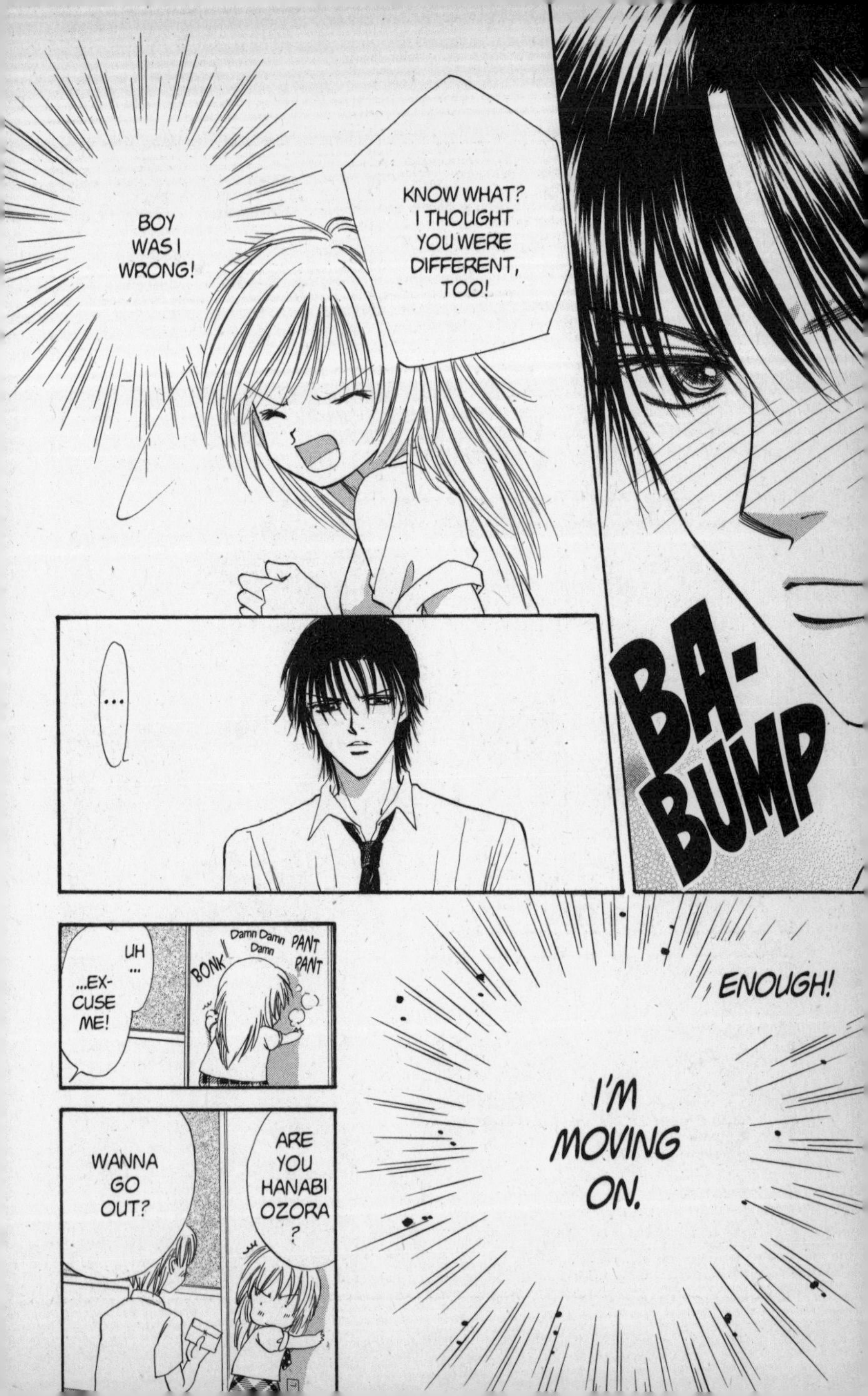
BA-BUMP
KNOW WHAT? I THOUGHT YOU WERE DIFFERENT, TOO!
BOY WAS I WRONG!
...
ENOUGH!
I'M MOVING ON.
PANT PANT
Damn Damn Damn
BONK
UH ...EX-CUSE ME!
ARE YOU HANABI OZORA?
WANNA GO OUT?

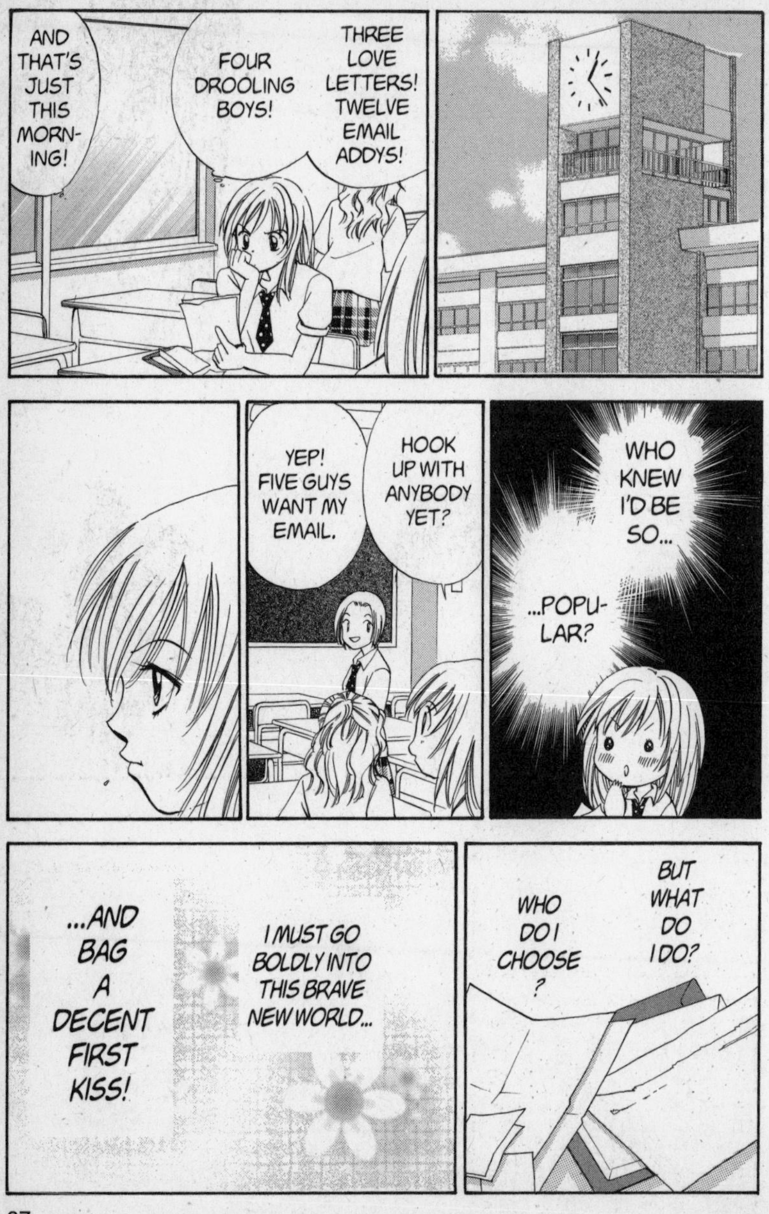
THREE LOVE LETTERS! TWELVE EMAIL ADDYS!
FOUR DROOLING BOYS!
AND THAT'S JUST THIS MORNING!
WHO KNEW I'D BE SO...
...POPULAR?
HOOK UP WITH ANYBODY YET?
YEP! FIVE GUYS WANT MY EMAIL.
BUT WHAT DO I DO?
WHO DO I CHOOSE?
I MUST GO BOLDLY INTO THIS BRAVE NEW WORLD...
...AND BAG A DECENT FIRST KISS!

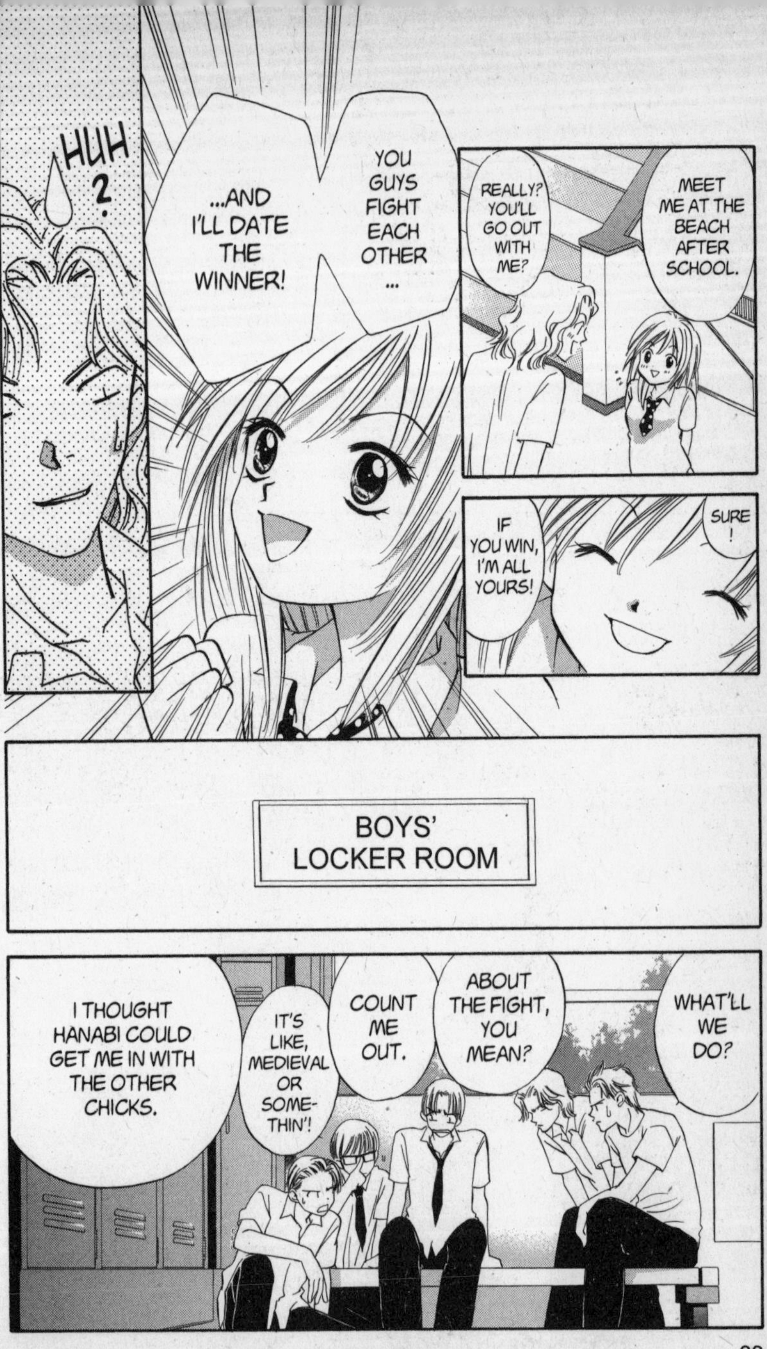
MEET ME AT THE BEACH AFTER SCHOOL.
REALLY? YOU'LL GO OUT WITH ME?
SURE!
IF YOU WIN, I'M ALL YOURS!
YOU GUYS FIGHT EACH OTHER ...
...AND I'LL DATE THE WINNER!
HUH?
BOYS' LOCKER ROOM
WHAT'LL WE DO?
ABOUT THE FIGHT, YOU MEAN?
COUNT ME OUT.
IT'S LIKE, MEDIEVAL OR SOME-THIN'!
I THOUGHT HANABI COULD GET ME IN WITH THE OTHER CHICKS.

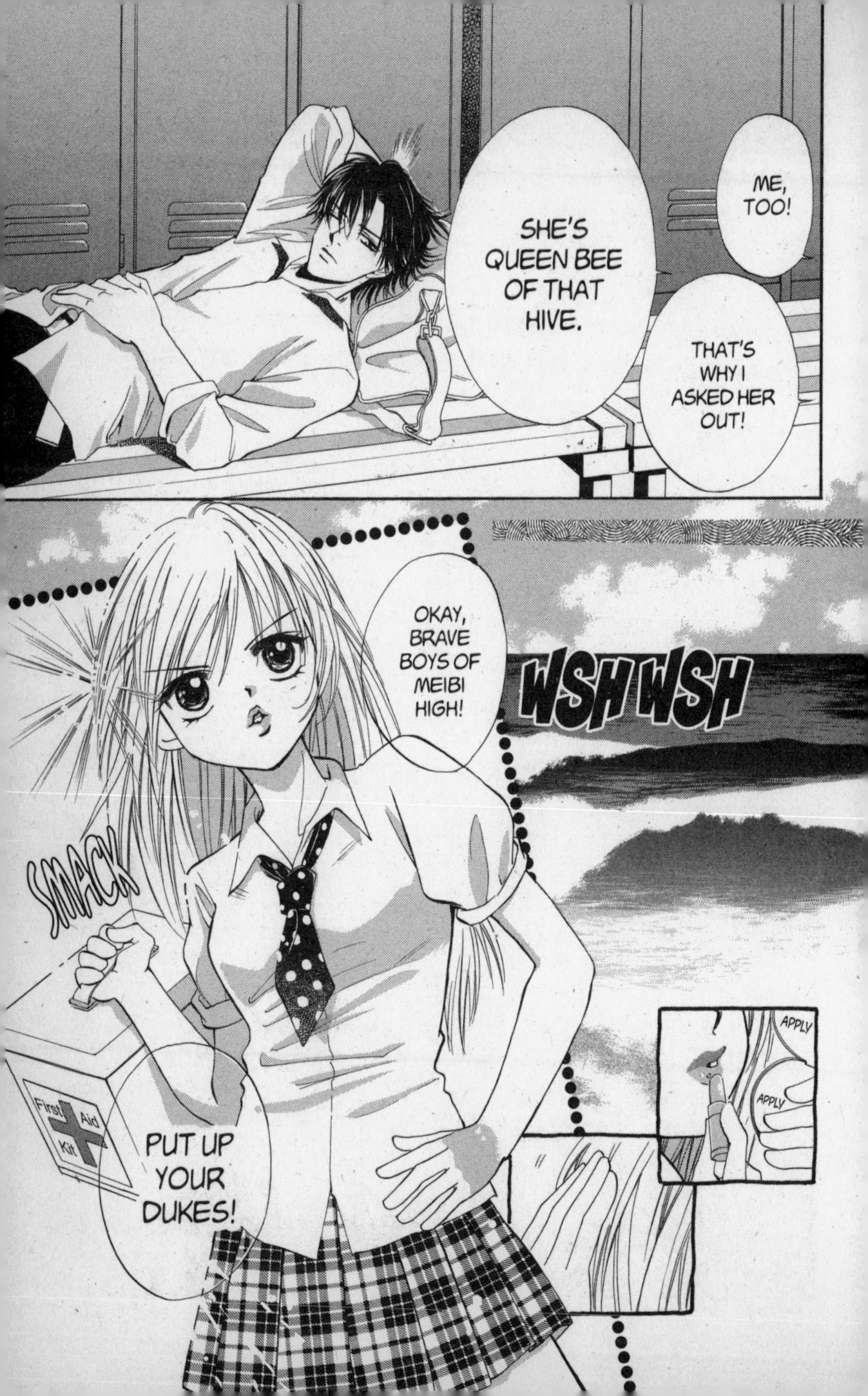
SHE'S QUEEN BEE OF THAT HIVE.
ME, TOO!
THAT'S WHY I ASKED HER OUT!
WSH WSH
APPLY
APPLY
OKAY, BRAVE BOYS OF MEIBI HIGH!
SMACK
First Aid Kit
PUT UP YOUR DUKES!

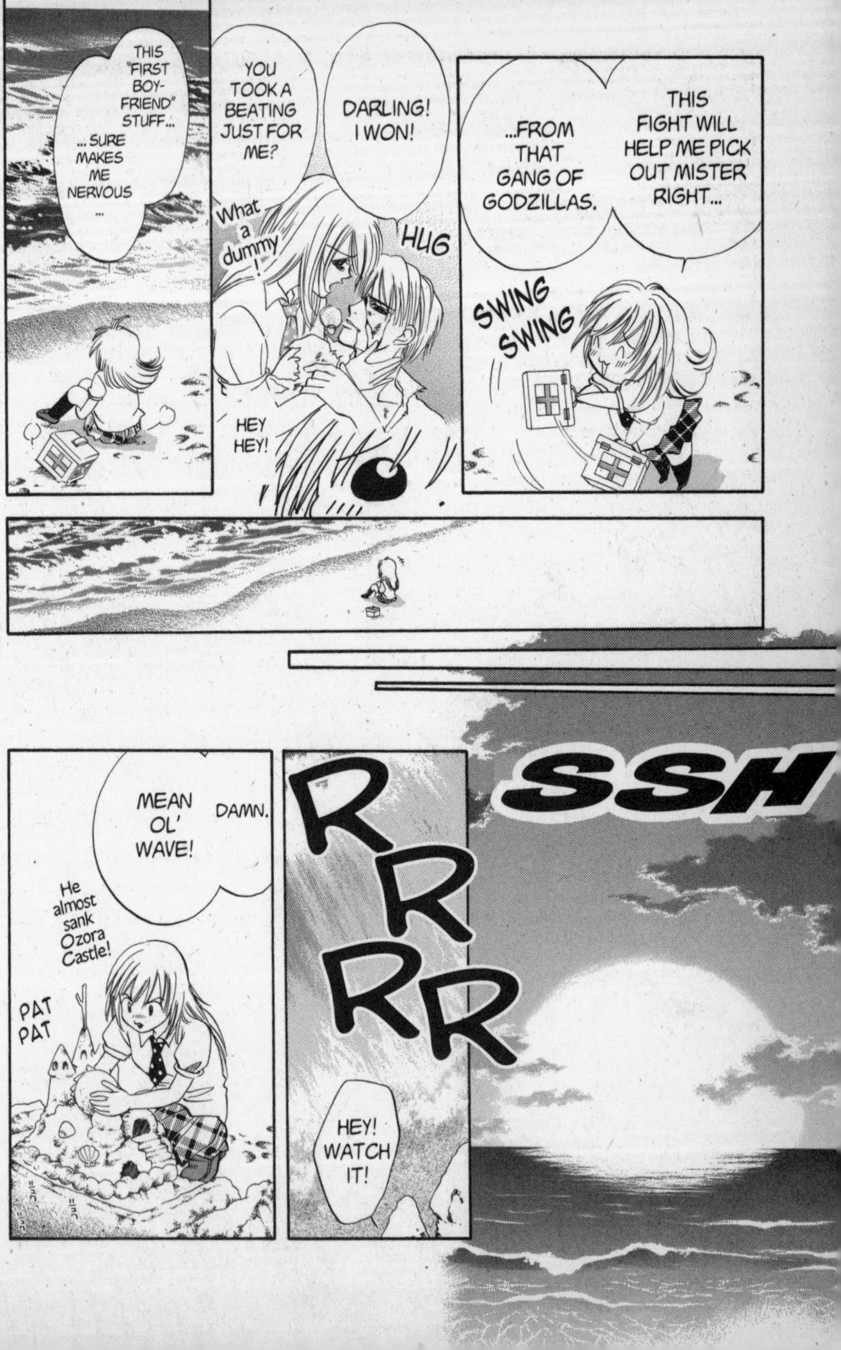
THIS FIGHT WILL HELP ME PICK OUT MISTER RIGHT...
...FROM THAT GANG OF GODZILLAS.
SWING SWING
DARLING! I WON!
YOU TOOK A BEATING JUST FOR ME?
What a dummy!
HUG
HEY HEY!
THIS "FIRST BOY-FRIEND" STUFF...
... SURE MAKES ME NERVOUS ...
SSH
RRRR
HEY! WATCH IT!
MEAN OL' WAVE!
DAMN.
He almost sank Ozora Castle!
PAT PAT

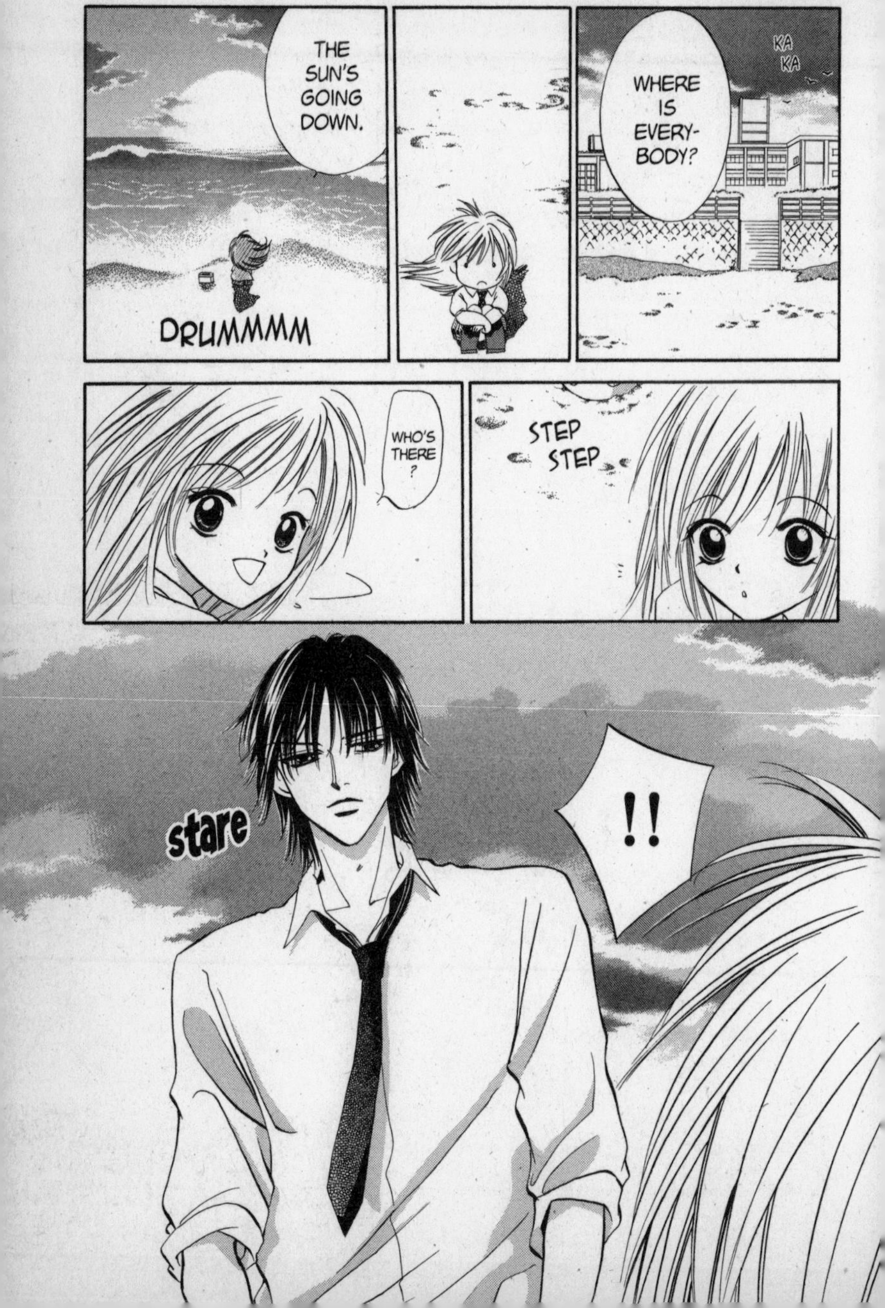
WHERE IS EVERY-BODY?
KA KA
THE SUN'S GOING DOWN.
DRUMMMM
STEP STEP
WHO'S THERE?
!!
stare

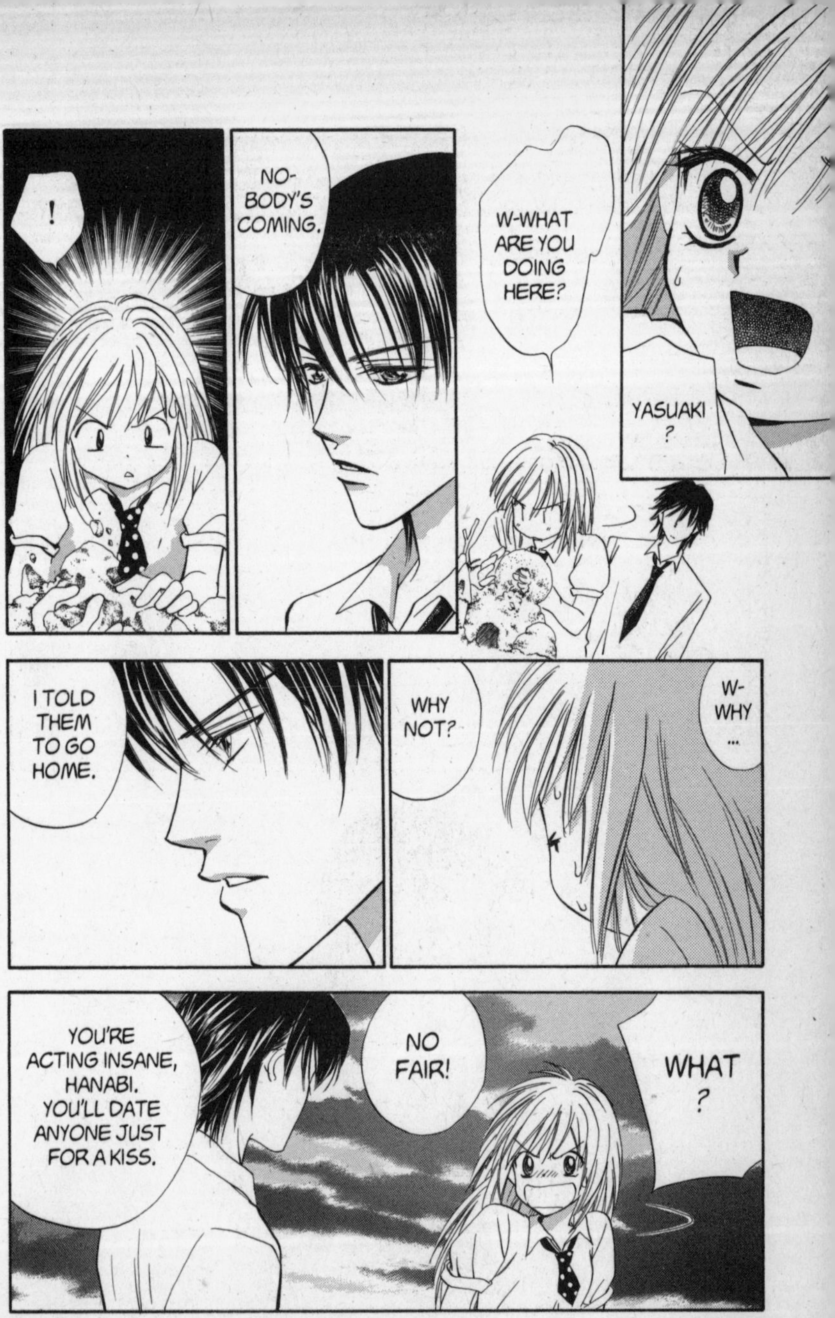
YASUAKI ?
W-WHAT ARE YOU DOING HERE?
NO-BODY'S COMING.
!
W-WHY ...
WHY NOT?
I TOLD THEM TO GO HOME.
WHAT ?
NO FAIR!
YOU'RE ACTING INSANE, HANABI. YOU'LL DATE ANYONE JUST FOR A KISS.

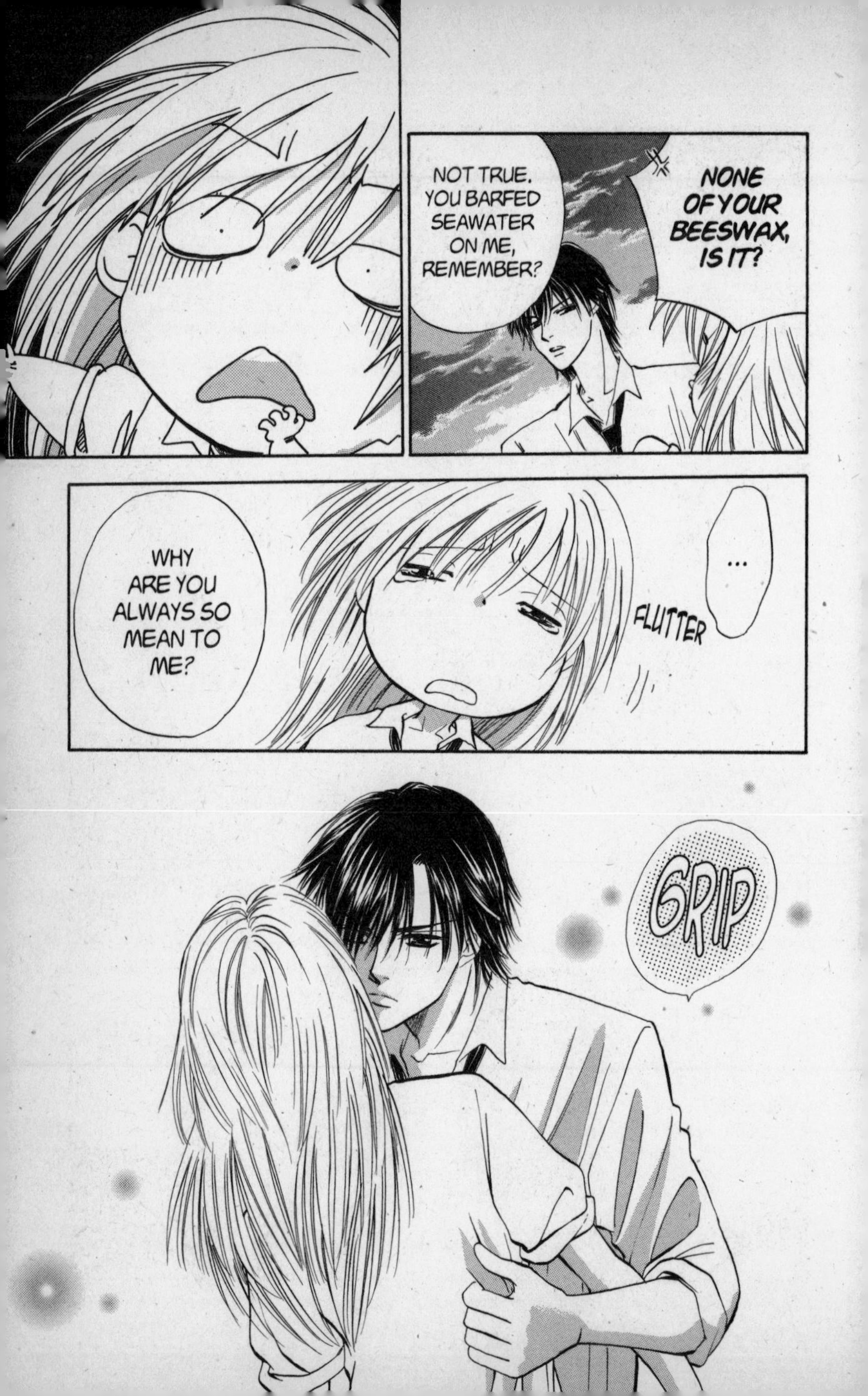
NONE OF YOUR BEESWAX, IS IT?
NOT TRUE. YOU BARFED SEAWATER ON ME, REMEMBER?
...
FLUTTER
WHY ARE YOU ALWAYS SO MEAN TO ME?
GRIP

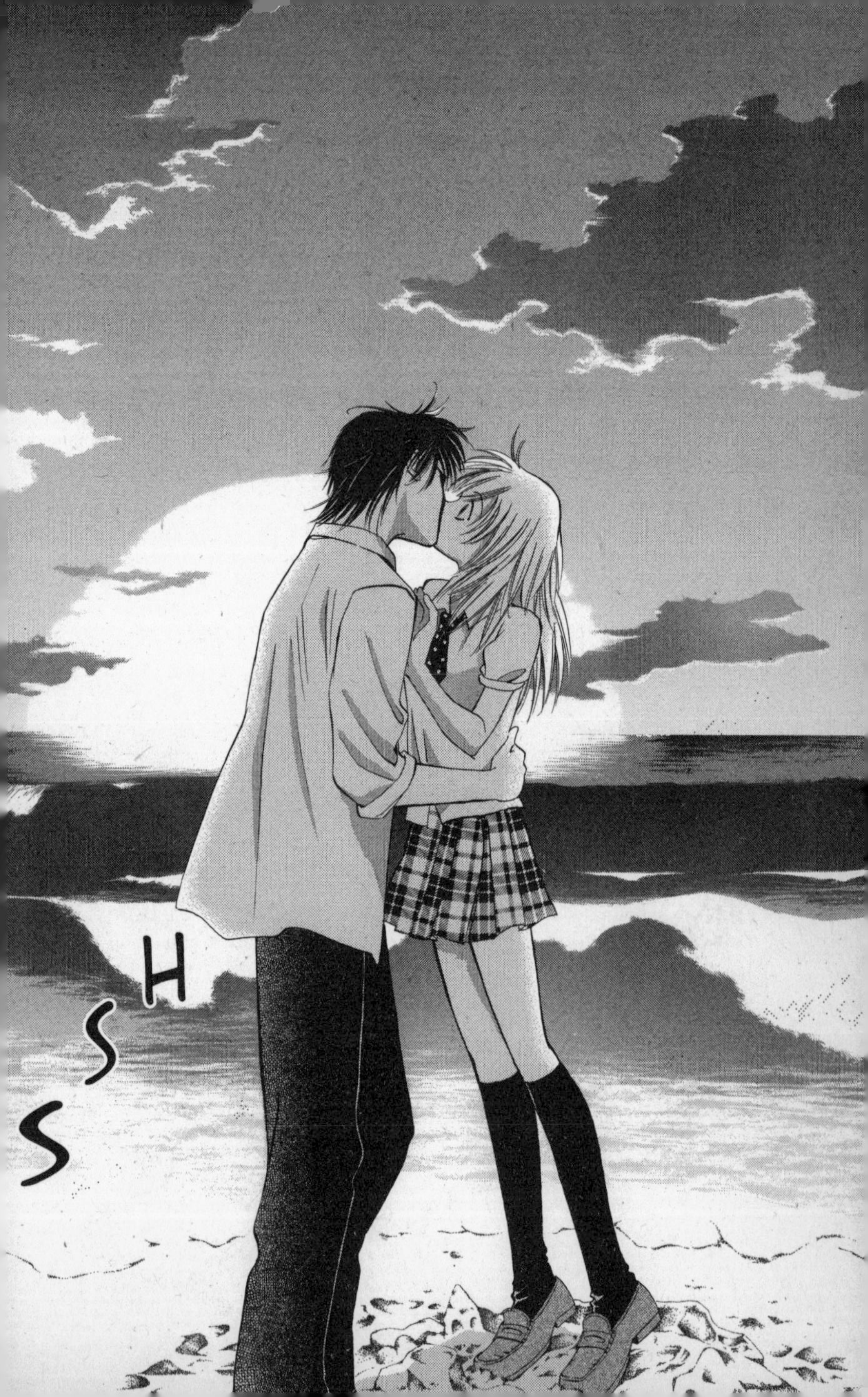
SSH

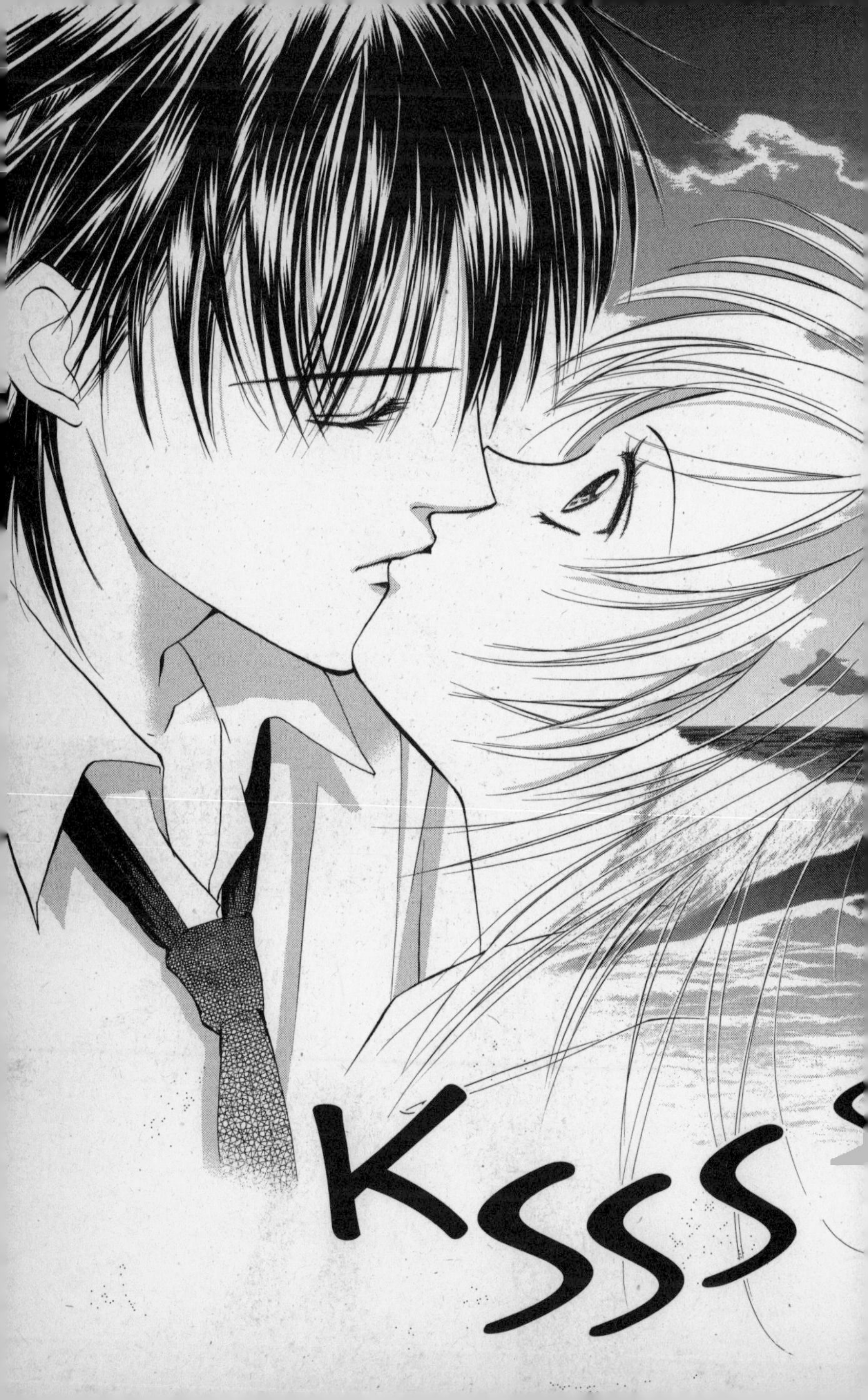
KSSS

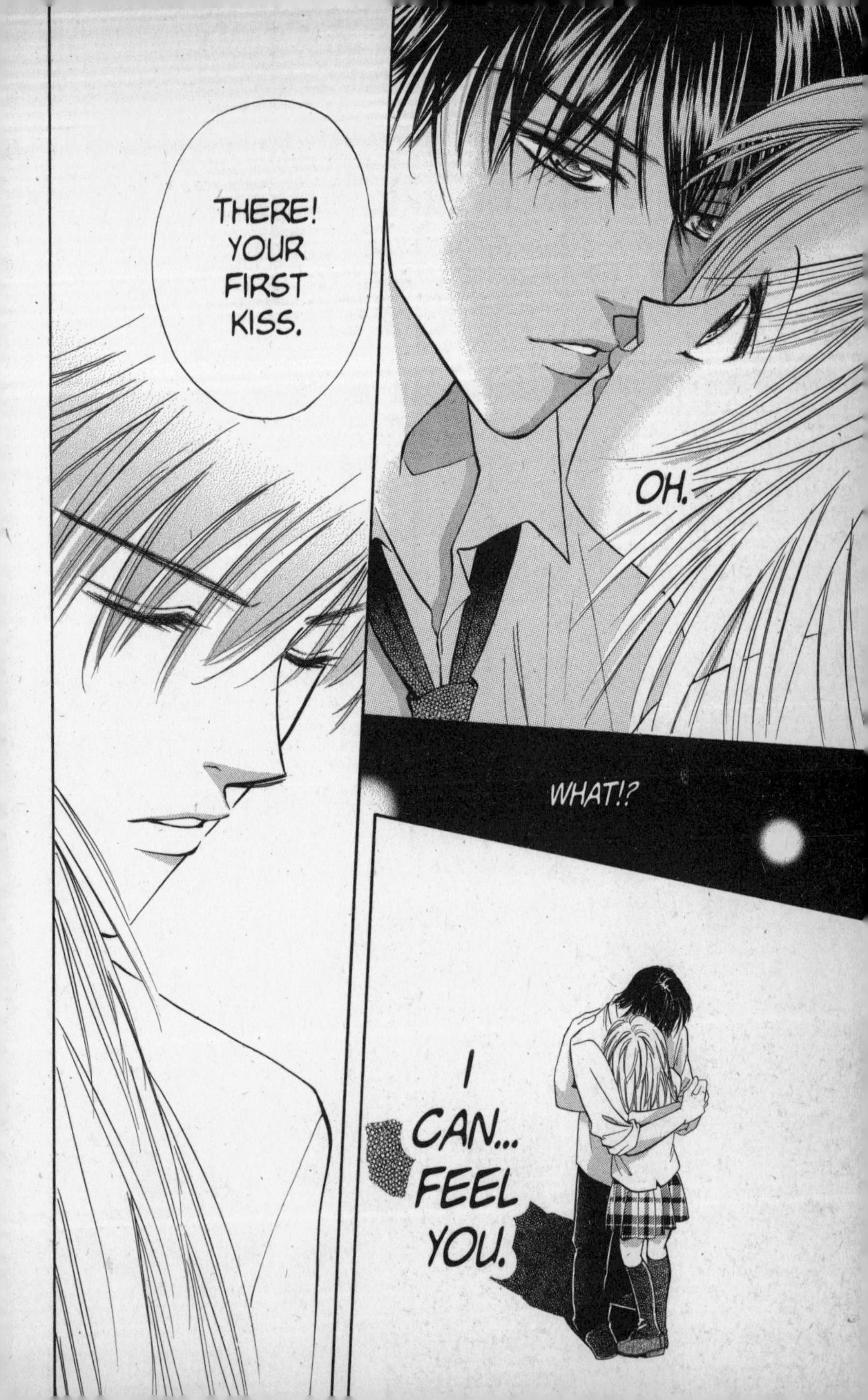
OH.
WHAT!?
I CAN... FEEL YOU.
THERE! YOUR FIRST KISS.

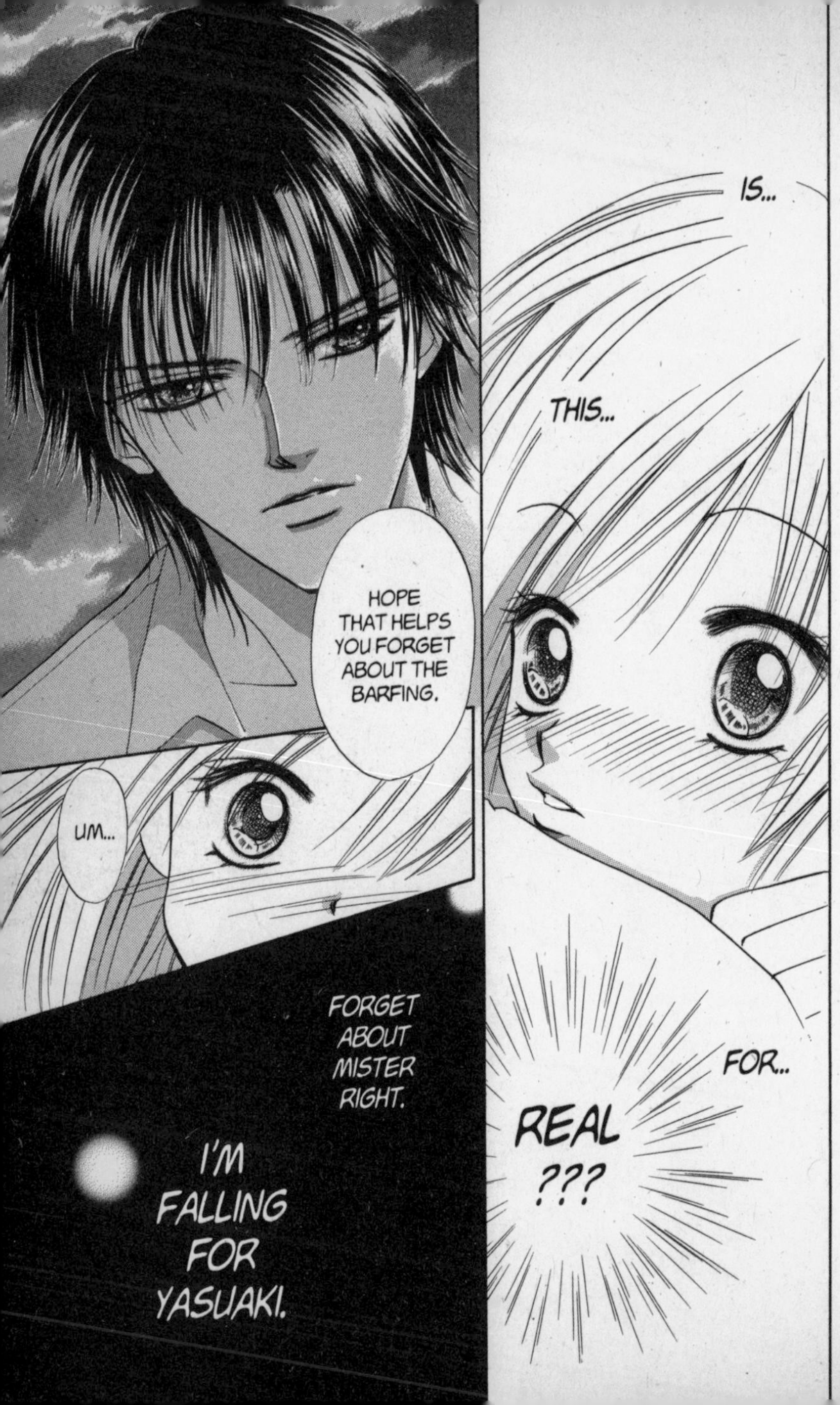
IS...
THIS...
FOR...
REAL ???
HOPE THAT HELPS YOU FORGET ABOUT THE BARFING.
UM...
FORGET ABOUT MISTER RIGHT.
I'M FALLING FOR YASUAKI.

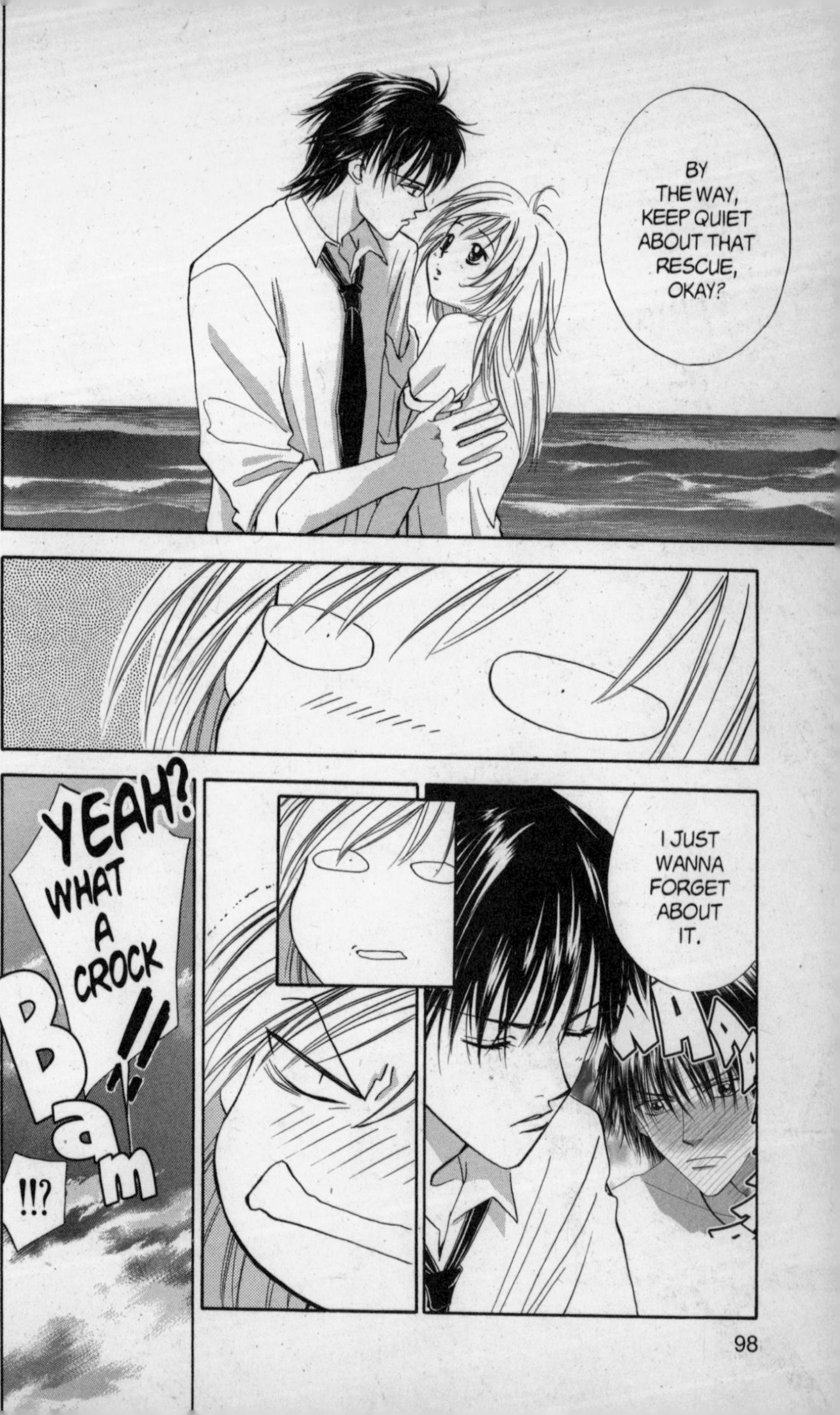
BY THE WAY, KEEP QUIET ABOUT THAT RESCUE, OKAY?
I JUST WANNA FORGET ABOUT IT.
YEAH? WHAT A CROCK!!
Bam
!!?

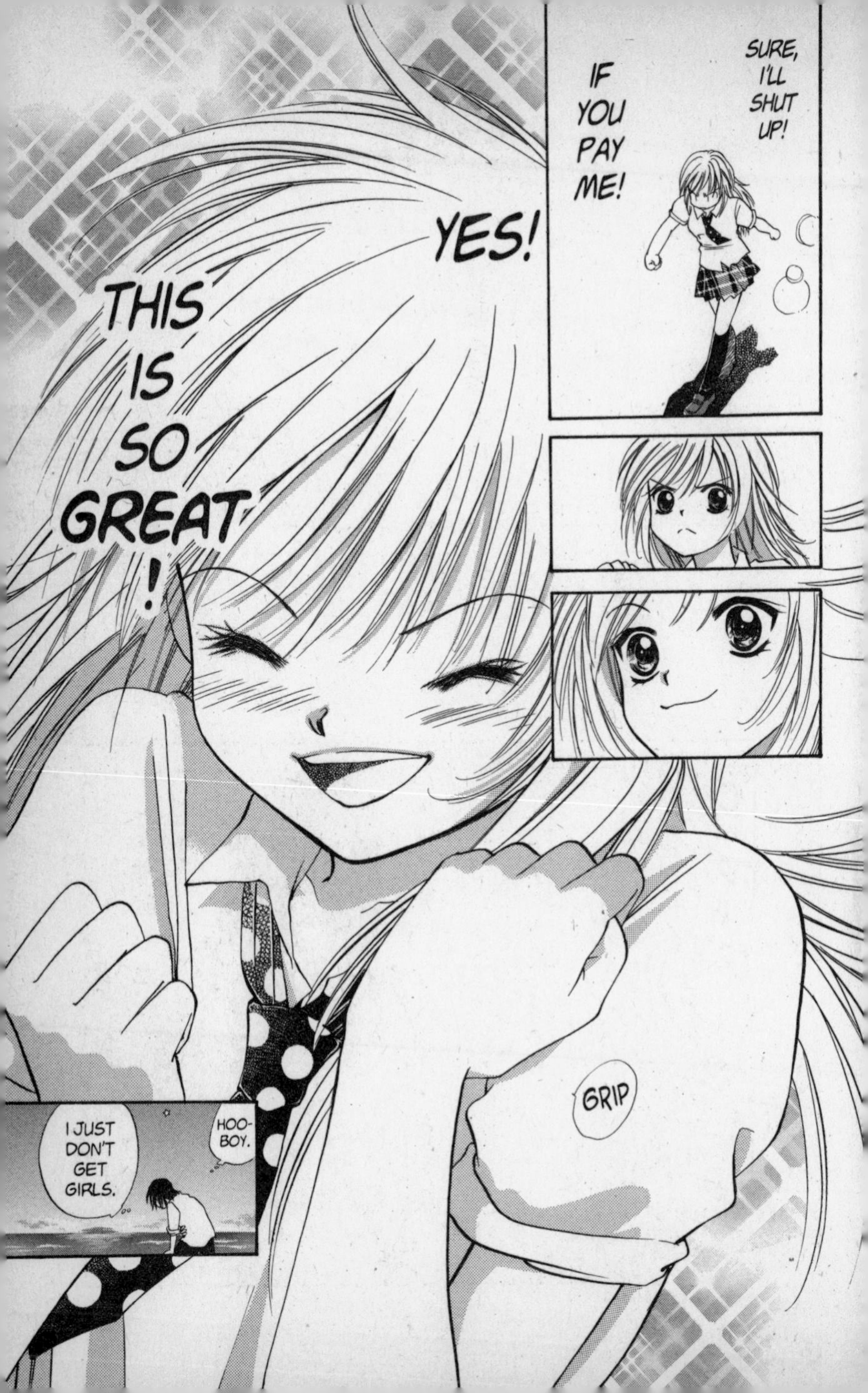
SURE, I'LL SHUT UP!
IF YOU PAY ME!
YES!
THIS IS SO GREAT!
GRIP
HOO-BOY.
I JUST DON'T GET GIRLS.

HAPPY
HUSTLE
HIGH

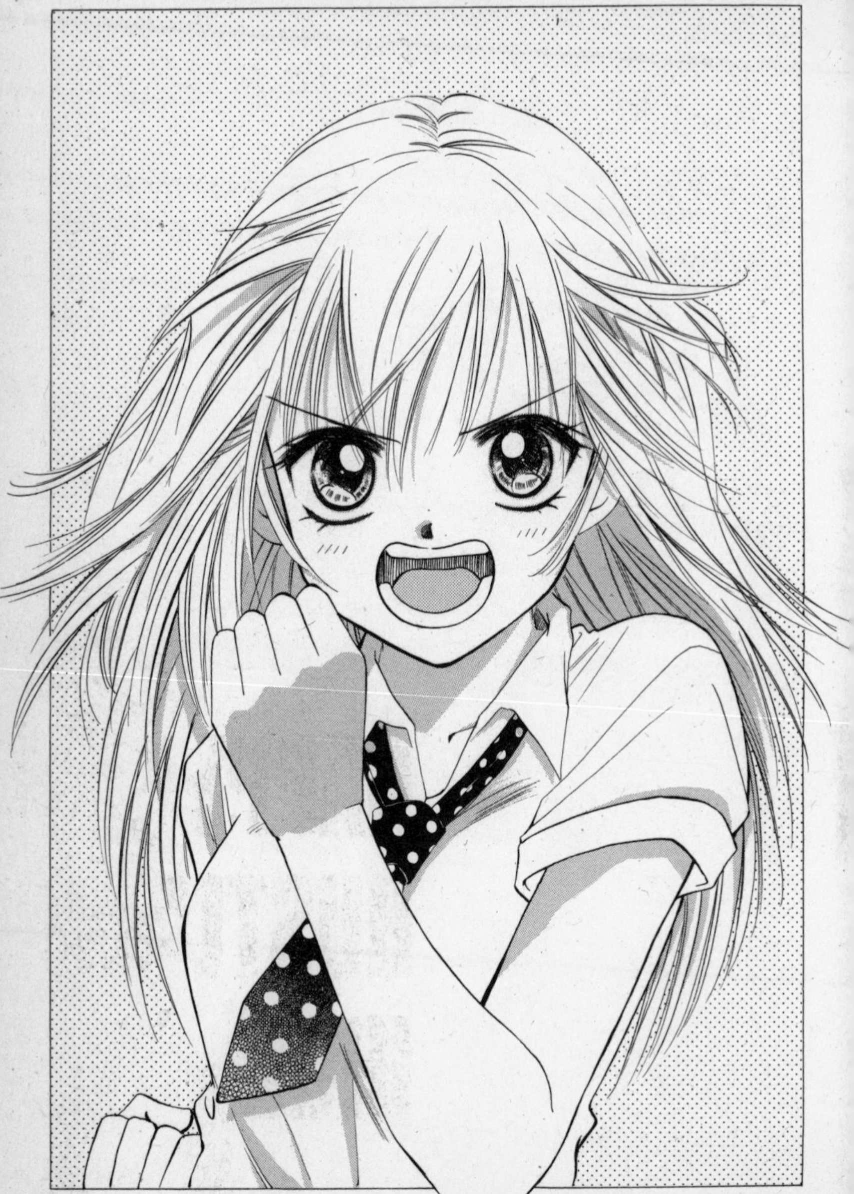

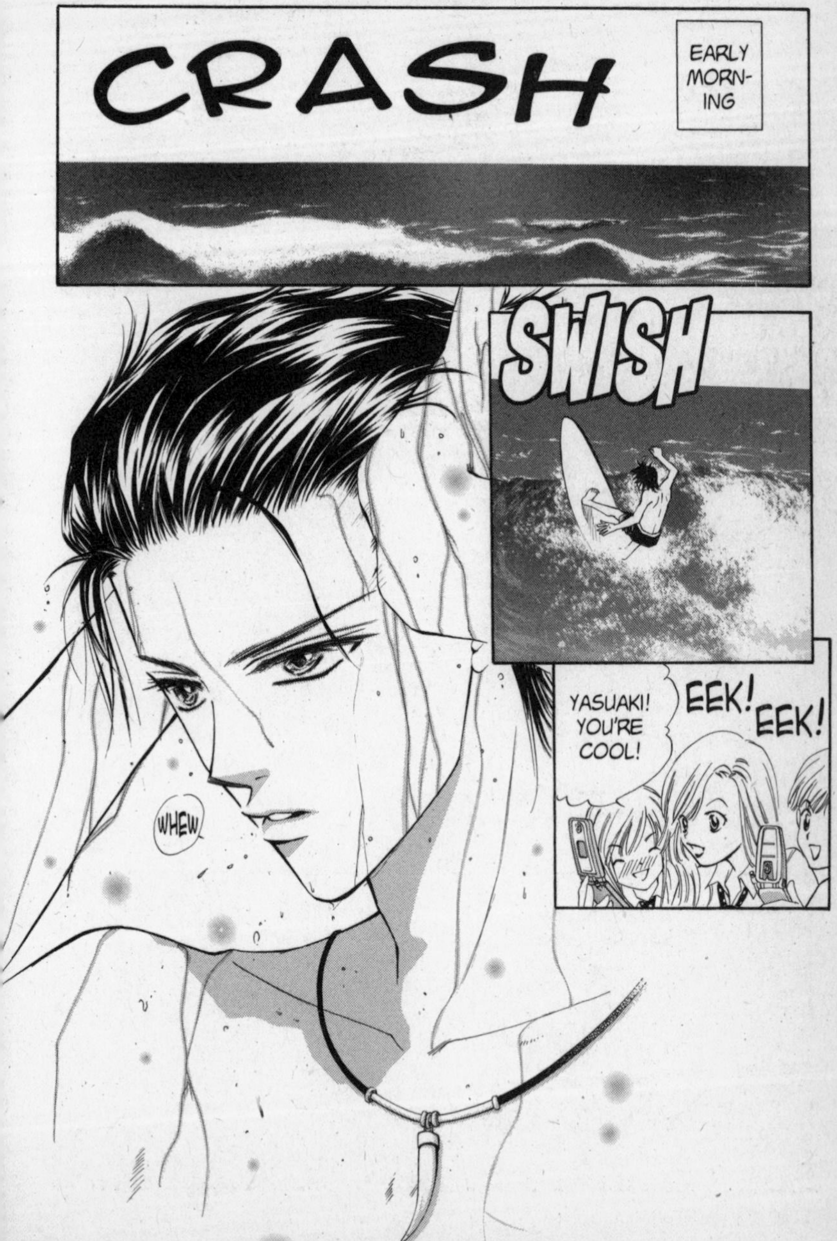
CRASH
EARLY MORNING-ING
SWISH
EEK!
EEK!
YASUAKI! YOU'RE COOL!
WHEW

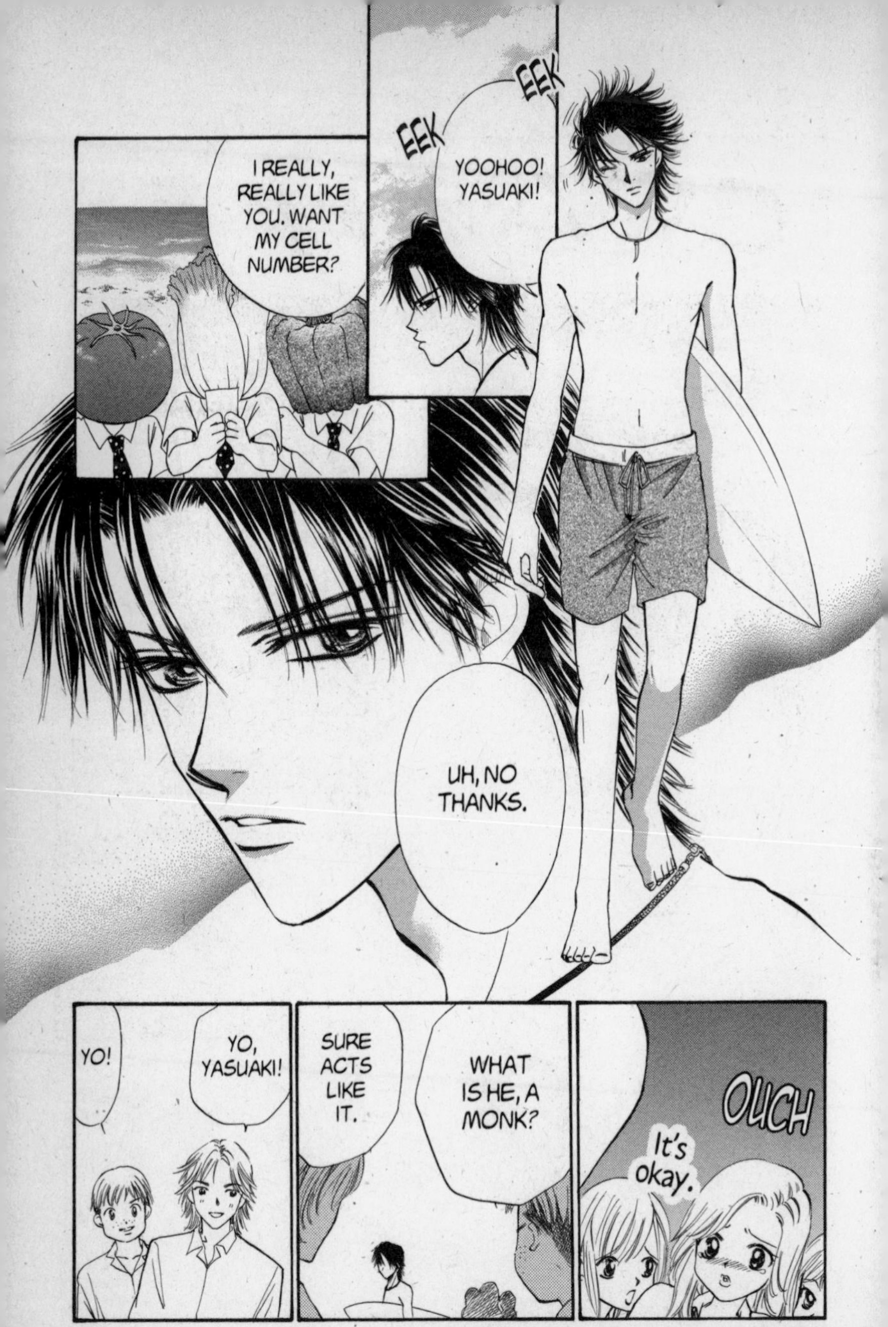
EEK
EEK
YOOHOO! YASUAKI!
I REALLY, REALLY LIKE YOU. WANT MY CELL NUMBER?
UH, NO THANKS.
OUCH
It's okay.
WHAT IS HE, A MONK?
SURE ACTS LIKE IT.
YO, YASUAKI!
YO!

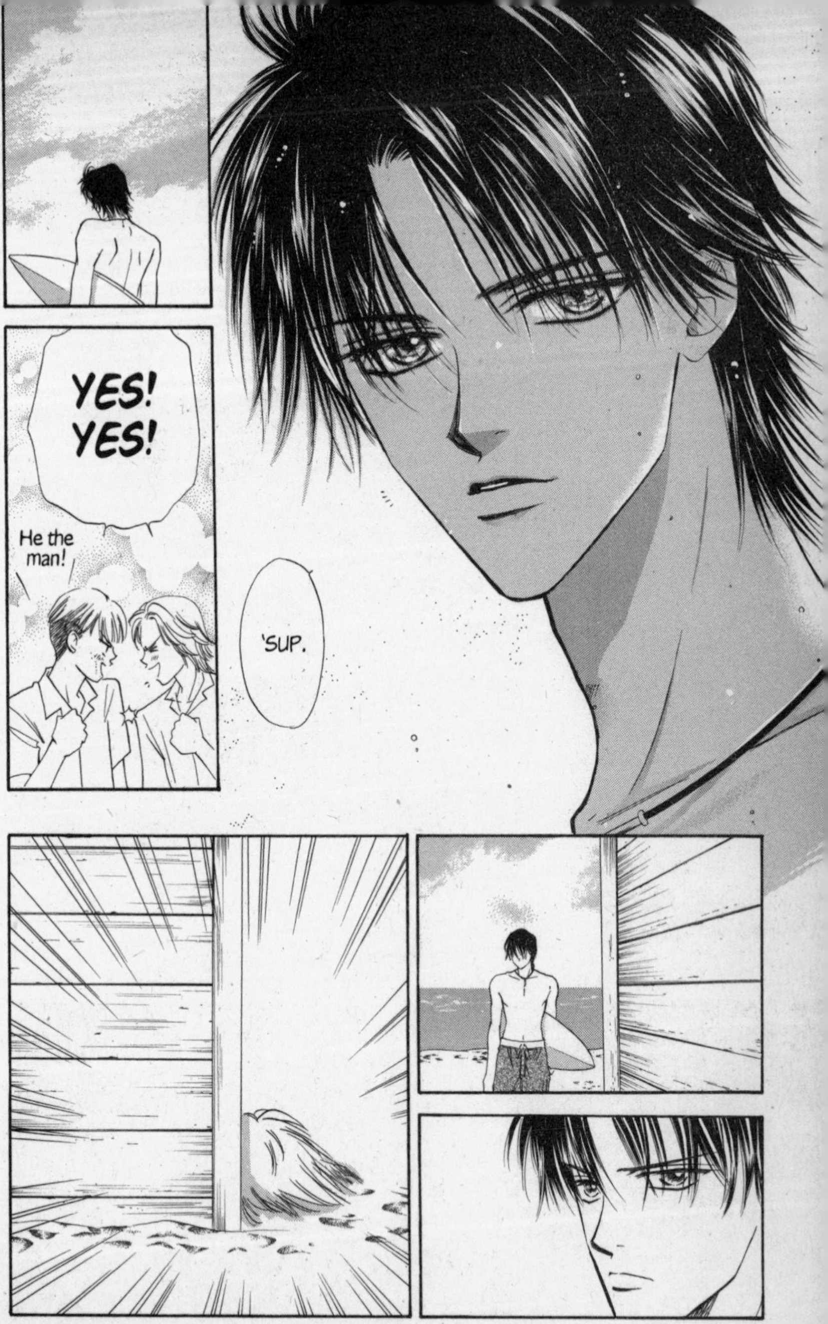
'SUP.
YES! YES!
He the man!

HERE.

HEY! WHAT ARE YOU DOING—

SPSH

CRUNCH

YASUAKI'S QUIET, PEACEFUL LIFE IS ABOUT TO GO BLOOEY.

CRASH

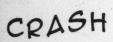

...

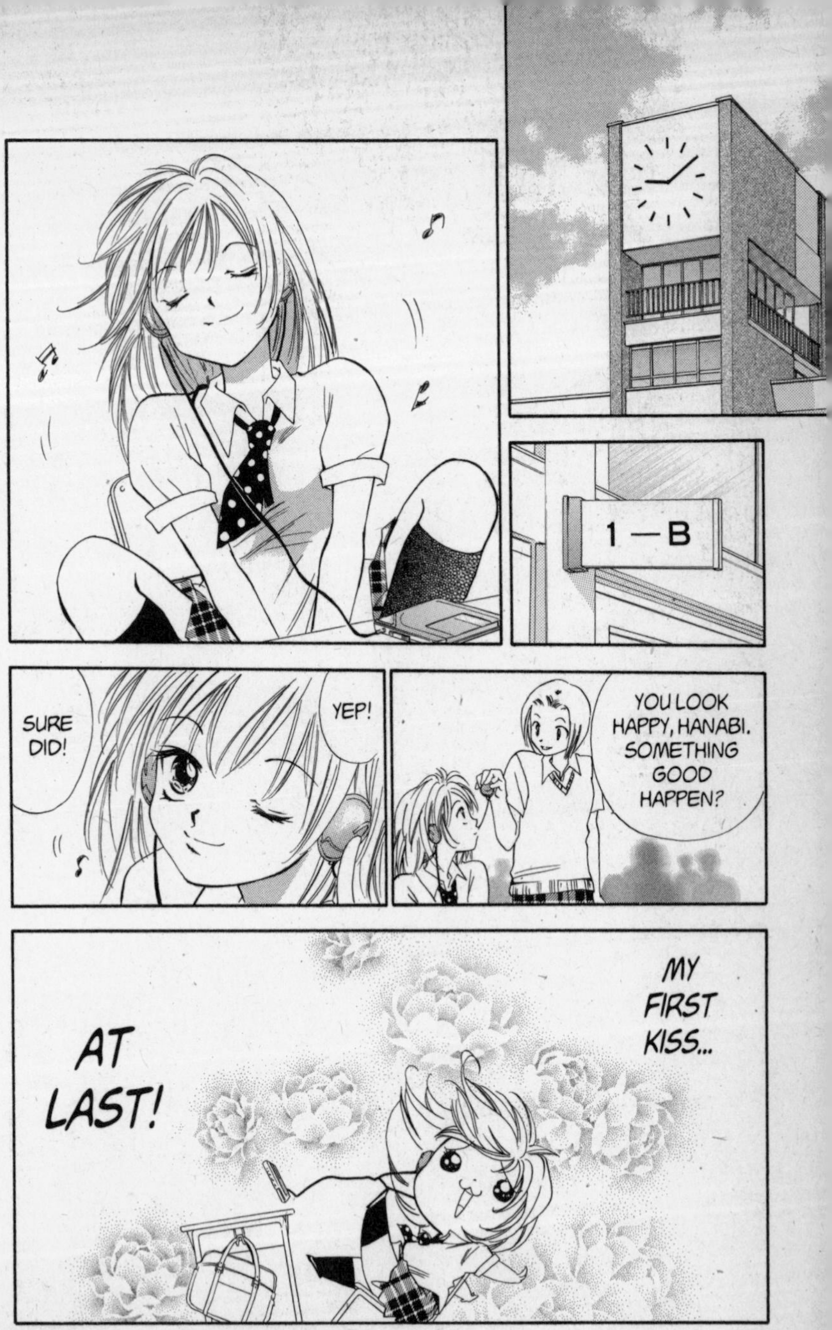
1—B
YOU LOOK HAPPY, HANABI. SOMETHING GOOD HAPPEN?
YEP!
SURE DID!
MY FIRST KISS...
AT LAST!

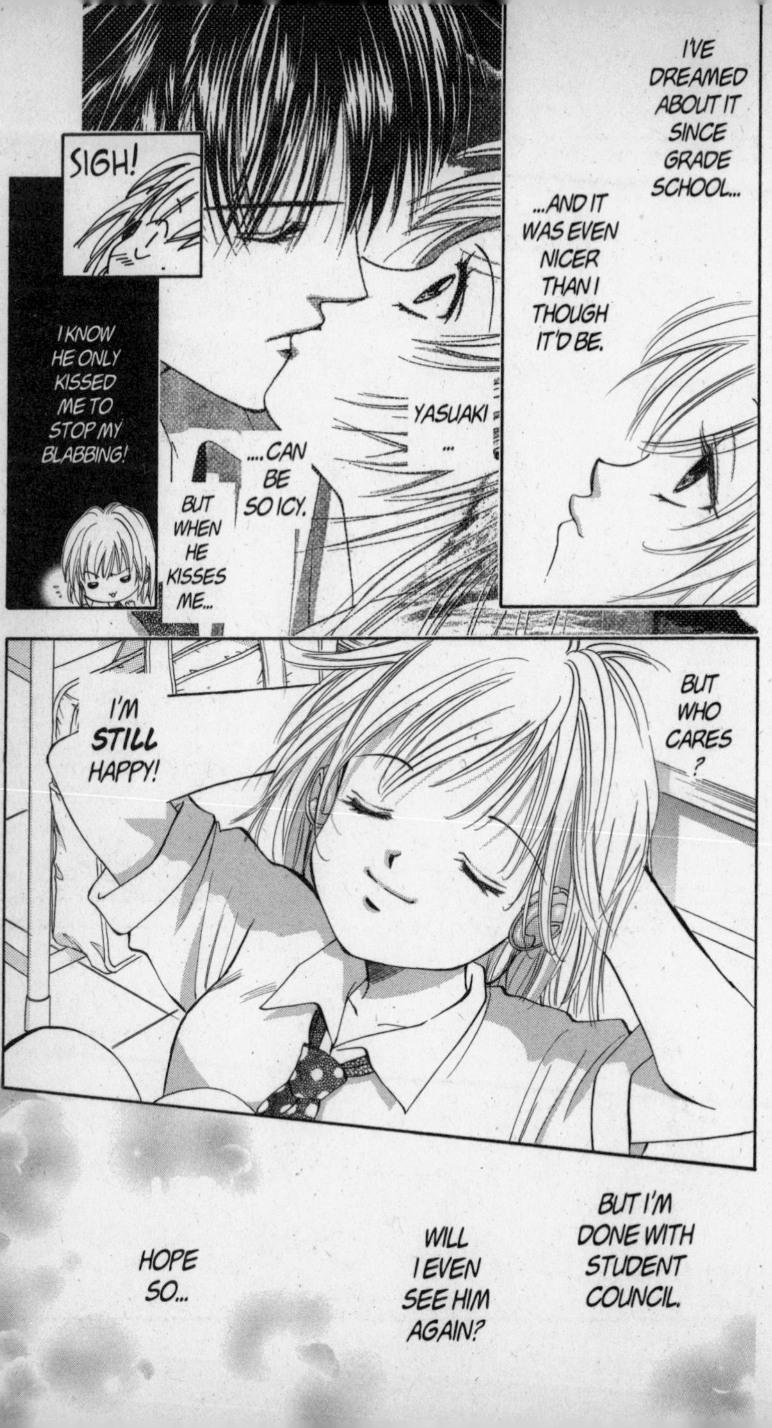
I'VE DREAMED ABOUT IT SINCE GRADE SCHOOL...
...AND IT WAS EVEN NICER THAN I THOUGH IT'D BE.
YASUAKI ...
....CAN BE SO ICY.
BUT WHEN HE KISSES ME...
SIGH!
I KNOW HE ONLY KISSED ME TO STOP MY BLABBING!
BUT WHO CARES?
I'M **STILL** HAPPY!
BUT I'M DONE WITH STUDENT COUNCIL.
WILL I EVEN SEE HIM AGAIN?
HOPE SO...

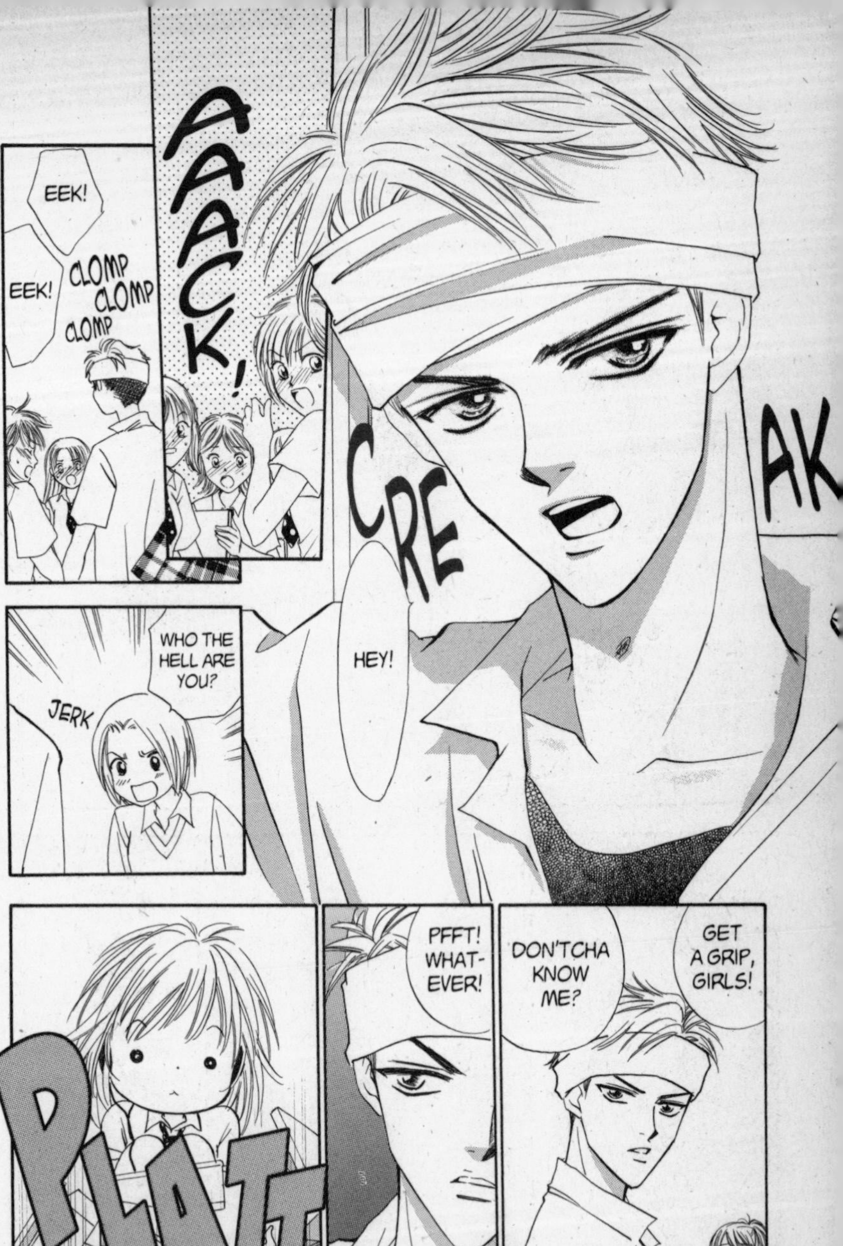

CREAK
HEY!
AAACK!
EEK!
EEK!
CLOMP CLOMP CLOMP
WHO THE HELL ARE YOU?
JERK
GET A GRIP, GIRLS!
DON'TCHA KNOW ME?
PFFT! WHAT-EVER!
PLATT

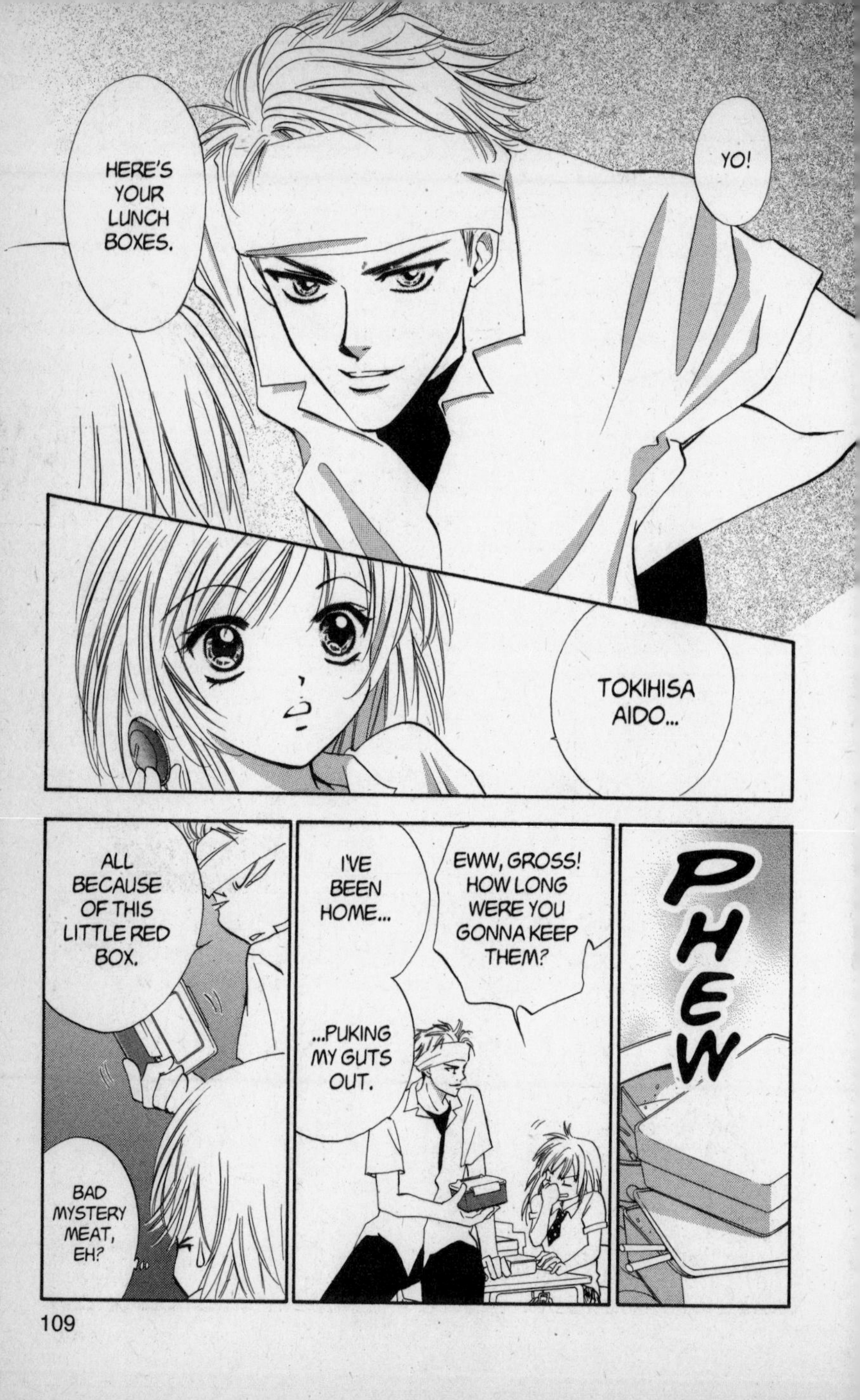
YO!
HERE'S YOUR LUNCH BOXES.
TOKIHISA AIDO...
PHEW
EWW, GROSS! HOW LONG WERE YOU GONNA KEEP THEM?
I'VE BEEN HOME...
...PUKING MY GUTS OUT.
ALL BECAUSE OF THIS LITTLE RED BOX.
BAD MYSTERY MEAT, EH?

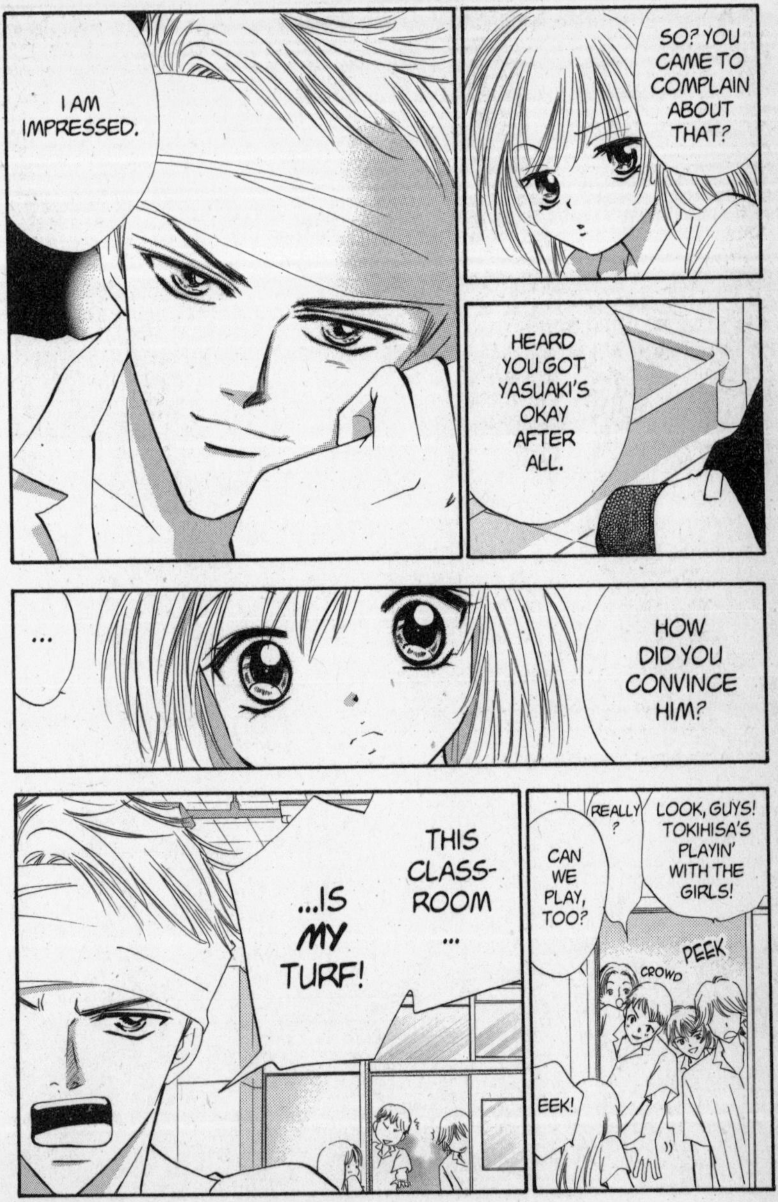

SO? YOU CAME TO COMPLAIN ABOUT THAT?
HEARD YOU GOT YASUAKI'S OKAY AFTER ALL.
I AM IMPRESSED.
HOW DID YOU CONVINCE HIM?
...
LOOK, GUYS! TOKIHISA'S PLAYIN' WITH THE GIRLS!
REALLY?
CAN WE PLAY, TOO?
PEEK
CROWD
EEK!
THIS CLASS-ROOM...
...IS MY TURF!

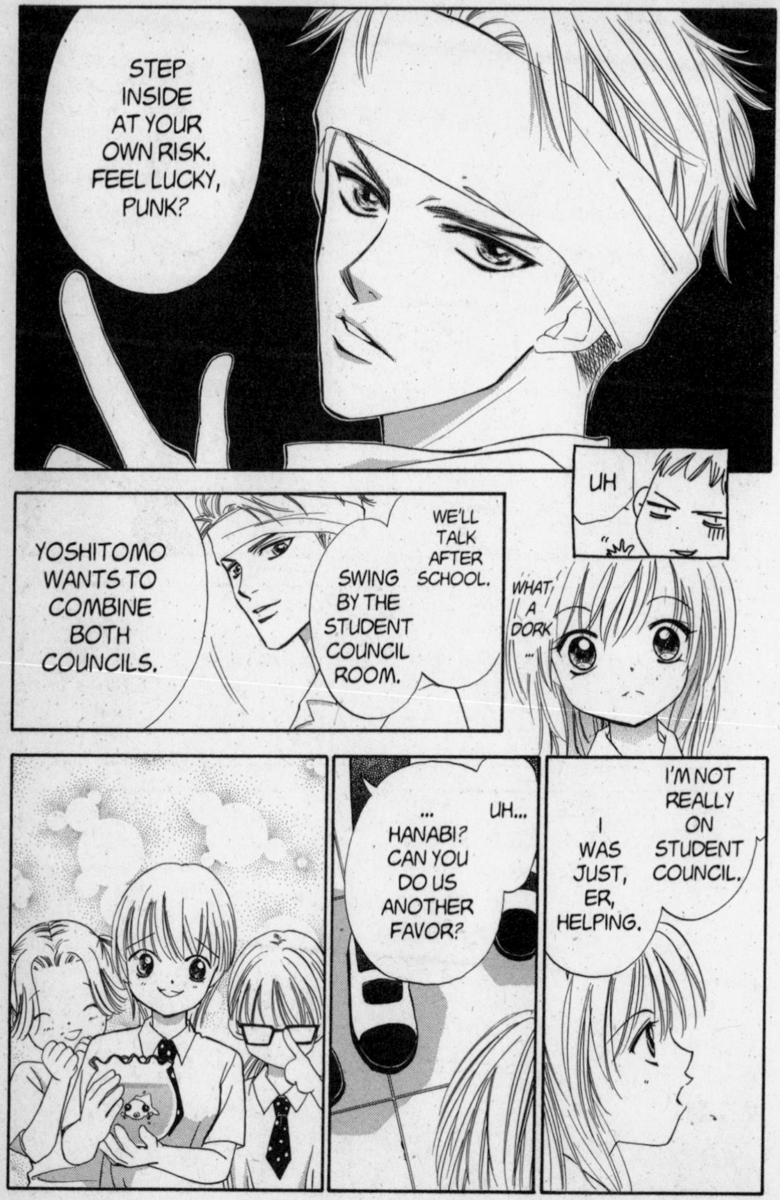
STEP INSIDE AT YOUR OWN RISK. FEEL LUCKY, PUNK?
UH
WHAT A DORK...
WE'LL TALK AFTER SCHOOL.
SWING BY THE STUDENT COUNCIL ROOM.
YOSHITOMO WANTS TO COMBINE BOTH COUNCILS.
I'M NOT REALLY ON STUDENT COUNCIL.
I WAS JUST, ER, HELPING.
UH...
...HANABI? CAN YOU DO US ANOTHER FAVOR?

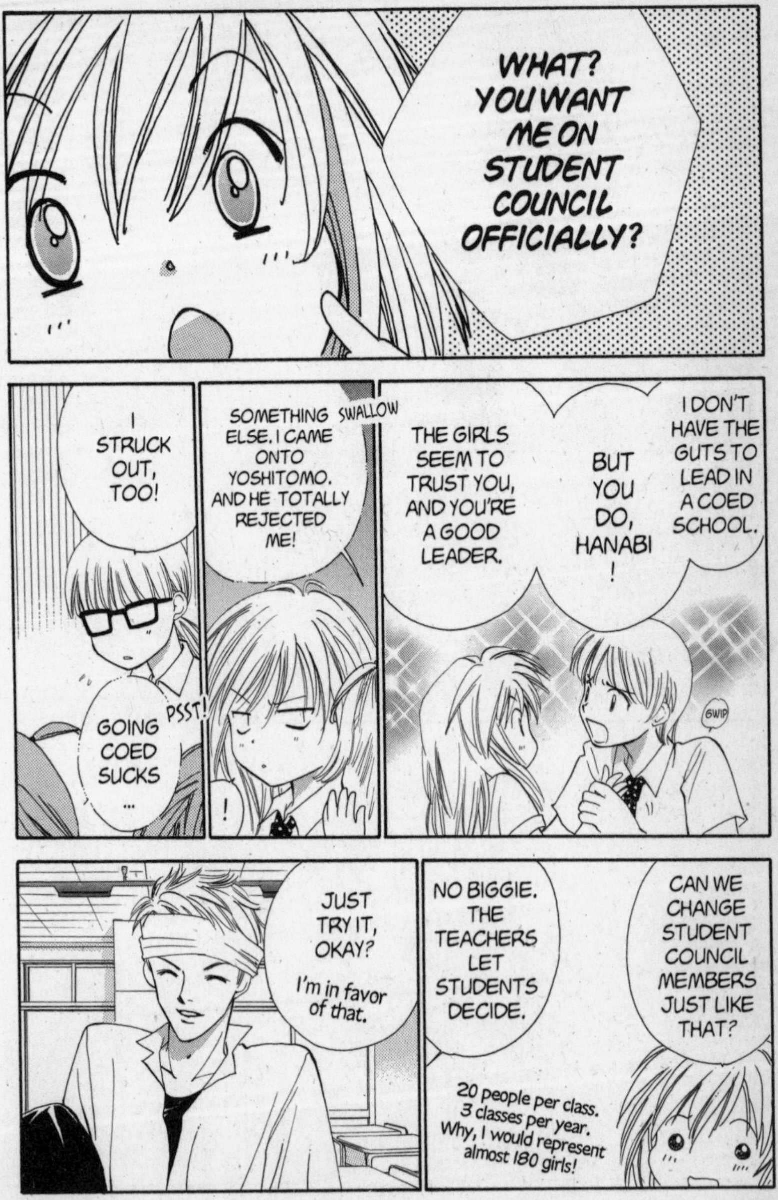
WHAT? YOU WANT ME ON STUDENT COUNCIL OFFICIALLY?
I DON'T HAVE THE GUTS TO LEAD IN A COED SCHOOL.
BUT YOU DO, HANABI!
THE GIRLS SEEM TO TRUST YOU, AND YOU'RE A GOOD LEADER.
GWIP
SOMETHING ELSE. I CAME ONTO YOSHITOMO. AND HE TOTALLY REJECTED ME!
SWALLOW
!
I STRUCK OUT, TOO!
PSST!
GOING COED SUCKS ...
CAN WE CHANGE STUDENT COUNCIL MEMBERS JUST LIKE THAT?
NO BIGGIE. THE TEACHERS LET STUDENTS DECIDE.
20 people per class. 3 classes per year. Why, I would represent almost 180 girls!
JUST TRY IT, OKAY?
I'm in favor of that.

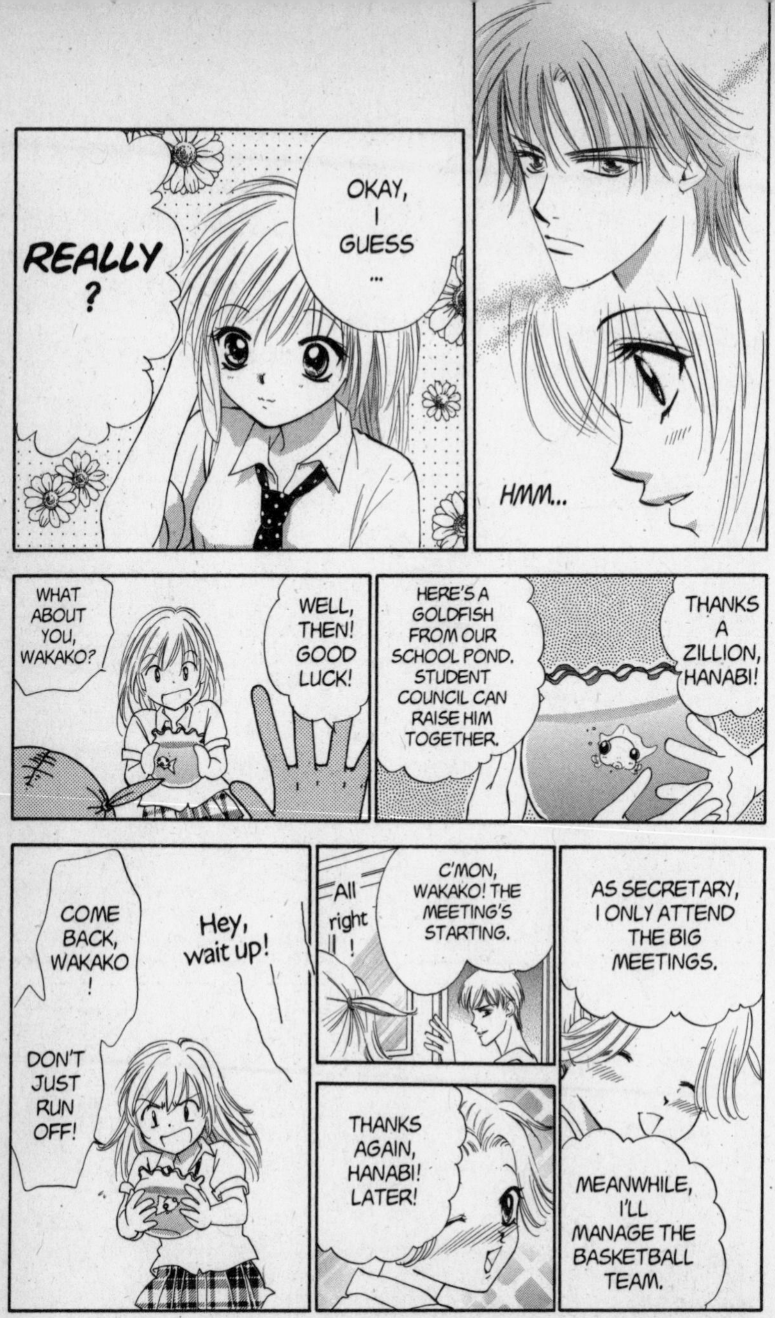
HMM...
OKAY, I GUESS ...
REALLY ?
THANKS A ZILLION, HANABI!
HERE'S A GOLDFISH FROM OUR SCHOOL POND. STUDENT COUNCIL CAN RAISE HIM TOGETHER.
WELL, THEN! GOOD LUCK!
WHAT ABOUT YOU, WAKAKO?
AS SECRETARY, I ONLY ATTEND THE BIG MEETINGS.
MEANWHILE, I'LL MANAGE THE BASKETBALL TEAM.
C'MON, WAKAKO! THE MEETING'S STARTING.
All right!
THANKS AGAIN, HANABI! LATER!
Hey, wait up!
COME BACK, WAKAKO!
DON'T JUST RUN OFF!

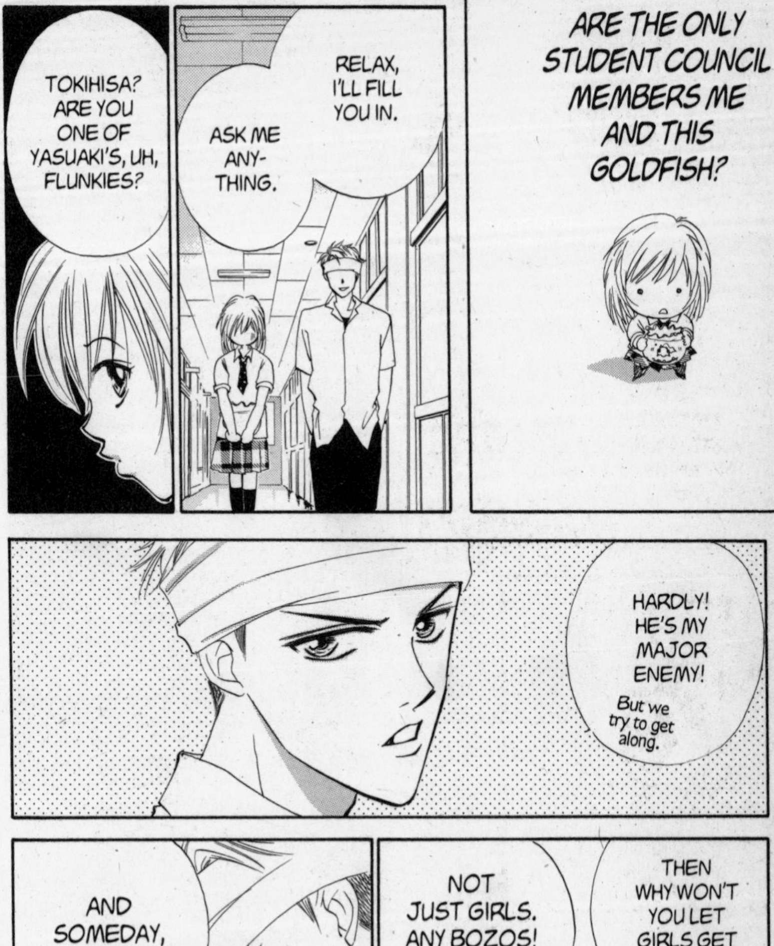
ARE THE ONLY STUDENT COUNCIL MEMBERS ME AND THIS GOLDFISH?
RELAX, I'LL FILL YOU IN.
ASK ME ANY-THING.
TOKIHISA? ARE YOU ONE OF YASUAKI'S, UH, FLUNKIES?
HARDLY! HE'S MY MAJOR ENEMY!
But we try to get along.
THEN WHY WON'T YOU LET GIRLS GET CLOSE TO HIM?
NOT JUST GIRLS. ANY BOZOS! HE'S *MY* PREY!
AND SOMEDAY, I'LL GET HIM!!
CLENCH
Why?

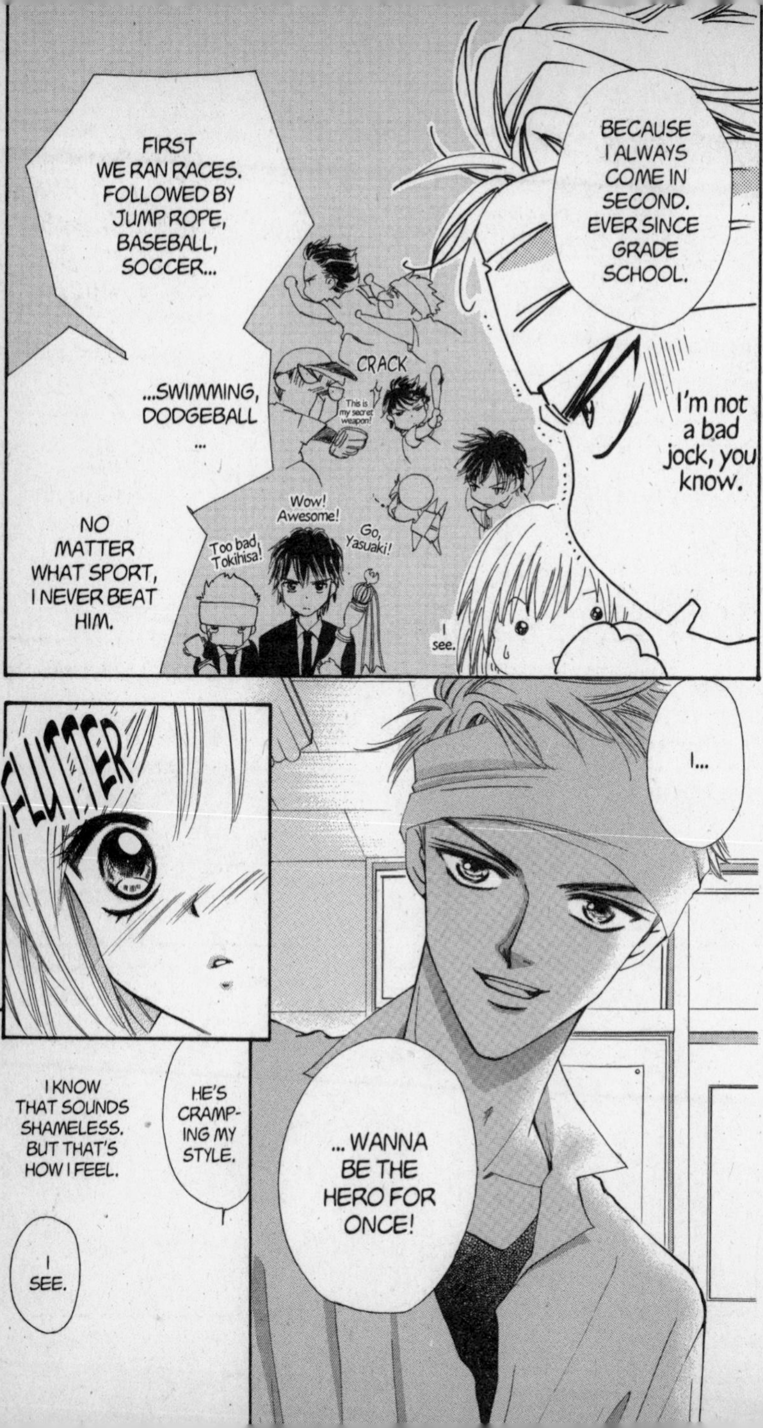
BECAUSE I ALWAYS COME IN SECOND. EVER SINCE GRADE SCHOOL.
I'm not a bad jock, you know.
FIRST WE RAN RACES. FOLLOWED BY JUMP ROPE, BASEBALL, SOCCER...
CRACK
This is my secret weapon!
...SWIMMING, DODGEBALL ...
Go, Yasuaki!
Wow! Awesome!
Too bad Tokihisa!
NO MATTER WHAT SPORT, I NEVER BEAT HIM.
I see.
I...
... WANNA BE THE HERO FOR ONCE!
FLUTTER
HE'S CRAMPING MY STYLE.
I KNOW THAT SOUNDS SHAMELESS. BUT THAT'S HOW I FEEL.
I SEE.

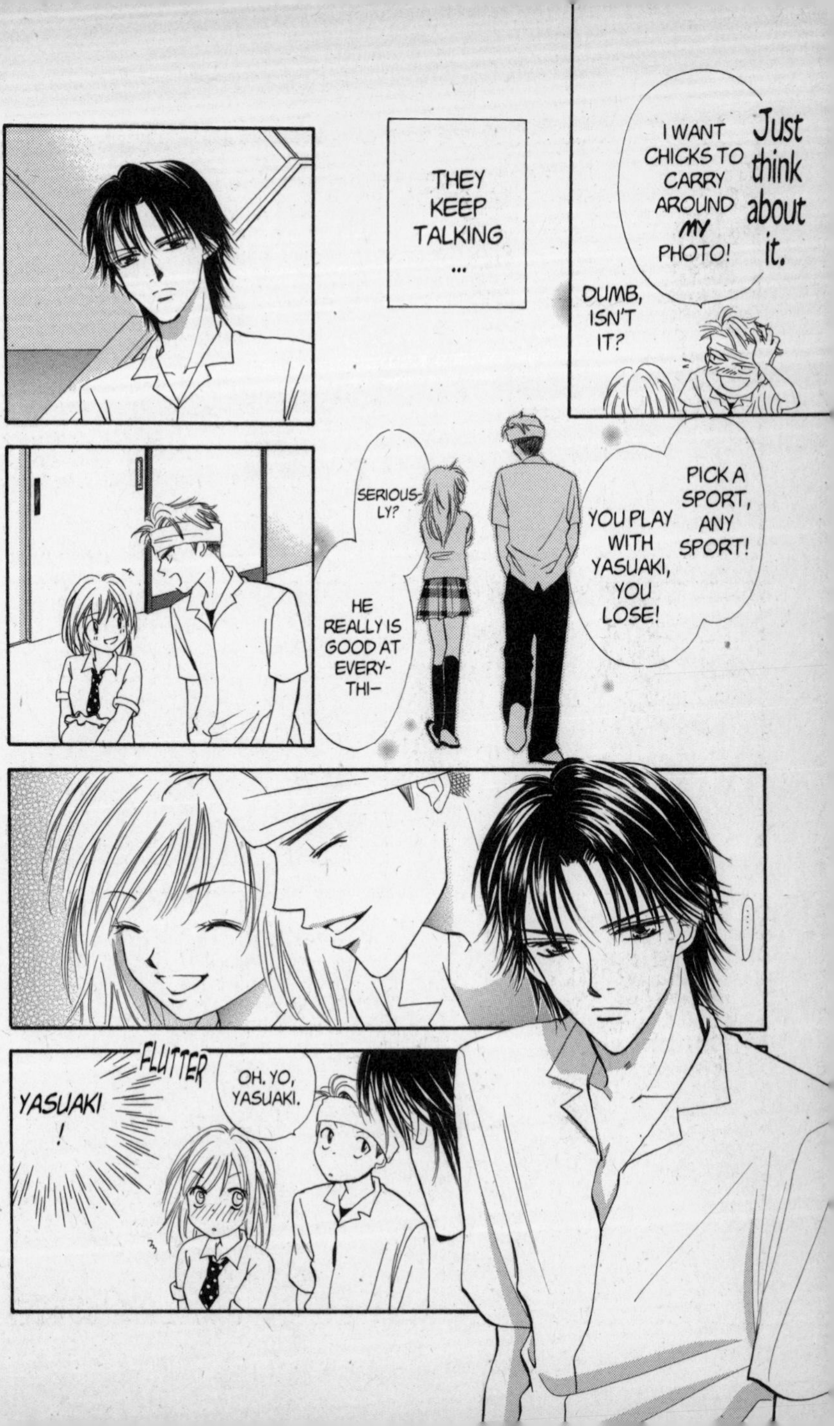

I WANT CHICKS TO CARRY AROUND MY PHOTO!
Just think about it.
DUMB, ISN'T IT?
THEY KEEP TALKING ...
PICK A SPORT, ANY SPORT!
YOU PLAY WITH YASUAKI, YOU LOSE!
SERIOUS-LY?
HE REALLY IS GOOD AT EVERY-THI–
......
OH. YO, YASUAKI.
FLUTTER
YASUAKI!

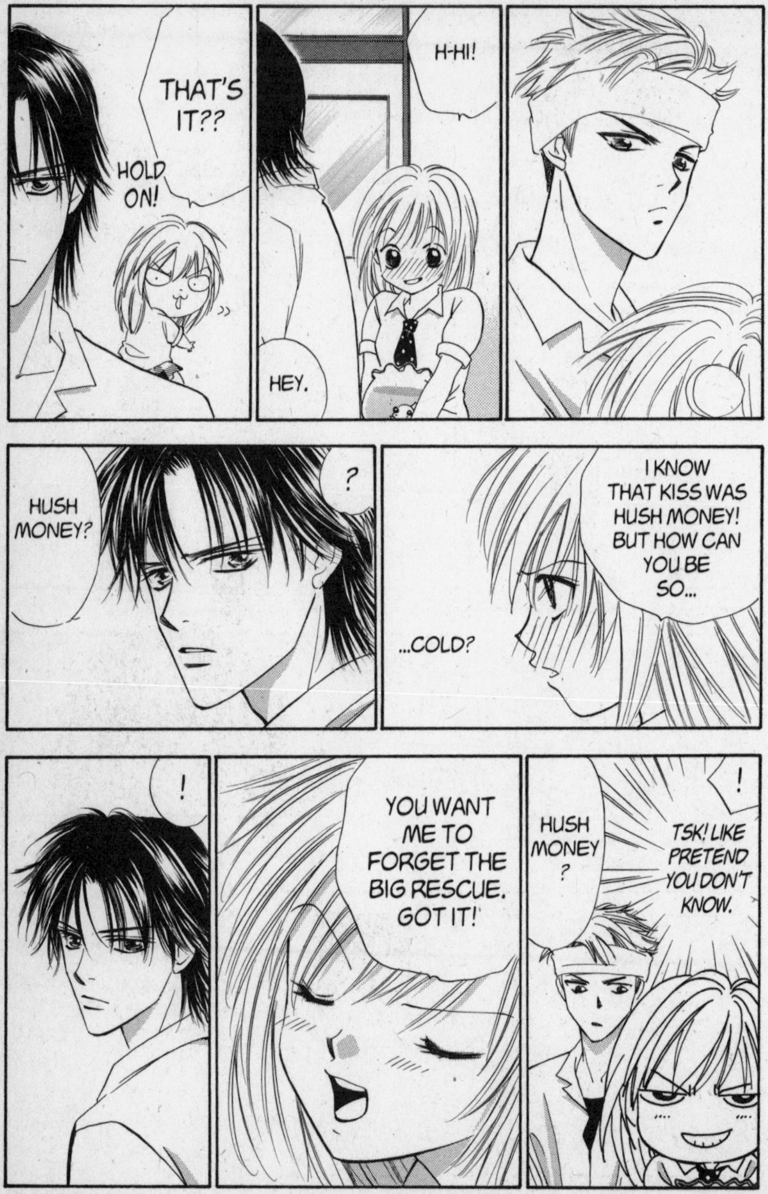
H-HI!
HEY.
THAT'S IT??
HOLD ON!
I KNOW THAT KISS WAS HUSH MONEY! BUT HOW CAN YOU BE SO...
...COLD?
?
HUSH MONEY?
!
TSK! LIKE PRETEND YOU DON'T KNOW.
HUSH MONEY?
YOU WANT ME TO FORGET THE BIG RESCUE. GOT IT!
!

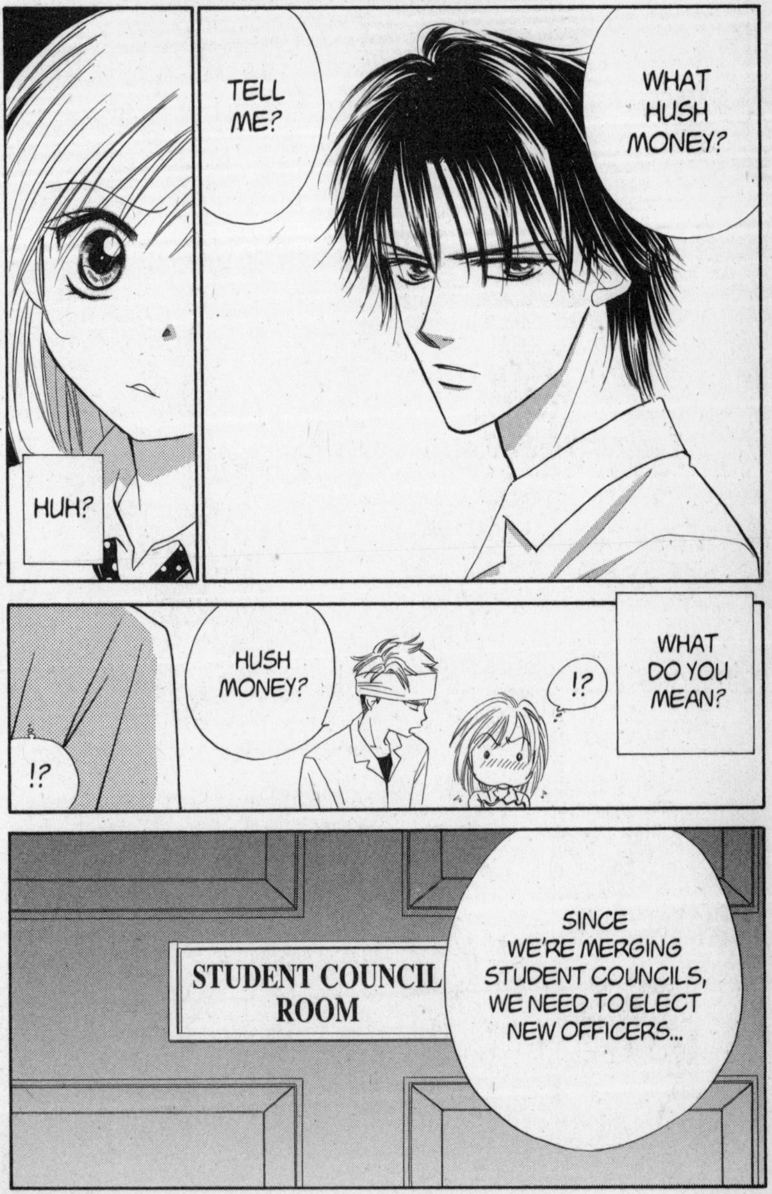
WHAT HUSH MONEY?
TELL ME?
HUH?
WHAT DO YOU MEAN?
!?
HUSH MONEY?
!?
SINCE WE'RE MERGING STUDENT COUNCILS, WE NEED TO ELECT NEW OFFICERS...
STUDENT COUNCIL ROOM

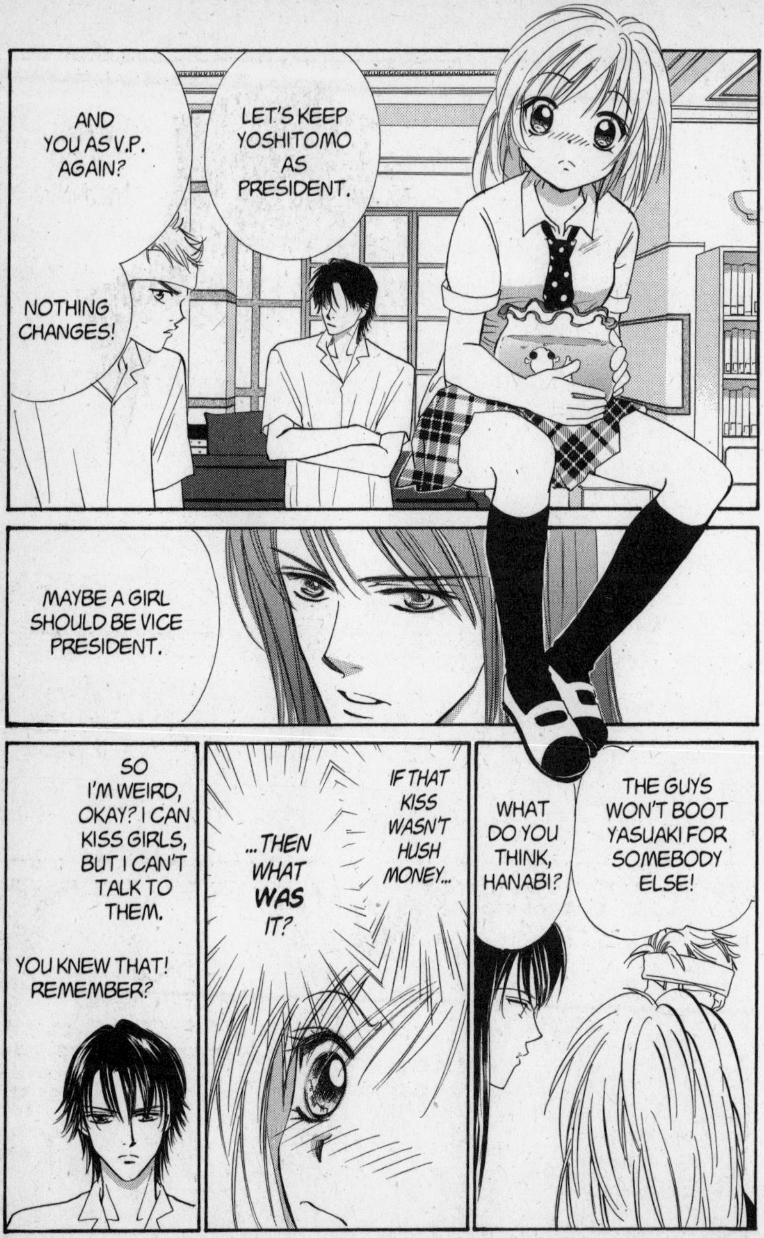
LET'S KEEP YOSHITOMO AS PRESIDENT.
AND YOU AS V.P. AGAIN?
NOTHING CHANGES!
MAYBE A GIRL SHOULD BE VICE PRESIDENT.
THE GUYS WON'T BOOT YASUAKI FOR SOMEBODY ELSE!
WHAT DO YOU THINK, HANABI?
IF THAT KISS WASN'T HUSH MONEY...
...THEN WHAT **WAS** IT?
SO I'M WEIRD, OKAY? I CAN KISS GIRLS, BUT I CAN'T TALK TO THEM.
YOU KNEW THAT! REMEMBER?

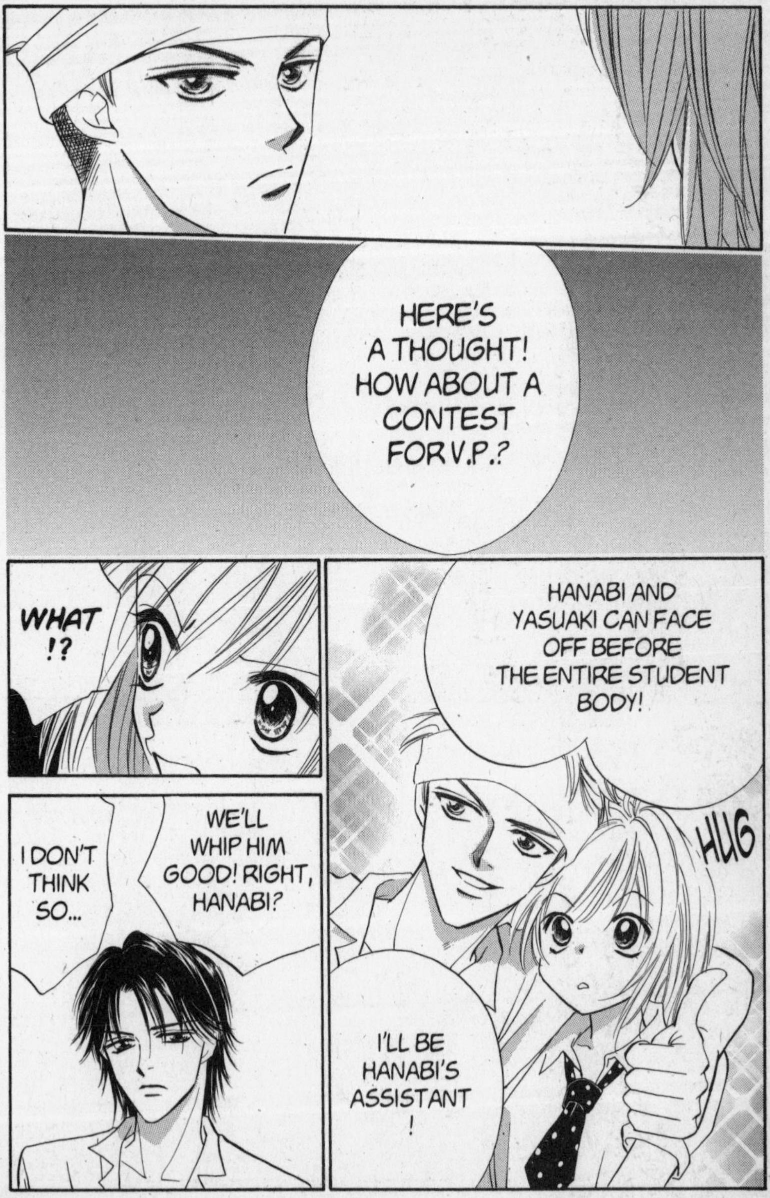
HERE'S A THOUGHT! HOW ABOUT A CONTEST FOR V.P.?
HANABI AND YASUAKI CAN FACE OFF BEFORE THE ENTIRE STUDENT BODY!
HUG
I'LL BE HANABI'S ASSISTANT!
WHAT!?
WE'LL WHIP HIM GOOD! RIGHT, HANABI?
I DON'T THINK SO...

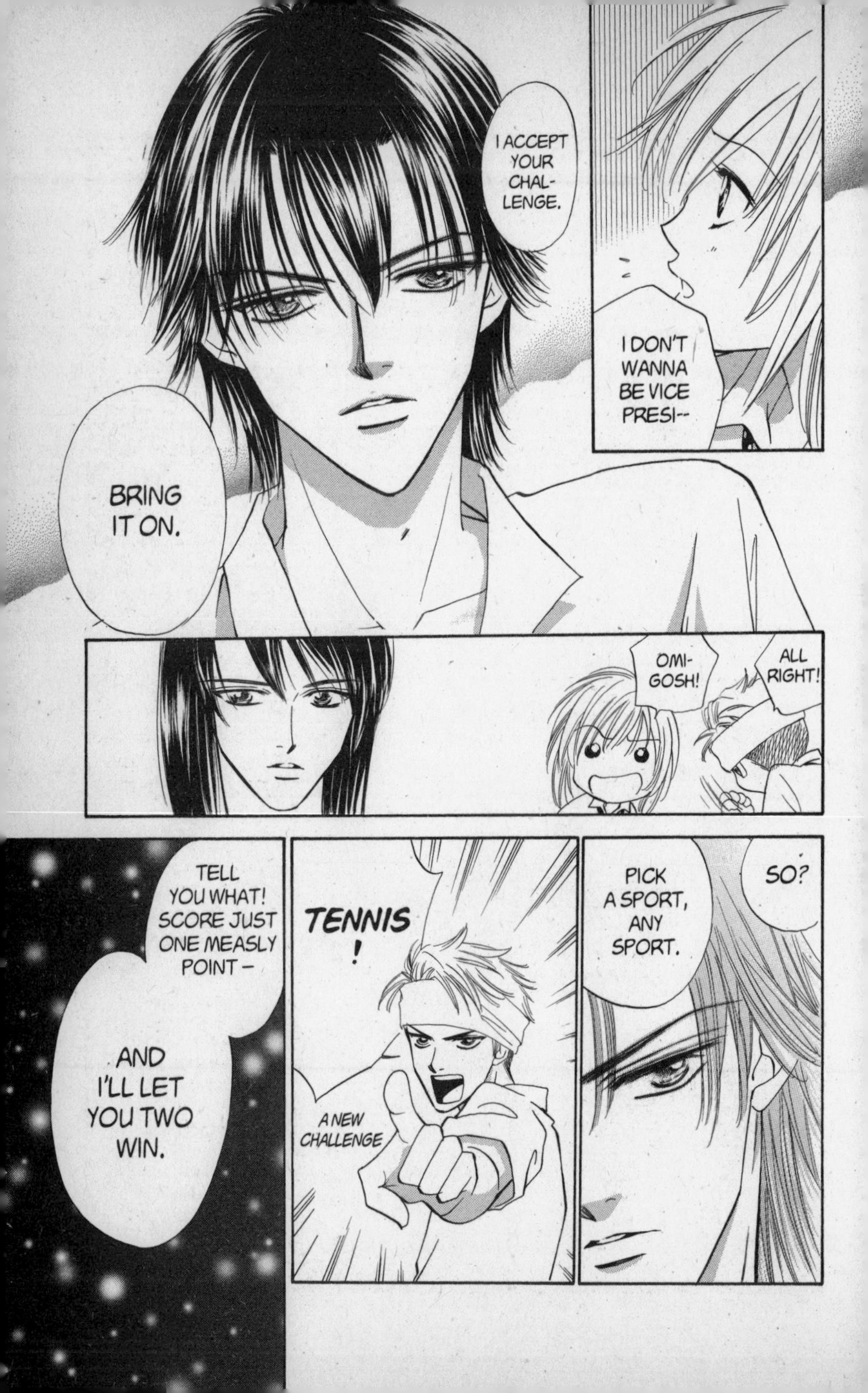
I DON'T WANNA BE VICE PRESI--
I ACCEPT YOUR CHAL- LENGE.
BRING IT ON.
ALL RIGHT!
OMI- GOSH!
SO?
PICK A SPORT, ANY SPORT.
TENNIS!
A NEW CHALLENGE
TELL YOU WHAT! SCORE JUST ONE MEASLY POINT –
AND I'LL LET YOU TWO WIN.

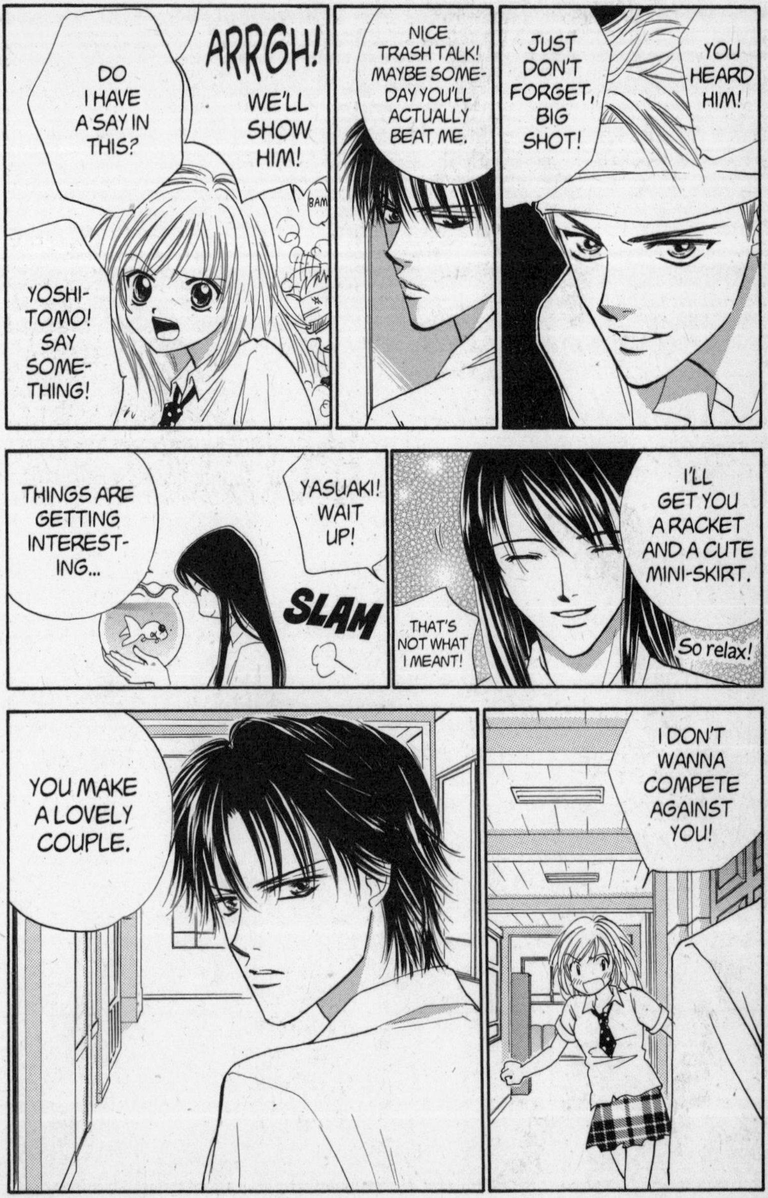
YOU HEARD HIM!
JUST DON'T FORGET, BIG SHOT!
NICE TRASH TALK! MAYBE SOME-DAY YOU'LL ACTUALLY BEAT ME.
ARRGH!
WE'LL SHOW HIM!
DO I HAVE A SAY IN THIS?
BAM
YOSHI-TOMO! SAY SOME-THING!
I'LL GET YOU A RACKET AND A CUTE MINI-SKIRT.
So relax!
THAT'S NOT WHAT I MEANT!
YASUAKI! WAIT UP!
SLAM
THINGS ARE GETTING INTEREST-ING...
I DON'T WANNA COMPETE AGAINST YOU!
YOU MAKE A LOVELY COUPLE.

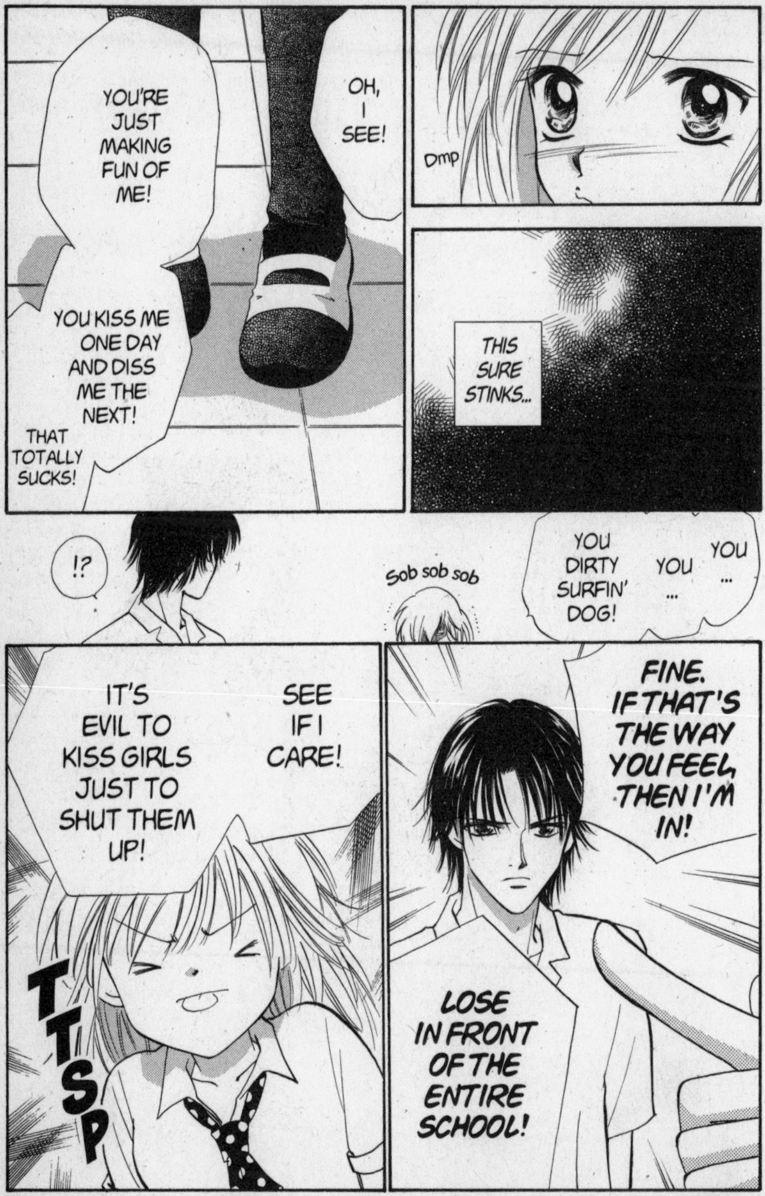

Dmp
THIS SURE STINKS...
OH, I SEE!
YOU'RE JUST MAKING FUN OF ME!
YOU KISS ME ONE DAY AND DISS ME THE NEXT!
THAT TOTALLY SUCKS!
YOU ... YOU ... YOU DIRTY SURFIN' DOG!
Sob sob sob
!?
FINE. IF THAT'S THE WAY YOU FEEL, THEN I'M IN!
LOSE IN FRONT OF THE ENTIRE SCHOOL!
SEE IF I CARE!
IT'S EVIL TO KISS GIRLS JUST TO SHUT THEM UP!
TTSP

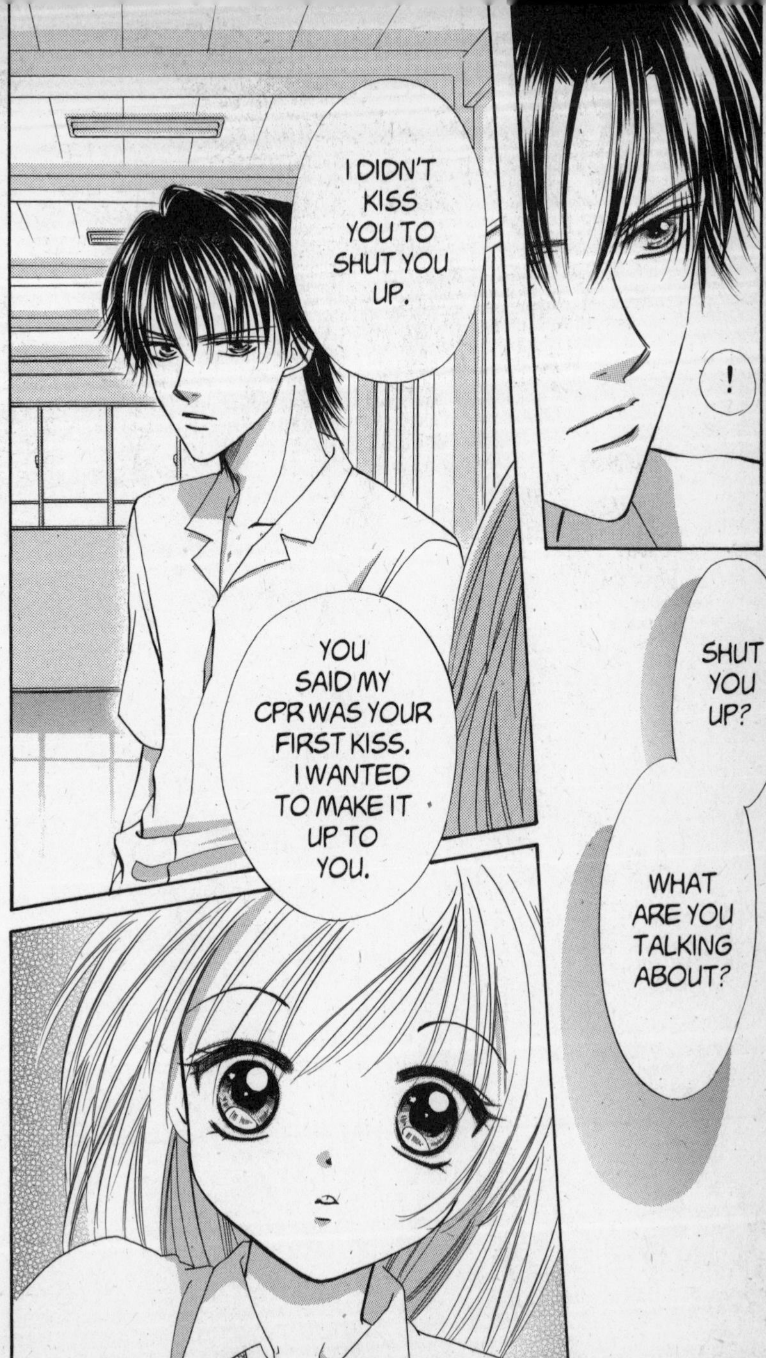
!
SHUT YOU UP?
WHAT ARE YOU TALKING ABOUT?
I DIDN'T KISS YOU TO SHUT YOU UP.
YOU SAID MY CPR WAS YOUR FIRST KISS. I WANTED TO MAKE IT UP TO YOU.

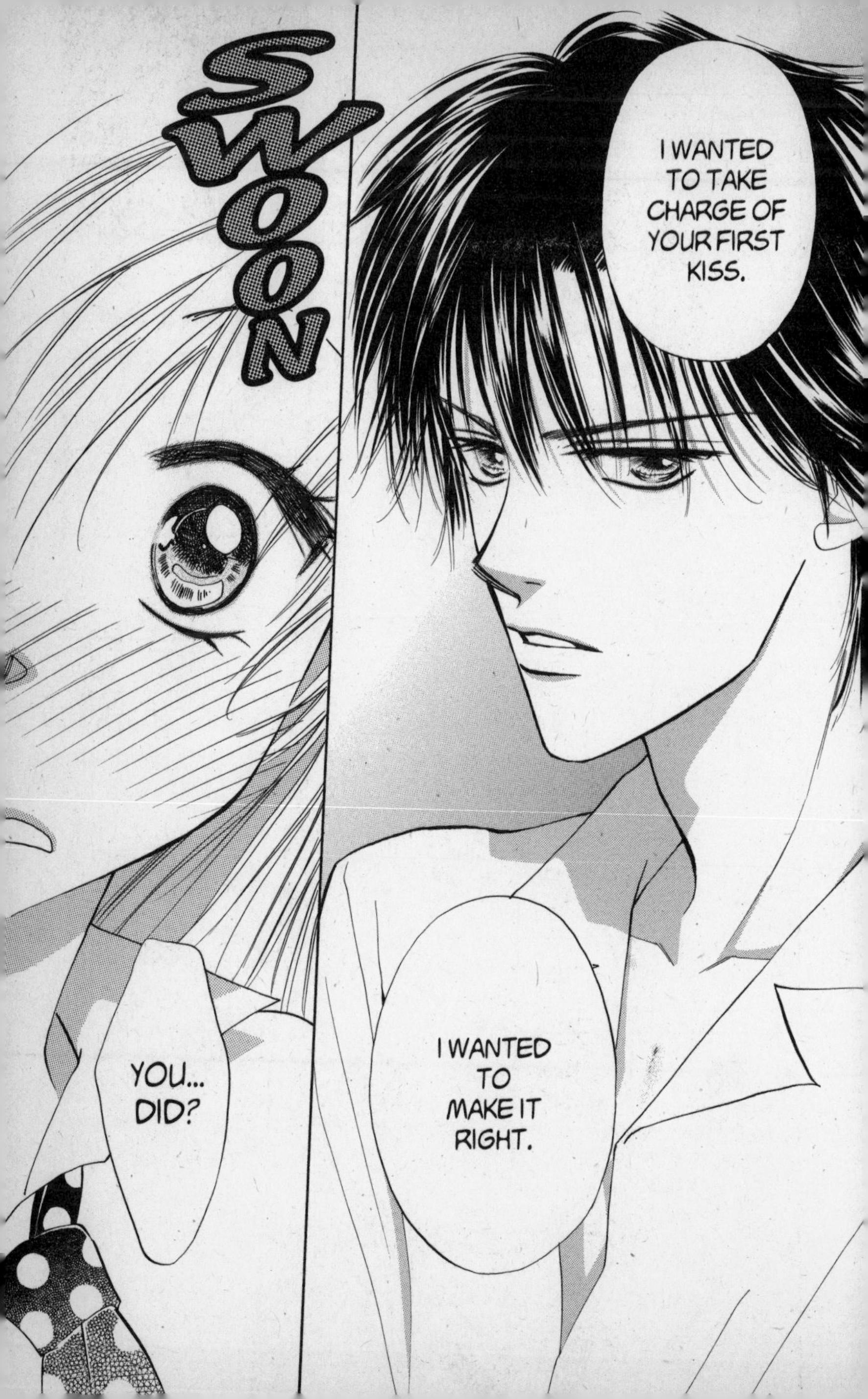
I WANTED TO TAKE CHARGE OF YOUR FIRST KISS.
I WANTED TO MAKE IT RIGHT.
SWOON
YOU... DID?

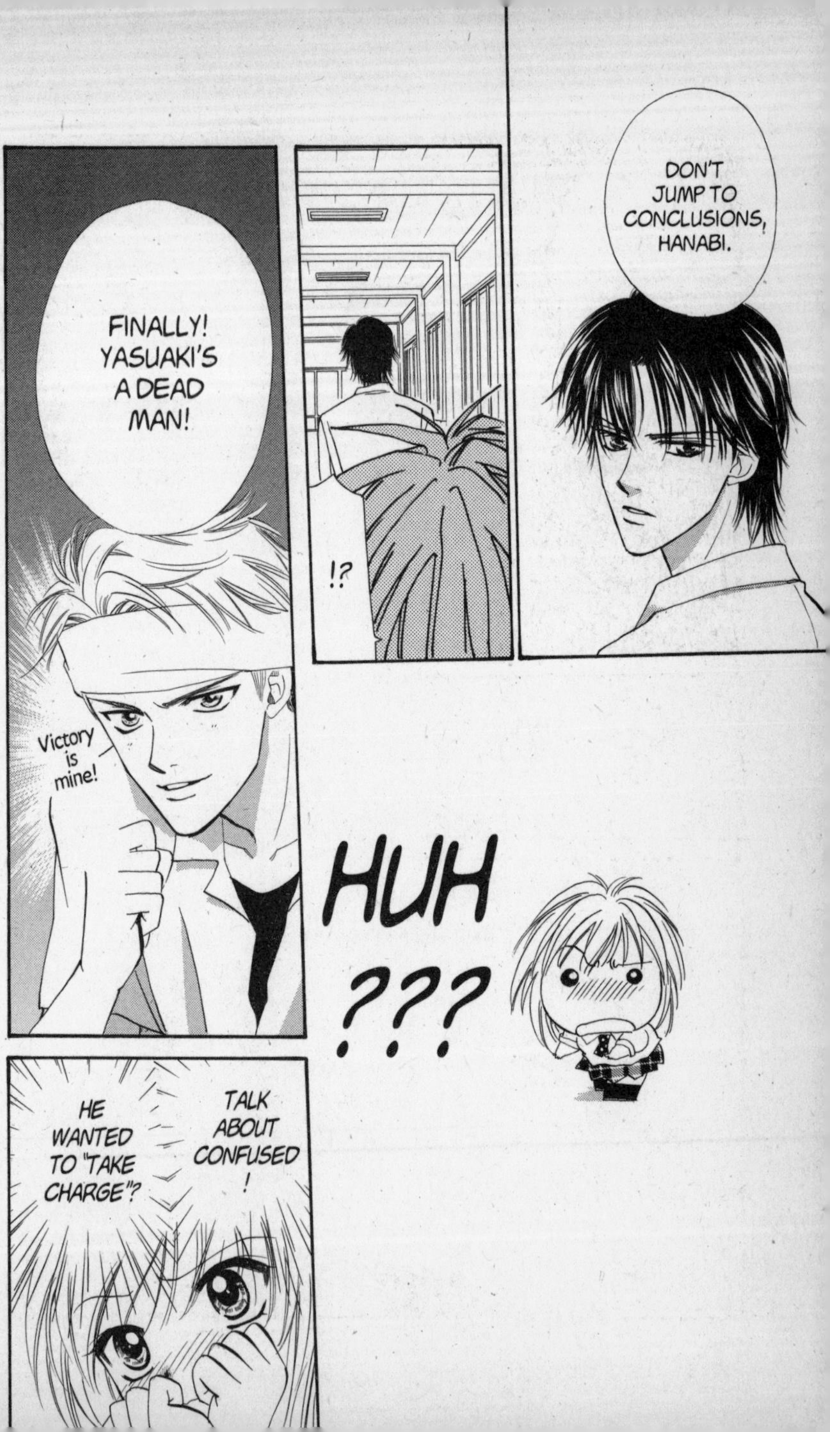

DON'T JUMP TO CONCLUSIONS, HANABI.
!?
FINALLY! YASUAKI'S A DEAD MAN!
Victory is mine!
HUH ???
HE WANTED TO "TAKE CHARGE"?
TALK ABOUT CONFUSED !

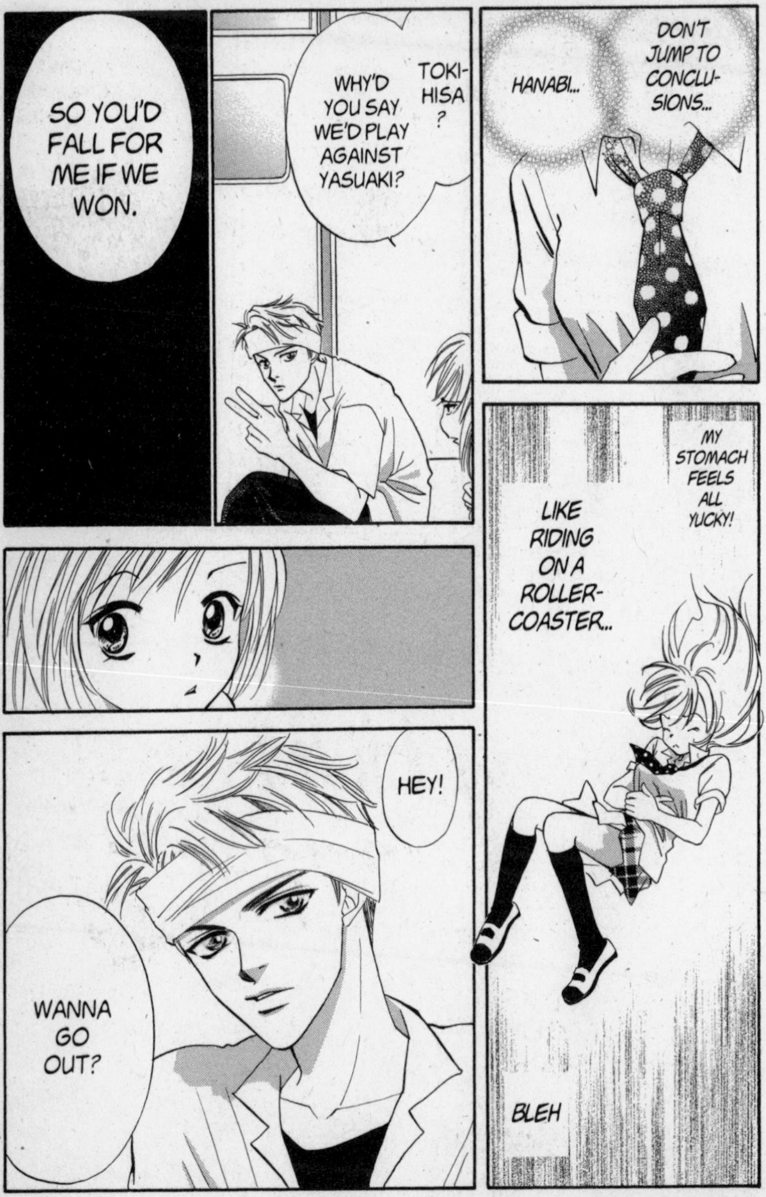
HANABI...
DON'T JUMP TO CONCLUSIONS...
TOKI-HISA?
WHY'D YOU SAY WE'D PLAY AGAINST YASUAKI?
SO YOU'D FALL FOR ME IF WE WON.
MY STOMACH FEELS ALL YUCKY!
LIKE RIDING ON A ROLLER-COASTER...
BLEH
HEY!
WANNA GO OUT?

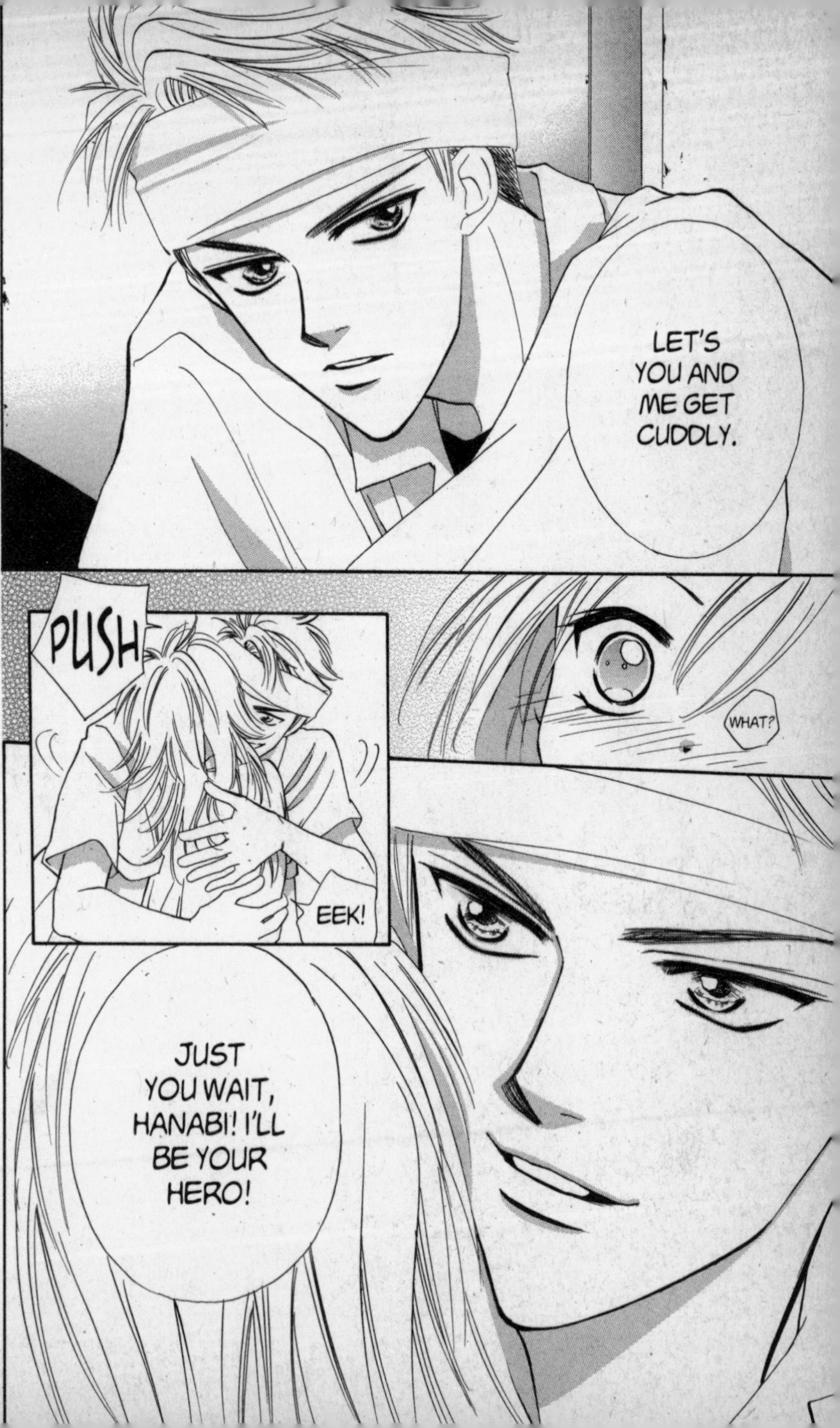
LET'S YOU AND ME GET CUDDLY.
WHAT?
PUSH
EEK!
JUST YOU WAIT, HANABI! I'LL BE YOUR HERO!

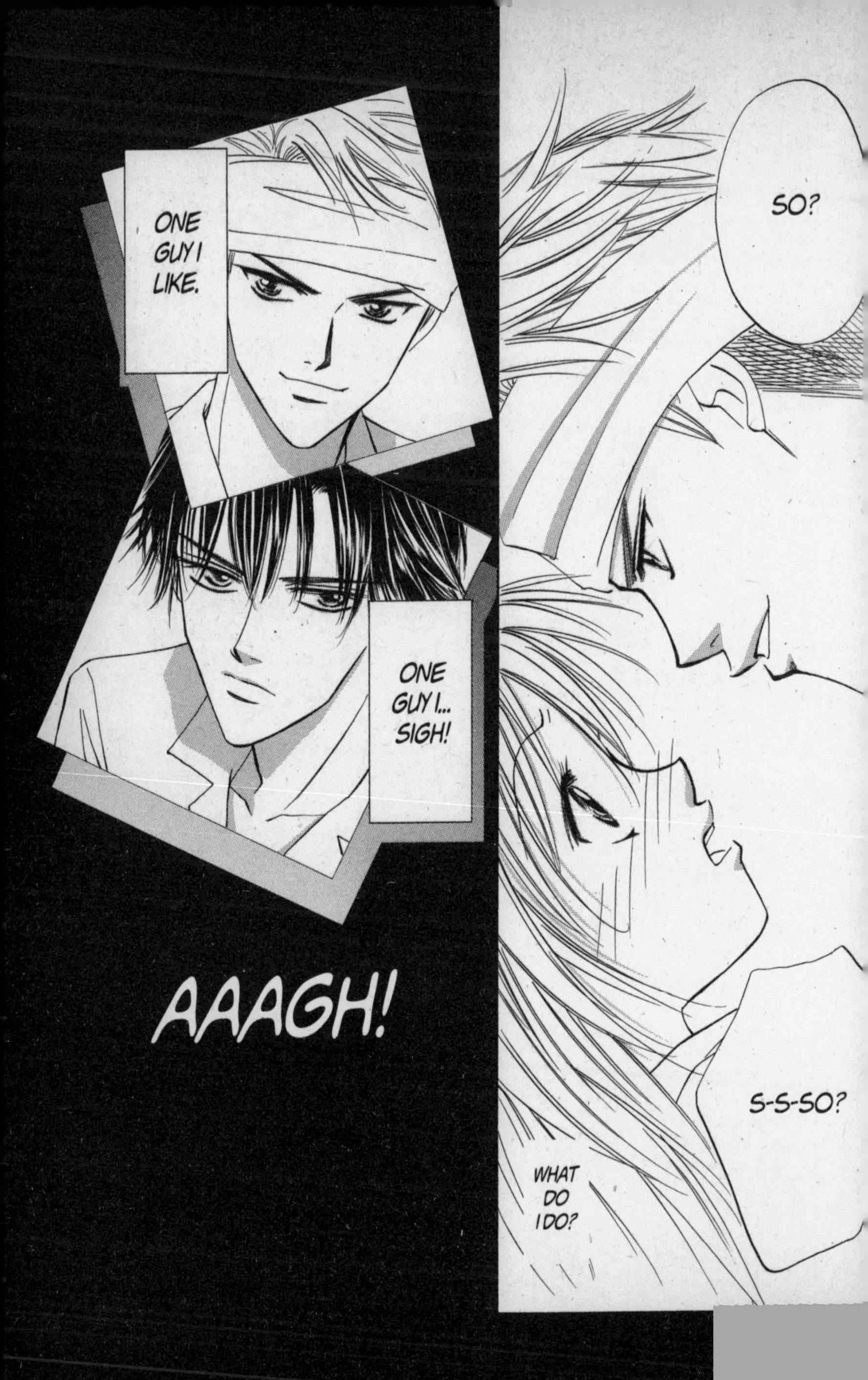
SO?
S-S-SO?
WHAT DO I DO?
ONE GUY I LIKE.
ONE GUY I... SIGH!
AAAGH!

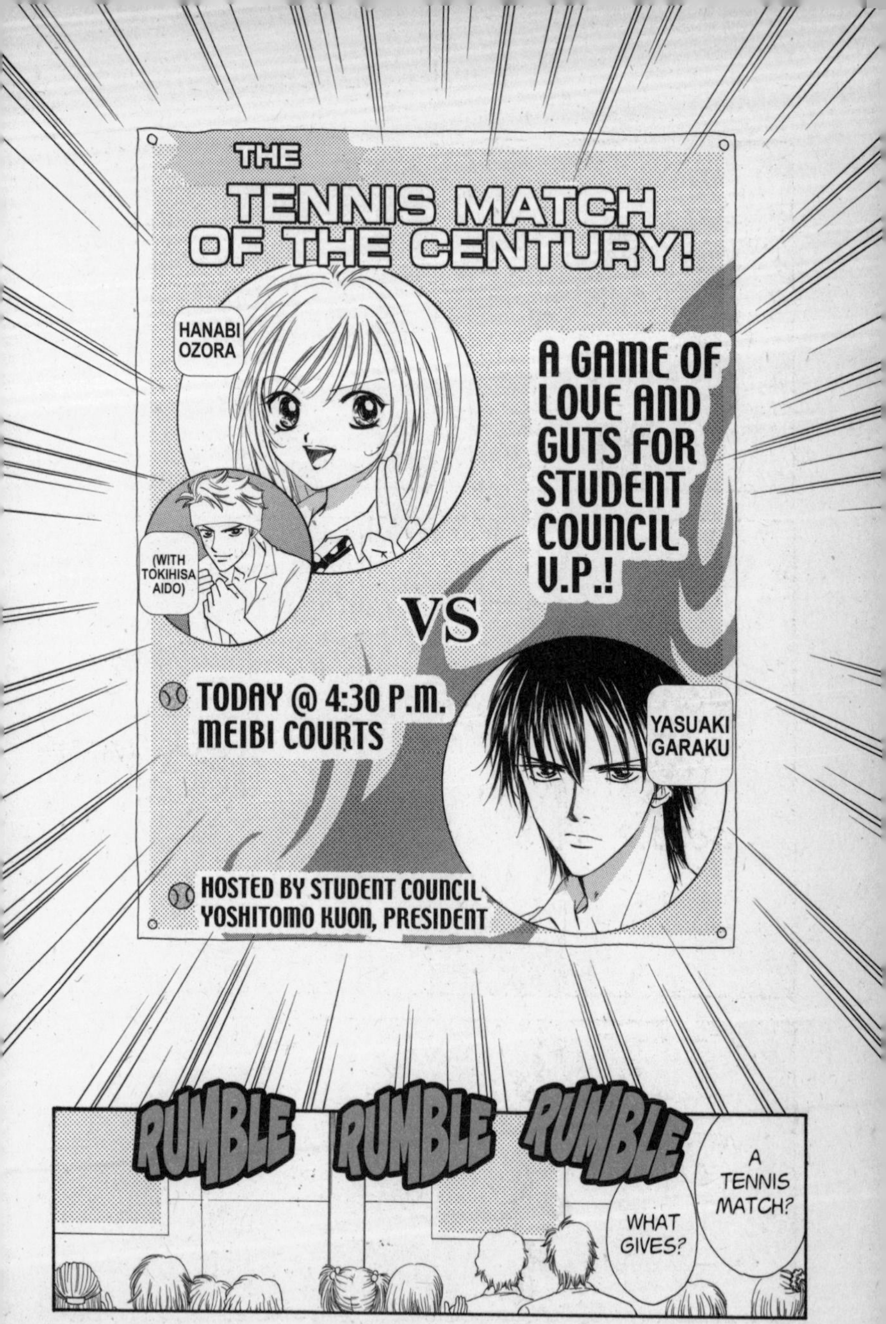
THE
TENNIS MATCH OF THE CENTURY!
HANABI OZORA
(WITH TOKIHISA AIDO)
A GAME OF LOVE AND GUTS FOR STUDENT COUNCIL V.P.!
VS
YASUAKI GARAKU
TODAY @ 4:30 P.M.
MEIBI COURTS
HOSTED BY STUDENT COUNCIL
YOSHITOMO KUON, PRESIDENT
RUMBLE RUMBLE RUMBLE
A TENNIS MATCH?
WHAT GIVES?

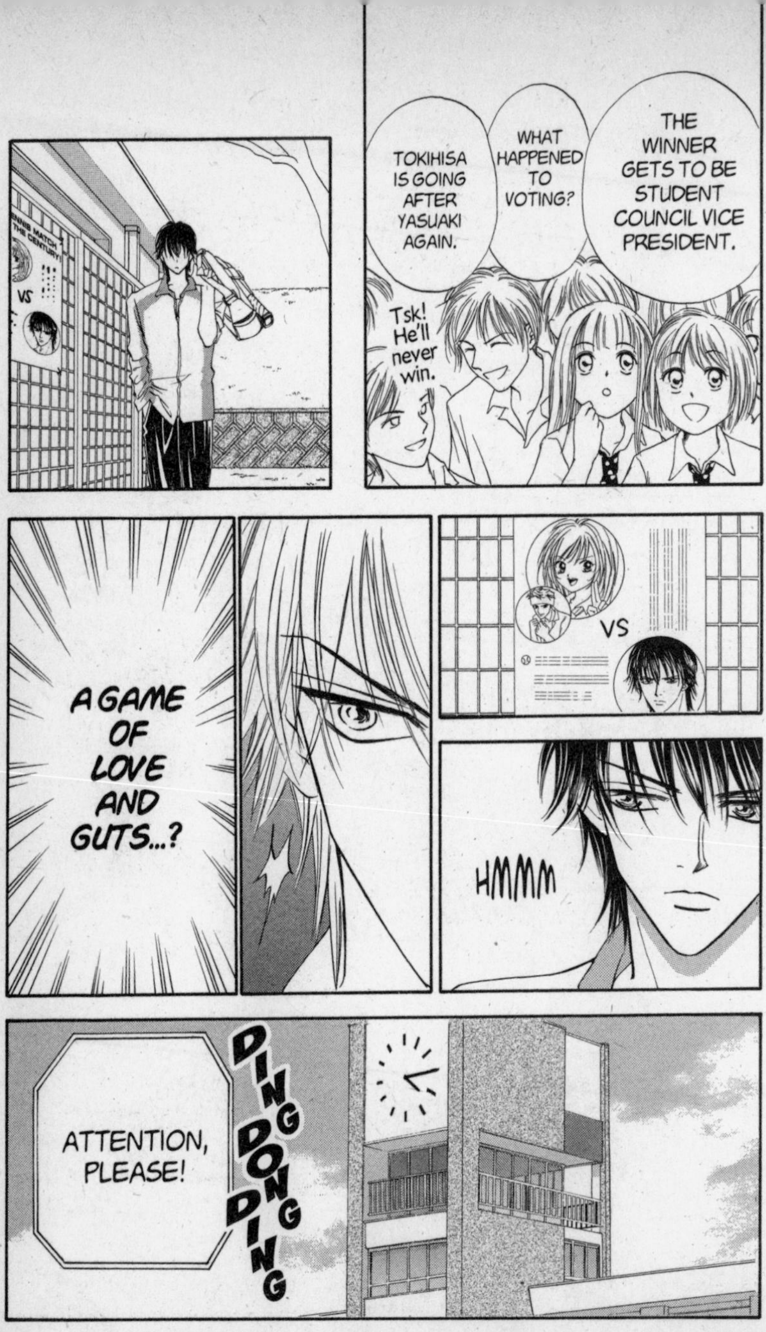

THE WINNER GETS TO BE STUDENT COUNCIL VICE PRESIDENT.
WHAT HAPPENED TO VOTING?
TOKIHISA IS GOING AFTER YASUAKI AGAIN.
Tsk! He'll never win.
VS
VS
HMMM
A GAME OF LOVE AND GUTS...?
DING DONG DING
ATTENTION, PLEASE!

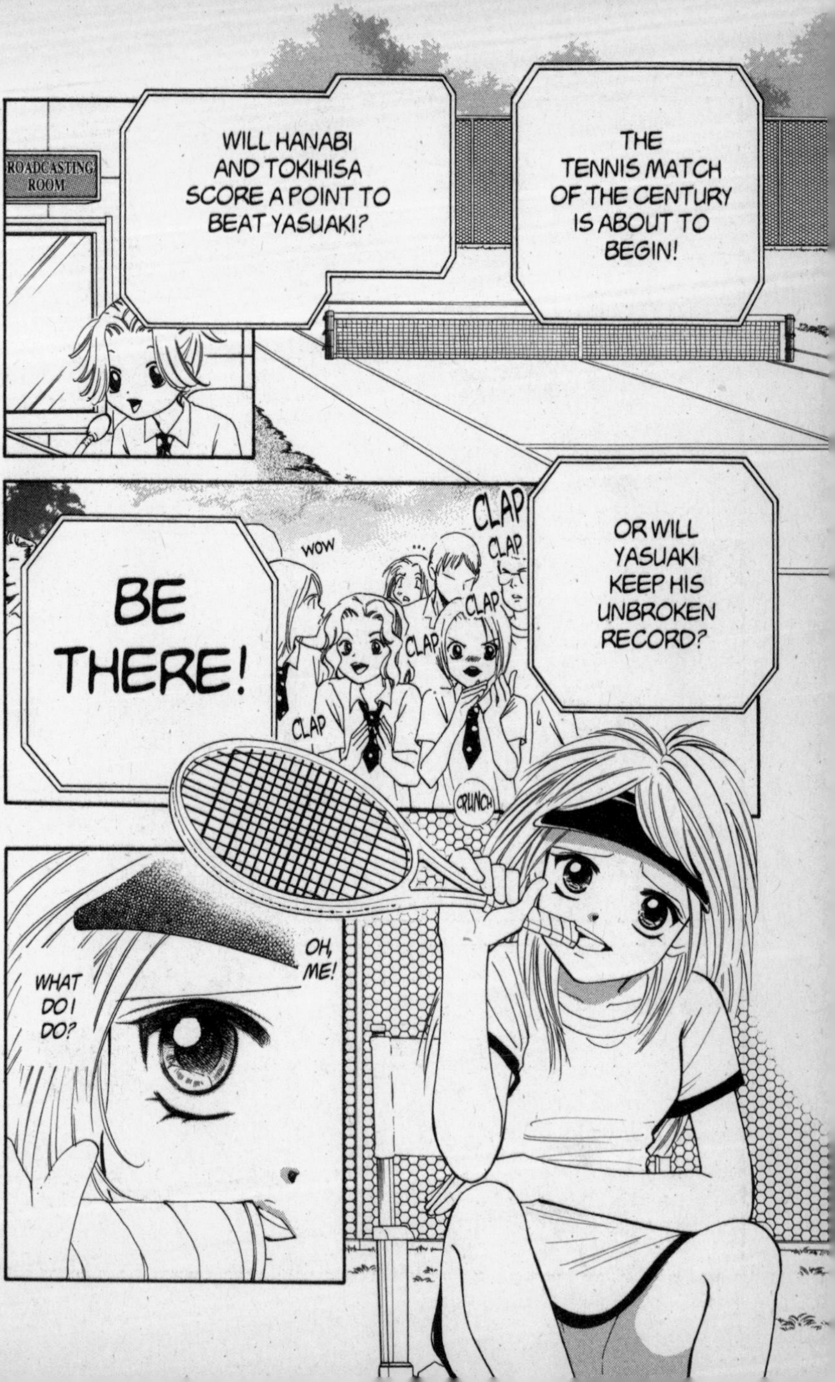
THE TENNIS MATCH OF THE CENTURY IS ABOUT TO BEGIN!
WILL HANABI AND TOKIHISA SCORE A POINT TO BEAT YASUAKI?
ROADCASTING ROOM
OR WILL YASUAKI KEEP HIS UNBROKEN RECORD?
CLAP
CLAP
CLAP
CLAP
WOW
CLAP
BE THERE!
CRUNCH
OH, ME!
WHAT DO I DO?

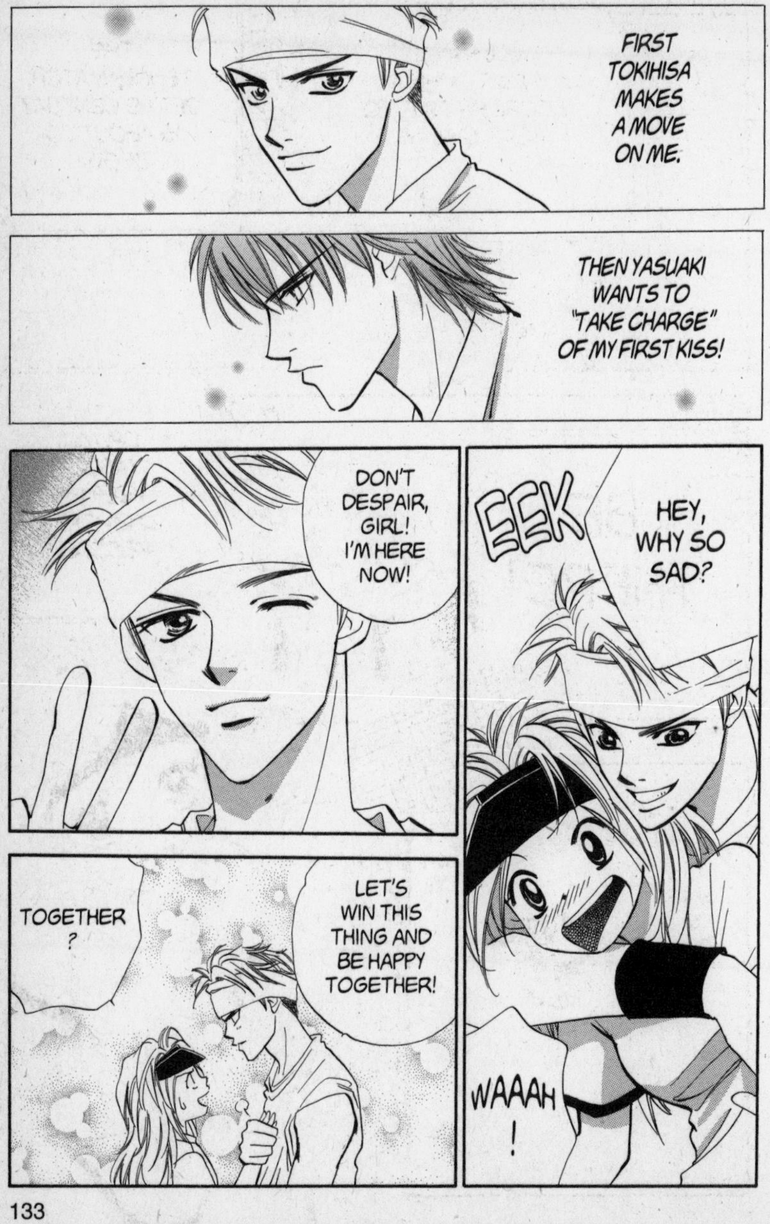
FIRST TOKIHISA MAKES A MOVE ON ME.
THEN YASUAKI WANTS TO "TAKE CHARGE" OF MY FIRST KISS!
EEK
HEY, WHY SO SAD?
WAAAH!
DON'T DESPAIR, GIRL! I'M HERE NOW!
LET'S WIN THIS THING AND BE HAPPY TOGETHER!
TOGETHER?

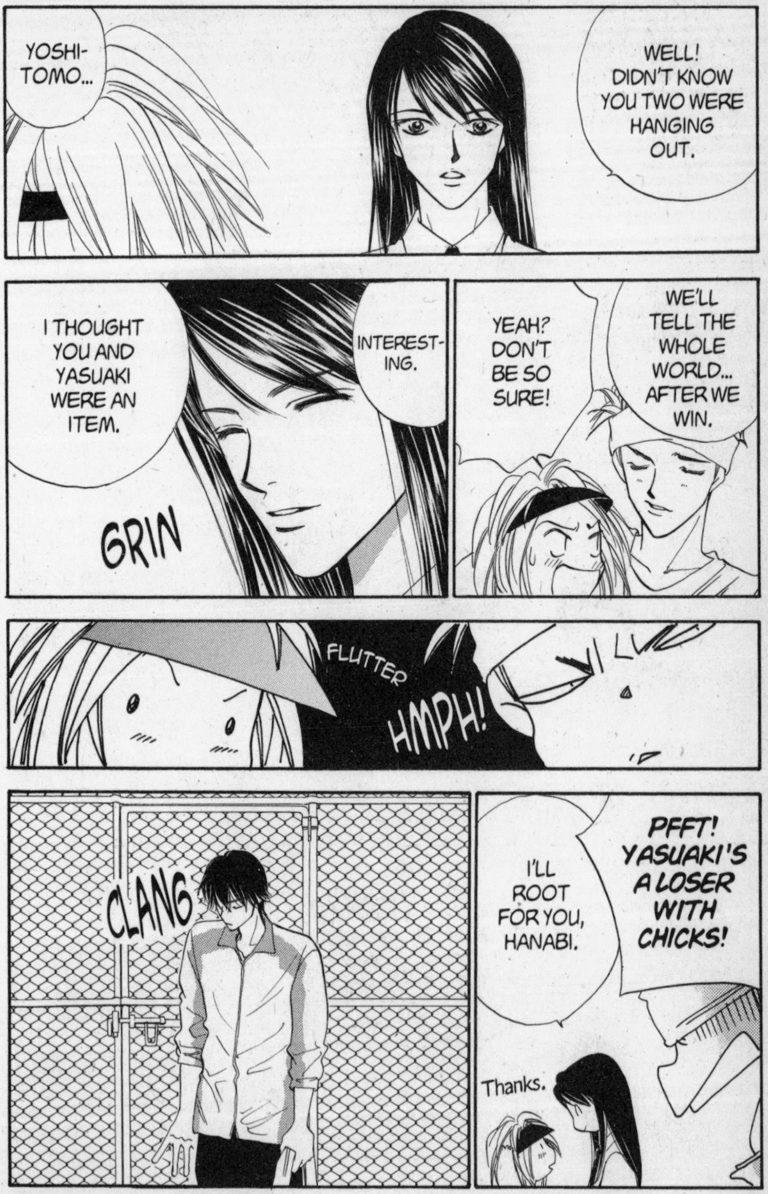
WELL! DIDN'T KNOW YOU TWO WERE HANGING OUT.
YOSHI-TOMO...
WE'LL TELL THE WHOLE WORLD... AFTER WE WIN.
YEAH? DON'T BE SO SURE!
INTEREST-ING.
I THOUGHT YOU AND YASUAKI WERE AN ITEM.
GRIN
FLUTTER
HMPH!
PFFT! YASUAKI'S A LOSER WITH CHICKS!
I'LL ROOT FOR YOU, HANABI.
Thanks.
CLANG

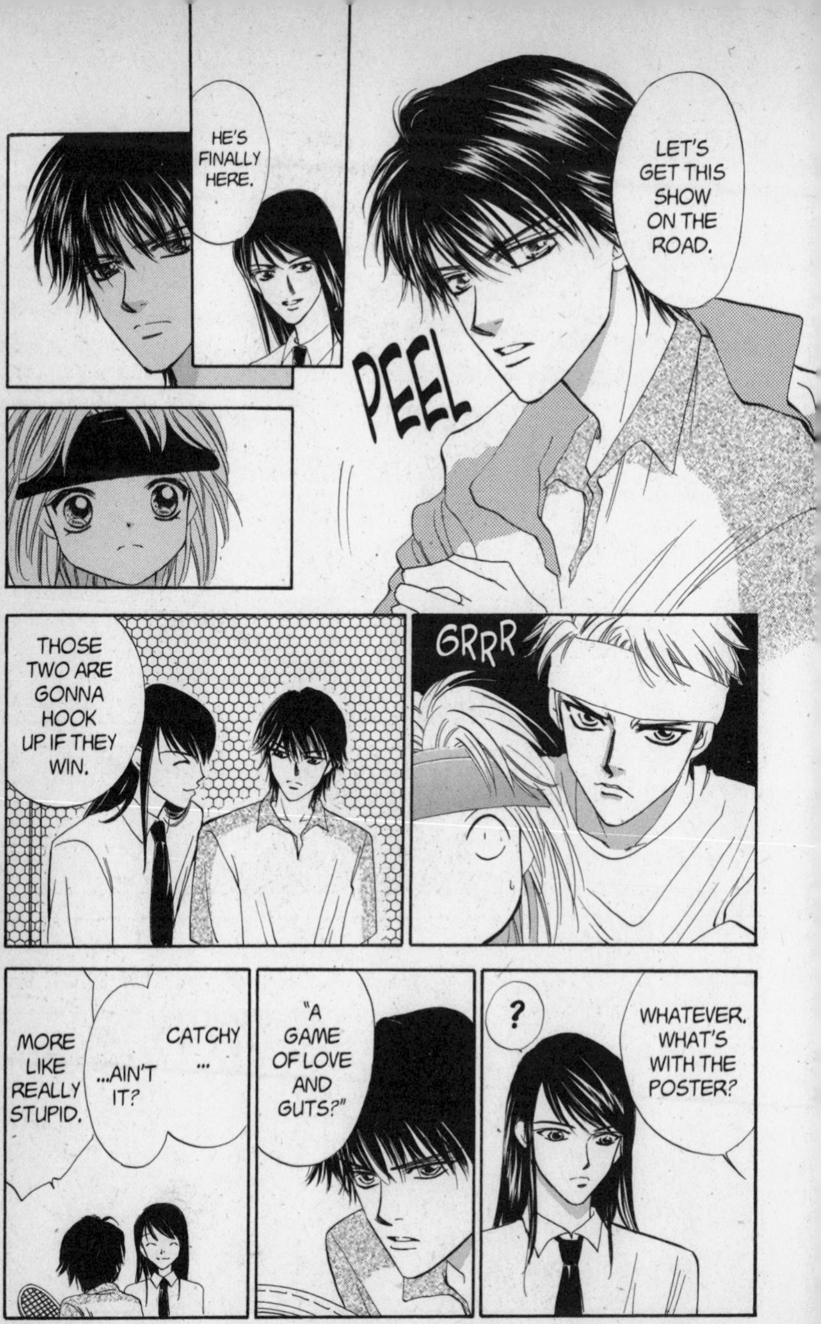
LET'S GET THIS SHOW ON THE ROAD.
PEEL
HE'S FINALLY HERE.
GRRR
THOSE TWO ARE GONNA HOOK UP IF THEY WIN.
WHATEVER. WHAT'S WITH THE POSTER?
?
"A GAME OF LOVE AND GUTS?"
CATCHY ...
...AIN'T IT?
MORE LIKE REALLY STUPID.

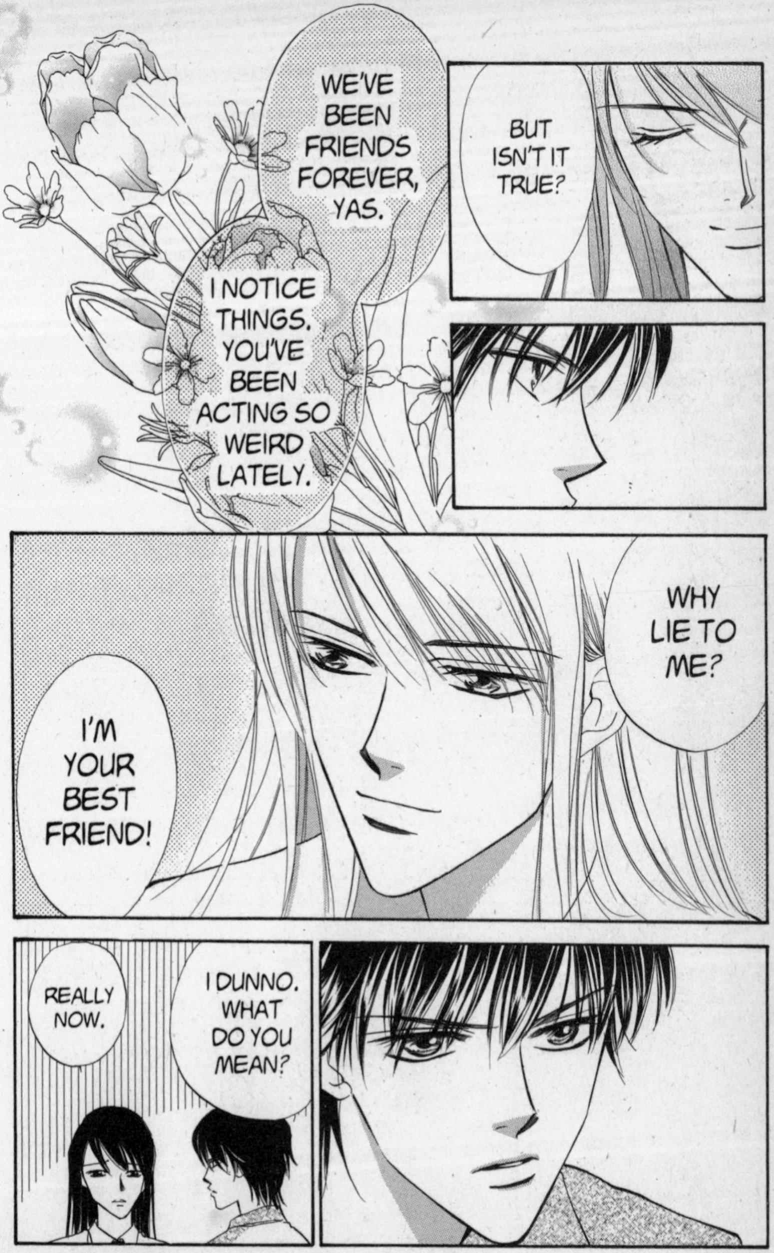
BUT ISN'T IT TRUE?
WE'VE BEEN FRIENDS FOREVER, YAS.
I NOTICE THINGS. YOU'VE BEEN ACTING SO WEIRD LATELY.
WHY LIE TO ME?
I'M YOUR BEST FRIEND!
I DUNNO. WHAT DO YOU MEAN?
REALLY NOW.

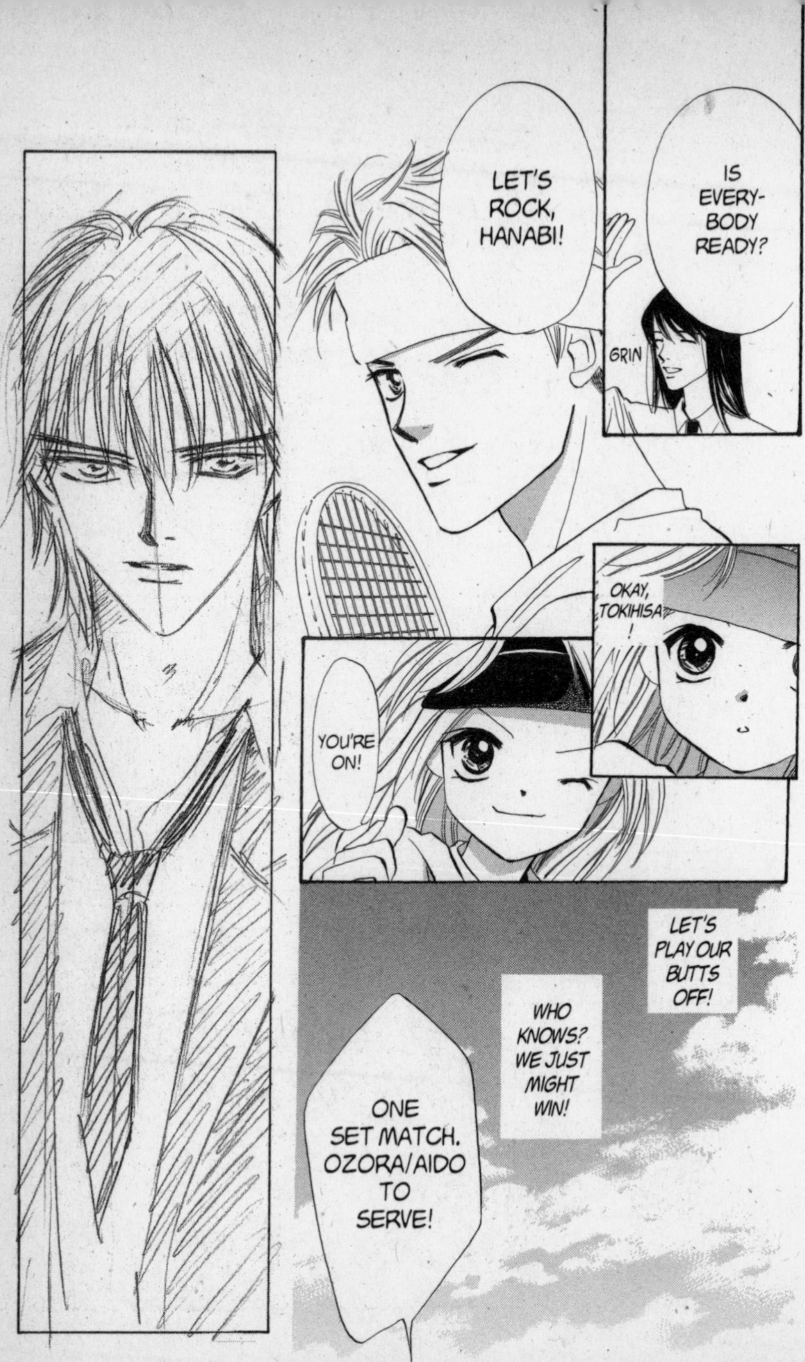
IS EVERYBODY READY?
GRIN
LET'S ROCK, HANABI!
OKAY, TOKIHISA!
YOU'RE ON!
LET'S PLAY OUR BUTTS OFF!
WHO KNOWS? WE JUST MIGHT WIN!
ONE SET MATCH. OZORA/AIDO TO SERVE!

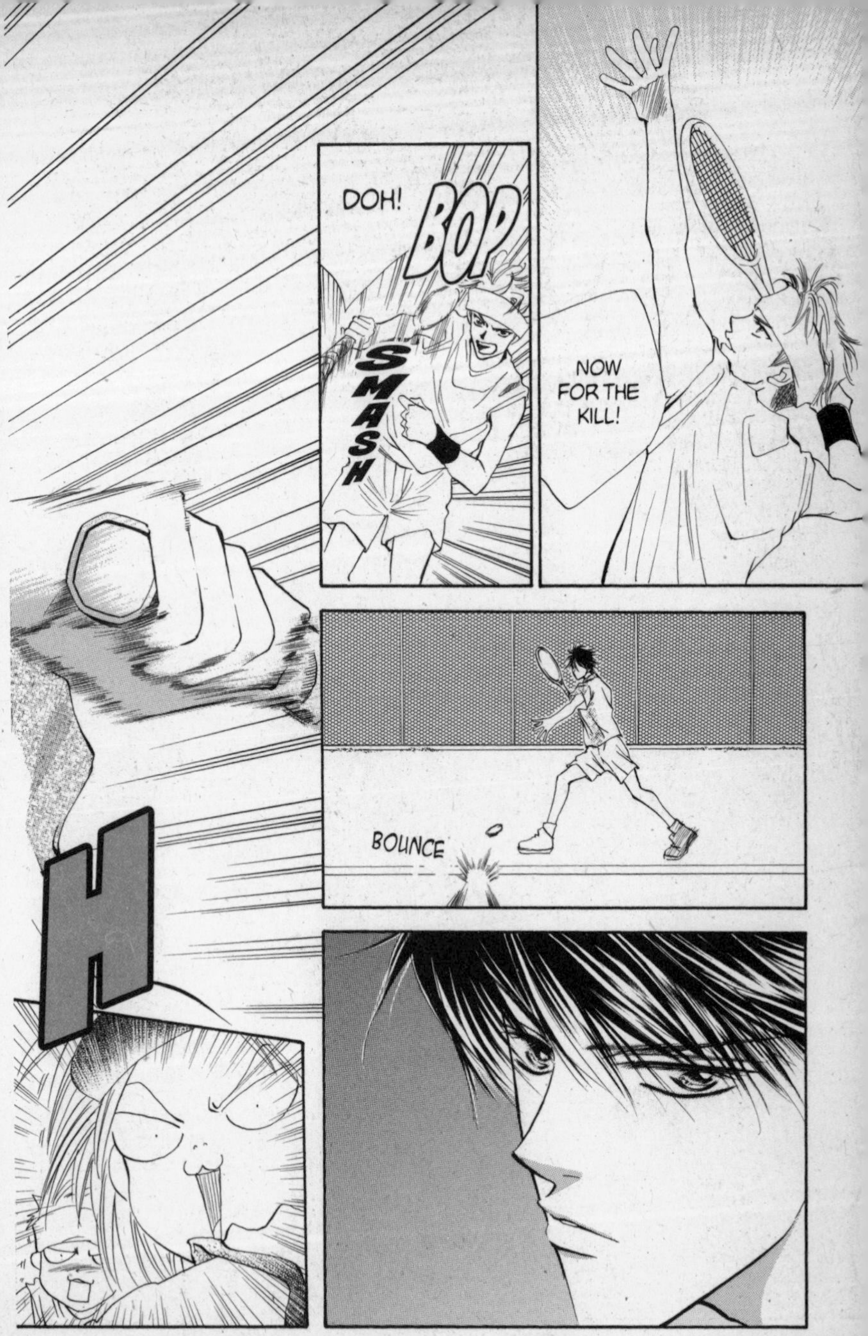
NOW FOR THE KILL!
DOH!
BOP
SMASH
BOUNCE
H

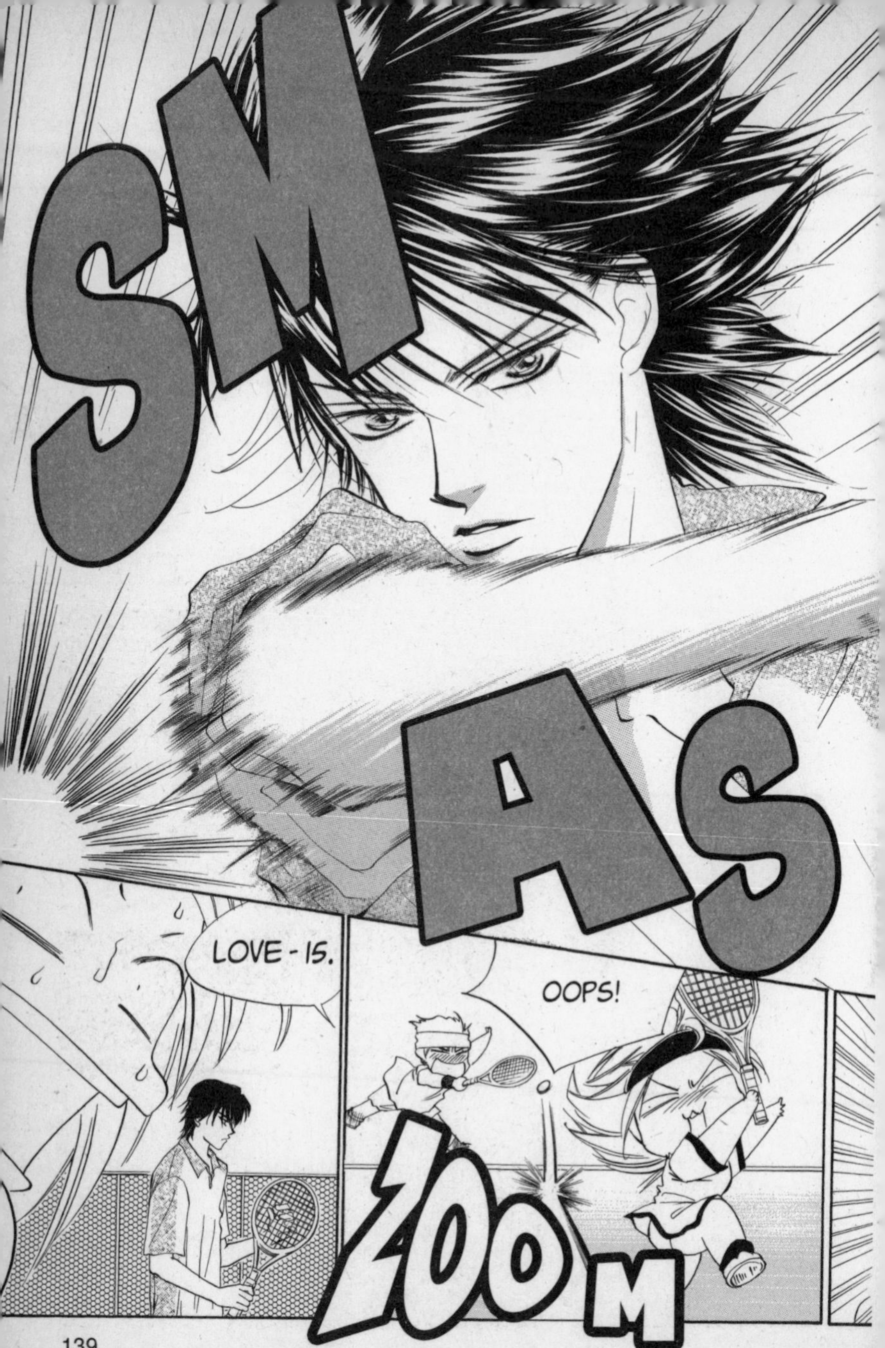
SMAS
OOPS!
ZOOM
LOVE - 15.

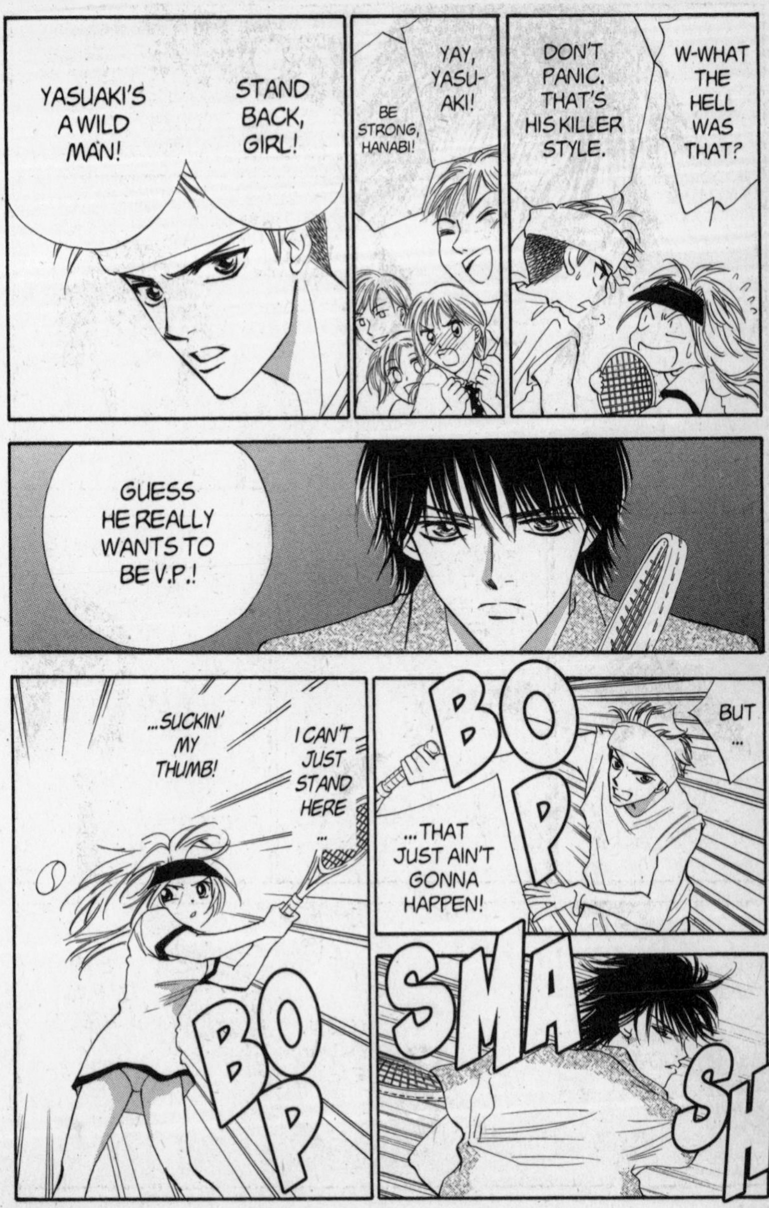
W-WHAT THE HELL WAS THAT?
DON'T PANIC. THAT'S HIS KILLER STYLE.
YAY, YASU-AKI!
BE STRONG, HANABI!
STAND BACK, GIRL!
YASUAKI'S A WILD MAN!
GUESS HE REALLY WANTS TO BE V.P.!
BOP
BUT ...
...THAT JUST AIN'T GONNA HAPPEN!
SMASH
I CAN'T JUST STAND HERE ...
...SUCKIN' MY THUMB!
BOP

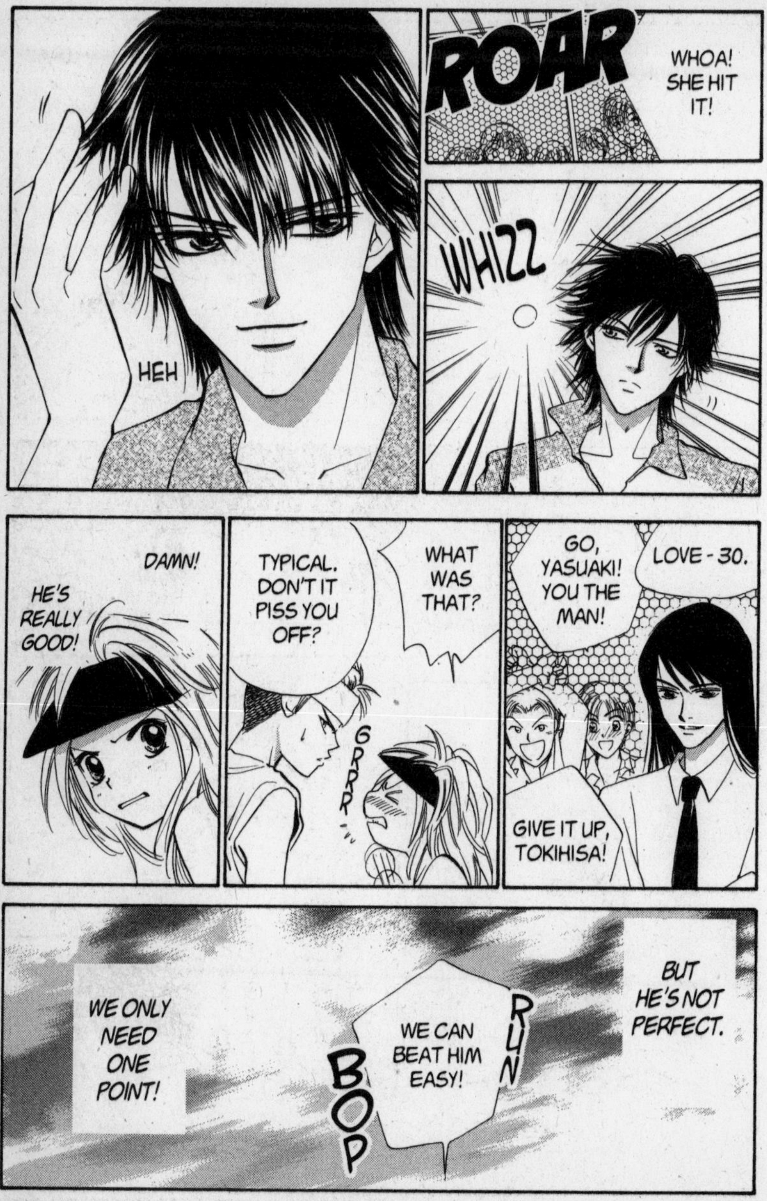
ROAR
WHOA! SHE HIT IT!
WHIZZ
HEH
LOVE - 30.
GO, YASUAKI! YOU THE MAN!
GIVE IT UP, TOKIHISA!
WHAT WAS THAT?
TYPICAL. DON'T IT PISS YOU OFF?
GRRR
DAMN!
HE'S REALLY GOOD!
BUT HE'S NOT PERFECT.
RUN
WE CAN BEAT HIM EASY!
BOP
WE ONLY NEED ONE POINT!

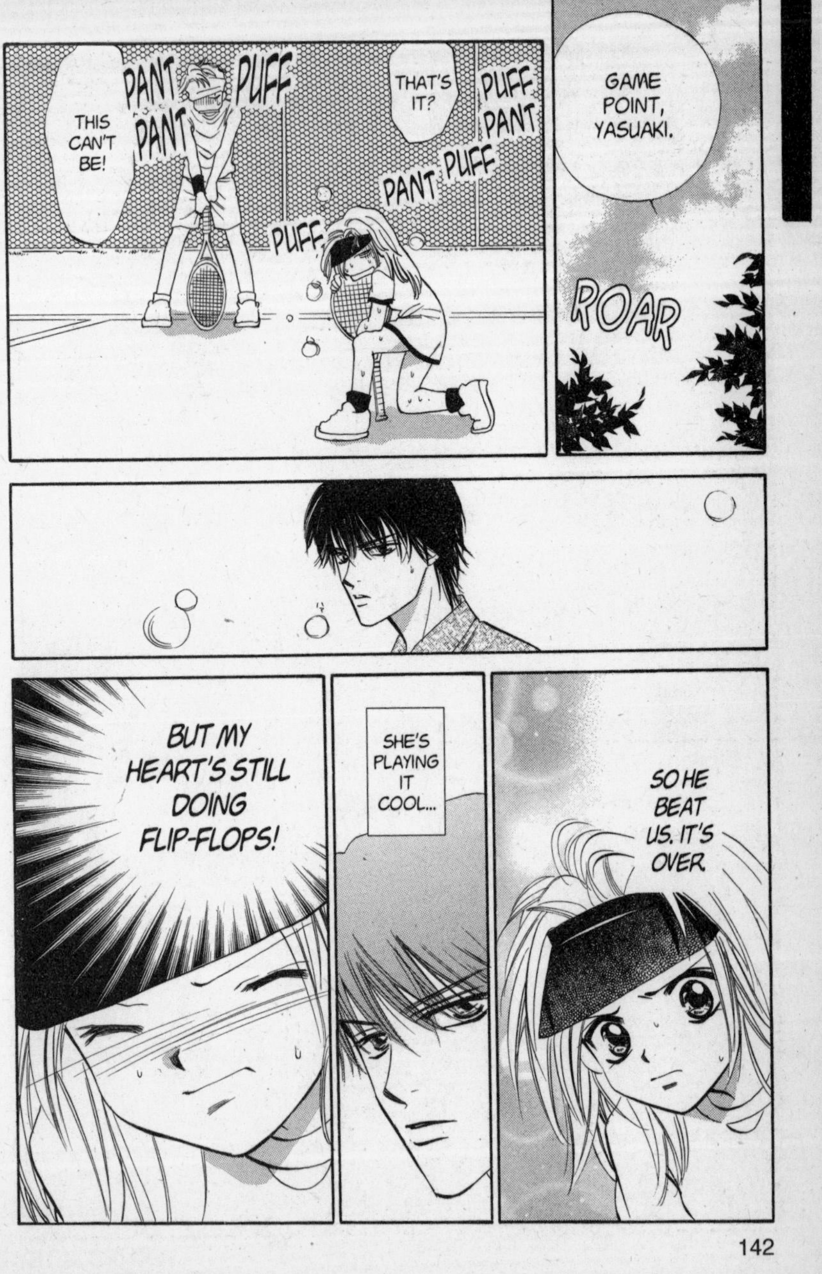
GAME POINT, YASUAKI.
ROAR
PUFF PANT
THAT'S IT?
PANT PUFF
PUFF
PANT PUFF
PANT PANT
THIS CAN'T BE!
SO HE BEAT US. IT'S OVER.
SHE'S PLAYING IT COOL...
BUT MY HEART'S STILL DOING FLIP-FLOPS!

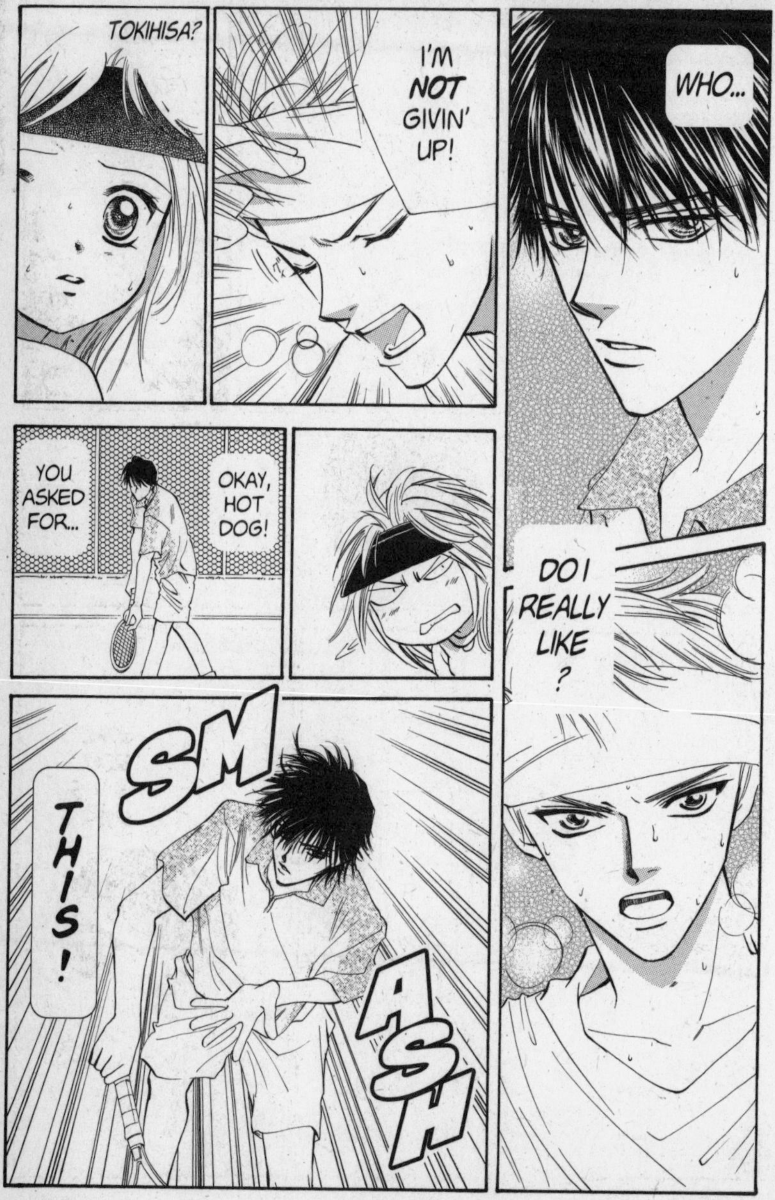
WHO...
DO I REALLY LIKE ?
I'M NOT GIVIN' UP!
TOKIHISA?
OKAY, HOT DOG!
YOU ASKED FOR...
SMASH
THIS!

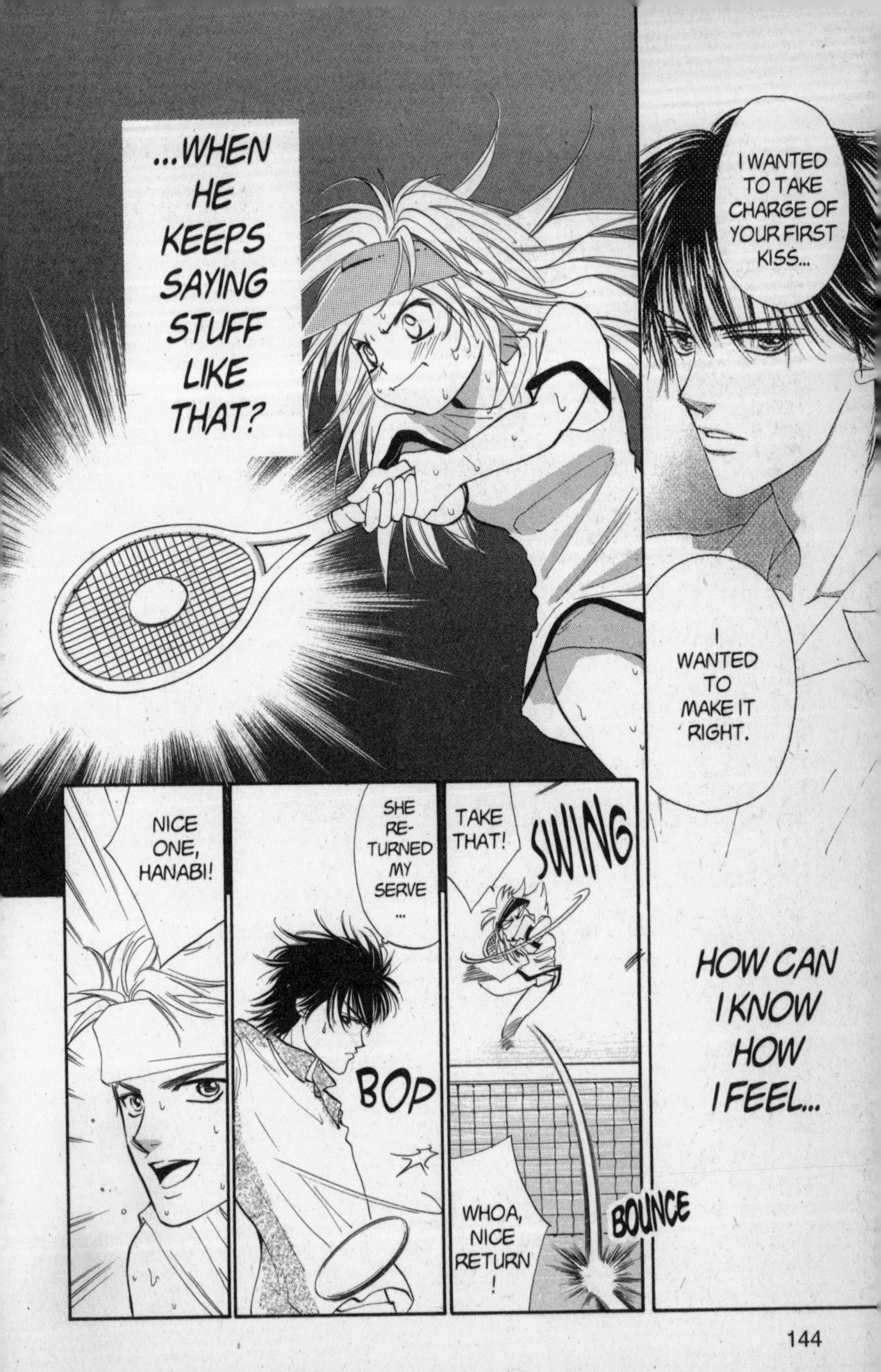
I WANTED TO TAKE CHARGE OF YOUR FIRST KISS...
I WANTED TO MAKE IT RIGHT.
HOW CAN I KNOW HOW I FEEL...
...WHEN HE KEEPS SAYING STUFF LIKE THAT?
TAKE THAT!
SWING
WHOA, NICE RETURN!
BOUNCE
SHE RE-TURNED MY SERVE...
BOP
NICE ONE, HANABI!

!
YESSS !
TWIST
TAKE THAT!
SMASH
!
BOP
OOPS !
FWA

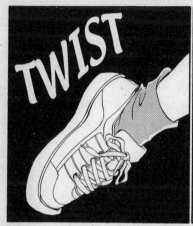

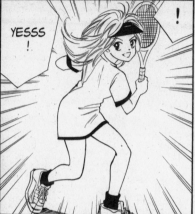

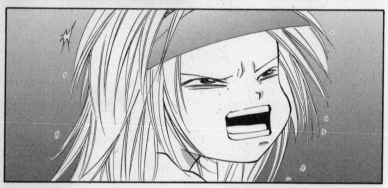

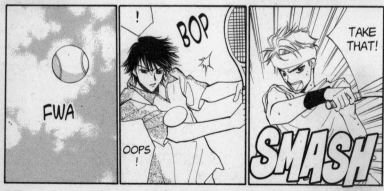

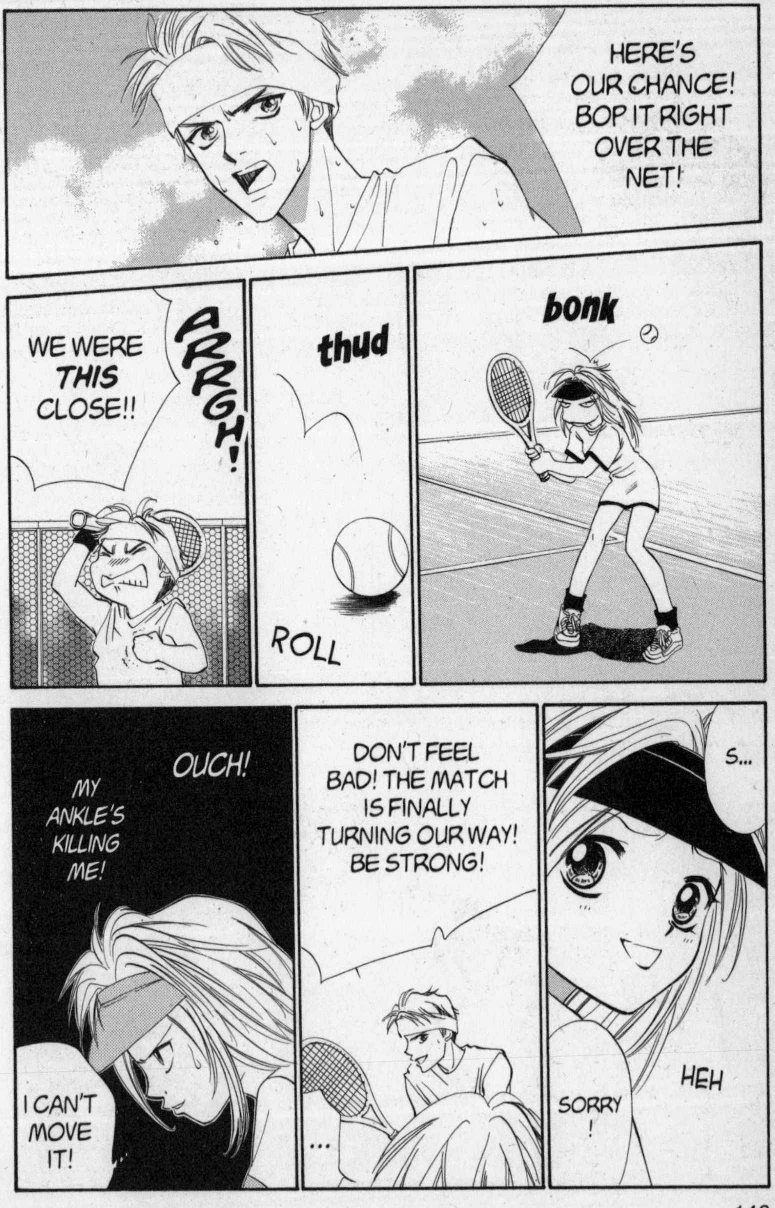
HERE'S OUR CHANCE! BOP IT RIGHT OVER THE NET!
bonk
thud
ROLL
ARRGH!
WE WERE THIS CLOSE!!
S...
HEH
SORRY!
DON'T FEEL BAD! THE MATCH IS FINALLY TURNING OUR WAY! BE STRONG!
...
OUCH!
MY ANKLE'S KILLING ME!
I CAN'T MOVE IT!

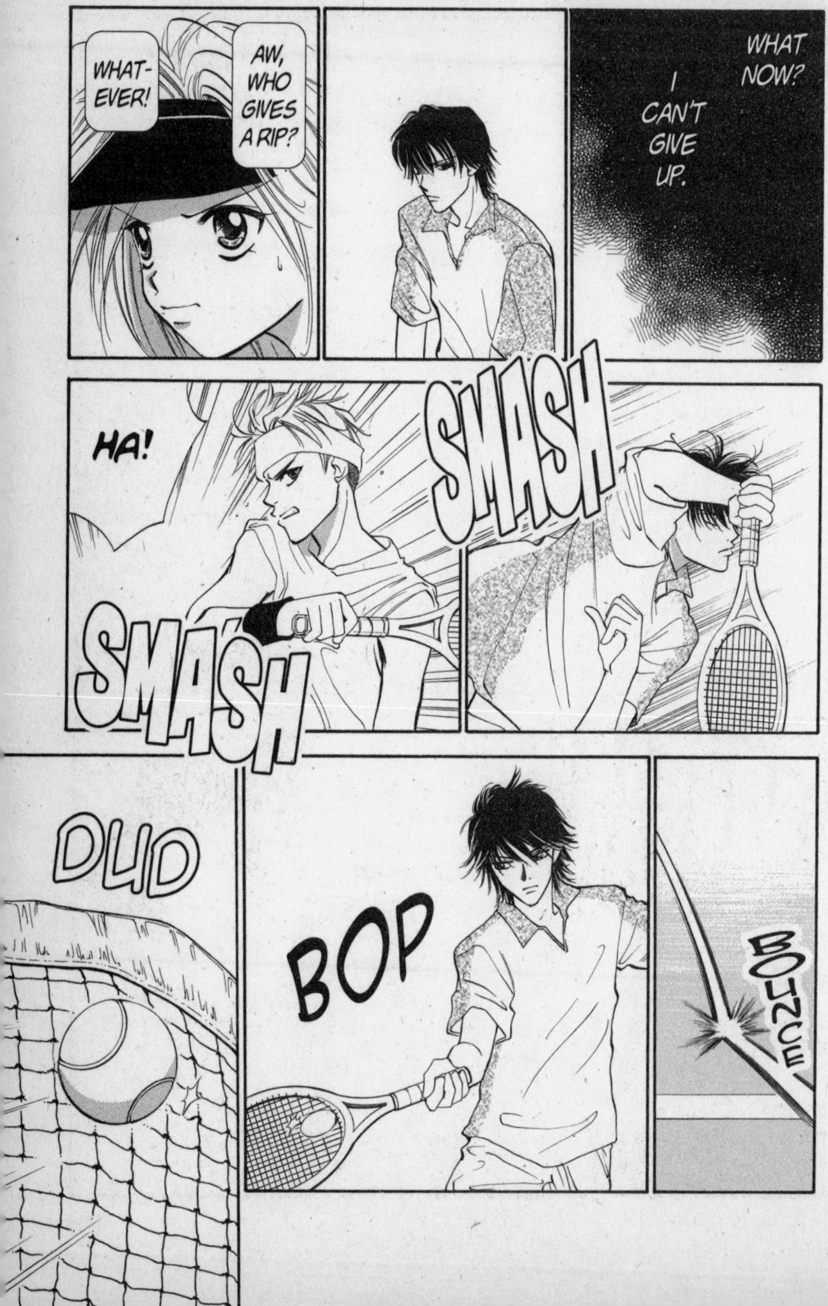
WHAT NOW?
I CAN'T GIVE UP.
AW, WHO GIVES A RIP?
WHAT-EVER!
SMASH
HA!
SMASH
BOUNCE
BOP
DUD

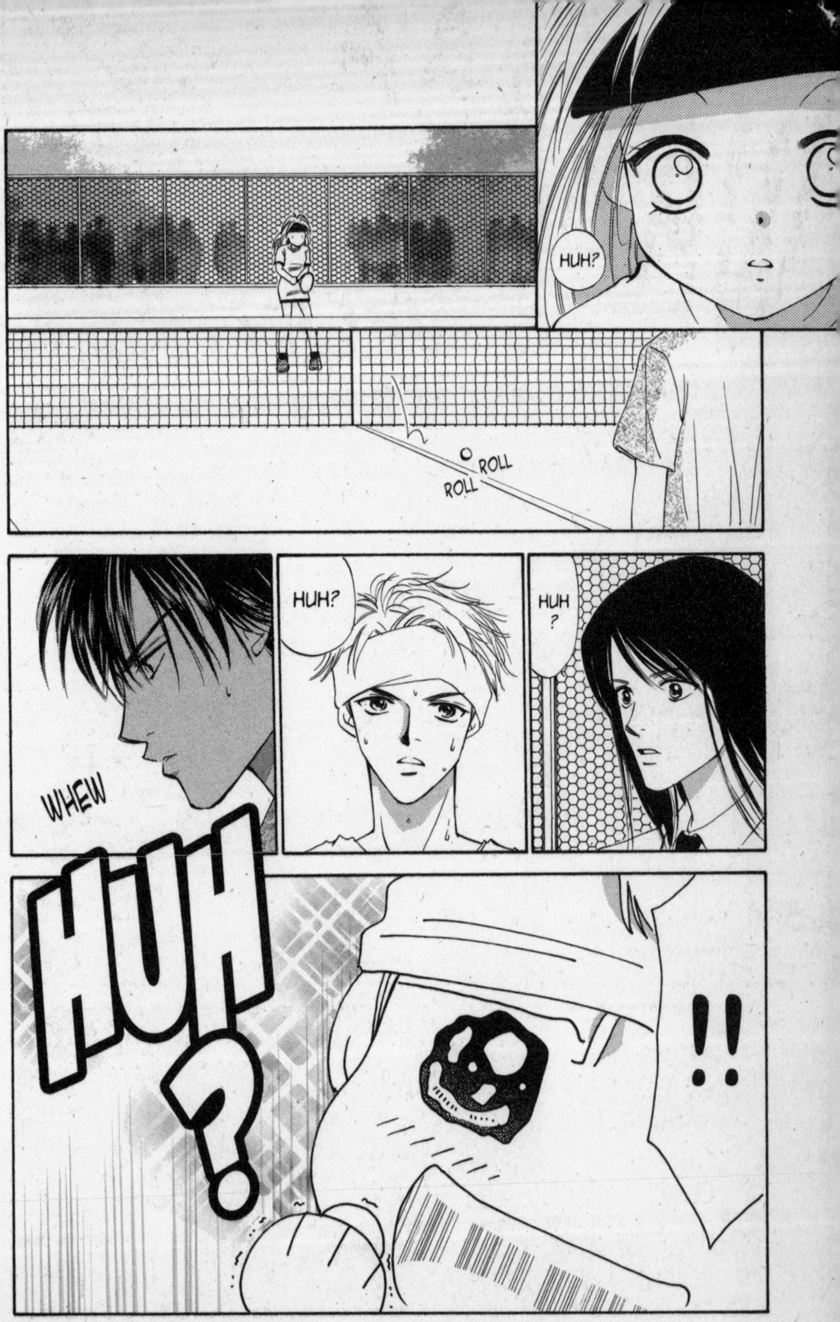
HUH?
ROLL
ROLL
HUH ?
HUH?
WHEW
!!
HUH ?

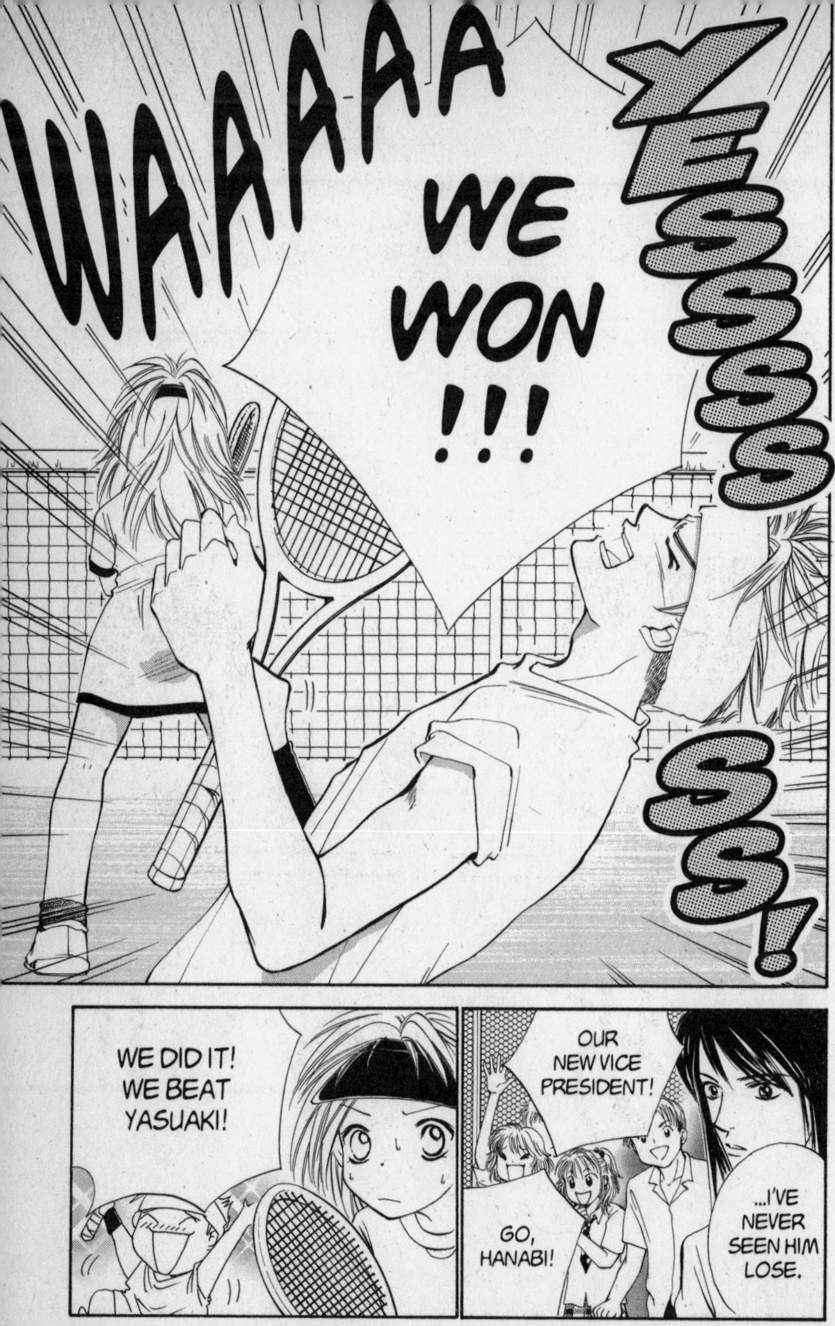
YESSSSSSS!
WE WON !!!
WAAAAAA
OUR NEW VICE PRESIDENT!
...I'VE NEVER SEEN HIM LOSE.
GO, HANABI!
WE DID IT! WE BEAT YASUAKI!

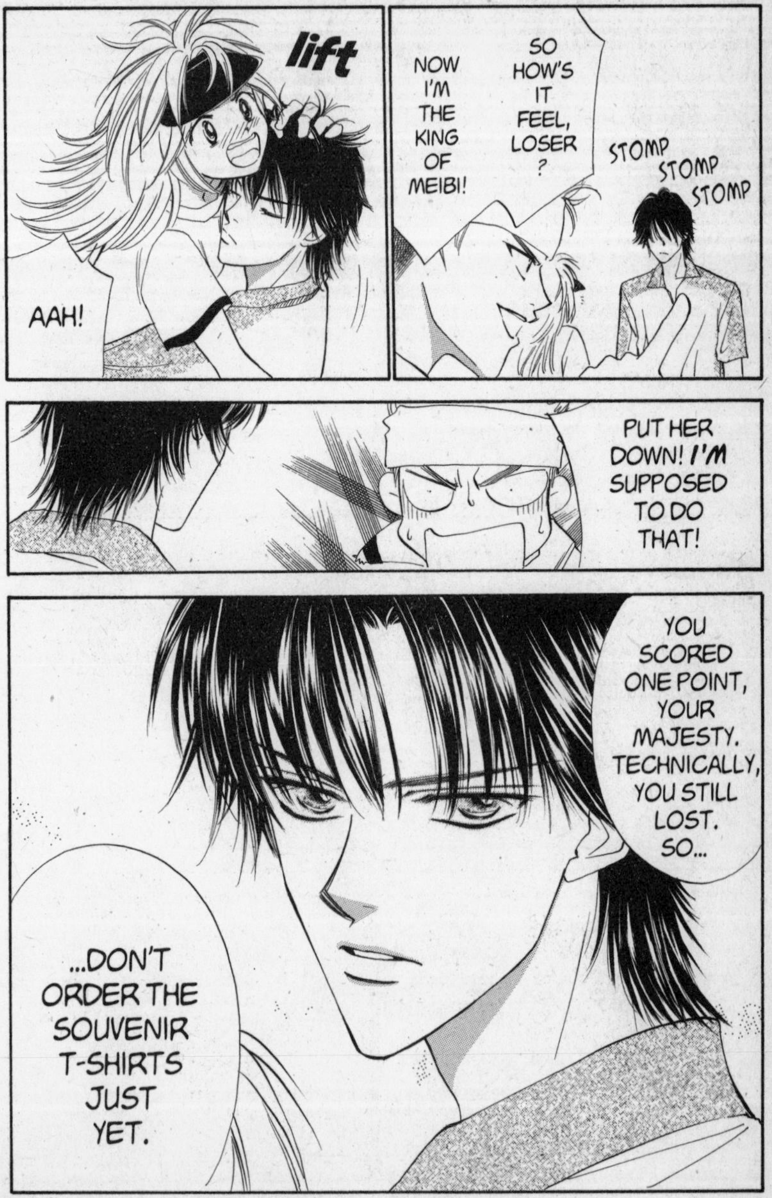
SO HOW'S IT FEEL, LOSER?
NOW I'M THE KING OF MEIBI!
STOMP STOMP STOMP
lift
AAH!
PUT HER DOWN! I'M SUPPOSED TO DO THAT!
YOU SCORED ONE POINT, YOUR MAJESTY. TECHNICALLY, YOU STILL LOST. SO...
...DON'T ORDER THE SOUVENIR T-SHIRTS JUST YET.

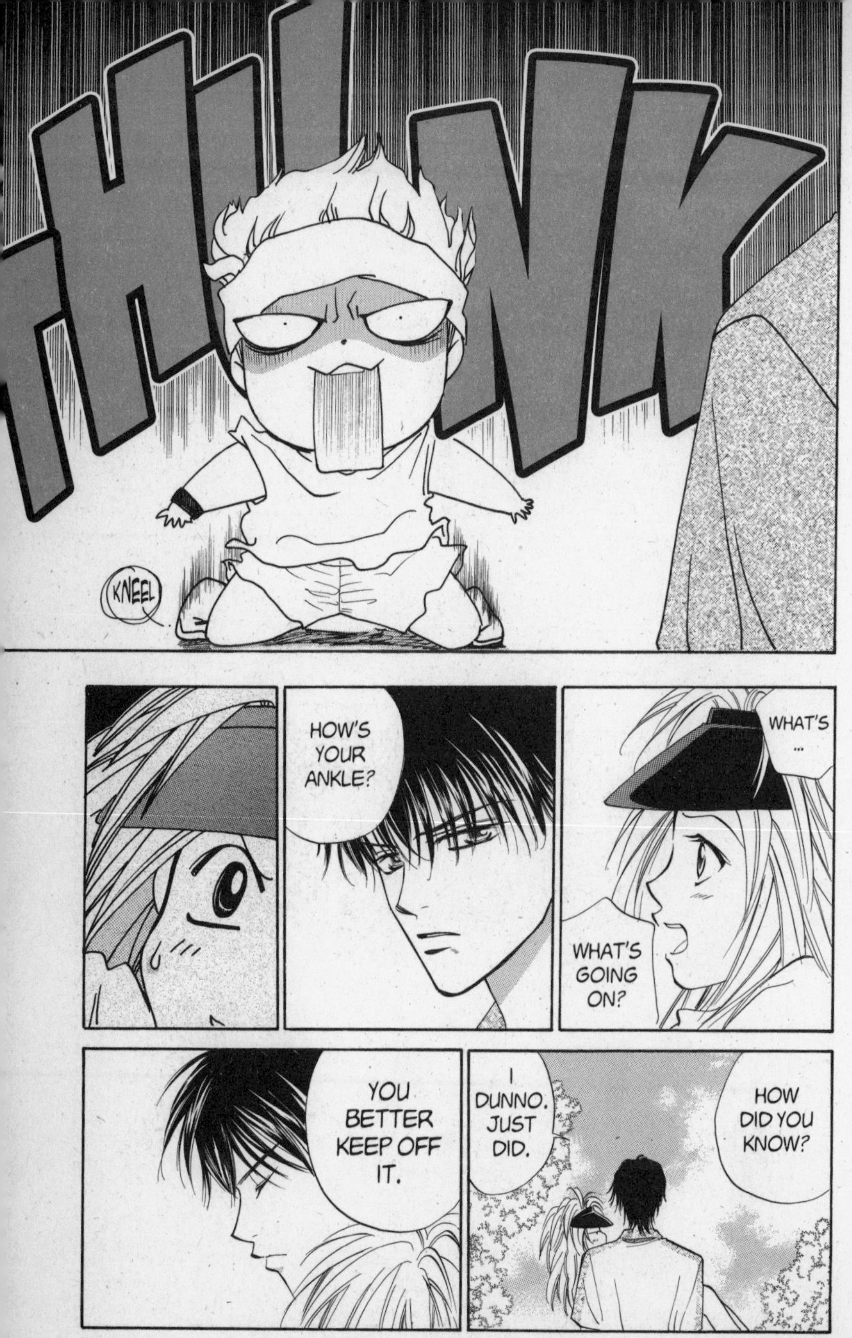
THUNK
KNEEL
WHAT'S ...
WHAT'S GOING ON?
HOW'S YOUR ANKLE?
HOW DID YOU KNOW?
I DUNNO. JUST DID.
YOU BETTER KEEP OFF IT.

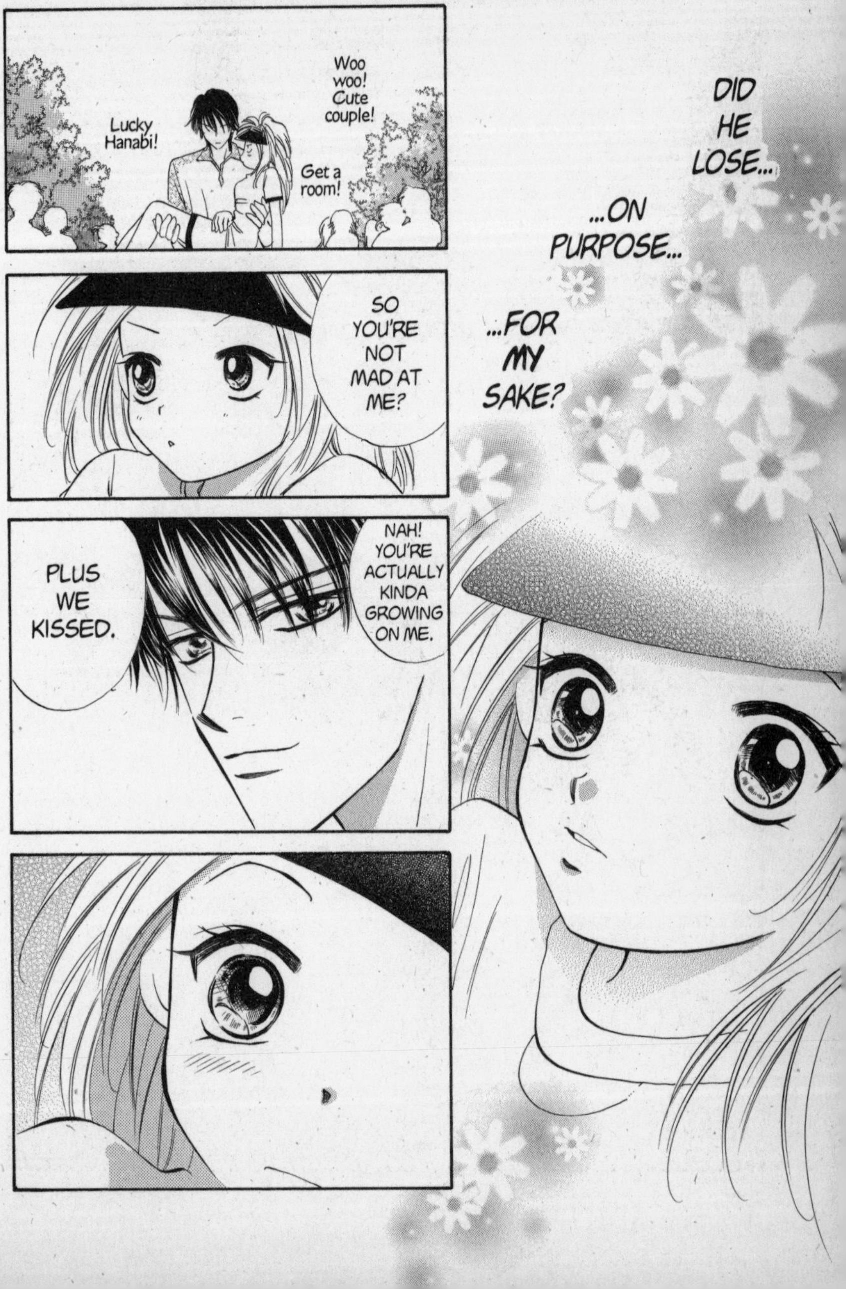
DID HE LOSE...
...ON PURPOSE...
...FOR MY SAKE?
Woo woo! Cute couple!
Get a room!
Lucky Hanabi!
SO YOU'RE NOT MAD AT ME?
NAH! YOU'RE ACTUALLY KINDA GROWING ON ME.
PLUS WE KISSED.

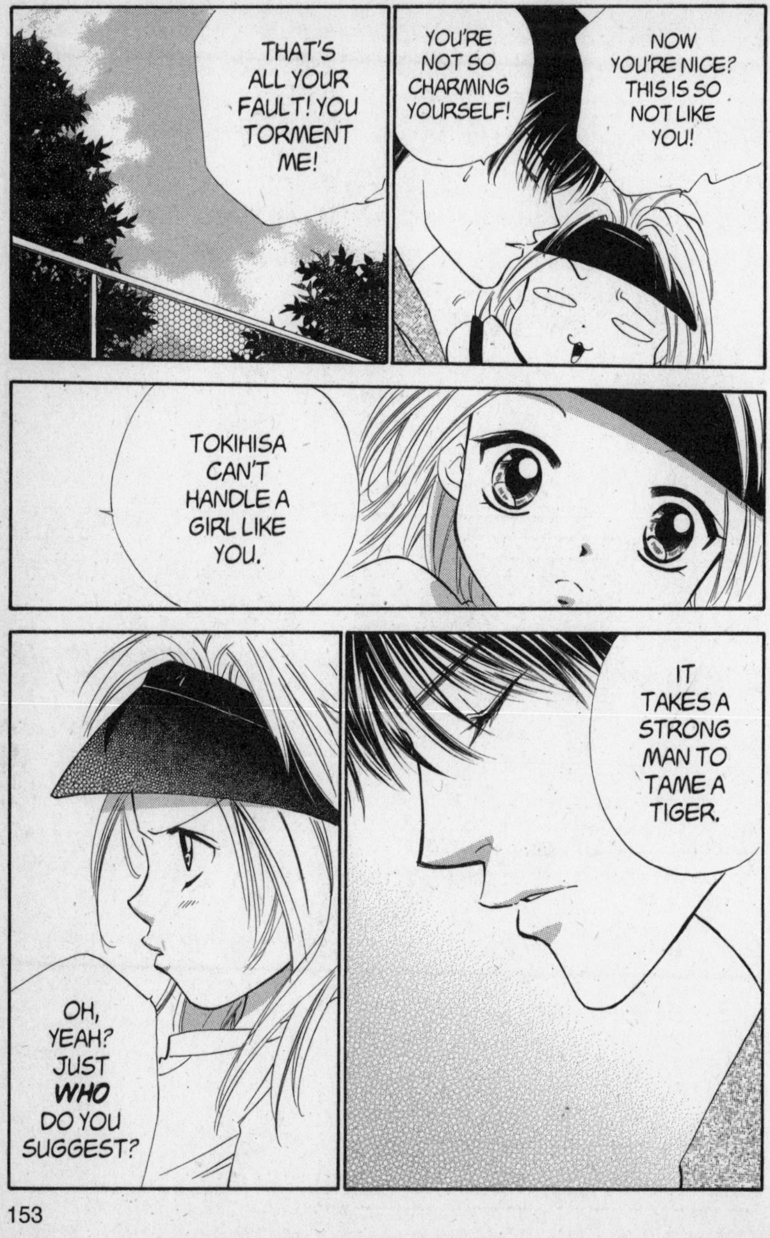
NOW YOU'RE NICE? THIS IS SO NOT LIKE YOU!
YOU'RE NOT SO CHARMING YOURSELF!
THAT'S ALL YOUR FAULT! YOU TORMENT ME!
TOKIHISA CAN'T HANDLE A GIRL LIKE YOU.
IT TAKES A STRONG MAN TO TAME A TIGER.
OH, YEAH? JUST **WHO** DO YOU SUGGEST?

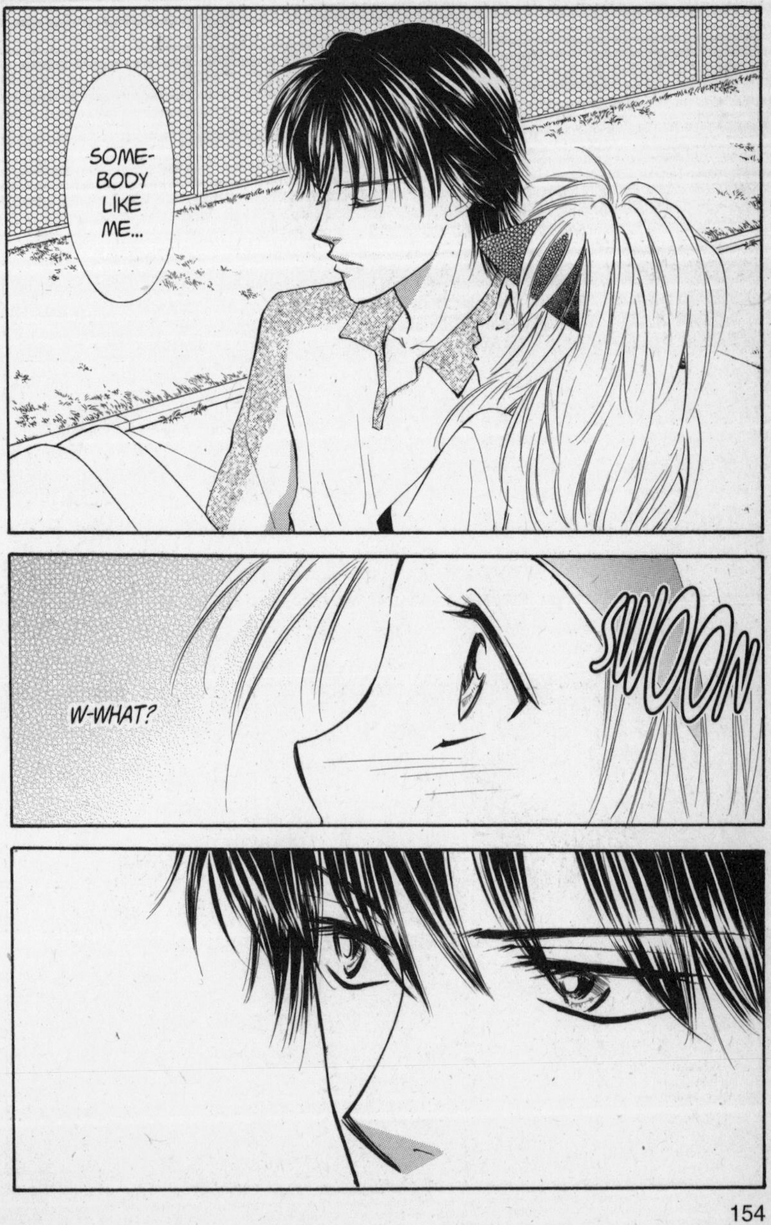
SOME-BODY LIKE ME...
SWOON
W-WHAT?

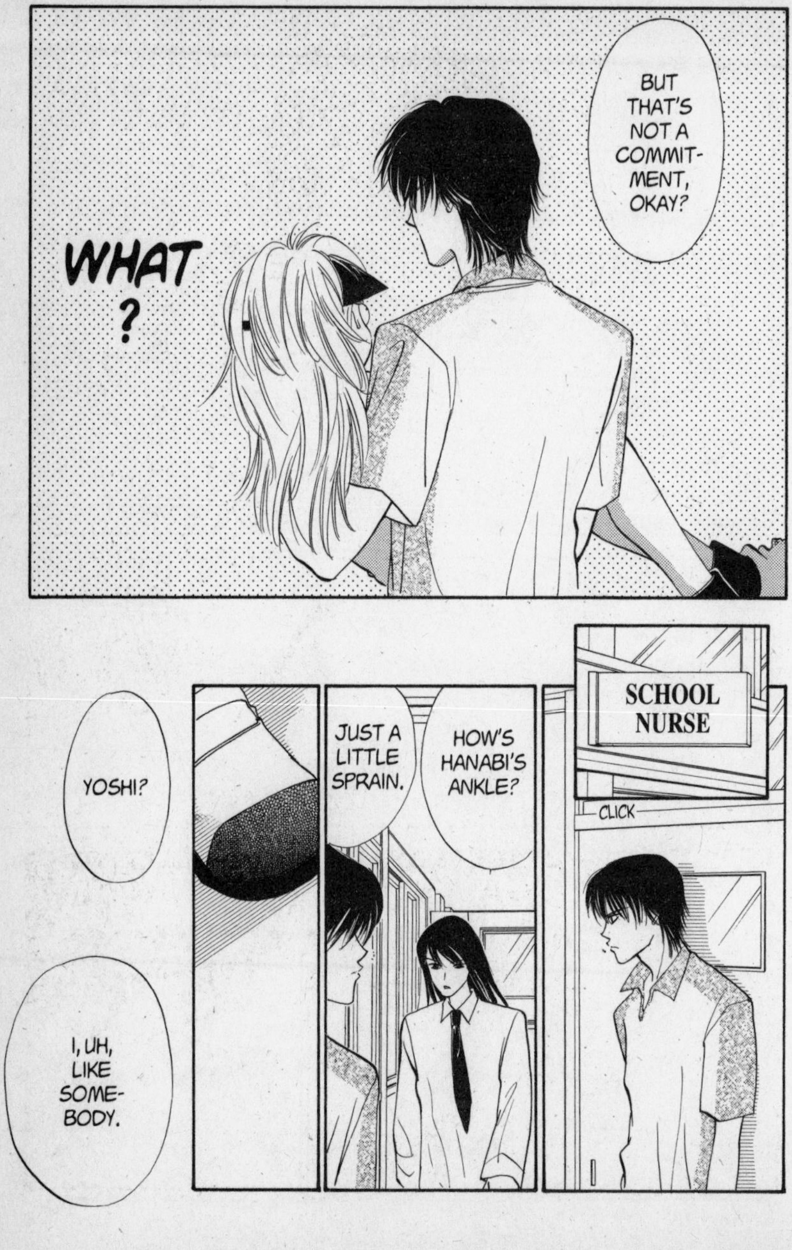
BUT THAT'S NOT A COMMIT-MENT, OKAY?
WHAT?
SCHOOL NURSE
CLICK
HOW'S HANABI'S ANKLE?
JUST A LITTLE SPRAIN.
YOSHI?
I, UH, LIKE SOME-BODY.

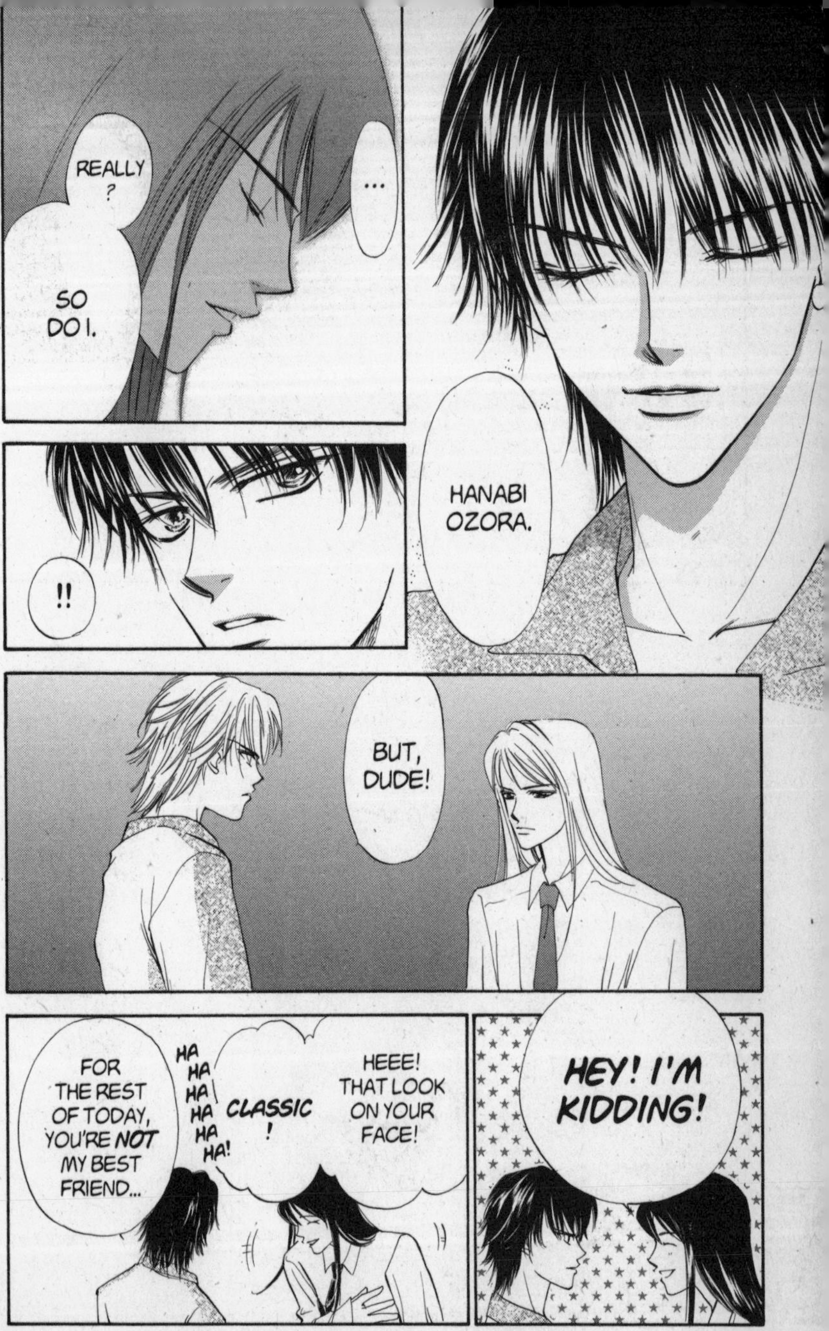
HANABI OZORA.
...
REALLY ?
SO DO I.
!!
BUT, DUDE!
HEY! I'M KIDDING!
HEEE! THAT LOOK ON YOUR FACE!
CLASSIC !
HA HA HA HA HA HA!
FOR THE REST OF TODAY, YOU'RE NOT MY BEST FRIEND...

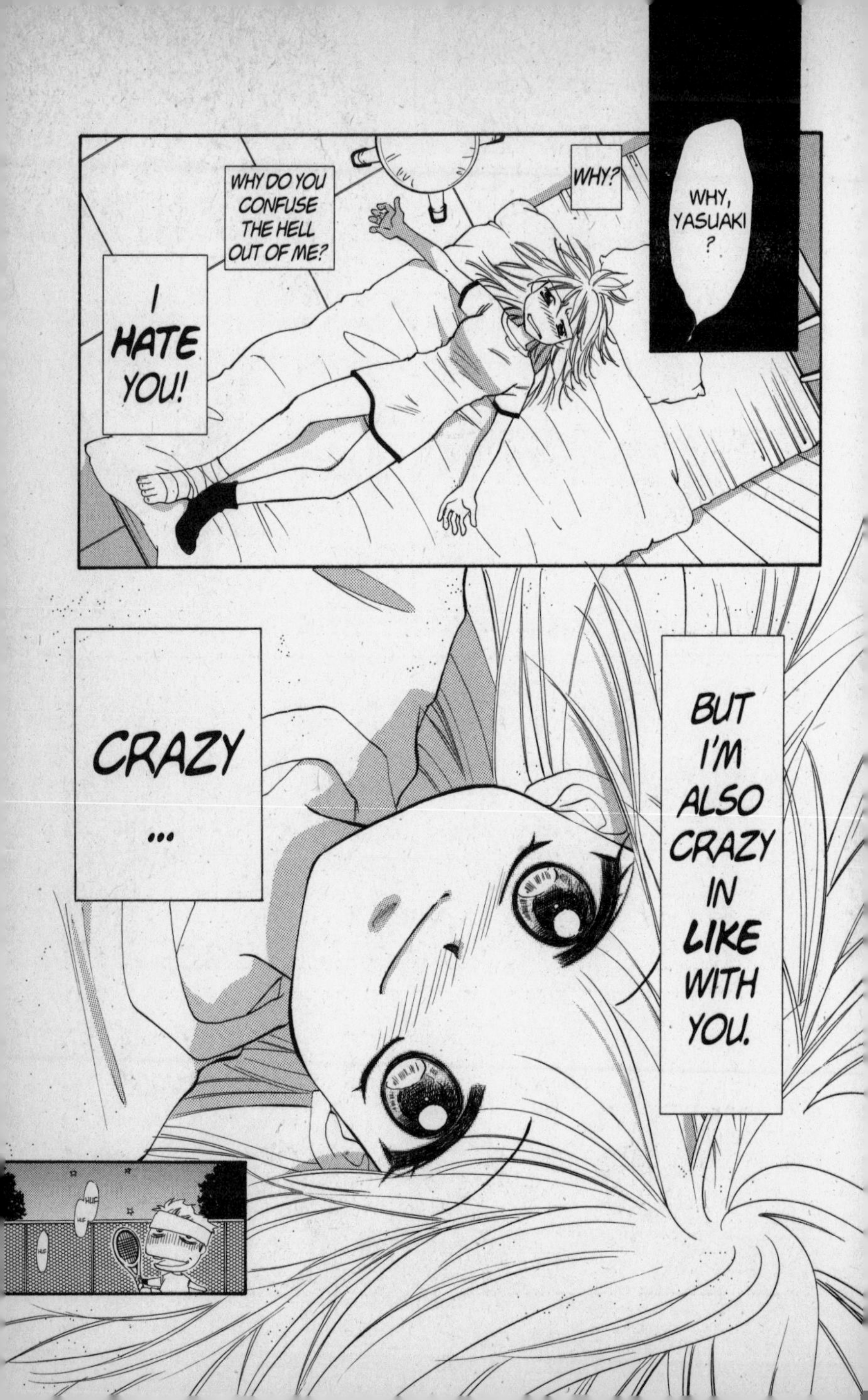
WHY, YASUAKI ?
WHY?
WHY DO YOU CONFUSE THE HELL OUT OF ME?
I HATE YOU!
BUT I'M ALSO CRAZY IN LIKE WITH YOU.
CRAZY ...

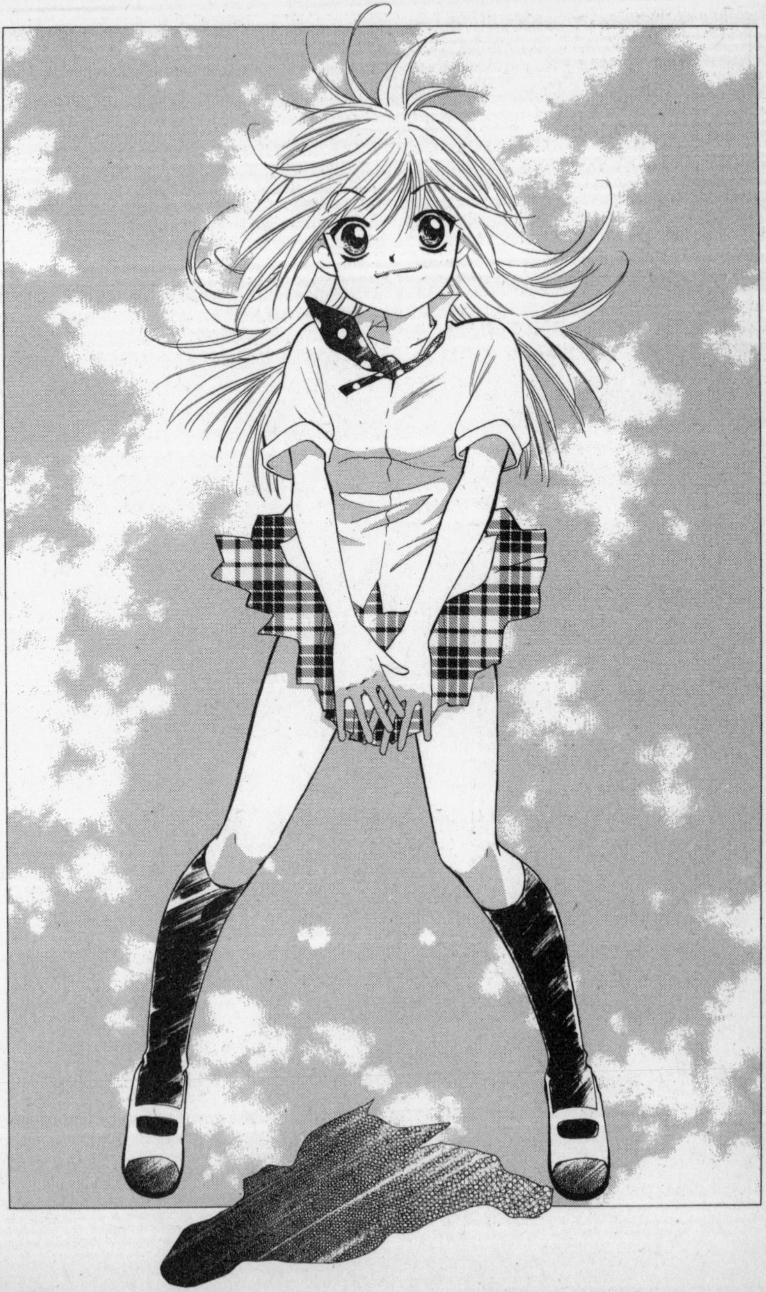

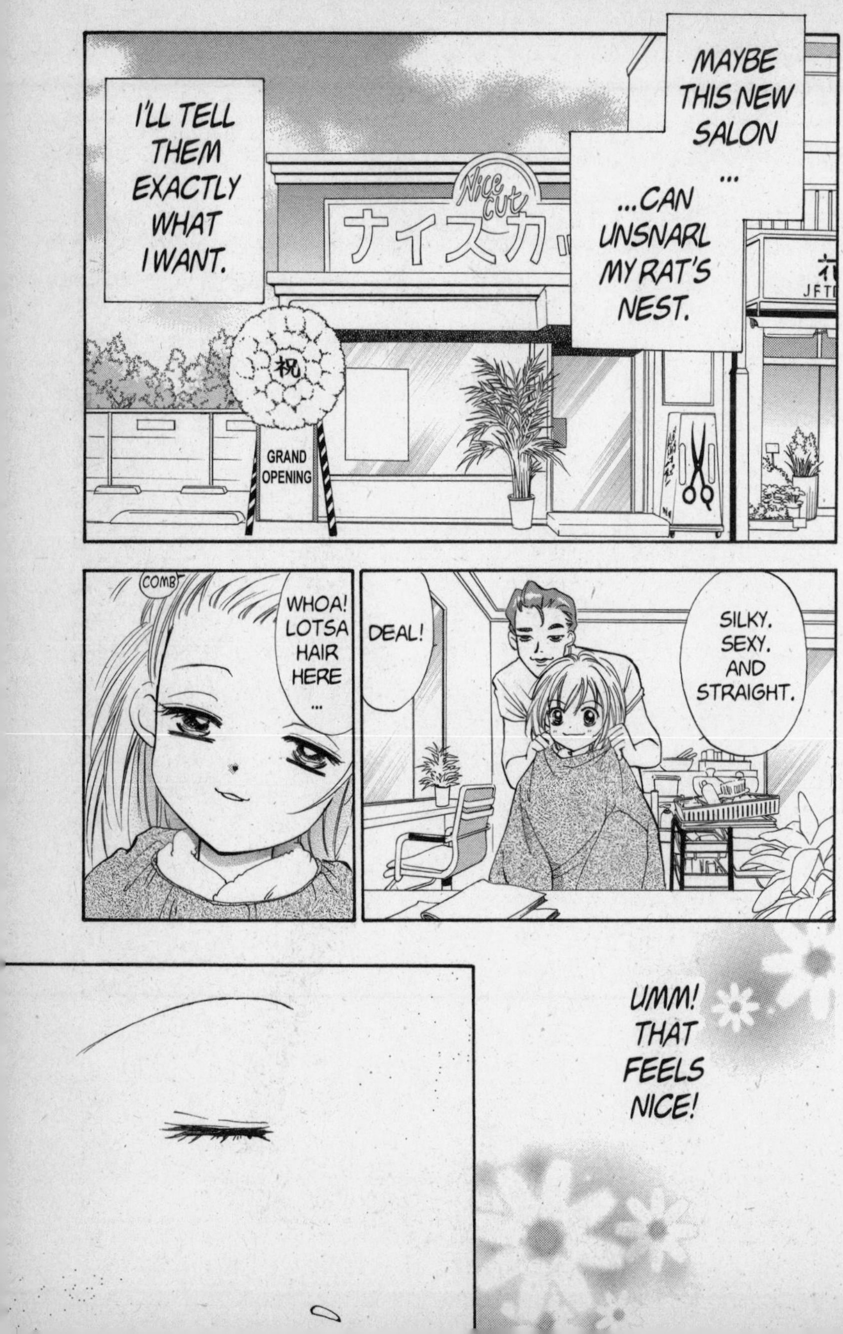
MAYBE THIS NEW SALON ...
...CAN UNSNARL MY RAT'S NEST.
I'LL TELL THEM EXACTLY WHAT I WANT.
Nice cut
祝
GRAND OPENING
SILKY. SEXY. AND STRAIGHT.
DEAL!
WHOA! LOTSA HAIR HERE ...
COMB
UMM! THAT FEELS NICE!

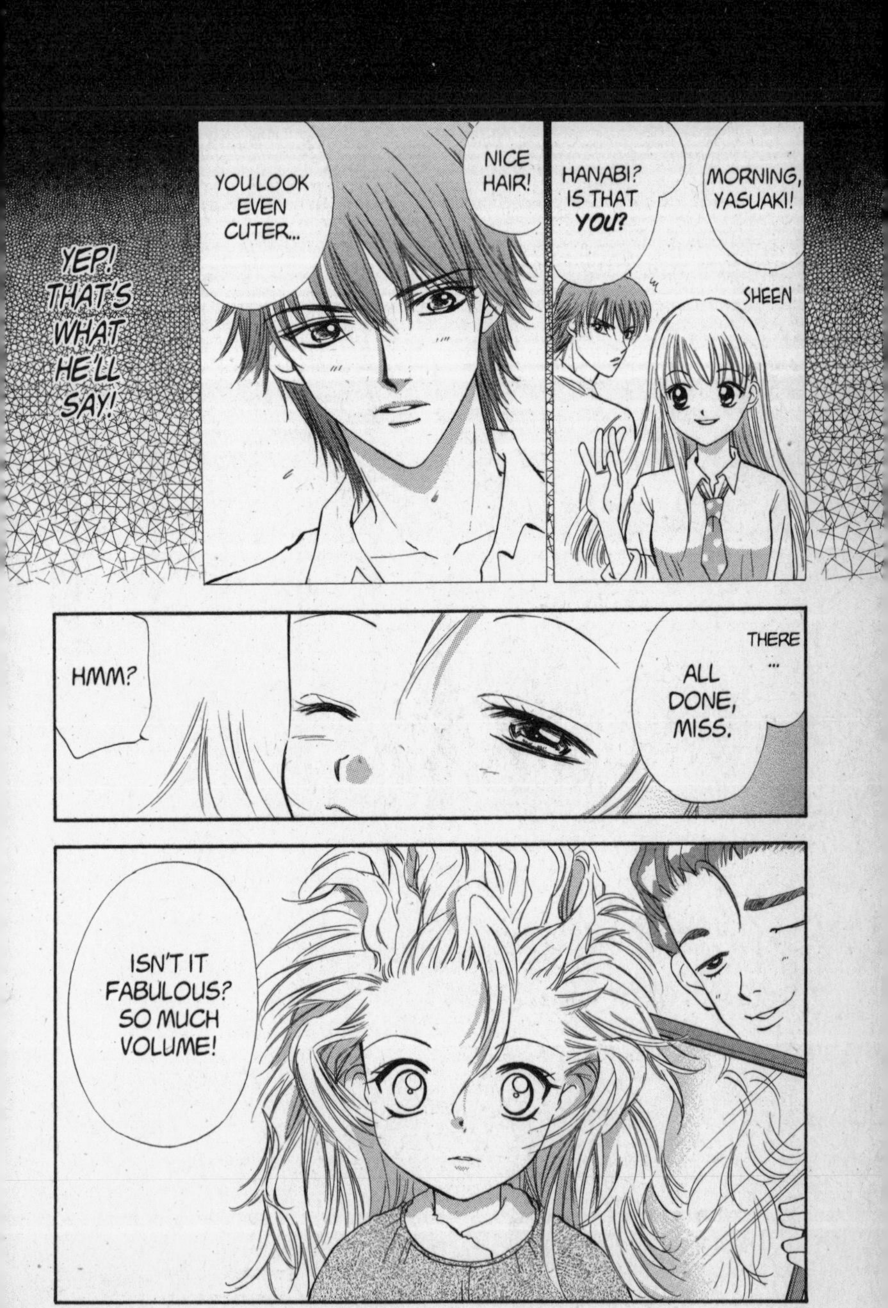
MORNING, YASUAKI!
SHEEN
HANABI? IS THAT YOU?
NICE HAIR!
YOU LOOK EVEN CUTER...
YEP! THAT'S WHAT HE'LL SAY!
THERE...
ALL DONE, MISS.
HMM?
ISN'T IT FABULOUS? SO MUCH VOLUME!

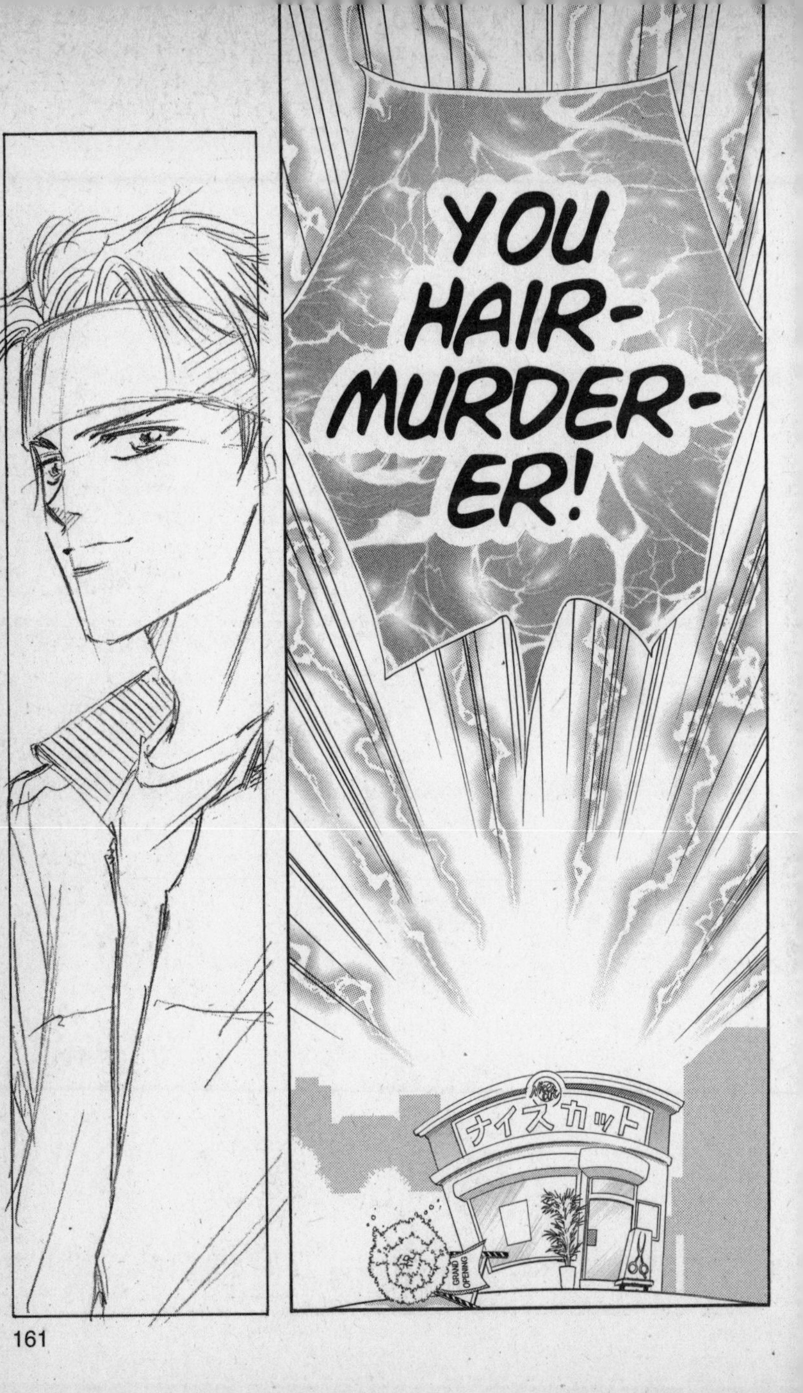
YOU HAIR-MURDER-ER!
ナイスカット
GRAND OPENING

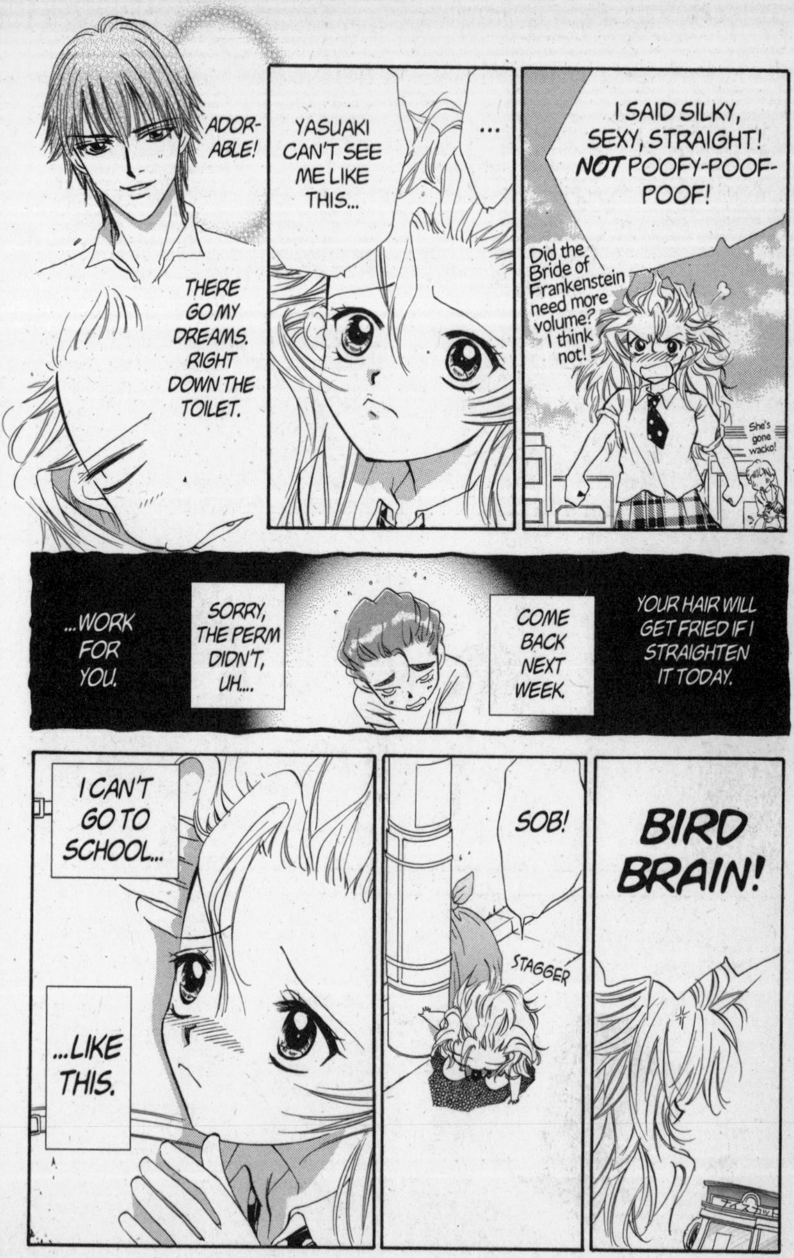
I SAID SILKY, SEXY, STRAIGHT! NOT POOFY-POOF-POOF!
Did the Bride of Frankenstein need more volume? I think not!
She's gone wacko!
...
YASUAKI CAN'T SEE ME LIKE THIS...
ADOR-ABLE!
THERE GO MY DREAMS. RIGHT DOWN THE TOILET.
YOUR HAIR WILL GET FRIED IF I STRAIGHTEN IT TODAY.
COME BACK NEXT WEEK.
SORRY, THE PERM DIDN'T, UH...
...WORK FOR YOU.
BIRD BRAIN!
SOB!
STAGGER
I CAN'T GO TO SCHOOL...
...LIKE THIS.

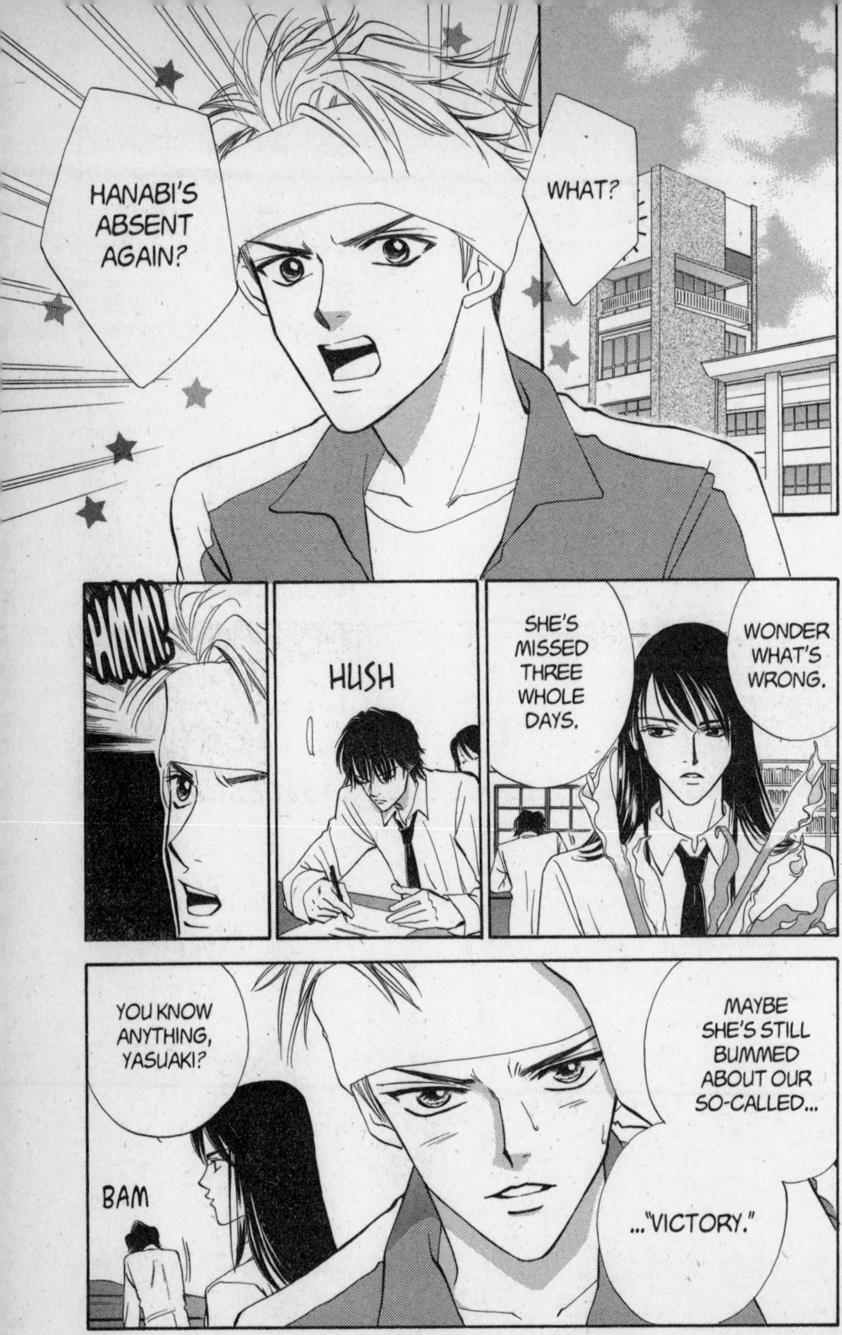
WHAT?
HANABI'S ABSENT AGAIN?
WONDER WHAT'S WRONG.
SHE'S MISSED THREE WHOLE DAYS.
HUSH
MAYBE SHE'S STILL BUMMED ABOUT OUR SO-CALLED...
..."VICTORY."
YOU KNOW ANYTHING, YASUAKI?
BAM

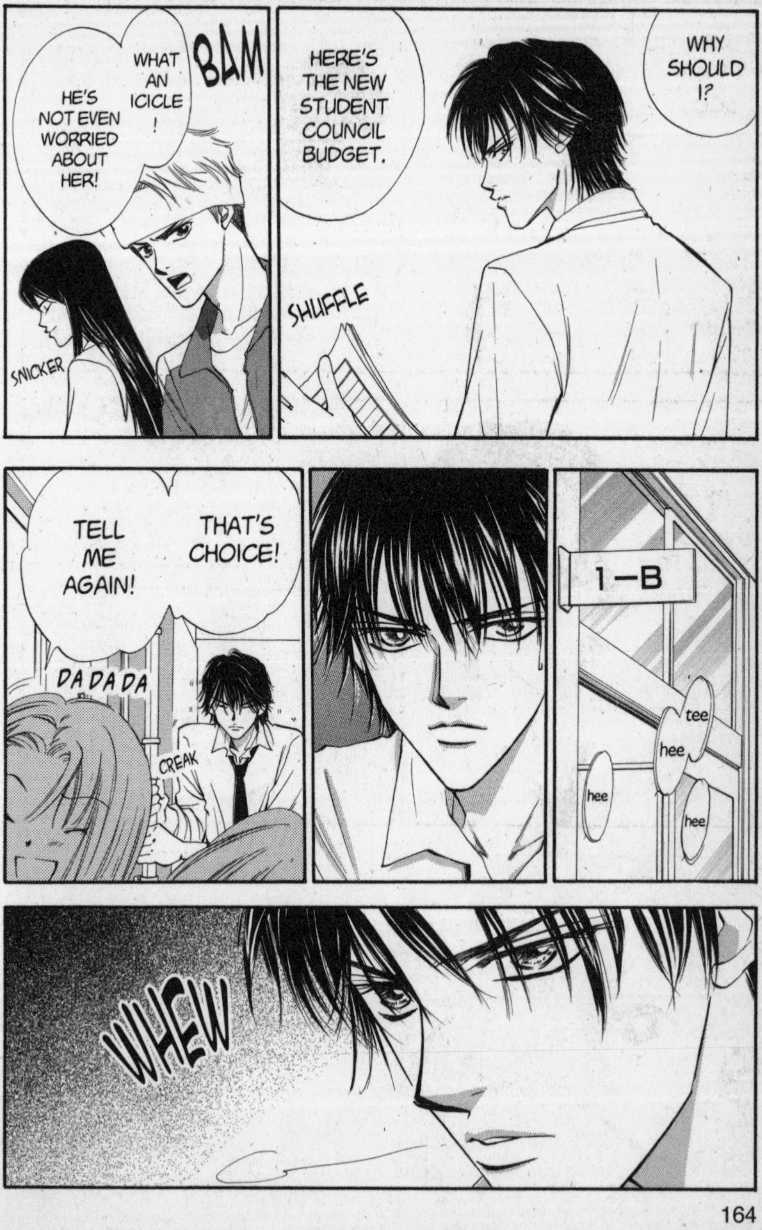
WHY SHOULD I?
HERE'S THE NEW STUDENT COUNCIL BUDGET.
SHUFFLE
BAM
WHAT AN ICICLE!
HE'S NOT EVEN WORRIED ABOUT HER!
SNICKER
1—B
tee hee
hee
hee
THAT'S CHOICE!
TELL ME AGAIN!
DA DA DA
CREAK
WHEW

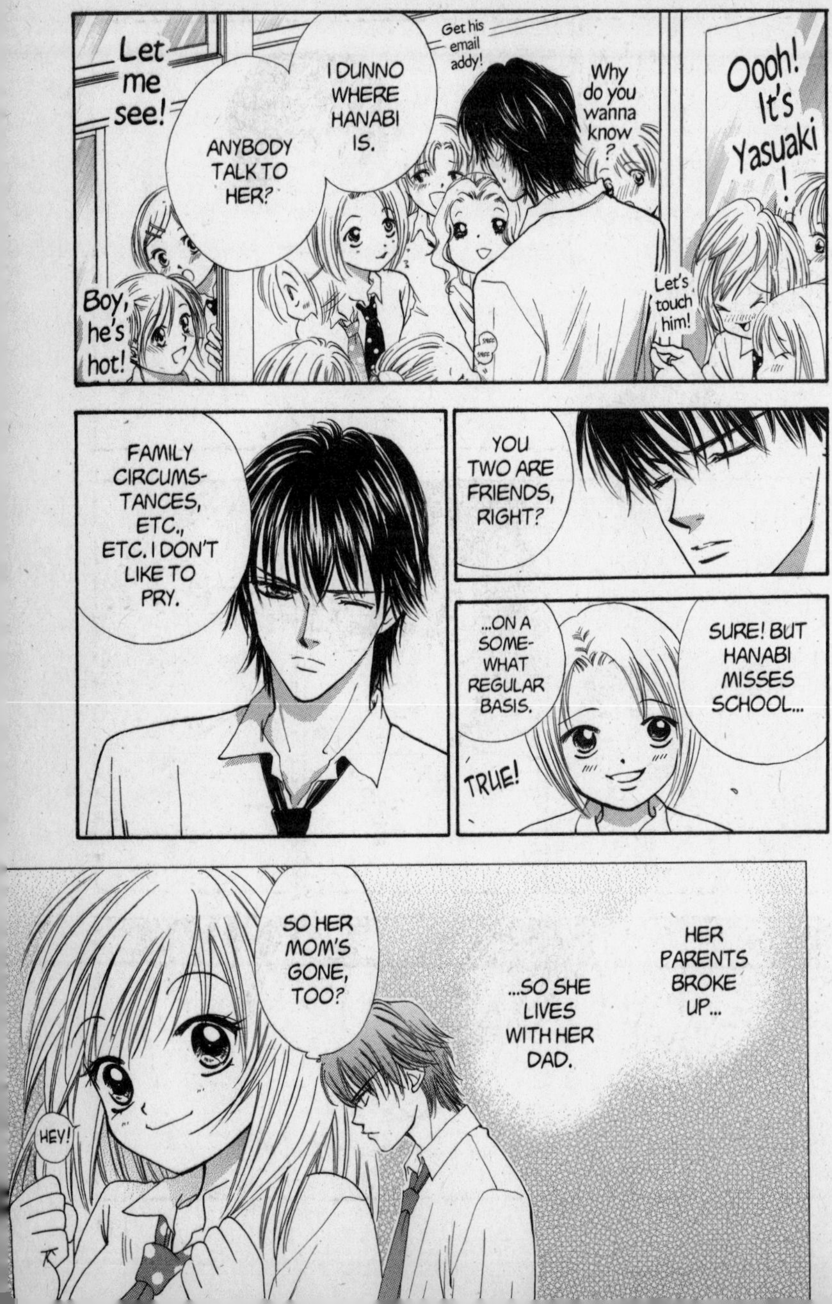
Oooh! It's Yasuaki!
Why do you wanna know?
Get his email addy!
I DUNNO WHERE HANABI IS.
Let's touch him!
ANYBODY TALK TO HER?
Let me see!
Boy, he's hot!
YOU TWO ARE FRIENDS, RIGHT?
SURE! BUT HANABI MISSES SCHOOL...
...ON A SOME-WHAT REGULAR BASIS.
TRUE!
FAMILY CIRCUMS-TANCES, ETC., ETC. I DON'T LIKE TO PRY.
HER PARENTS BROKE UP...
...SO SHE LIVES WITH HER DAD.
SO HER MOM'S GONE, TOO?
HEY!

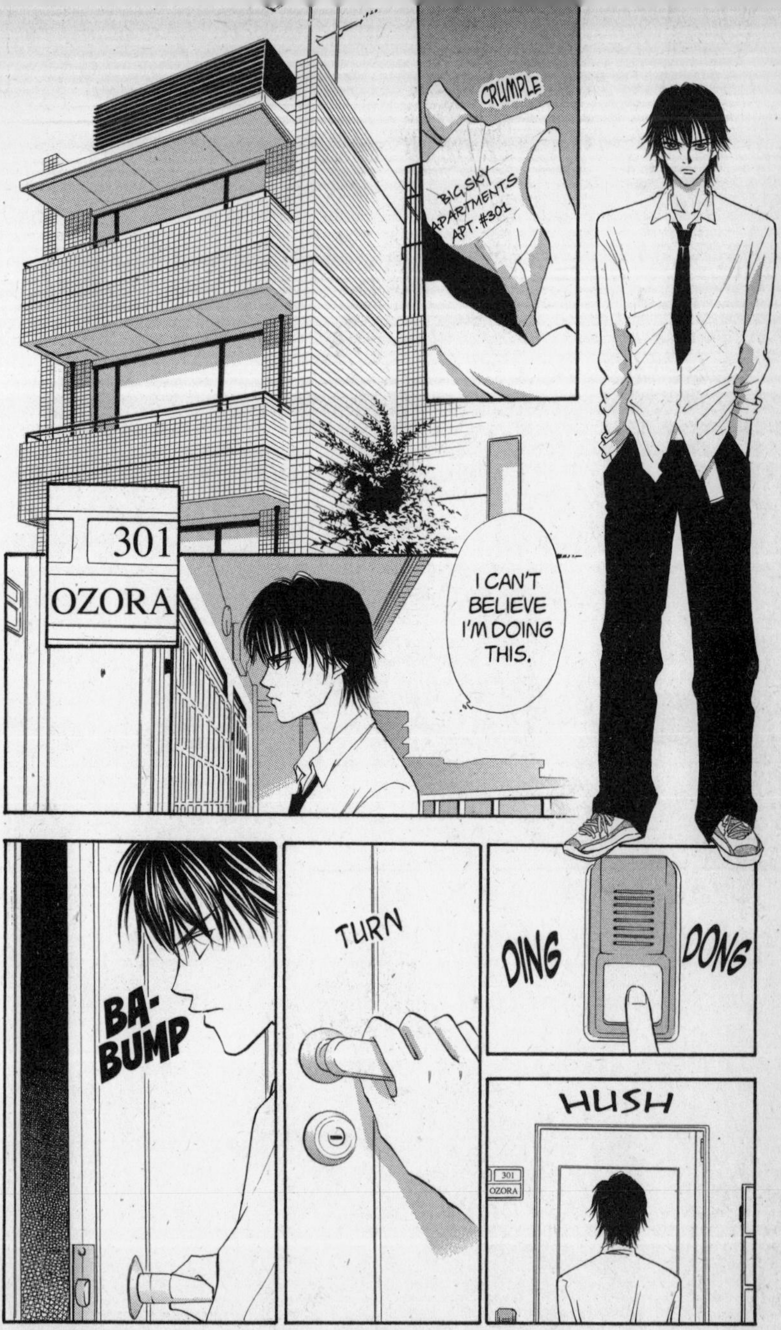
CRUMPLE
BIG SKY APARTMENTS APT. #301
I CAN'T BELIEVE I'M DOING THIS.
301
OZORA
DING
DONG
HUSH
TURN
BA-BUMP

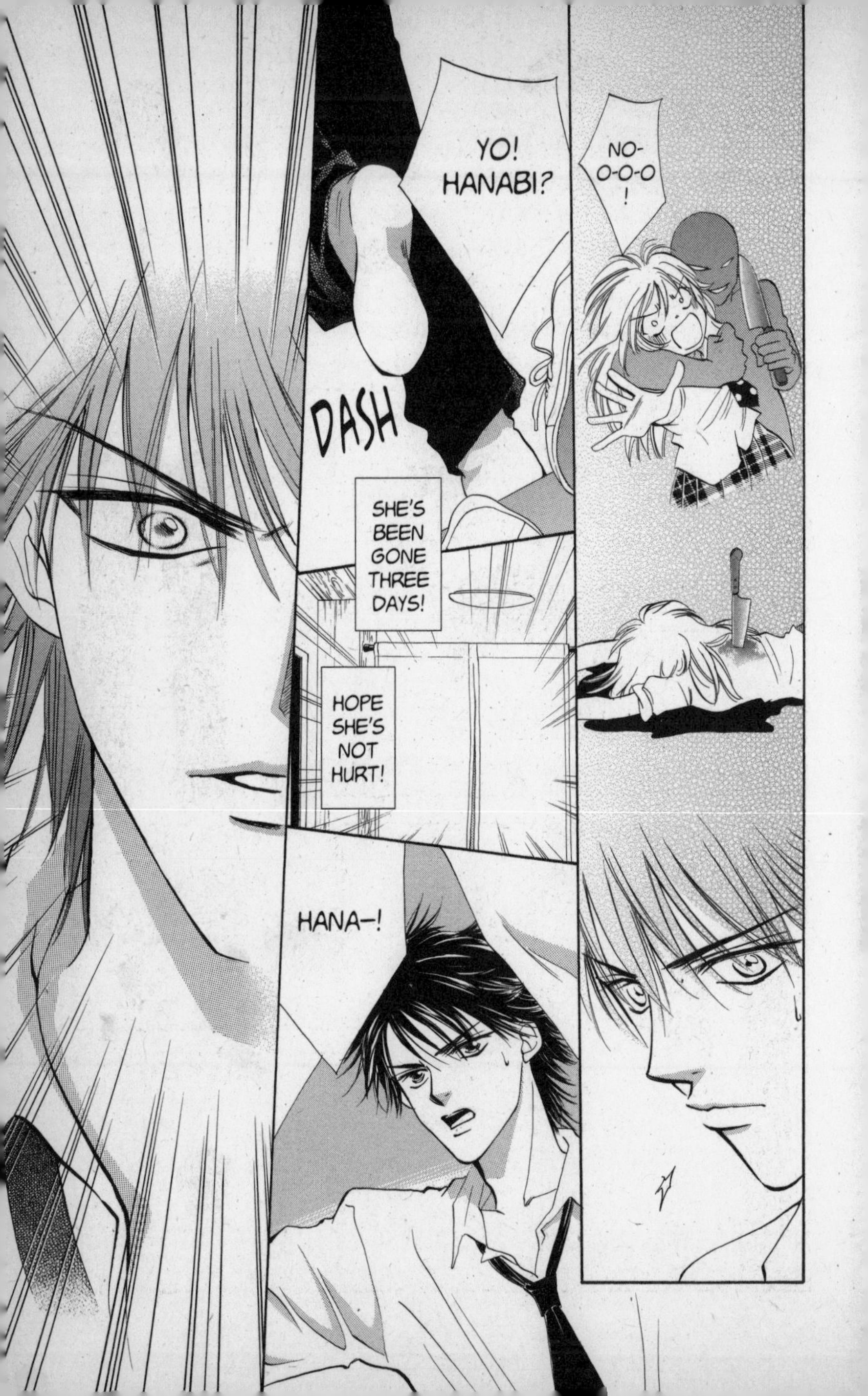
NO-O-O-O!
YO! HANABI?
DASH
SHE'S BEEN GONE THREE DAYS!
HOPE SHE'S NOT HURT!
HANA-!

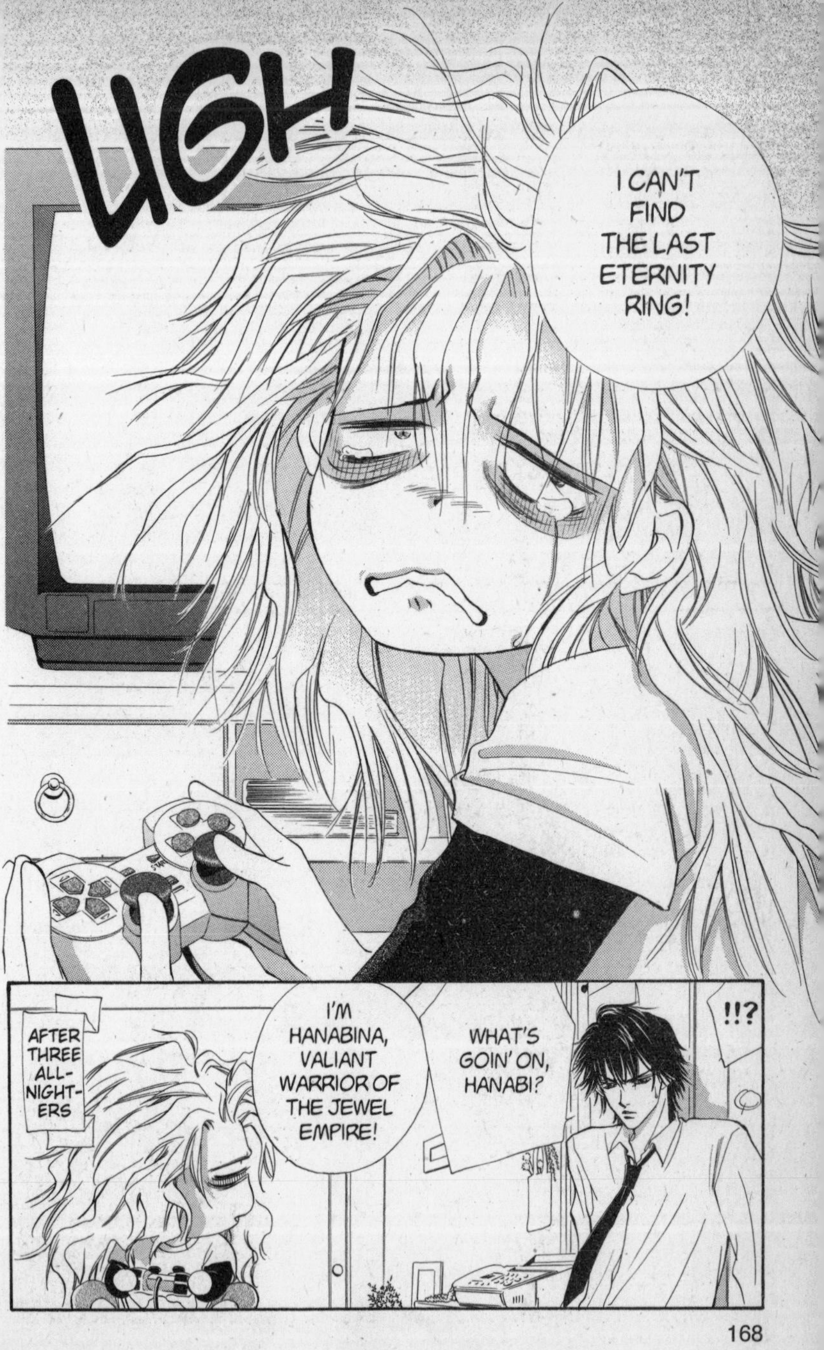
UGH
I CAN'T FIND THE LAST ETERNITY RING!
!!?
WHAT'S GOIN' ON, HANABI?
I'M HANABINA, VALIANT WARRIOR OF THE JEWEL EMPIRE!
AFTER THREE ALL-NIGHTERS

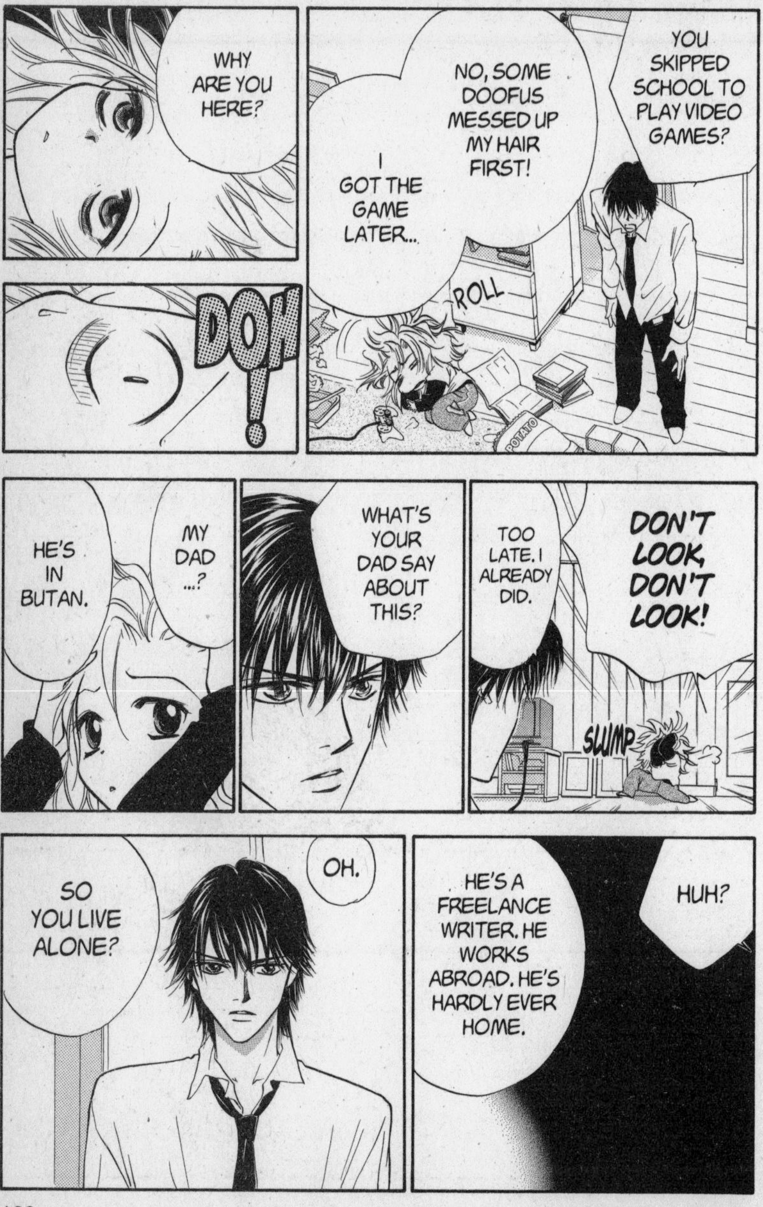
YOU SKIPPED SCHOOL TO PLAY VIDEO GAMES?
NO, SOME DOOFUS MESSED UP MY HAIR FIRST!
I GOT THE GAME LATER...
ROLL
POTATO
WHY ARE YOU HERE?
DOH!
DON'T LOOK, DON'T LOOK!
TOO LATE. I ALREADY DID.
SLUMP
WHAT'S YOUR DAD SAY ABOUT THIS?
MY DAD ...?
HE'S IN BUTAN.
HUH?
HE'S A FREELANCE WRITER. HE WORKS ABROAD. HE'S HARDLY EVER HOME.
OH.
SO YOU LIVE ALONE?

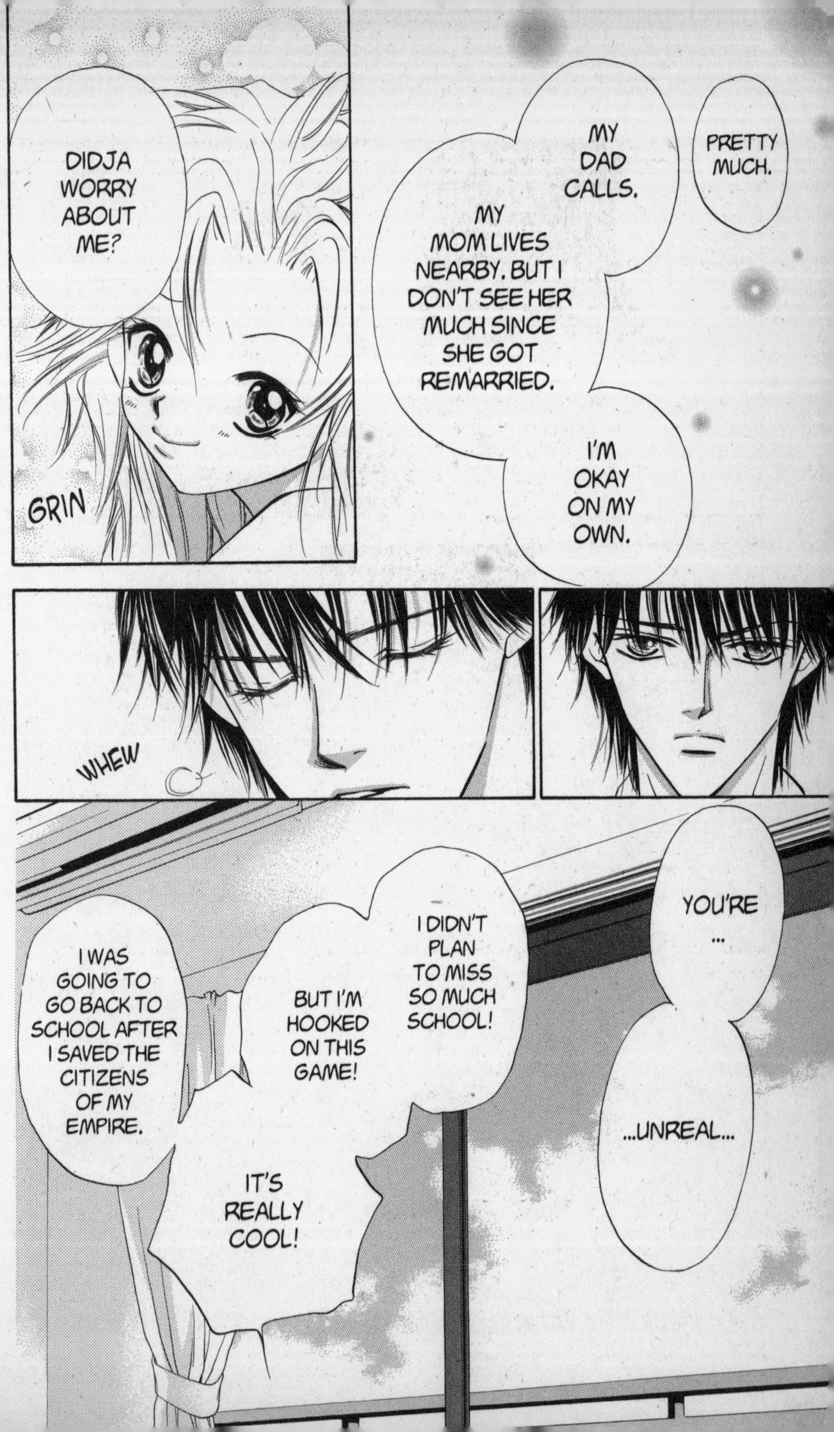
PRETTY MUCH.
MY DAD CALLS.
MY MOM LIVES NEARBY. BUT I DON'T SEE HER MUCH SINCE SHE GOT REMARRIED.
I'M OKAY ON MY OWN.
DIDJA WORRY ABOUT ME?
GRIN
WHEW
YOU'RE ...
...UNREAL...
I DIDN'T PLAN TO MISS SO MUCH SCHOOL!
BUT I'M HOOKED ON THIS GAME!
IT'S REALLY COOL!
I WAS GOING TO GO BACK TO SCHOOL AFTER I SAVED THE CITIZENS OF MY EMPIRE.

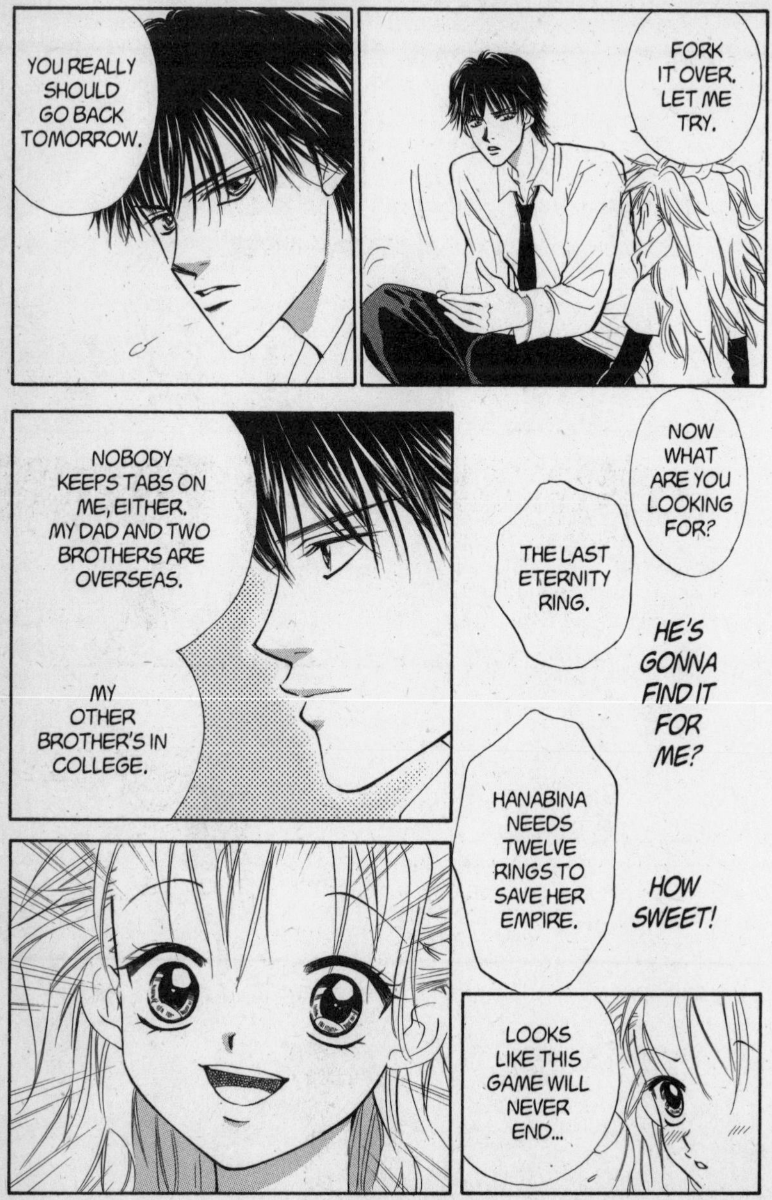
FORK IT OVER. LET ME TRY.
YOU REALLY SHOULD GO BACK TOMORROW.
NOW WHAT ARE YOU LOOKING FOR?
THE LAST ETERNITY RING.
HE'S GONNA FIND IT FOR ME?
NOBODY KEEPS TABS ON ME, EITHER. MY DAD AND TWO BROTHERS ARE OVERSEAS.
MY OTHER BROTHER'S IN COLLEGE.
HANABINA NEEDS TWELVE RINGS TO SAVE HER EMPIRE.
HOW SWEET!
LOOKS LIKE THIS GAME WILL NEVER END...

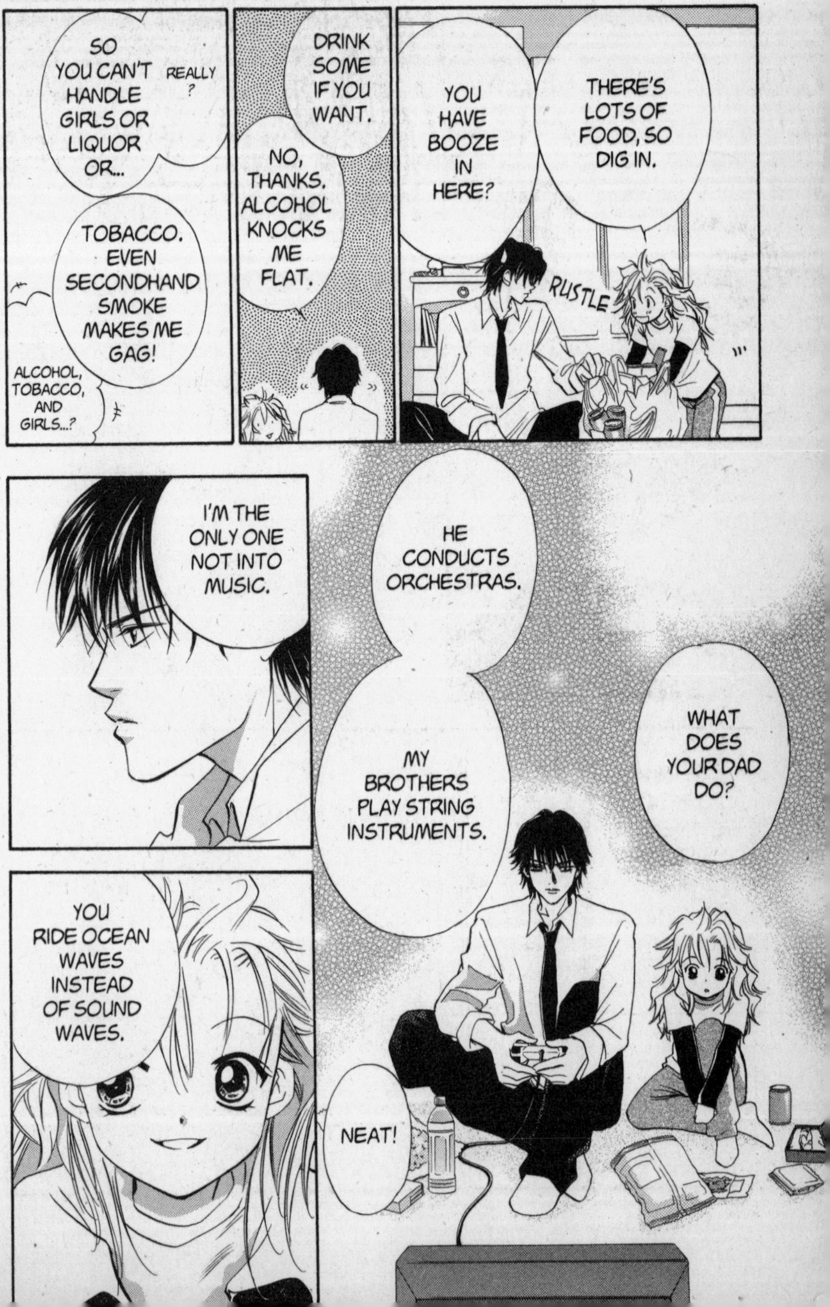
THERE'S LOTS OF FOOD, SO DIG IN.
YOU HAVE BOOZE IN HERE?
RUSTLE
DRINK SOME IF YOU WANT.
NO, THANKS. ALCOHOL KNOCKS ME FLAT.
SO YOU CAN'T HANDLE GIRLS OR LIQUOR OR...
REALLY?
TOBACCO. EVEN SECONDHAND SMOKE MAKES ME GAG!
ALCOHOL, TOBACCO, AND GIRLS...?
WHAT DOES YOUR DAD DO?
HE CONDUCTS ORCHESTRAS.
MY BROTHERS PLAY STRING INSTRUMENTS.
NEAT!
I'M THE ONLY ONE NOT INTO MUSIC.
YOU RIDE OCEAN WAVES INSTEAD OF SOUND WAVES.

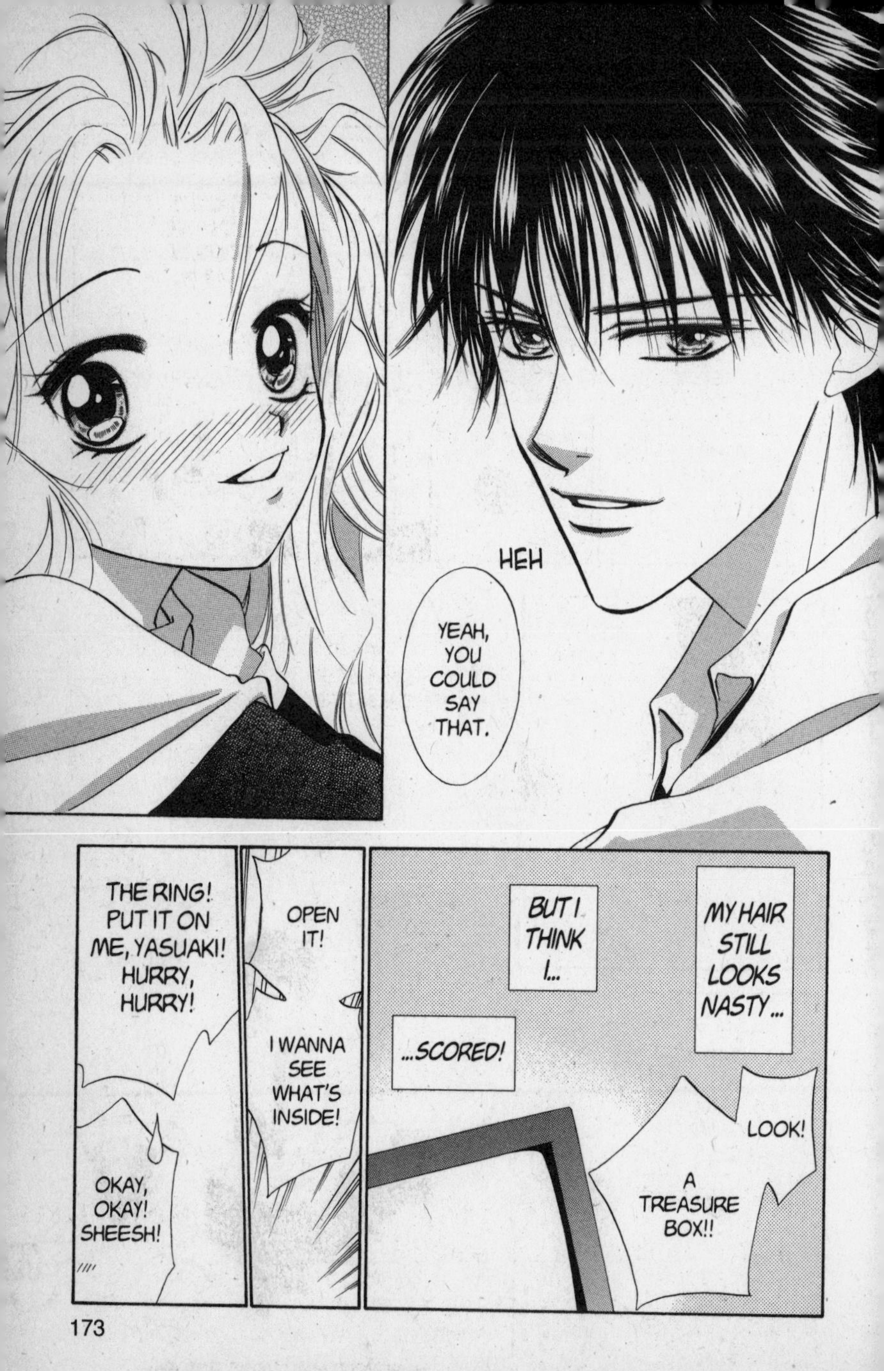
HEH
YEAH, YOU COULD SAY THAT.
MY HAIR STILL LOOKS NASTY...
BUT I THINK I...
...SCORED!
LOOK!
A TREASURE BOX!!
OPEN IT!
I WANNA SEE WHAT'S INSIDE!
THE RING! PUT IT ON ME, YASUAKI! HURRY, HURRY!
OKAY, OKAY! SHEESH!

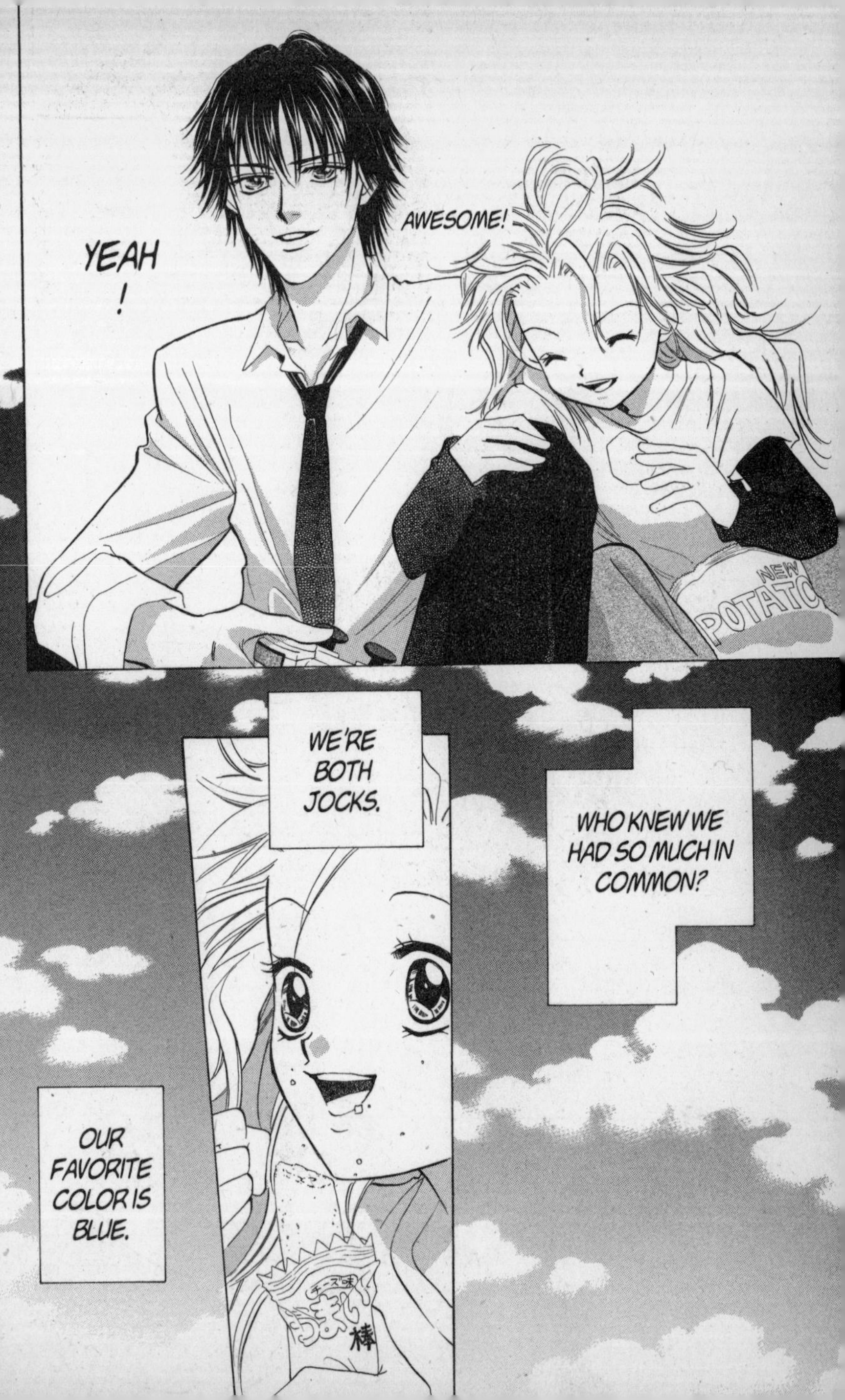
AWESOME!
YEAH!
NEW POTATO
WHO KNEW WE HAD SO MUCH IN COMMON?
WE'RE BOTH JOCKS.
OUR FAVORITE COLOR IS BLUE.
チーズ味
うまい棒

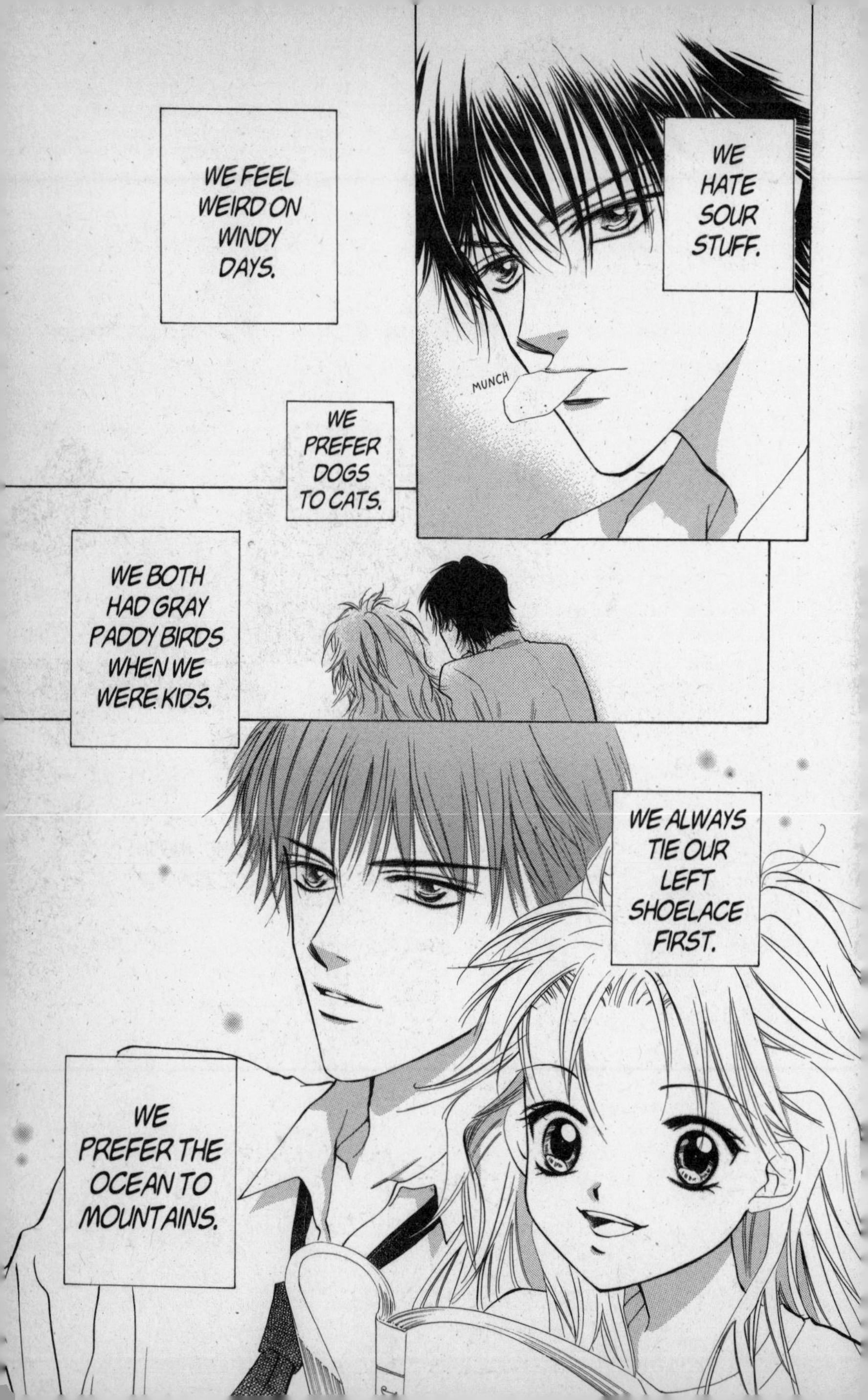
WE HATE SOUR STUFF.
MUNCH
WE FEEL WEIRD ON WINDY DAYS.
WE PREFER DOGS TO CATS.
WE BOTH HAD GRAY PADDY BIRDS WHEN WE WERE KIDS.
WE ALWAYS TIE OUR LEFT SHOELACE FIRST.
WE PREFER THE OCEAN TO MOUNTAINS.

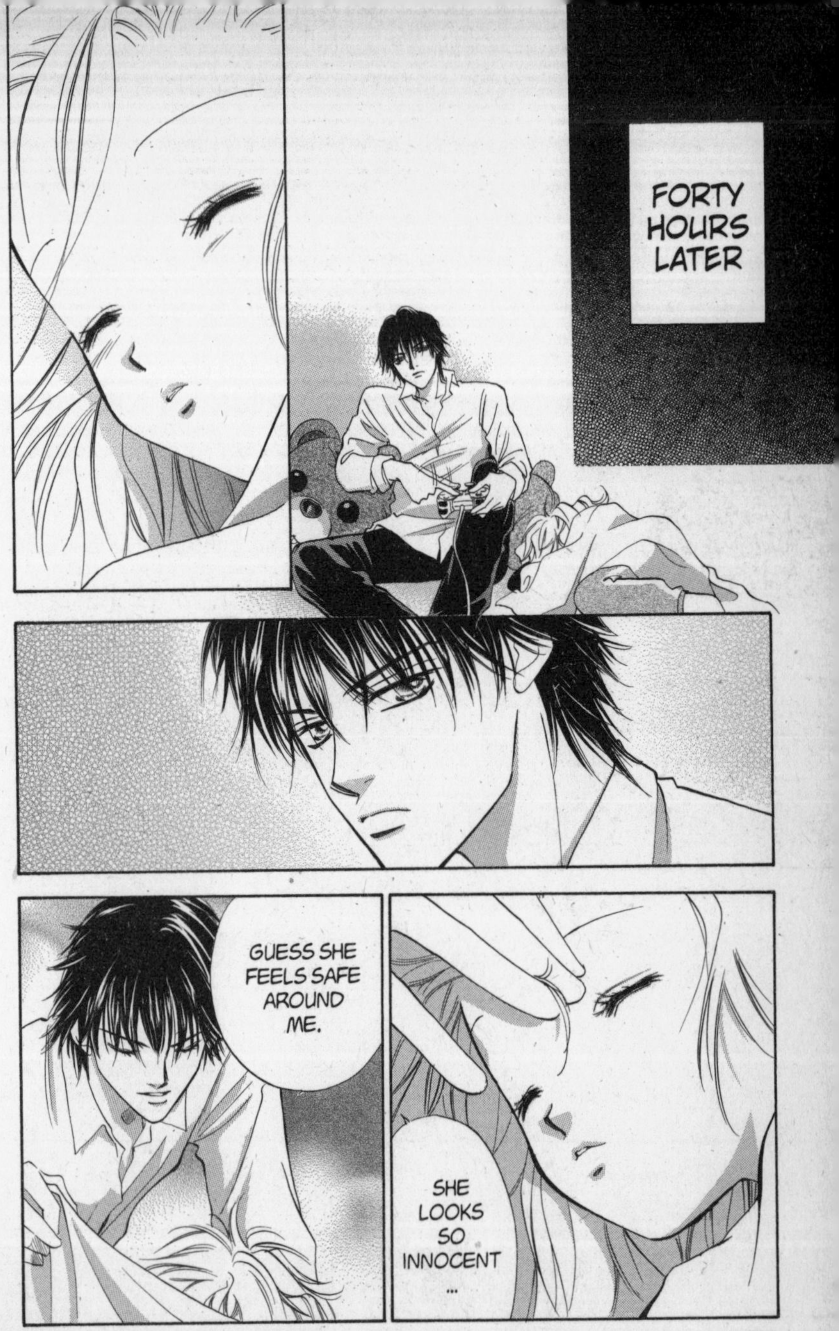
FORTY HOURS LATER
SHE LOOKS SO INNOCENT ...
GUESS SHE FEELS SAFE AROUND ME.

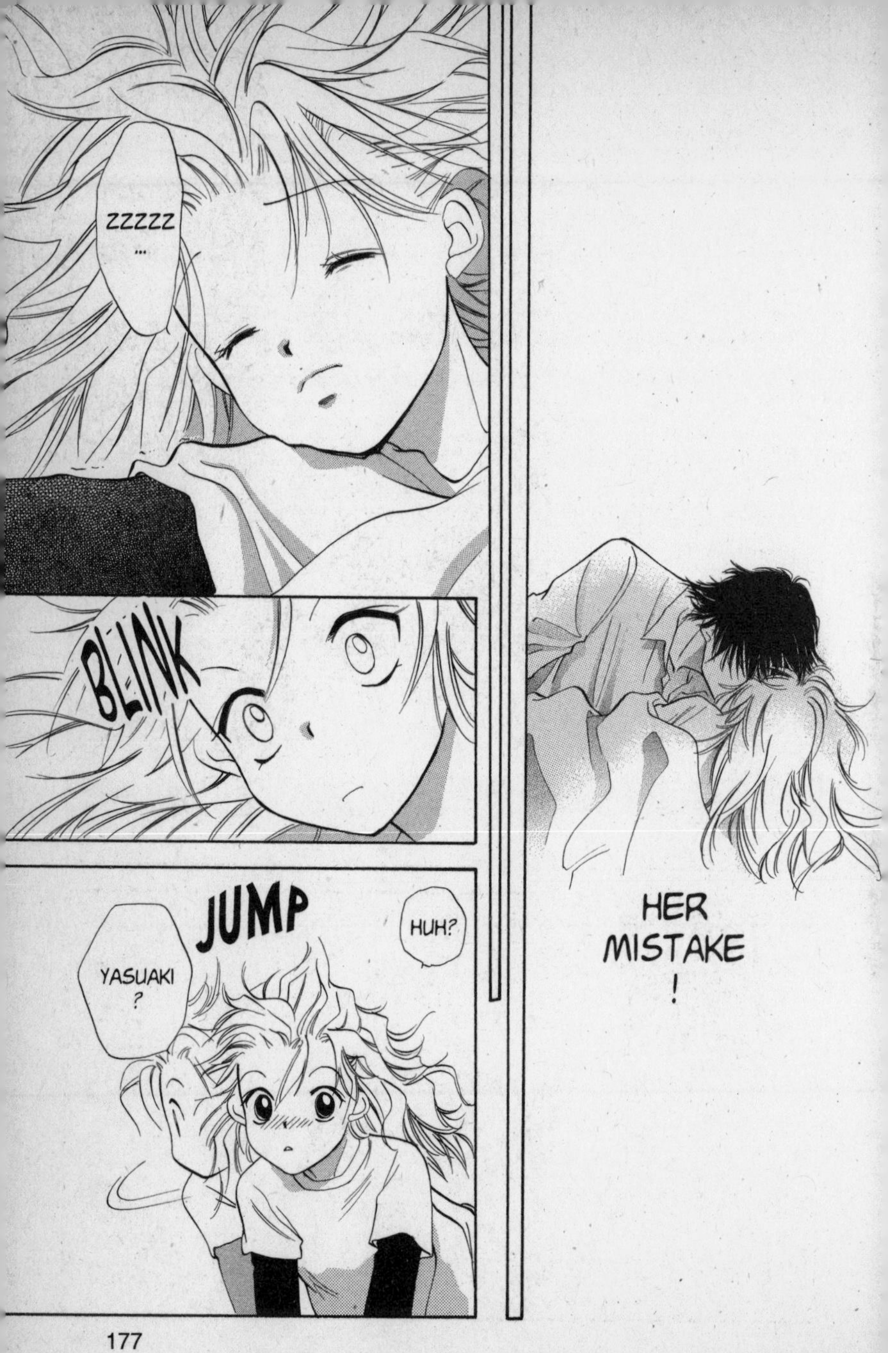
HER MISTAKE !
ZZZZZ ...
BLINK
HUH?
JUMP
YASUAKI ?

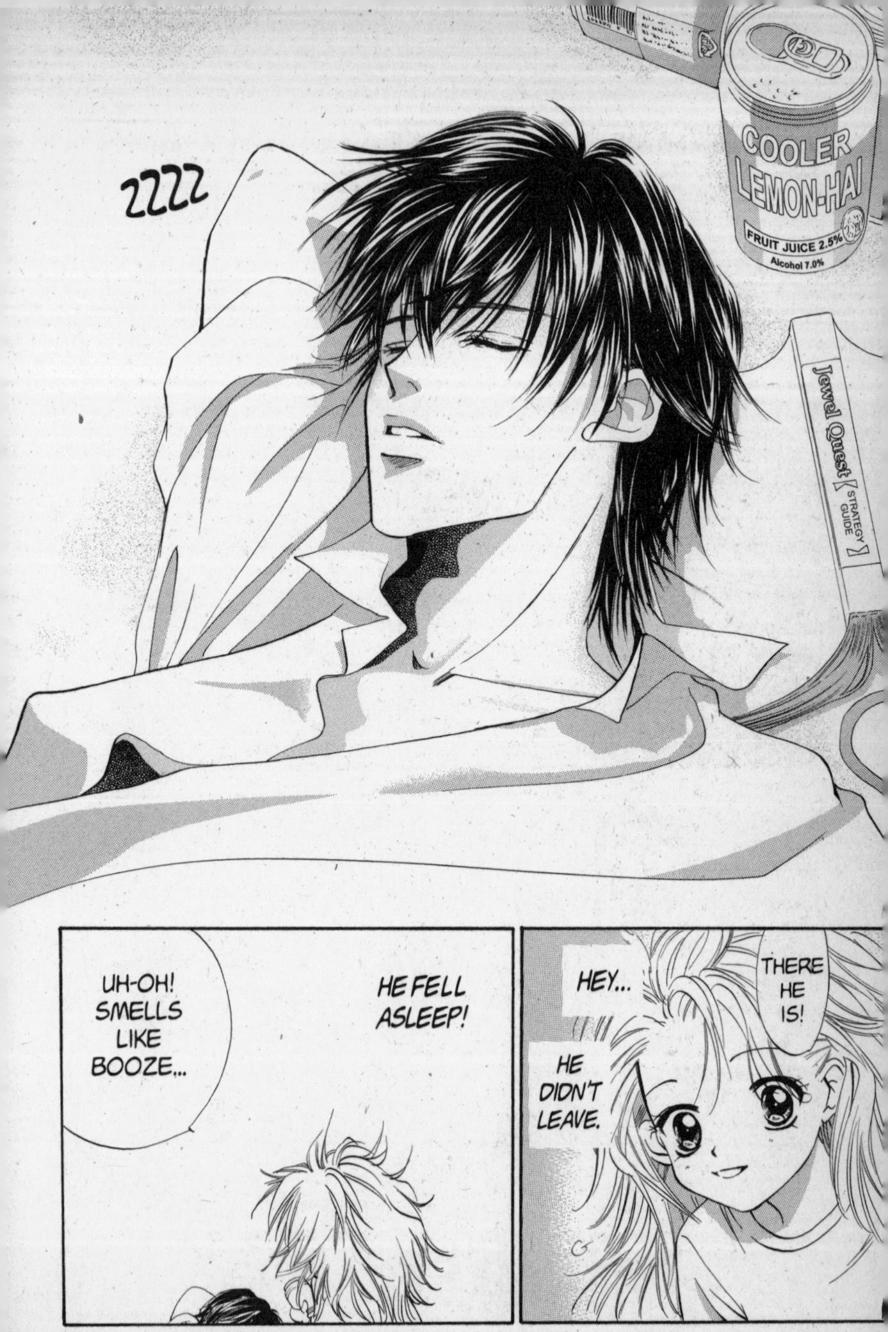
COOLER
LEMON-HAI
FRUIT JUICE 2.5%
Alcohol 7.0%
Jewel Quest
STRATEGY GUIDE
ZZZZ
THERE HE IS!
HEY...
HE DIDN'T LEAVE.
HE FELL ASLEEP!
UH-OH! SMELLS LIKE BOOZE...

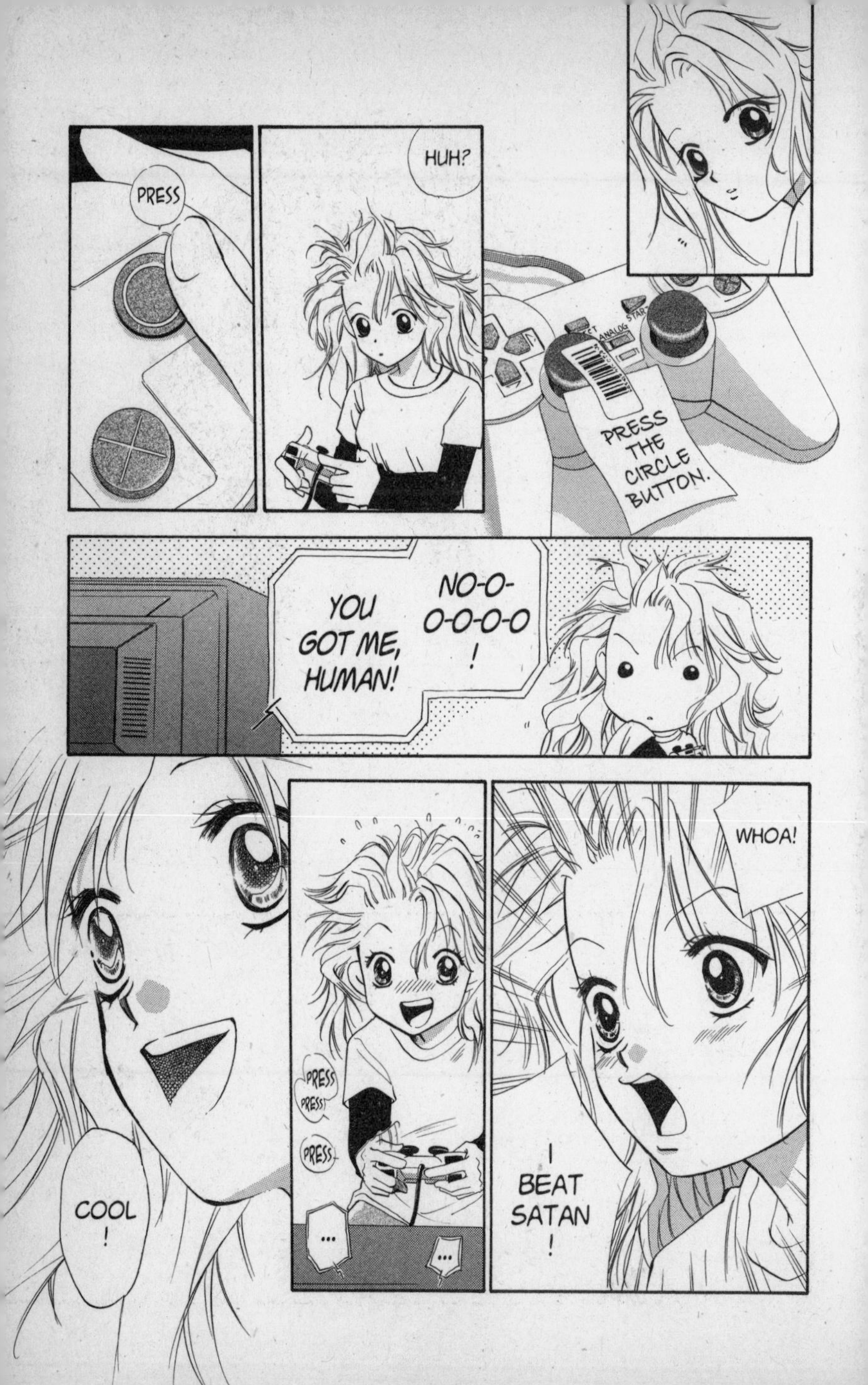
PRESS THE CIRCLE BUTTON.
HUH?
PRESS
NO-O-O-O-O-O!
YOU GOT ME, HUMAN!
WHOA!
I BEAT SATAN!
PRESS PRESS
PRESS
...
...
COOL!

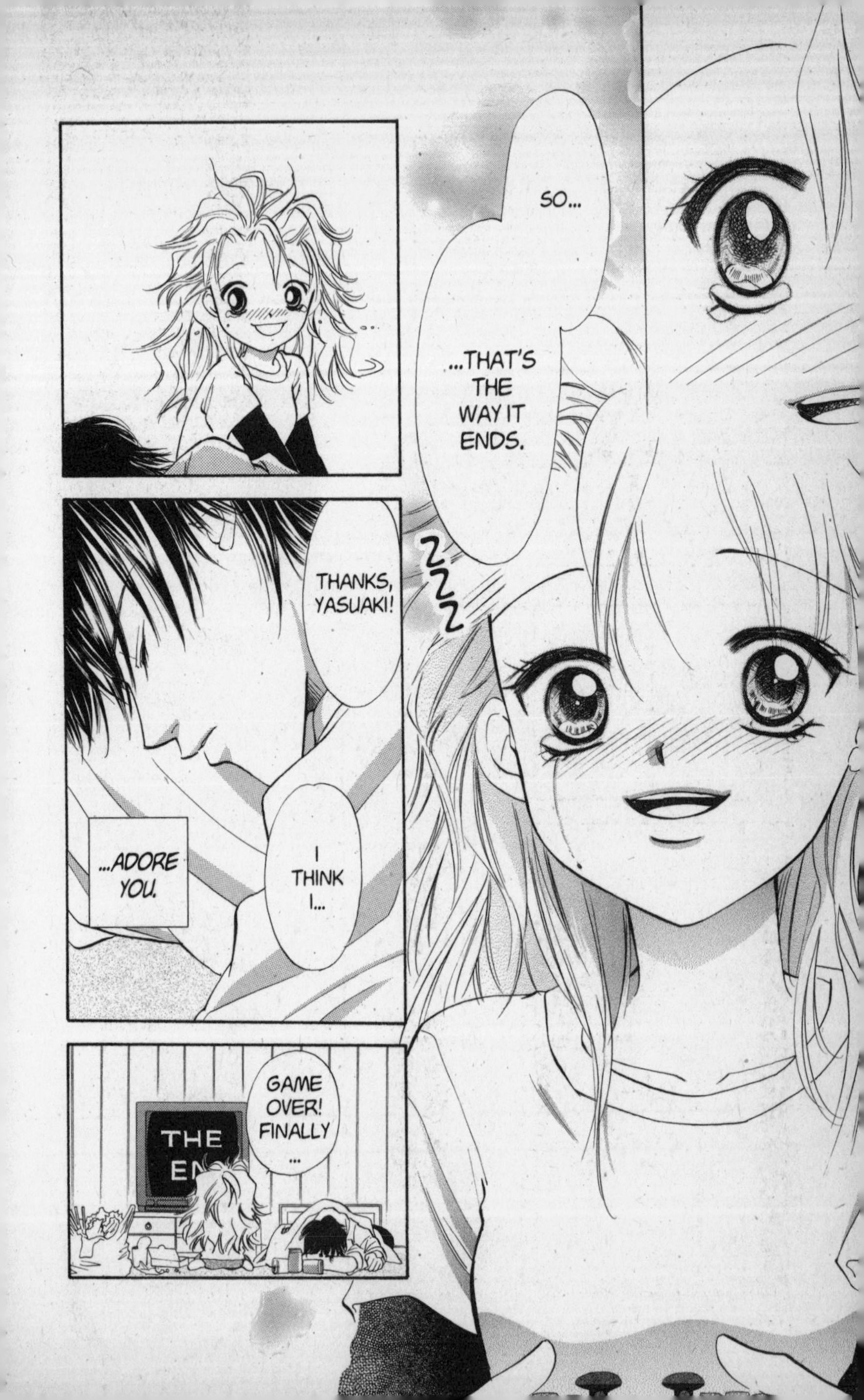
SO...
...THAT'S THE WAY IT ENDS.
ZZZ
THANKS, YASUAKI!
I THINK I...
...ADORE YOU.
GAME OVER! FINALLY ...
THE E

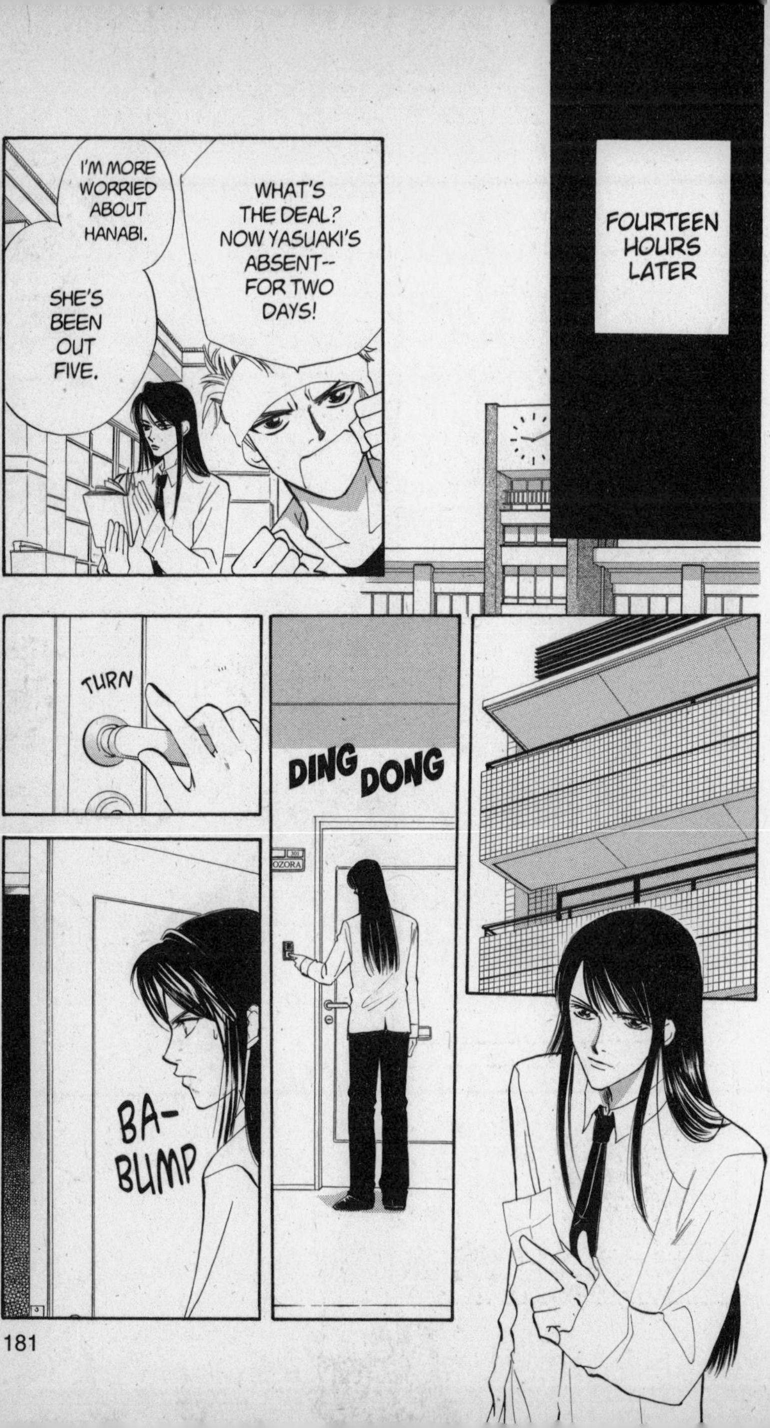
FOURTEEN HOURS LATER
WHAT'S THE DEAL? NOW YASUAKI'S ABSENT-- FOR TWO DAYS!
I'M MORE WORRIED ABOUT HANABI.
SHE'S BEEN OUT FIVE.
DING DONG
TURN
...
BA-BUMP

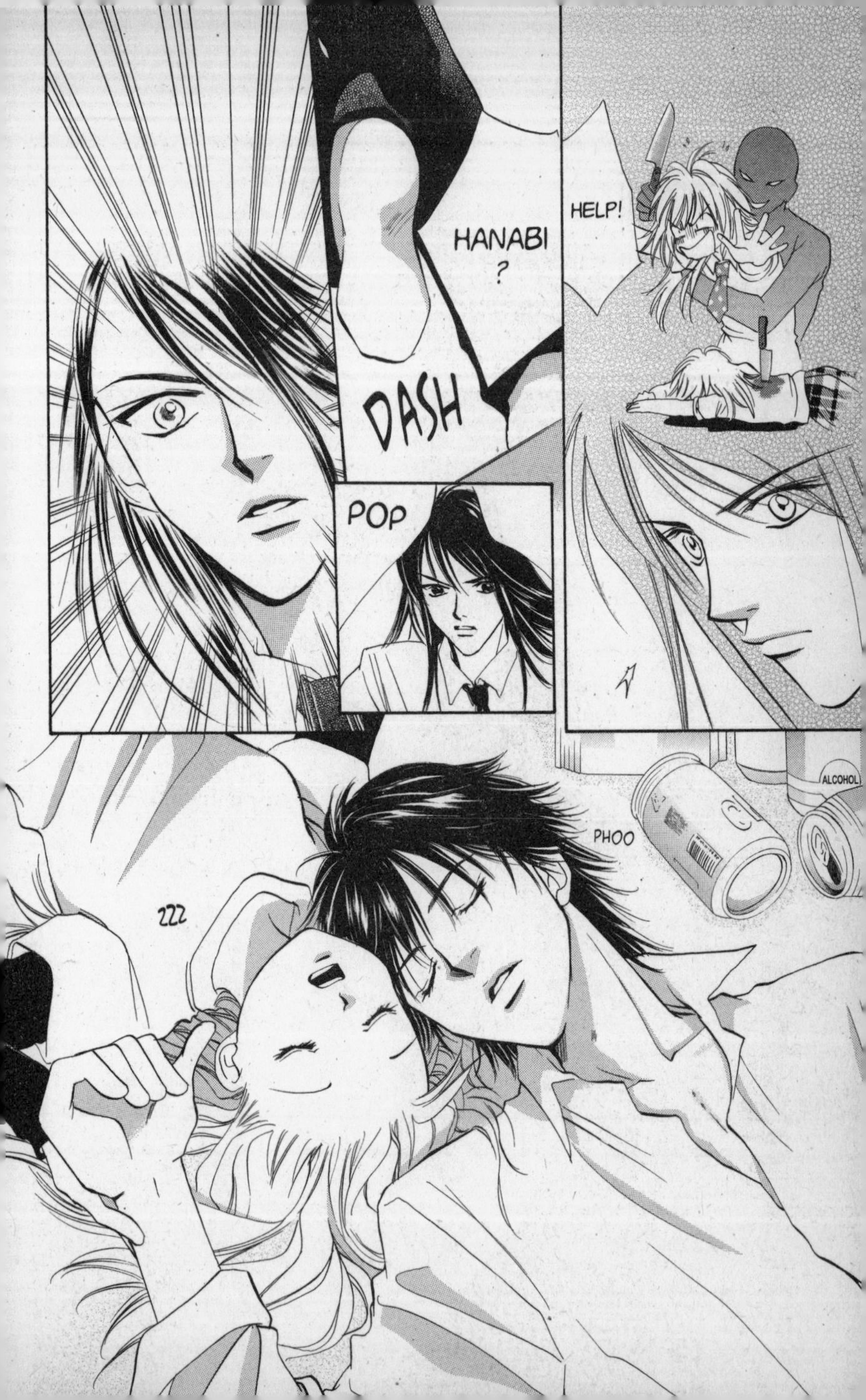
HELP!
HANABI ?
DASH
POP
ALCOHOL
PHOO
ZZZ

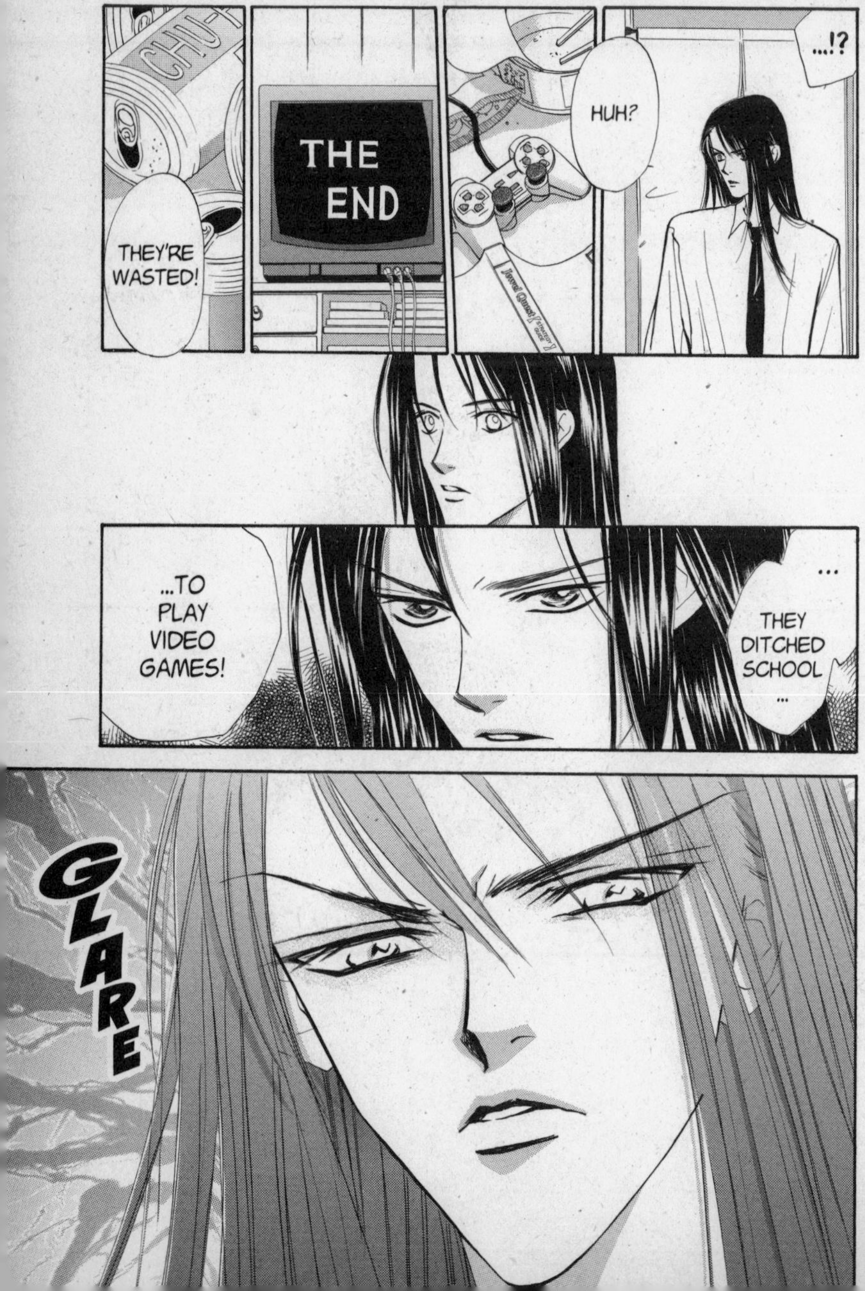
...!?
HUH?
THE END
THEY'RE WASTED!
...
THEY DITCHED SCHOOL
...
...TO PLAY VIDEO GAMES!
GLARE

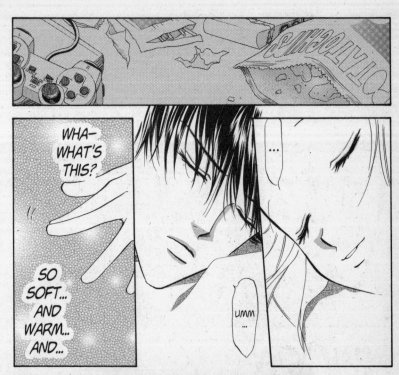

WHA— WHAT'S THIS?

...

SO SOFT... AND WARM... AND...

UMM ...

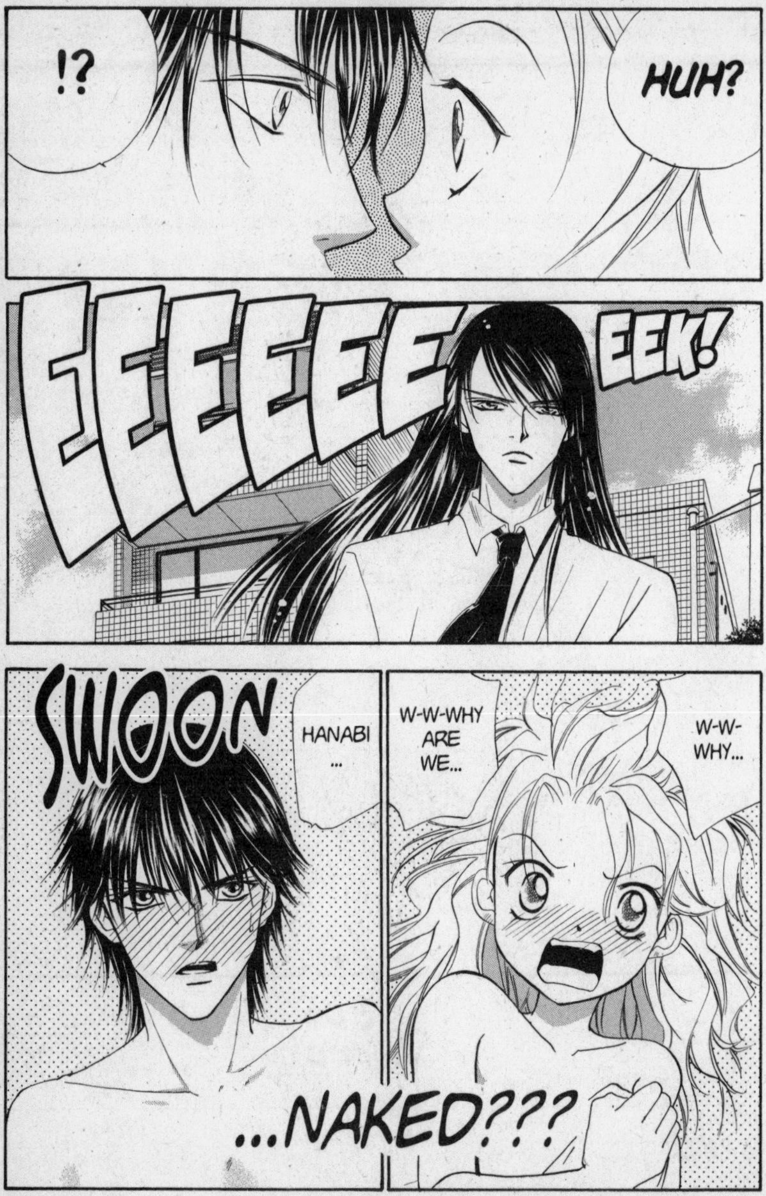
HUH?
!?
EEEEEEEEK!
W-W-WHY...
W-W-WHY ARE WE...
...NAKED???
HANABI ...
SWOON

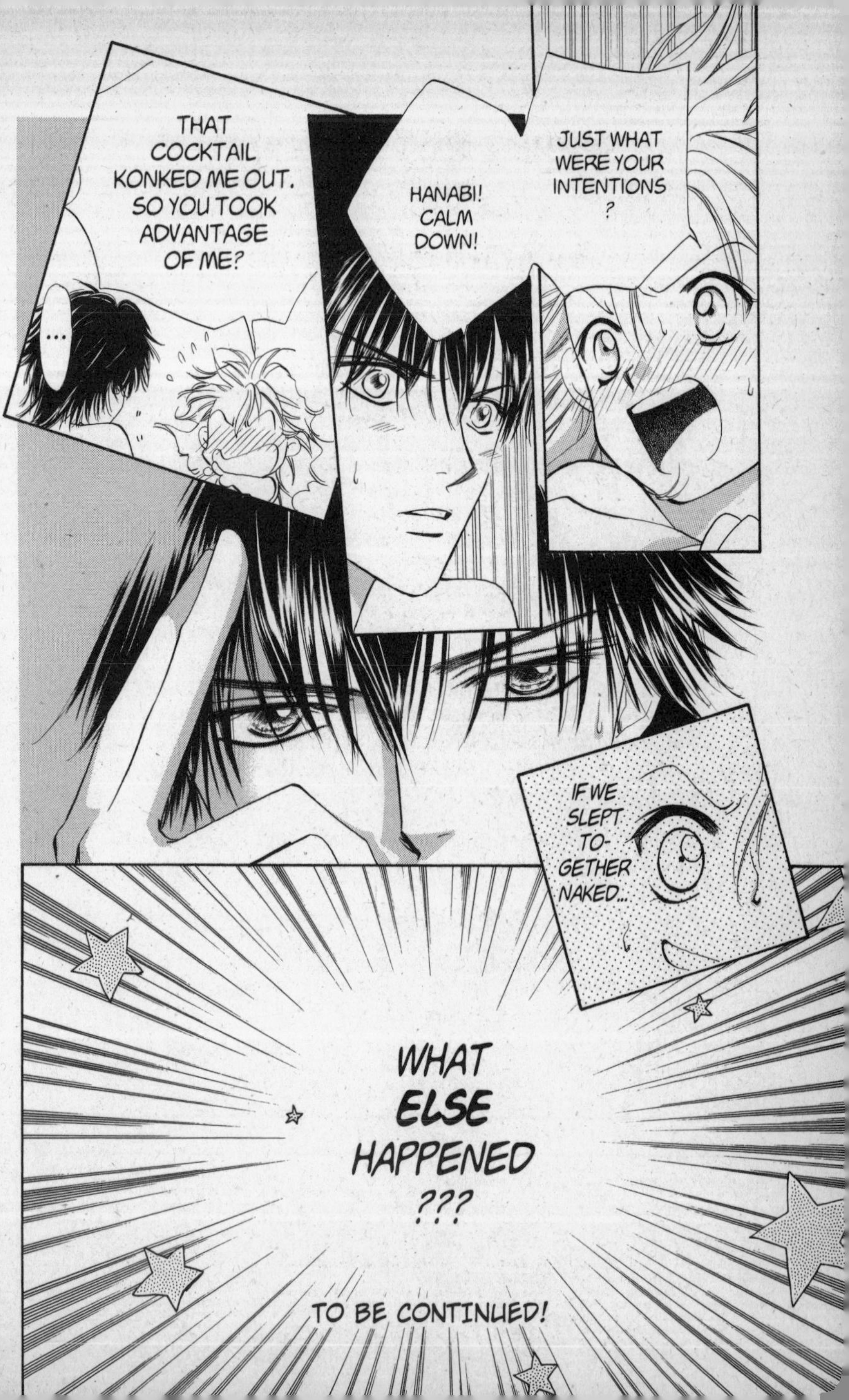
JUST WHAT WERE YOUR INTENTIONS ?
HANABI! CALM DOWN!
THAT COCKTAIL KONKED ME OUT. SO YOU TOOK ADVANTAGE OF ME?
...
IF WE SLEPT TO-GETHER NAKED...
WHAT ELSE HAPPENED ???
TO BE CONTINUED!

HAPPY HUSTLE HIGH
Vol. 1

Story and Art by Rie Takada

English Adaptation/Janet Gilbert
Translation/June Honma
Touch-up Art & Lettering/Rina Mapa
Design/Izumi Evers
Editor/Kit Fox

Managing Editor/Megan Bates
Editorial Director/Elizabeth Kawasaki
Editor in Chief/Alvin Lu
Sr. Director of Acquisitions/Rika Inouye
Sr. VP of Marketing/Liza Coppola
Exec. VP of Sales & Marketing/John Easum
Publisher/Hyoe Narita

Printed in the U.S.A.

Published by VIZ Media, LLC
P.O. Box 77010
San Francisco, CA 94107

10 9 8 7 6 5 4 3 2
First printing, February 2005
Second printing, August 2006

VIZ MEDIA

www.viz.com
store.viz.com

RATED T+ FOR OLDER TEEN

PARENTAL ADVISORY
HAPPY HUSTLE HIGH is rated T+ for Older Teen and is recommended for ages 16 and up. Contains strong language and sexual themes.

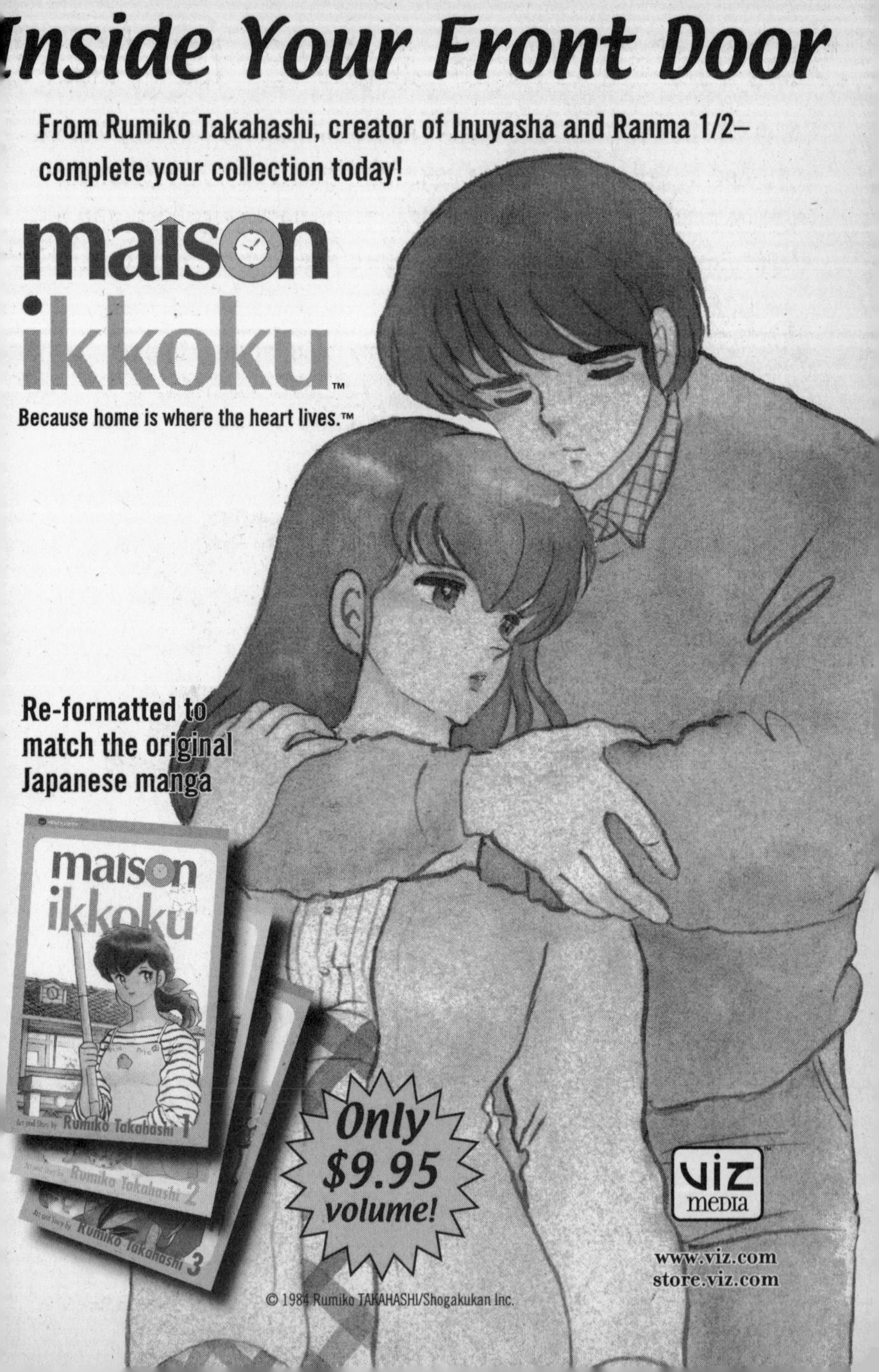
Inside Your Front Door
From Rumiko Takahashi, creator of Inuyasha and Ranma 1/2–
complete your collection today!
maison ikkoku™
Because home is where the heart lives.™
Re-formatted to match the original Japanese manga
maison ikkoku
Rumiko Takahashi 1
Rumiko Takahashi 2
Rumiko Takahashi 3
Only $9.95 volume!
VIZ MEDIA
www.viz.com
store.viz.com
© 1984 Rumiko TAKAHASHI/Shogakukan Inc.

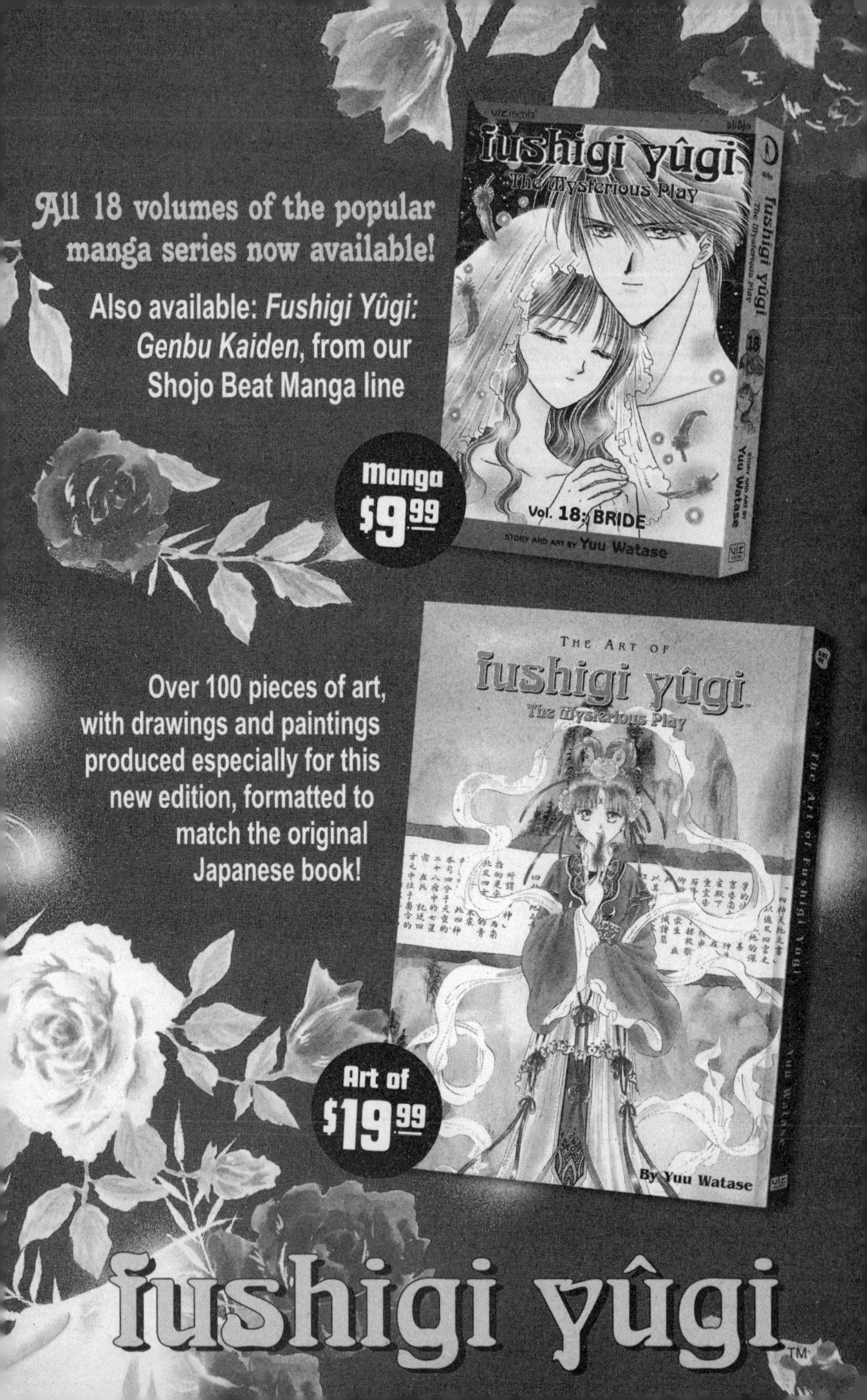
All 18 volumes of the popular manga series now available!
Also available: Fushigi Yûgi: Genbu Kaiden, from our Shojo Beat Manga line
fushigi yûgi
The Mysterious Play
Vol. 18: BRIDE
STORY AND ART BY Yuu Watase
Manga $9.99
Over 100 pieces of art, with drawings and paintings produced especially for this new edition, formatted to match the original Japanese book!
THE ART OF
fushigi yûgi
The Mysterious Play
By Yuu Watase
Art of $19.99
fushigi yûgi™

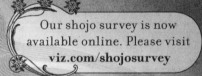